THE ACHIEVEMENT
OF ROME

LONDON : HUMPHREY MILFORD

OXFORD UNIVERSITY PRESS

VIEW FROM HORACE'S SABINE FARM

(*Photo by W. C. Greene*)

THE ACHIEVEMENT OF ROME

A CHAPTER IN CIVILIZATION

BY

WILLIAM CHASE GREENE, Ph.D.

ASSOCIATE PROFESSOR OF GREEK AND LATIN
IN HARVARD UNIVERSITY

Et quasi cursores vitai lampada tradunt

CAMBRIDGE

HARVARD UNIVERSITY PRESS

1933

PRINTED AT THE HARVARD UNIVERSITY PRESS
CAMBRIDGE, MASS., U. S. A.

LIBERIS VXORIQVE

H. T. G.

M. C. G. A. M. G.

M. E. G.

ROMAE MECVM COMITIBVS

LIBRVM

D. D.

PREFACE

IN MOST of the activities that enable the individual to lead a rich and satisfying life, in the discovery of beauty and in rational conduct, the ancient Greeks are still our masters. They learned so much and expressed so directly what they learned that it is not only a pleasure but a wise economy to rehearse their experience as a preliminary to experiment in our modern world. Some of these matters I attempted to set forth not many years ago in a book entitled *The Achievement of Greece: A Chapter in Human Experience* (Harvard University Press, 1923).

The Romans, though less original than the Greeks, were their heirs, as we in turn are the Romans' heirs; and they succeeded better than the Greeks in consolidating the gains of civilization in lasting forms. If the individual can learn more from Greece, organized society can learn more from Rome. Again, whatever we may think of the achievement of Rome in its various phases, there it is, a tremendous fact from which we can no more escape than we can evade the revelations of astronomy. It demands our effort to understand it, and it proves to be a strangely fascinating subject. Freeman hardly overstates the case: "The history of Rome is the greatest of all historical subjects, for this simple reason, that the history of Rome is in truth synonymous with the history of the world." [1]

The present book, though in general a companion and a complement to my earlier book, is nevertheless an inde-

---

[1] E. A. Freeman, Introduction to English translation of Mommsen's *History of Rome*, Everyman Edition, p. vii.

pendent work and can be read separately. I have refrained
from making any references to the earlier book in text and
in notes, except in one passage (p. 328) in which I have borrowed a few sentences from it. The general plan is similar,
though in the nature of the case it has seemed desirable to
devote more space to narrative and exposition. The spirit is,
however, likewise critical, and I have ventured again to write
a final chapter of a more speculative character. After all,
one can no more dismiss the Romans without attempting
to define the meaning of civilization than one can leave the
Greeks without inquiring into the meaning of humanism.
Even though the results can be only tentative, such an undertaking is a practical one, and is important.

One is sometimes confronted with the interesting but difficult task of trying to show an intelligent foreigner what is
most significant in a modern country, — for example, the
United States. One tries perhaps to bring out the geographical variety, the racial diversity, the historical trends; one
attempts to convey an idea of the industrial and economic
and political structure, the intellectual and artistic and religious movements; one seeks to reckon with social standards, with family life, with amusements, with the influence
of journalism and moving pictures and the radio. One
courageously recognizes the mediocre and the bad along
with the good. But one hesitates, if one is wise, to suggest
anything more than a provisional judgment on the whole
trend of American civilization or on its peculiar contribution
to the world. Except that we see the ancient civilization in
a longer perspective, it is hardly less difficult to select what
is most significant in the achievement of Rome; for there
have been many Romes, each with its special character.
There was the primitive Rome of the Monarchy and the
early Republic; the strong, expanding Rome of Scipio; the

turbulent, triumphant Rome of the Gracchi and Sulla and
Caesar. There followed the disciplined empire of Augustus
and the Antonines, already harboring secret germs of dissolution; and presently the weary empire of Diocletian. There
has been the Rome of the Popes; the Rome that remained
as an idea throughout nearly two millennia of change; and
the Rome of modern Italy. There is also the perennial, universal Rome, speaking in church and law courts and in
popular speech in many parts of the world to-day, and
among educated men almost everywhere.

To select amid all this record of achievements what deserves to be called "the achievement of Rome" has been a
task of compression, of exclusion, and of emphasis. The
chronicle of ancient Rome's influence in later ages has been
confined to occasional allusion. For the rest, I have devoted
most space to the period between the Punic Wars and the
Age of the Antonines. I have drawn most freely on the most
important and therefore most familiar ancient authors; in
referring to modern works I have preferred those which are
most readily available (usually in English), with the exception of some recent books and articles in periodicals representing matter not yet generally available in English books.
Remembering the needs of those who are not professional
students, I have given quotations from Latin authors usually
in English translation. There are many omissions, and I
cannot pretend to have been wholly consistent in applying
my own principles. Chapter VII is not a history of Roman
literature, and neither oratory nor historical writing receives
the treatment which both deserve in any full survey. A considerable portion of the discussion of Virgil will be found, for
what seem to me to be good reasons, in the chapter dealing
with religion. Some of the pages on Virgil are borrowed from
a paper which I contributed to the *Classical Weekly* (April

20 and 27, 1931). On the other hand, it will be seen that I
have not hesitated to indulge in a certain amount of repetition, discussing a topic in more than one context, usually
with cross references; this method has its advantages for one
whose aim is to give emphasis to what seems most significant.

The completion of this book, which has occupied the
leisure of several years, was made possible by two grants
from the fund established at Harvard University by the
General Education Board for the encouragement of studies
in the humanities. For this aid I express my cordial gratitude. To individual scholars, with whom I have discussed
many of the subjects dealt with in these pages, I am conscious of owing far more than I can acknowledge in detail;
among them I may be permitted to mention in particular
two Harvard colleagues, the late and much-lamented Professor Clifford H. Moore, and Professor E. K. Rand, the
latter of whom kindly read and criticized my manuscript.
In certain details I have benefited by the criticism and advice of other friends, though they are not responsible for
what errors may remain: Professor A. W. Van Buren, of the
American Academy in Rome (archaeology); Professor A. D.
Nock of Harvard (the worship of Roman emperors); Mr.
Mason Hammond, also of Harvard (the constitution of
Augustus); and Professor J. A. O. Larsen, of the University
of Chicago (provincial assemblies). During the past year,
while completing this book, I have enjoyed the unique advantage of residence in Rome, serving as Annual Professor in
the School of Classical Studies of the American Academy in
Rome.

In this place, and in this year, I cannot conclude without
referring to two other matters. Although it would be pre-
sumptuous to anticipate the verdict of history on the Fascist
era, now in its tenth year, at least one cannot view it at close

range without realizing that it is no isolated phenomenon in
the history of Rome. In its insistence on the discipline of the
individual, in its awakening of a spirit of energy and sacrifice
and nationalism, in its realistic cutting of red tape, in its
ruthless treatment of opposition, as well as in its preservation of forms and its desire to conciliate public opinion, it is
in the Roman tradition; the nearest analogy, despite differences, would be the rule of Augustus. Finally, in a year
when the tragic consequences of the World War are still alive
and all nations are apparently helpless to escape from the
vicious circle of international debts and international trade-
barriers and economic depression, one turns almost with a
sense of relief to the spectacle of the Roman Empire at its
best, an effective society of nations, free from practically all
trade-barriers, enjoying a common law within the Pax
Romana. Yet passive contemplation of the spectacle is not
enough; indeed the Roman Empire itself at last decayed.
What our present plight may lead us to undertake is a more
effective recognition of the interdependence of all nations
and of the futility of all wars (even of trade wars), and a
more deliberate cultivation of mutual understanding. To
accomplish this without having recourse to an imperialistic
system is a task for enlightened leadership. A good omen for
the success of this undertaking would be such a sense of a
common civilization among leaders in all countries as would
come from their fuller understanding of the achievement of
Rome.

W. C. G.

ROME
June, 1932

CONTENTS

SYNOPSIS

LIST OF ILLUSTRATIONS

LIST OF ABBREVIATIONS

THE following abbreviations are used in referring to certain periodicals and other works. For a further bibliography, see pages 537–546.

Am. Hist. Rev.	*American Historical Review.*
A. J. P.	*American Journal of Philology.*
C. A. H.	*Cambridge Ancient History.*
C. I. L.	*Corpus Inscriptionum Latinarum.*
C. J.	*Classical Journal.*
C. P.	*Classical Philology.*
C. Q.	*Classical Quarterly.*
H. S. C. P.	*Harvard Studies in Classical Philology.*
J. R. S.	*Journal of Roman Studies.*
Mem. Am. Acad. Rome	*Memoirs of the American Academy in Rome.*
Mon. Ant.	*Monumenti Antichi.*
T. A. P. A.	*Transactions of the American Philological Association.*

THE ACHIEVEMENT
OF ROME

CHAPTER I

ITALY : THE LAND AND ITS ANCIENT PEOPLES

Salve, magna parens frugum, Saturnia tellus,
Magna virum.   Virgil, *Georgics* II, 173 f.

Rerum facta est pulcherrima Roma,
Septemque una sibi muro circumdedit arces.
Georgics II, 534 f.

1. THE LAND

SURROUNDED by the sunny lands of southern Europe and western Asia and the coasts of northern Africa lies the Mediterranean Sea. A mighty water, nearly as wide as the United States, it is nevertheless an inland sea on the shores of which have dwelt peoples always sharing certain common ways of living and forced to find, in hostility or in friendship, some division of territory. Nearly at the middle of this sea, like a great bridge, stretches the Italian peninsula with its continuation, Sicily, and the strategic island of Malta, dividing the sea into two basins and almost connecting Europe with Africa. From the Alps to the toe of the peninsula, Italy measures nearly seven hundred miles; but at no point is it more than one hundred miles in width. Embracing an area of about one hundred thousand square miles, it is somewhat larger than New England, and slightly larger than Great Britain. Though the northern portions are of Alpine climate, and the most southerly part of Sicily overlaps a part of Africa, the climate is in the main tempered by winds from the sea; if the mountains are very cold in winter, snow is seldom to be seen in Rome, which is in the same latitude as Providence, Rhode Island.

Varied as is the climate of Italy because of its situation, the landscape is still more varied by the contrasts of mountain and plain, of land and sea. The great backbone of the Apennines swings first in a southeasterly direction across from the west coast of Italy nearly to the east coast, and then turns in a more southerly direction along the main axis of the peninsula, finally crossing again to the west coast, and finds its rugged continuation in the mountains of Sicily.[1] It rises to its greatest height in central Italy, at a little over ten thousand feet; but the volcano of Aetna, in Sicily, reaches nearly eleven thousand feet. Many are the massive tablelands, thousands of feet above the sea, divided by narrow passes and defiles. Between the northern Apennines and the Alps extends a vast plain, watered by the Po, the "king of rivers," [2] down to the level coast of the Adriatic; but this fruitful region was not politically a part of Italy till the end of the Roman Republic, and was properly named Cisalpine Gaul. Of other lowlands on the east coast there are few except short and narrow valleys and the plain of Calabria at the heel of Italy, and there are few good harbors; those of Brindisi and Ravenna owed much to the work of man. Very few Greek settlements were ever made on the east coast. On the west coast, however, are more abundant and more fertile plains, notably those of Etruria, Latium, and Campania. The west coast contains also several good harbors, as well as the only really navigable river in Italy proper, the Tiber. But the mouth of the Tiber, as of the Po and other rivers, has been silted up as forests have been cut down.

In contrast with Greece, whose mountain valleys slope in general to the southeast, and whose many islands and land-

---

[1] The Greeks emphasized in the name of "Rhegion" (= Regium, now Reggio), at the strait, the fact that Sicily was "broken off" from Italy.

[2] Virgil, *Georg.* I, 481.

locked harbors invited seafaring and trade with the East, Italy's mountain barrier on her eastern side and her scarcity of good harbors seemed to predestine her for many centuries to the development of her own territory and to trade within the western Mediterranean, where her chief rival was to be Carthage. It was of the greatest importance for civilization that Greece and Italy faced in opposite directions, and developed their own types of culture before they came closely into contact with each other, and that Rome had succeeded in consolidating a large part of Italy before she met any considerable Greek power on the battlefield. And if the inhabitants of Italy were not forced by the poverty of their country to turn to foreign trade, they found ample compensation in the extent of their rich alluvial plains and their upland pastures, in both of which Italy surpasses Greece. Indeed they were inclined to believe that the very name of their land came from their pastures: Italia (i.e. Vitalia) = the land of cattle (*vituli*).[1] At all events, the Italian cattle are still driven to and from their summer grazing lands in the mountains over the same tracks that were used two or three thousand years ago. The mountain spurs and the river torrents of Italy, however, like those of Greece, divided the country into small compartments; and it became a serious problem whether these small divisions would remain, as they generally remained in Greece, politically distinct, or whether some single power would be able to build roads through these barriers so as to unite the sundered parts of the peninsula, and would at the same time have the political sagacity needed to unite its various peoples.

Nature has been kind to Italy in the gift of beauty. The elder Pliny, usually prosaic enough in his voluminous treatise on "Natural History," becomes almost lyric in his de-

---

[1] Oscan *Viteliú*, a name used first of the toe of the peninsula. Cf. p. 12.

scription of Italy. He enumerates "the climate, with its eternal freshness, and abounding in health and vitality, the enchanting serenity of the weather, the fertile fields, the sunny hillsides, the thickets free from every danger, the cool and shady groves, the forests with their varying and luxuriant vegetation, the fruitfulness of the grain, the vines, and the admirable olives, the flocks with noble fleeces, the bulls with sinewy necks; the lakes coming ever one after another, the numerous rivers and springs which refresh the land on every side with their waters, the numerous gulfs of the sea with their havens, and the bosom of the lands opening everywhere to the commerce of the wide world, yes, eagerly reaching out, as it were, into the very midst of the waves for the purpose of aiding, so it seems, the efforts of the Immortals!" [1] But Pliny hardly helps one to picture the typical Italian landscape: brown plain, softened by masses of grey-green olive trees, and broken by the soaring walls of the houses, pink and yellow, of some little hill town that rises abruptly on a crag, the distance bounded on one side by the sparkling of the blue Mediterranean, on the other by the purple of the Apennines, and over all a sky of clear and intense blue. Nor has he remembered the volcanoes, some of the most characteristic features of Italy, whether they be slumbering and only occasionally active, like Vesuvius and Aetna, or whether they be long dead and hold in their craters deep and crystalline lakes. For much of the land from Etruria to Sicily is volcanic, and has given not only building stone and fertile soil but caves and earthquakes and sulphurous vapors, — sure signs that the entrance to the lower world is near!

It may be that Pliny's eulogy of the Italian climate was truer in his day than it would be to-day; for there is some

[1] Pliny the Elder, *N. H.* III, 6.

reason to believe that the climate of Italy, except in the northern part, is now less moist and variable and is hotter and less healthful and stimulating than in earlier times.[1] But Pliny justly mentions the ancient glory of Italy's crops, and in particular of those three crops that have been called "the Mediterranean Triad": grain, the vine, and the olive. Practically all the peoples bordering on the Mediterranean have made these three the staples of their diet, thus differing from northern Europeans in this as in dress and houses and other habits; and it is not unreasonable to see in these common ways of living, as well as in homogeneous racial stocks, one element that assisted in the Romanization of the Mediterranean world and in causing a certain amount of racial approximation to a single human type.[2] Nor does Virgil indulge in idle rhetoric in the climax of his magnificent "Praise of Italy," when he hails the land as "mighty mother of harvests, mighty mother of men." [3] For, to speak now only of the crops, it is true that in fertility and in variety of crops Italy surpassed then, as now, all other Mediterranean lands.[4] Virgil writes first of the all-important triad, and of

[1] Cf. Ellsworth Huntington, *Civilization and Climate*[3] (New Haven, 1924), and *World Power and Evolution* (New Haven, 1919). Huntington infers from the rate of growth of sequoia trees in California a sudden aridity in Italy between 400 and 200 B.C., an improvement from the last century B.C. till about 200 A.D., followed by other pulsations. One of the consequences of the sluggish drainage would be the invasion of Italy by the mosquito, and therefore by malaria, with a consequent decline of the health and morale of the people. See also W. H. S. Jones, *Malaria: A Neglected Factor in the History of Greece and Rome* (Cambridge, 1907).

[2] Cf. A. E. Zimmern, *The Greek Commonwealth*[3], pp. 49 ff.; J. L. Myres, *Greek Lands and the Greek People*, pp. 19–23; R. G. Collingwood, *Roman Britain*, pp. 14 f.

[3] Virgil, *Georg.* II, 173 f. The words of this apostrophe stand at the head of the present chapter.

[4] We are not concerned here with the problem of the exhaustion of the soil. The fertility of the Nile valley is, for a special reason, inexhaustible; northern Africa and southern France have large fertile tracts. But in variety all these yield to Italy. Greece and Spain, rocky and mountainous, afford only a small area to the plough.

the incessant spring, in which two crops a year could be harvested. Other writers boast of the roses that blossomed twice a year at Paestum in Campania; probably this means the intermittent, perennial blossoming, still characteristic of some favored parts of Italy.

Many are the trees that clothe the Italian landscape. Of oaks there are several varieties: one, the *aesculus*, provided leaves for the "civic crown," earned by saving the life of a Roman citizen in battle; another, the *ilex*, or holm oak, keeps its glossy leaves in winter. The spreading beech tree (*fagus*) was valued for its shade, and grew in the Roman Campagna as late as the third century B.C.; it still clothes the upper slopes of the Alban Mount. The elm (*ulmus*) and a variety of poplar have been much used as a support for the vines that are "wedded" to it. Of the willow (*salix*) that grows in the lowlands, wicker baskets were made; and the mountain fir (*abies*) was valued for shipbuilding. Conspicuous today are the pruned, umbrella-shaped pine (*pinus*) and the spire-like cypress (*cypressus*), associated with cemeteries; both these were brought in ancient times from Greece or western Asia. The palm grows well in Italy as far north as Rome, and in favored spots still further north. The Romans were familiar with not a few kinds of shrubs, and prized especially the myrtle, the box, and the privet; the ivy (*hedera*) was sacred to Bacchus and to poets. It would be pleasant to linger over the many flowers, both wild and cultivated, whose names stud the pages of the Roman poets. Some, like the *hyacinthus* (most often a variety of lily), puzzle even the botanist; others we know well as violets, marigolds, narcissi, lilies, and roses (introduced from Asia). The Romans cut many of these for garlands; and in the streets of an Italian town to-day nothing is more beautiful than the flower markets.

In primitive times the Roman farmer grew a kind of wheat known as spelt (*far*), which was used in the marriage-cakes of the ancient patrician marriage ceremony (*confarreatio*) long after a better kind of wheat (*triticum*) was commonly grown. Barley (*hordeum*) and other grains were also raised. Various kinds of beans (*faba*), peas (*pisum*), and lentils (*lens*) found a place in the kitchen garden along with many of our common vegetables. A wild grape was known in Italy in prehistoric times, but the cultivated vine came later from Greek lands. So, too, the olive tree and most of the fruit trees were imported from Africa or Asia; pomegranate, quince, fig, black mulberry, pear, plum, peach, and cherry. The citron, the lemon, and the orange were introduced after the classical period, and flourish in Italy to-day. Walnuts and chestnuts were plentiful, and various small fruits and berries, including the strawberry (*fraga*), which may be picked near Rome to-day even in December.

We shall have occasion to notice later that Italy is rich in minerals, providing many kinds of building stone; and from the volcanic regions come sulphur and other mineral products. From the quarries near Luna, on the northwest coast, is cut the snowy marble of Carrara; and the ancient Romans delighted in the colored marbles of Greece and Africa.

The natural beauty of Italy, enhanced by the softness of the climate and the fascination of centuries of human associations, has won the hearts of all who have known it. Of its appeal to the Romans, something will be said in another chapter. Modern travellers find in Italy something even richer, contrasting it with the bleakness of a northern land or with the shallowness of a younger civilization. Here Greek column and Roman arch, Christian basilica and cloister, Byzantine mosaic and Florentine carving and painting, garden terrace and fountain, pagan manuscript and mediaeval shrine, music of Palestrina and poem of Dante, fill one with a sense both of the endless variety and of the continuity of civilization. Nor can one forget the charm of the Italians of to-day, perhaps especially of the peasants, — their vivacity and dignity and courtesy. It is no wonder that Italians abroad think with longing of this land. Sings the girl Mignon in Goethe's *Wilhelm Meisters Lehrjahre*:

"Kennst du das Land, wo die Zitronen blühn?
Dahin! Dahin
Möcht' ich mit dir, o mein Geliebter, ziehn!"

And northerners have found in Italy a spiritual home.[1] Sometimes its brilliancy has palled on them. Browning loved Italy well, and lived there for more than fifteen years; yet he writes, "Oh, to be in England now that April's there!" Perhaps Italy adopts in perfect kinship only those who, with their forebears, have found during several generations a congenial home within her borders; and perhaps only those people who belong to the Mediterranean type or to a kindred race will long make it their home. It is time for us to ask who were the people that dwelt there in ancient times.

2. The Peoples

Among the ancients it was believed that racial characters were fixed by climate and soil, and the Romans found in the natural advantages of Italy the chief cause of Roman greatness.[2] So Virgil hailed Italy as the mighty mother not only of harvests, of the vine, and of flocks, but of men, the Scipios and the Caesars. Yet but few of the peoples of Italy can be held to be in any sense aboriginal.

[1] Some mention of the tribute of several of them to Italy will be found in the List of Books at the end of this volume.
[2] Cf. E. E. Sikes, *Roman Poetry*, pp. 114 f.

Of the very earliest inhabitants, cave men who lived in Italy in the Old Stone Age, there are a few unimportant traces. In the Late Stone Age, we may picture Italy as inhabited by a primitive race, long-skulled and dark of complexion, which, like the similar inhabitants of the Balkan and the Spanish peninsulas, were swept along in the Bronze and the Iron Ages by successive waves of invasion on the part of more vigorous Indo-Europeans, men of shorter skulls and fairer complexion. In historic times we find some of the primitive race crowded into northwestern Italy and along the Riviera, and known as Ligurians; the Messapians, or Iapygians, near the heel of Italy, represent a similar survival of a primitive people; and doubtless many of these peoples were absorbed by their conquerors and became the substratum of the population of Italy. Whether the Ligurians were a "Mediterranean" or African people, as their skulls and their custom of burying their dead would indicate, or whether on the contrary they were Indo-Europeans, as the scanty survivals of their language would more plausibly argue, is still uncertain. Probably it was not they but rather the earliest bands of Indo-European invaders from the north who, during the Late Stone Age and the Bronze Age, inhabited the southern Alps, the northern Apennines, and the Po valley, and built pile dwellings over bodies of water or even over land surrounded by moats. Remains of these dwellings, at any rate, have been found in deposits known as "terramara"; the pile-built city of Venice preserves the type, and Roman military camps and frequently towns were built on a plan derived from it. The terramara peoples not only knew the use of bronze but cremated their dead before burying them in "cities of the dead" resembling those of the living. In the course of a few hundred years either they or, as is more likely, a new band of invading

Indo-Europeans of a similar stock developed the civilization known to us from graves found at Villanova, near Bologna, as well as elsewhere, even in Latium. These "Villanovans" also burned their dead; they could work metal, both bronze brooches and iron tools. And the urns in which the ashes of their dead were placed show the oblong form, with door and smoke-hole, of the later Italic and Roman house.[1] For these "Villanovans" represent the group of peoples whom we may fairly call Italic.[2]

The first wave of Italic invaders seems to have been rapidly driven along by its successor, and to have reached Sicily, where its people, known as Siculi, mingled with the aboriginal Sicani. The second wave included the main body of the Italic invaders, in two branches: the Umbrians, who settled in the northeastern Apennines, and the Sabellians, who dominated the central mountains, and whose various subdivisions, — Sabines, Latins, Samnites, and other minor tribes,— found homes in well-defined regions. From one small people near the toe of the peninsula, the Itali, came the name later to be used of the whole peninsula. The language of the Sabellians was the Safine or Oscan dialect; Latin, a kindred dialect, spoken by the Romans in historic times, preserved a large element of the tongue of the primitive, probably Indo-European Ligurians, and in time prevailed over all other Italic dialects. During the Italic invasions of Italy, a number of Greek invaders found their way into northeastern and central Italy; and Virgil's picture of the city of Pallanteum, ruled by the Greek Evander, on the site of what was one day to be the city of Rome, preserves the

[1] Cf. p. 125.
[2] See further T. E. Peet, *The Stone and Bronze Ages in Italy*; D. Randall-MacIver, *Italy before the Romans* (Oxford, 1928); *Villanovans and Early Etruscans* (Oxford, 1924); and *The Iron Age in Italy* (Oxford, 1927).

tradition of these early Greek settlers.[1] The great age of
Greek colonization in southern Italy was, of course, some
centuries later.

While the Italic tribes were still struggling for the possession of Italy, probably not long after 850 B.C., the Etruscans,
an alien race from Asia Minor, descended on the western
coast and seized the territory bounded by the Apennines and
the Tiber, and found footholds in Campania. A mysterious
and a warlike people, whose non-Indo-European language
can be only very imperfectly read, they built walled towns
and beat back the Italic tribes who still remained in loosely
organized cantons or leagues; with the Umbrians they probably mingled to some extent. For several centuries the
Etruscans seemed likely to win the whole of Italy. Their
rock-hewn chamber-tombs have been found in considerable numbers, sometimes containing large sarcophagi surmounted by figures of the dead reclining as at a banquet.
The contributions of the Etruscans to the early politics, the
religion, the art, and even the alphabet, of Rome, we shall
have occasion to notice in later chapters.[2]

Two other peoples made their way into Italy. Many times
during the centuries of Roman growth tribes of fair-haired
Celts (called by the Romans *Galli*), tall and short-skulled,
and armed with long iron swords, pushed down from their

---

[1] Virgil, to be sure, like Livy and his contemporary the Greek historian
Dionysius of Halicarnassus, was to a great extent dependent on the confused
traditions recorded by early Greek and Roman historians of Italy. Of these
the Greeks, such as the Sicilian Timaeus (350–256 B.C.), were especially interested in showing that Romans were an "ancient people and a Greek one"
(Dionysius); hence, probably, the stories of Evander and Hercules (= Her-
acles), and the attempts, by a fictitious dynasty of Alban kings, to bridge the
gap between the burning of Troy, from which Aeneas escaped, and the
founding of Rome. See further C. Saunders, *Vergil's Primitive Italy* (New
York, 1930), esp. pp. 39–46.

[2] Pp. 39–41, 159–161, 172 f., 321–323.

homes north of the Alps into the sunnier lands to the south. Probably they were kinsmen of the Umbrians. Fortunately for the Romans, these Celts served as a strong check on the power of the Etruscans, whom they outnumbered; and though Rome itself fell for a short time into the hands of the Gauls (390 B.C.), the invaders were bought off by the Romans and weakened by malaria, and retired in the main into the Po valley. But the threat of further Celtic invasions from the regions north of the Alps was not averted till the beginning of the first century B.C., and began again when the Roman Empire began to show signs of weakness. Finally, among the inhabitants of ancient Italy are to be numbered the Greek cities of the southern coasts reaching from the instep around to the shores of Campania and along the coast of Sicily; there were also Greek cities in southern Gaul. So important and so distinctively Greek were the cities of southern Italy, though constantly attacked by Italic tribes, that the region was known as *Magna Graecia*.

Except the Etruscans, then, probably all the peoples of ancient Italy were Indo-Europeans, and their qualities were well adapted to supplement each other and to form a single strong nation, if necessity or purpose demanded. But although the process of fusion and consolidation was slow, and was not completed till the end of the Roman Republic, the predominant character of this whole nation was stamped by that small people of central Italy which could borrow from Etruscan, Celt, and Greek without surrendering its peculiar nature.

The Romans themselves, indeed, clearly represent an early fusion of peoples; this not only is the ancient tradition, but is made probable by the evidence of archaeology and by the long conflict between plebeian and patrician. The tradition distinguishes between the "aboriginal" inhabitants of

Latium (who represent the stratum of people found in historic times chiefly in Liguria), the Greek (or "Pelasgian") settlers, and the newcomers of the Italic tribes (the Rutuli, and others). Thus Virgil's Aeneas finds an alliance with King Latinus, who rules over the Latini (thought of as aboriginal), and with the Greek Evander, against Turnus, chief of the Rutuli (who represent the turbulent Italic invaders). One of the most significant tasks of the *Aeneid*, nobly conceived and nobly carried out, as we shall see later, is to represent the conflict of the city of Rome and the primitive culture of the land with the rude vigor of the Italic tribes whom Turnus musters from their mountain fastnesses, and to hint prophetically at the final reconciliation. But Virgil, interested in fusing the legend of Troy with that of the foundation of Rome, makes Aeneas and Latinus (the primitive people) victorious over Turnus and the Italians; whereas the fact is certain that the Italians conquered the previous inhabitants, and the Trojans may here be dismissed as legendary. We must note once more in passing that it is the tongue of the Latini, not that of the other Italic tribes, that appears to be nearest to the language of the primitive "Ligurian" inhabitants of Italy; the conquering minority acquiesced in the tongue of the conquered majority.[1] Virgil deals with the victory of the language as a condition im-

---

[1] The conquerors did, to be sure, impose their ethnic suffixes, generally of the form -NO-, on peoples who had preferred names with the suffix -CO- or -TI-. Thus we have not only names like Sabi*ni* but Marruc*ini* replacing Marru*ci*, Roma*ni* (from an Etruscan stem) replacing Quiri*tes*, Lati*nus* superseding Latia*ris* (except in religious connections). Moreover many classical Latin words show the earlier pure Latin sound *q* changed to *p*, as in *lupus* (for *lucus*, wolf), and Pompilius (= Latin Quintilius, or even Quinquilius). Thus the Norman conquerors of England in the main accepted the language of the conquered minority, but not without impressing on it many of their own words. (Cf. R. S. Conway, in *C. A. H.*, Vol. IV, Ch. XIII; and Sir W. Ridgeway, "Who Were the Romans?" in *Proceedings of the British Academy*, 1907–08.)

posed by Juno before Aeneas shall conquer: the Latins shall not lose their name or their tongue.[1]

Nearer to historic times is the tradition that the people of Rome under Romulus provided themselves with wives by stealing them from the Sabines, and that after a war with the Sabines, under Titus Tatius, the two peoples were fused, two classes, the Titienses and the Ramnenses, being distinguished. Though these names, like that of the third class, the Luceres, are probably of Etruscan origin, it seems clear that the Romans did consist of at least two strains, a primitive plebeian strain, and a conquering, patrician, Italic strain from the Sabine hills to the east of Rome; the class warfare of plebeians and patricians continued the struggle. The plebeians, like the other primitive inhabitants of Italy, may have buried their dead; the Sabines clearly did. Most Romans, however, like the other Italic tribes, practised cremation. Both methods of disposing of the dead are found in the early graves in the Roman Forum, the inhumation graves being later than the cremation ones. The different methods of burial cannot be said, however, to prove differences of race.[2] In the attitude toward marriage, on the other hand, a divergence is more apparent. The plebeians had only a civil rite, and admitted divorce, and probably at first reckoned succession through the mother; the patricians held, at least in theory, a much stricter view of the sacred-

---

[1] Virgil, *Aen.* XII, 819–828.

[2] Cf. H. J. Rose, *Primitive Culture in Italy* (London, 1926), pp. 30 f.; A. Piganiol, *Essai sur les Origines de Rome* (Paris, 1917); Inez Scott, "Early Roman Traditions," in *Mem. Am. Acad. Rome*, Vol. VII (1929); F. von Duhn, *Italische Gräberkunde*, Vol. I (Heidelberg, 1924); Sir W. Ridgeway, "Who Were the Romans?" (But Ridgeway erroneously attributes cremation to the Sabines, who were generally inhumers, with the notable exception of the Claudian *gens*.) H. J. Rose, in "Patricians and Plebeians at Rome" (*J. R. S.*, XII (1922), 106–133), offers trenchant arguments against the idea that patricians and plebeians were in origin different peoples.

ness of marriage and of its indissolubility except through
death, and had sole claim to the religious form of marriage known as *confarreatio*, symbolized by the sharing of a
sacred cake, and introduced, as was believed, by the Sabine,
Numa Pompilius. Only those born of a marriage thus
solemnized could ever hold the major priesthoods, and these
were associated with gods of Sabine origin. In this high conception of the stability of marriage, and in tracing succession
through the father, as in many other customs, the patricians
show their common bond with Homer's "Achaeans" and
with the Celtic and Teutonic peoples of northern Europe.
In the use of armor, moreover, plebeians and patricians long
preserved the evidence of their different origins: the lower
classes in the Roman army long fought with the oblong
shield (*scutum*) that was indigenous in the Mediterranean
world, while those of the First Class and the *Equites* carried
the round shield (*clipeus*) found among northern peoples.
The Romans, then, were a fusion of the primitive inhabitants of Latium with the Italic Sabines, together with various less important accretions, probably from the Siculan,
Pelasgian, and Etruscan peoples, who formed a third element called by the Romans the Luceres. How they came to
live in Rome and how they gained control of their neighbors
must next be considered.

3. THE CITY

To the Roman nothing seemed more surely eternal than
the hills of Rome. Yet they are young hills, if measured by
the Apennines. Some thousands of years before the founding of Rome there was no Latin plain; the waves of the
Mediterranean dashed against the feet of the Apennines,
and the rivers fell directly into the Sea. In the course of

ages, great volcanic upheavals lifted the floor of the bay, and showered cinders and ashes on it to a depth of several hundred feet. Where the ashes fell in water they were compacted into rock, reddish or grey or brown. At length the rushing waters of glaciers further north channelled their way through the rock and ashes; along a volcanic crack, as the waters subsided, flowed the chief torrent, the river Tiber, fed by scores of tributaries. Another volcanic upheaval a little to the south hurled up the steep Alban Mount and later, along the slopes of its worn rim, the smaller craters that became the Alban Lake and the Lake of Nemi; and within the Alban crater appeared the cone of Monte Cavo, more than three thousand feet high. This same upheaval hurled against the course of the Tiber fragments of rock that blocked its channel and compelled it to wind about them or to wear them away, cutting gorges and leaving islands and fingers of rock that rose above the flood or projected into it. Another glacial age ensued, and when it receded its melting waters again flooded the plain, carrying down from the mountains rich soil and volcanic ash and spreading it over the slopes and level ground. Through it the Tiber wound its sinuous way, ever a narrower stream, and finding its marshy mouth ever farther from the mountains, as it carried the rich silt seawards. The Roman harbor of Ostia, once at the Tiber's mouth, is now four miles from the sea.

Such was the plain in which the earliest inhabitants of Latium lived and into which the Italic invaders came as they passed from the foothills of the Apennines. They still dwelt by choice on hilly sites for safety, but gradually spread out into the plain, then far more wooded than to-day. The strongest settlements were on the ridges and slopes of the Alban Mount. Yet there was no political organization to hold them together, or to enable them to assert lordship over their kinsmen who kept sheep or tilled farms down in the plain. The Latins did, to be sure, join in a common worship of Jupiter Latiaris on the Alban Mount; but it was only the danger of a common enemy that could persuade them to forget for a time their own quarrels. And chief among their enemies were the Etruscans just across the Tiber. Nevertheless they continued to push out their settlements of herdsmen and farmers and hunters toward the river, and presently reached the Tiber. Already they may have bartered their flocks and herds for the wares of the Etruscans, who had a trade route along the foot of the Sabine hills and down to the Greeks of Campania; and there was another route along the Tiber valley by which salt was carried from the flats at the mouth of the river up to the interior of Italy. To this day the salt road keeps its name, the Via Salaria. From time to time, moreover, trading ships made their way up the river.

Fourteen miles from the sea the Latins established on the Tiber a trading post, soon to become a military outpost, the city of Rome. The general course of the river at this point is from north to south, but its winding course past the hills of Rome forms a letter S. Just below the little island in the middle of the river, where it bends to follow the last part of the S, stood an ancient wooden bridge, the Pons Sublicius of historic times; on the low banks of the eastern shore were the cattle market (Forum Boarium) and later the vegetable market (Forum Holitorium). Above them rose the three low but steep hills, once islands in the flood, which the Romans called the Capitoline, the Palatine, and the Aventine. Between the first two of these hills drained from the finger-hills to the northeast the little stream that was later carried underground to the river by the Cloaca Maxima. By a true instinct Virgil brings his hero to the site of Rome up the river, so that his first glimpse of the site should include all that was most characteristic of the earliest city: wooded banks, market-place, and, just above, the citadel on the Palatine, which he presently ascends with the friendly king Evander. Here was doubtless the earliest Latin settlement at Rome, the Palatium, named for Pales, the Italic goddess of flocks;[1] and when its rectangular top of some twenty-five acres was walled, it was sometimes known as Roma Quadrata. Other settlements were soon made on other hills; possibly the inhabitants of the Esquiline, the spur projecting toward the Palatine from the northeast, with its blunt fingers (Quirinal, Viminal, Cispian, and Oppian), were Sabines.[2] Presently, by a fusion of Latin and Sabine settlements, the boundaries of the new city were extended to include what became known as the Septmontium, though it is uncertain precisely which seven hills were thus included. In the marshy valley between the Palatine and the Esquiline, soon called the Forum Romanum and used as the chief place of trade and other business, have been found graves, dating from as early as 1000 B.C., which show that both burial and cremation were known. Very recently there have been found in the Forum evidences of habitations of about the seventh century. The united settlements of Latins and Sabines now fortified the Capitoline, and used the more northerly of its two summits as their citadel (Arx), while on the other was built during the period of Etruscan domination the most august of Roman temples, that of Jupiter Optimus Maximus.[3]

[1] Cf. pascor, "feed."

[2] It is at least possible that the dwellers on these hills were distinguished, as out-habitants, from the in-habitants of the Palatine, esquilinus being the converse of inquilinus.

[3] Horace, prophesying the immortality of his poems, declares that they shall endure "dum Capitolium|scandet cum tacita virgine pontifex" (Odes III, 30, 9 f.).

About this enlarged city, which presently included also the Aventine to the southwest and the Caelian to the southeast, was built an earthen rampart and ditch, here and there reenforced with stone;[1] within this fortification, some five miles in circumference, were those hills, famous in the age of Virgil as "the seven hills of Rome": the Palatine, Capitoline, Aventine, Caelian, Esquiline, Viminal, and Quirinal. On the level fields to the northwest of this walled town, and bounded by the curve of the Tiber, was the Campus Martius, the ancient drill-ground of the Romans, and for many years the usual meeting-place of Roman assemblies. Across the river, above the island, rose the Janiculum; this hill the people of Rome early seized and fortified as a defense against attack from the north. So strong were the fortifications of Rome, and still more, the Roman armies in the field, that after the building of the wall just mentioned no other wall was needed till the days of the barbarian invasions, when the Emperor Aurelian (270–275 A.D.) and his successor Probus flung about the city the great wall, fourteen miles long, much of which stands to-day.[2] At each stage of the city's growth the Romans thought of a spiritual boundary, the *pomoerium*, approximately parallel to the physical boundary, marked out, in ritual fashion, by the furrow of a plough, the ploughshare being lifted over the places where gates were to be made. Within the sacred *pomoerium* the gods of the city were powerful, and the auspices must be taken within it; and round it moved the lustral processions of priests. As the

[1] A similar fortification may be seen at Ardea. The stone wall long called "Servian," of which fragments may be seen in several parts of Rome, is now known to have been built after the Gallic capture of Rome (390 B.C.). Cf. p. 44. The indispensable work on the republican wall of Rome is now that of Gösta Säflund, *Le Mura di Roma Repubblicana* (Lund, Sweden; and Oxford, 1932).

[2] For a full account of this wall, and the modifications of it, see I. A. Richmond, *The City Wall of Imperial Rome* (Oxford, 1930).

physical boundaries of the city were enlarged, the limits of the *pomoerium* were extended; later, the *pomoerium* might be extended as a symbol of the enlargement of distant frontiers.[1]

The site of Rome was well chosen for a people that was to extend its power over the whole of Italy. At the centre of Italy, on the side that was richest in agriculture, astride the chief river of Italy proper and indeed the only navigable river, at the intersection of two important trade routes, the site was of great economic advantage. Still more desirable was it from a military point of view. The early Romans were not a naval people, and the fourteen miles between Rome and the sea kept them from the danger of attack by Etruscan and Carthaginian navies. Indeed, before Genseric (455 A.D.) Rome was never captured by an invader from the sea. For the conditions of early warfare by land, the hills, low but steep and easily fortified by walls and escarpments, made an excellent defense; and the possession of fortresses on both sides of the Tiber enabled the Romans to beat back enemies whether from the south or from the north. In the days of the Samnite Wars and the Second Punic War the Romans had reason to be thankful for their position at the centre of Italy, for it gave them a strategic base of operations against enemies in every direction. They could launch armies, at the opportune moment, north, east, or south, using shorter and comparatively level lines of communication, while their enemies must move through mountainous country along more extended lines that made well-timed operations difficult.

Nevertheless the site of Rome was not in all respects perfect. The current of the Tiber is too swift for easy navigation; its bed is too shallow for large ships. The lower parts

---

[1] Tacitus, *Ann.* XII, 23. See further J. H. Oliver, "The Augustan Pomoerium," in *Mem. Am. Acad. Rome*, X (1932), 145–182.

of the city are often flooded, the level rising fifteen or even twenty feet in a few hours, and the water reaching at times to the Pantheon.[1] And the hills are not high enough to protect the Romans from the malaria that has sometimes been a deadly foe.[2] Though the Latin plain was once very fertile it was soon overpopulated, and food had to be imported; and there are few mineral resources in the immediate neighborhood. Rome could never become a great industrial city. In a word, the site was better for the early city than for a more developed people.

Some of the disadvantages of the site the Romans at times appreciated, and more than once there was thought of migrating to a better site. When Rome lay in ashes, after its capture by the Gauls (390 B.C.), there was a proposal that the Romans move to the Etruscan city of Veii, a dozen miles to the north, a crag fortress which they had captured a few years before. During the Civil Wars Horace dreamed of a better home for the Romans to be found across the seas in some Islands of the Blest;[3] there were those who believed that Julius Caesar intended to make Alexandria or Ilium his capital,[4] and that Augustus revived the idea, or that he considered Byzantium as a possible seat of government, which Constantine, of course, actually made it.[5] But the idea did

[1] Horace in the second ode of the First Book represents such a flood as the punishment of the gods for civil war. Tacitus tells of the panic and superstition caused by such a flood in the year 69 A.D. (*Hist.* I, 86).

[2] None of the hills rise more than 200 feet above the river. The Palatine and the Capitoline are both 165 feet high; the various spurs of the Esquiline, the highest of the hills, are only a few feet higher. In ancient times the hills were about 30 feet higher than to-day, but have been weathered away, while the level of the valleys between them has been raised.

[3] Horace, Epode 16.

[4] Suetonius, *Julius,* 79; cf. Horace, *Odes* III, 3; Virgil, *Aen.* XII, 819–828; and see further R. S. Conway, *New Studies of a Great Inheritance,* pp. 59–62, and C. Pascal, *Feste e Poesie Antiche* (Milan, 1926), pp. 229–257.

[5] Cf. pp. 84, 260.

violence to all the deepest instincts of the older Romans;
and Livy, recounting the proposal to begin a new city at
Veii, has put in the mouth of the general Camillus a moving
speech in which the veteran enlists the Romans against such
a migration. And what strikes the reader most forcibly in his
plea is that it is not primarily the economic and military advantages of the site of Rome that Camillus invokes, but the
hallowed associations of religion; the gods will not suffer a
removal. Toward the end of his speech, however, he does
make much of the site. "Not without reason did gods and
men choose this spot for the founding of the city; the healthful hills, the convenient river, by which harvests are carried
down from inland regions and trade is brought from the sea,
our position conveniently near the coast, and yet not exposed by an excessive propinquity to peril from foreign
fleets, our situation in the middle of Italy, a place destined,
as no other, for the expansion of a city." [1] Thus both material reasons and the ever deeper affections of men for
places in which their fathers and their gods were rooted
bound the Romans firmly to their city.

The early city grew rapidly. The simple farmer population was swollen by all sorts of newcomers: prosperous
farmers from the outlying districts of Latium, who directed
their farms, but lived at Rome; artisans from Etruria,
veteran soldiers, slaves captured in the wars. The rude huts
of wood and wattles that had crowned the hills and spread
along narrow and irregular streets into the valleys were replaced by houses of wood and brick, and temples and shrines

[1] Livy, V, 54. Like Cicero (De Rep. II, 6), Livy exaggerates the health-
fulness of the site. Early Rome built many shrines to the Goddess of Fever;
in spite of adverse natural changes (cf. p. 7), better drainage and water supply improved conditions during the late Republic and the Empire; in the
Dark Ages primitive conditions returned with the breaking of the aqueducts,
not to be greatly improved till very recent times.

sprang up. Successive fires, floods, and earthquakes repeatedly levelled the houses, and new ones were built; but till late in the Republic private houses were of a humble sort,[1] and even the public buildings aroused the patronizing contempt of those who knew the fair cities of Campania and Greece. The ancient landmarks were kept with jealous pride: the Cave on the Aventine where Hercules had wrestled with the giant Cacus,[2] and the Altar of Hercules (the Ara Maxima) near the river; the thatched Hut of Romulus on the Palatine (a modern reconstruction of which may be seen on the same hill); the Cave of the Lupercal, also on the Palatine, where Romulus and Remus had been found, suckled by the wolf,[3] and in the Forum near it the Ruminal Fig Tree, a scion of the tree that had sheltered them; [4] the Grave of Romulus in the Forum; the Sister's Beam, beneath which passed in penance the surviving Horatius who killed his sister in anger for her grief at the death of her betrothed, a Curiatius, whom he had slain as a foe, and outside the city the graves of the two Horatii and the three Curiatii; [5] the statue of the augur, Attius Navius, who had proved the efficacy of his art by cutting a stone with a razor, — the statue might still confute those who doubted the story; [6] the

[1] Horace, *Odes* II, 15, 13–20.

[2] Livy, I, 7; Virgil, *Aen.* VIII, 190–305. It need hardly be added that this and most of the following legends are aetiological, — that is, they were invented to explain sites and landmarks of which the real origin had been forgotten. As usual, such legends, however untrue as history, have much of the truth of poetry as an interpretation of history and of the Roman character. Some of the landmarks (e.g. the House of Romulus) may have been built to lend credibility to ancient legends already generally believed. How some of the legends may have taken form is considered by E. Pais, in *Ancient Legends of Roman History* (New York, 1905), an interesting and ingenious book, to be taken not without a grain of salt.

[3] Livy, I, 5.

[4] Livy, I, 4; Ovid, *Fasti* II, 412.

[5] Livy, I, 25–26; cf. below, p. 36.

[6] Livy, I, 36.

horns, in Diana's Temple on the Aventine, of the beautiful
Sabine cow that a shrewd Roman priest had sacrificed, and
so kept sovereignty at Rome;[1] the cliff, on the southern
brow of the Capitoline, near which the maiden Tarpeia, who
had opened the citadel to the Sabines, was crushed to death
by their shields, whether a traitress to Rome or a shrewd but
ill-starred heroine the Romans were not certain;[2] the statue
of Horatius Cocles, famous defender of the wooden bridge
against the Etruscans and Tarquin the Proud.[3] At the head
of the Forum, a little to the southeast of the Arx on the
Capitoline, may be seen to-day the underground prison[4] in
which from the days of the early kings of Rome were kept
those who awaited trial or punishment; here were im-
prisoned, among many others, Jugurtha, the accomplices of
Catiline, and Vercingetorix, and, according to tradition, St.
Peter and St. Paul. A few yards to the east was the Senate
House (*Curia*), and, in front of it, an early meeting place of
the Assembly (*Comitia*) and the orators' *Rostra*.[5]

When Evander and Aeneas looked down from the Palatine into the marshy valley to the north and across to the
wooded slopes beyond it, the region was filled with lowing
cattle; but Virgil's eye saw in the valley and on the hills the
stately Rome that was to be.[6] The valley, now the Forum
Romanum, for a time was a busy market-place, after it had
been drained by the Cloaca Maxima. But its scant three
acres were too precious to remain a place of barter, and the
cattle market and the vegetable market soon were found
only by the river. Business was still done in the Forum, but
it tended to become the business of the banker, the lawyer,

---

[1] Livy, I, 45.   [2] Livy, I, 11.   [3] Livy, II, 10.
[4] The Mamertine Prison; the lowest part is the Robur Tullianum.
[5] Named from the bronze beaks of captured ships formerly fastened to it.
[6] *Passimque armenta videbant | Romanoque foro et lautis mugire Carinis*
(*Aen.* VIII, 360 f.).

and the statesman. Just below the northwestern corner of
the Palatine was the round Temple of Vesta, and next to it
the Regia, once the abode of the Rex, and later the office of
the Pontifex Maximus, his successor, and of the Vestal Virgins, who were under his special protection. Numerous other
temples rose in or near the Forum: at the eastern end, that of
Jupiter Stator,[1] and in other parts of it an ancient shrine of
the city Penates, and temples of Castor, of Saturn,[2] and of
Concord. Indeed, so hallowed were the associations of this
region that the devious street that extended for half a mile
from the Temple of Jupiter Stator to the foot of the Capitoline was known as the Sacra Via. Along it passed the triumphal processions of victorious generals, their faces painted
with vermilion, on their way to the great Temple of Jupiter
Optimus Maximus on the Capitoline, to pay homage to the
god, whose statue was likewise painted.[3] It was on this same
street, too, that the poet Horace met and outwitted the
famous bore.[4] Crowded, unsymmetrical, never deliberately
planned, the Forum grew almost as chance would have it;
and indeed a part of its fascination lies in the picturesque
charm of its oddly jumbled landmarks. It is no wonder that
it was in the Forum that the Romans revered the "Navel"
(*Umbilicus*) of the City, or that Augustus placed a few

---

[1] To Jupiter as founder of the city; but the Romans believed that Romulus had built it in gratitude to the "Stayer" who turned the tide of battle in
the Forum against the Sabines (Livy, I, 12). Cicero could make an impressive appeal to Jupiter Stator to save Rome from Catiline (*In L. Catilinam*, I,
33; cf. I, 11); his third speech against Catiline tells (20–22) of the new statue
of Jupiter, that very day installed on the Capitoline, facing east so that it
could behold the Temple of Concord just below and bring to light the guilt of
the Catilinarian conspirators who were there being tried before the Senate.

[2] God of sown fields; the temple later became an important treasury.

[3] Cf. p. 322.

[4] *Sat.* I, 9. A new interpretation of the name Sacra Via would explain
it as an ancient Street of Tombs in the Forum, outside the primitive settlement on the Palatine. See Gösta Säflund, in *Corolla Archaeologica* (Lund,
Sweden, and Oxford, 1932), p. 70.

yards from it the "Golden Milestone" (*Miliarium Aureum*) on which were inscribed the distances from Rome to many Italian and provincial cities. In a true sense this was the hub of the world.

At the sides of the Forum, for the shelter of the courts and other legal business, were built basilicas, rectangular halls with central nave and side aisles and colonnades. Of these one of the most important was that begun by Julius Caesar and finished by Augustus; its ground-plan may be seen toward the western end of the Forum, between the temples of Castor and Saturn. The records of the state were housed in a building (the Tabularium) just below the Capitol. Thus the most important edifices that were to be associated both with religion and with the state were grouped within the view of one standing, like Aeneas and Evander, on the vantage-ground of the Palatine. Meanwhile the Palatine itself became the home of nobles and well-to-do burghers, while it was chiefly the humbler folk who found homes on the less aristocratic Aventine and Caelian hills, on the slopes of the northern hills, or in the Campus Martius. In the valley between the Palatine and the Aventine was erected the wooden Circus Maximus, later magnificently rebuilt in stone; and until the late Republic the theatres, in the southern part of the Campus Martius, were still temporary wooden structures. Down the river, a little below the island, docks and granaries had been built, and behind them was rising the enormous rubbish heap of broken jars and other *débris* now known as the Monte Testaccio. The river itself was now spanned by several more bridges, and water was brought to Rome from the hills by several aqueducts.

If we would picture to ourselves the growth of republican Rome to the Rome of the emperors, we must imagine many changes. The Palatine has become the dwelling of the emperors, as the modern word "palace" suggests, and includes the new Temple of Apollo. For a time the vast Golden House of Nero, with its gardens, has stretched from the Palatine across the eastern end of the Forum, and up the slope of the Esquiline. Old temples have been restored; Augustus declares in his autobiography, the Monumentum Ancyranum,[1] that he restored no less than eighty-two. New temples have been built; besides that of Apollo, just mentioned, Augustus, aided by his minister, Agrippa, built the great Pantheon in the Campus Martius, which was now rapidly filling with houses and public buildings. To relieve the congestion in the Forum Romanum, several of the Caesars built great new forums to the northwest. The new public buildings, and many of the private houses, were of more durable and more beautiful materials than of old. Familiar is the boast of Augustus that he found Rome of brick and left it of marble; but it should be added that much of the marble was destroyed in fires and that because the marble was used chiefly as a thin veneer it became a convenient quarry for the purposes of later builders, pagan or Christian, often being burned in kilns to provide lime. Thus it is chiefly the brick and concrete, which were beneath the marble, that meet the eye of the traveller to-day.

Yet of solidity much, but of splendor little is extant:
"Brickwork I found thee, and marble I left thee!" their Emperor vaunted;
"Marble I thought thee, and brickwork I find thee!" the tourist may answer.[2]

---

[1] So named because a copy of it has been found inscribed on stone in Ancyra, in Asia Minor; another copy has been found at Antioch in Pisidia. The original was in Rome.   See also p. 233.

[2] A. H. Clough, in "Amours de Voyage." Goethe's impressions of Rome were less disillusioned (*Italienische Reise* and *Römische Elegien*), as were Byron's (*Childe Harold*, Canto IV, especially stanzas 25–26, 78–80, 112 ff.; and *Manfred*, III, 4).

So wrote an English poet; but it is not difficult in the presence of these massive ruins to see them reclothed with splendor. The new stone and brick theatres rose in the Campus Martius, the magnificent Circus Maximus was rebuilt, and other circuses were built; enormous public baths were erected by several of the emperors; the Flavian Amphitheatre, or Colosseum, still stands at the eastern end of the Sacra Via; just outside the northeastern corner of the old wall, and later to be enclosed by the wall of Aurelian, were built the barracks of the Praetorian Guard that policed the city. New bridges and docks and warehouses, new aqueducts and fountains, and well-paved streets were added; and the victories of the emperors were commemorated by triumphal arches and columns.[1] In the Campus Martius, near the Tiber, Augustus built a lordly mausoleum for his family (now used as a concert hall), and not far from it the great Altar of Peace (*Ara Pacis Augustae*), bearing the finest reliefs ever carved on Roman stone.[2] On the northern hills and across the Tiber were spacious gardens, sometimes laid out where burial grounds or crowded slums had been. Such were the gardens on the Esquiline on Maecenas, the trusted adviser of Augustus. Not less than one-eighth of the area of Rome was given up to these breathing-places, green with pines and palm trees. The *pomoerium* was again and again enlarged, till the city nearly reached the limits of the walls of Aurelian; it was divided by Augustus into fourteen *regiones*, and was entered by thirty-seven gates. Probably a million souls now thronged Rome. It was a city of undulating roofs

[1] Of arches the most notable now standing are those of Titus, at the east end of the Forum; of Constantine, just below the northeastern end of the Palatine; and of Septimius Severus, at the west end of the Forum hard by the Rostra. Of columns, that of Trajan, in his Forum, is the finest; that of Marcus Aurelius, rising above the great northern highway of the city, gives the name to the modern Piazza della Colonna. See further pp. 168–170.
[2] Cf. pp. 178–180.

with open squares and colonnades, dotted with fountains and obelisks and thousands of statues, crowded with toilers and pleasure-seekers, Romans and foreigners alike.

Beneath the surface of pagan Rome was growing, scarcely suspected, a Christian Rome. As the Romans in historic times buried the ashes of their dead beside the roads outside the city, the Christians, obscure and in danger of persecution, excavated in numerous places in the rock under the Campagna the burial places for their dead. In the course of two hundred years these catacombs had been so far extended that they would make, if they were continuous, a tunnel of more than five hundred miles. Here and there in the city the Christians held their services, at first in private houses, later in churches that preserved something of the form of the secular basilicas and of the subterranean basilicas used by the pagan mystery-cults. As Christianity won its way and at last conquered Rome, churches were often built into pagan temples and into secular buildings; and during the next seventeen hundred years Rome saw rise several hundred new churches, at least one for every day in the year, as the saying goes.

But the city suffered incredible vicissitudes. Civil wars, barbarian invasions, struggles between the Papacy and temporal powers, Italian and foreign; fires and floods innumerable; ruthless pillage and the slow hand of time, — all these left little of the proud city of the Caesars. Wars and fevers again and again decimated the wretched population. The hills were desolate; the Forum Romanum, choked with half-buried ruins, was again the pasturage of cattle, as in Evander's day.[1] During the early Middle Ages, the Popes, entrenched in the Lateran Palace on the southeastern edge of

[1] So it appears in the etchings of Piranesi in the eighteenth century, when it was known as the *Campo Vaccino*.

the city, were able to keep at times some semblance of order; and various princely houses, lodged in ancient buildings, — tombs, theatres, and the like, — or in feudal fortresses in the Campagna, maintained their turbulent society. But during the absence of the Popes at Avignon, during the fourteenth century, human misery could hardly sink lower than did Rome and her few remaining inhabitants. Only the memory of her great past still claimed the loyalty of pilgrim and crusader. With the return of the Popes and the Renaissance came better days, though tardily; and it is chiefly to the architects of the next three hundred years, under the patronage of the Popes, that Rome owes the present appearance of many of her principal buildings. Churches and palaces, the new St. Peter's and the Vatican on the hill across the river, statues and fountains, were gradually erected; the inspiration of the ancient Roman architecture was strong, and the very stones of the ancient buildings were gathered up to build the new Rome. But many of the streets were still squalid and ill-lighted; and it was not until after the stormy struggles of the nineteenth century, in which the French and the Austrians were driven out and the Papacy submitted to the claims of a reunited Italy, that the modern city was able to put in order her streets and dwellings. Italy had long been divided into warring states; now, thanks to the crusading spirit of Garibaldi and Cavour and the devotion of the royal house of Savoy, Rome became the capital of the kingdom of Italy. Broad avenues, flanked by substantial houses and new public buildings and monuments, were constructed in the long-desolate quarters of the city; during the past decade a vigorous plan of excavation, city-planning, and building has been undertaken; and Rome now contains a population of about a million.

Nevertheless, for one who treads the streets of Rome and climbs its hills with leisurely foot, she is unique among all cities. There, as nowhere else, one reads history in every stone. The hills and the plain speak of geologic ages; the walls tell of the first settlers and warriors; ruined temple and basilica and palace are eloquent of priest and lawyer and emperor in days when men were learning to replace war by law and a common allegiance; Christian churches testify to the growth of a single faith held by men of many races in all parts of the world; and across the Campagna still stretch the roads by which the Romans carried their civilization to their furthest possessions and gave it to us, who are their heirs to-day. How they spread from the seven hills to their distant frontiers in Asia and Africa and northern Europe, we must now observe.

CHAPTER II

THE EXPANSION OF ROME : FROM VILLAGE TO EMPIRE

Urbem fecistis quod prius orbis erat.
Rutilius Claudius Namatianus, *De Reditu Suo* I, 66.

1. FROM VILLAGE TO CITY-STATE

THERE have been many empires in the history of the world, and each has had a different story. Some have arisen when a single strong race, more fortunate in geographical position than its neighbors, has absorbed other peoples and their lands and kept them in servitude; some have arisen when a sturdy people, living in a poor country, has seized the richer lands of older peoples whose character has grown softer; sometimes an individual conqueror, an Alexander or a Napoleon, has deliberately embarked on a career of conquest and empire-building; occasionally, as in the case of the British, empire has seemed to grow undesignedly from the varied purposes of explorers, traders, missionaries, and colonists. A theory of empire and a system of government relating the possessions in some manner to the ruling power have usually followed the fact of empire. But empires have seldom lasted long unless they have embodied a plausible political idea, aided by fortunate external circumstances, in a people (not merely an individual) gifted with strength of character. No purely military autocracy or despotism based merely on material resources has long endured.

The theory of Roman government was the product of Roman experience, and will concern us later; the Roman character, though essential to the growth of the empire, may also be reserved most conveniently as the subject of separate consideration. But the fact of empire, which preceded the theory of empire, was so largely the result of external circumstances, of geography and the order of events which no man could have foreseen, that we must first trace the stages in the expansion of Roman territory. We have already noted the advantage given the Romans in the site of their city. We shall see, moreover, that they were fortunate in being able to meet their various enemies successively, in the main, rather than at the same time, and in finding a few great leaders at the most critical moments. And inasmuch as the Romans have deservedly the reputation of being a military nation, we must notice particularly that for several centuries (until the age of Pompey) the expansion of the Roman territory was seldom due to any special aggressiveness on their part. They were not, of course, averse on moral grounds to fighting, if the occasion seemed to require fighting; but they had a ritual, conducted by the fetial priests, that served to delay the outbreak of war, and for a long time there was not a deliberate policy of expansion that required offensive wars.[1] And if the following pages necessarily are concerned to a large extent with wars, we are not interested primarily in military history as such, but rather in the occasions of the successive wars and their effects on the Roman territory. In a word, our interest is in tracing the steps by which the map of the ancient world saw Rome grow from village to city-state, from city-state to world-empire; and furthermore in observing how she was forced eventually to relinquish most of her empire.

The earliest period of Roman history, though hidden in mist, shines with the splendor of heroic legend. Historians like Livy, poets like Virgil, joined in celebrating the foundation of Alba Longa by Ascanius, son of Trojan Aeneas, on

---

[1] See T. Frank, *Roman Imperialism, passim.*

the ridge of the Alban Hills, where his line ruled for three hundred years.[1] It was his descendant Romulus who led a band of adventurers to found the new city by the Tiber.[2] The legend told how a later successor, Tullus Hostilius, waged war with the parent city, and the three Roman Horatii met the three Alban Curiatii in combat to determine the fates of the cities. Two Romans fell; all the Albans were wounded, but unequally; and the Roman survivor, by pretending to run away, was able to dispatch his foes severally.[3] The Roman people, thus victorious, became the masters of Alba Longa; and when the Albans proved treacherous, in a war with the Etruscans, the Romans sent their cavalry to raze the city, now four hundred years old, and transferred the inhabitants to Rome.[4] There was now only one mistress of Latium.

[1] Livy, I, 3; Virgil, *Aen.* I, 267–274. Alba Longa was supposed to be an overflow from Lavinium, the city founded by Aeneas near the coast. It now seems probable that Alba Longa, which to the Romans meant the "Long White City," preserves rather an old, possibly pre-Latin, word signifying a height. Cf. *Alpes.* (See W. Helbig, *Die Italiker in der Poebene*, Leipzig, 1879, p. 31; A. Walde, *Lateinisches Etymologisches Wörterbuch*[3] [Heidelberg, 1930], p. 27.)

[2] The Romans supposed that Rome took its name from Romulus; but it is probably derived from that of an Etruscan tribe or chieftain, and the names of Romulus and Remus were derived from that of the city. (See W. Schulze, *Zur Geschichte der lateinischen Eigennamen* [Berlin, 1904], pp. 579–582.) The adventures of Romulus and Remus (exposed in infancy by a usurping great-uncle, saved by a she-wolf, found and reared as shepherds, living for a time the life of Robin Hoods, restored to royal station by their kingly qualities, and avenging their grandfather's exile) remind one somewhat of the story of the infant Moses (*Exodus*, ii, 1–10), still more of the boyhood of Cyrus the Great (Herodotus, I, 107–130). Other stories, familiar to the Greeks, probably explain the origin of the present myth.

[3] Livy, I, 24–26. Three mounds may still be seen on the Appian Way, of which two, near together, are supposed by some to cover the slain Horatii, and the third to be that of one of the Curiatii. In Livy's day there were five such mounds. (See also p. 25.)

[4] Livy's account of the destruction of Alba (I, 29) has something in common with Virgil's story of the last hours of Troy (*Aen.* II, esp. ll. 298 ff., 363 ff., 486 ff., 624 ff.).

We may disregard, if we please, the heroes of the legend, and even the forcible destruction of Alba and other cities; but the legend itself surely preserves much of truth. The earliest Italic settlements in Latium were certainly the villages on the Alban heights; there was, as we have seen, a loose federation of Latin tribes banded together for defense and for the worship of Jupiter Latiaris on the Alban Mount, and probably there were other Latin leagues. The cult and the principal Latin league lasted in historic times, and came under the leadership of Rome. But although the earliest Romans were, like the other Latins, herdsmen and farmers, it cannot be doubted that two facts gave them an immediate advantage over the other Latins. They began very soon to add to their strength by including immigrants of various sorts. Legend affirmed that Romulus opened the city as an asylum for refugees, vigorous outlaws from other towns; and we have already observed that there was an early coalition with the warlike Sabines from the neighboring hills. Other aliens flocked to Rome along the trade routes, by land or by river. And the second advantage of Rome over the other Latin towns came from her position on the river, which brought her a growing commerce. It is significant that according to tradition the earliest Roman colony was the ancient harbor fort of Ostia, at the Tiber's mouth, founded, the Romans believed, by King Ancus Martius only some hundred years after the death of Romulus.[1] Rome was becoming a mixed population, and was a city of traders as well as of farmers and herdsmen.

It was not only in the eclipse of Alba Longa that the Roman domination over the Latins appeared. During anxious

---

[1] The earliest walls that have been found at Ostia, however, belong to the fourth century B.C. A *colonia* is in origin a settlement in which each member (*colonus*) receives an allotment of land to cultivate (*colere*).

centuries Rome led armies of Latins against Etruscans and against Italic tribes to the east and south, and recruited her own population and its armies from the Latin towns. At many a dangerous spot, commanding roads that led to Rome, she placed colonies, garrisoned with Roman citizens or with Latins who had a partial citizenship; and in later times the "Latin status" was often given to distant towns, and marked a transitional or probationary stage in their progress toward complete Roman citizenship. But the Latin League, as such, had become less important; in 385 the Romans insisted that new Latin colonies must have relations not with the League but only with Rome; and in 338, after a war fought by the Latins who demanded equality with Rome,[1] a Roman victory resulted in the enforced dissolution of the League. The importance of this event can hardly be overestimated. From this time we may fairly date the emergence of Rome as a city-state, a city legislating for a considerable territory, in which the several isolated communities henceforth had in common nothing but their common relation with Rome. Already the Romans were learning the value of the principle made famous in the phrase "Divide et impera"; with the united powers of Latium, of central Italy, of the Mediterranean world, Rome could hardly cope; with each power severally she could and did maintain in war and in peace a sovereign relation. Whether the form of government of the little city would be found capable of dealing fairly with a vast empire is a question that Rome was compelled later to face. But in following the story of the Latin League we have passed over other matters, to which we must now return.

[1] During this war the consul Manlius Torquatus was reputed to have put to death his own son for killing in single combat a Latin warrior, the acceptance of such challenges being forbidden (Livy, VIII, 7). And his colleague, P. Decius Mus, the story runs, in order to save his army from defeat, "devoted" himself to certain death in battle (Livy, VIII, 9).

Just across the Tiber, all these years, the Etruscans held their hill fortresses; indeed, their pirate ships harried the coasts, their traders pushed past the foothills of the mountains to their towns further south, and they even captured Praeneste, twenty miles east of Rome, and established a fortress at Fidenae, on the eastern bank of the Tiber only seven miles from Rome. From the Janiculum the Romans could almost see the powerful town of Veii, a dozen miles to the north; and still further north, beyond the dark Ciminian forest, there were numerous other towns. Many times the Etruscans raided the Roman territory. But probably Etruscan merchants and artisans and soothsayers were finding their way into Rome and settled in the Etruscan quarter (*Vicus Tuscus*); and perhaps now and then an Etruscan prince found reason to leave his native land and settle in the new city. How it came to pass, we shall in all probability never know; but it is certain that the Romans, lying between the Etruscans of the north and the Etruscans in Campania, found themselves under the rule of an Etruscan king. The patriotism of later Romans forbade them to suppose that the Etruscan domination began much more than a hundred years before it fell (about 509); recent archaeological investigations tend to support this belief. The legend told how an Etruscan adventurer, Romanizing his name as Lucius Tarquinius Priscus,[1] won the kingship by intrigue; how he and his successors, Servius Tullius and Tarquinius Superbus, led the Romans in war and in the building of walls and temples and sewers; and how the arrogance of the last Tarquin and the wrong done to Lucretia by his son caused the Romans to drive out the royal house, never again to admit

---

[1] Tarquinius = the man of the city of Tarquinii. Virgil invents an eponymous Tarchon to give his name to the city. The name Tarchnas (and Tarquitius) has been found in Etruscan tombs. (Cf. p. 157, n. 1.)

the title of king.[1] However that may be, the Romans, in spite of their hatred of the alien Etruscans, had cause to thank them not only for buildings and crafts, for rites of divination and the triumph and the art of land surveying, for a livelier trade and contact with the Greeks of Campania,[2] but also for a tribal organization and a closely knit army that enabled the Romans to subdue the Latin cities and not a few Etruscan cities. Fidenae had fallen to Rome, as well as Gabii, to the east, and Praeneste, too. Wealth and splendor began to clothe the drab city of Rome, and her prestige grew abroad under the efficient Etruscan monarchy; she controlled a territory of some three hundred and fifty square miles.

With the fall of the monarchy, something of Roman prestige was lost for a time, and Rome had to battle hard to hold off her enemies. According to tradition, the exiled Tarquin, aided by the Etruscan prince Lars Porsenna, made a desperate effort to regain Rome. It may be that the Etruscans won some temporary success, and this Roman reverse was veiled by the patriotic legend that represented the heroic Horatius and his two comrades as holding the wooden bridge till it could be cut down and Rome could thus be saved. But

---

[1] Etruscan arrogance, sensuality, corpulence, cruelty, and a preoccupation with death and the underworld seem to be characteristic; Virgil suggests some of these traits in his portrait of Mezentius. The Etruscans were also given to human sacrifices and the massacre of captives, both of which the Romans sometimes imitated; gladiatorial fights they also borrowed from the Etruscans in 264 B.C., and did not abandon for more than four hundred years. On the other hand, H. Last does well to call attention to the limited extent of Rome's Etruscan period, and to the comparative scantiness of her borrowings from the culture of Etruria (C. A. H., VII, 378–399).

[2] From these Greeks, via the Etruscans, the Romans acquired a finer pottery and, more important, the alphabet. Some peculiarities of Roman spelling and pronunciation come from the Etruscans' influence: the redundant letters c, q, and k; words like persona (Etruscan φερσυ, Greek πρόσωπον), "mask"; triumpus (Greek θρίαμβος). Cf. R. S. Conway, in C. A. H., IV, 395 ff.

luck was on the side of Rome; for it was only a few years after the expulsion of the kings that an Etruscan navy was crushed, off Cumae in Campania, by the Greeks of Syracuse (474 B.C.), and the power of the Etruscans in Campania died away. In Etruria, too, the Etruscans were now hard pressed by a great invasion of Gallic tribes, which was later to reach Rome. This double blow to Etruscan power, in the south and in the north, doubtless saved Rome from destruction; and the wars with the Etruscans resolved themselves into a deadly duel between Rome and Veii. For the first time, Rome found it necessary to keep a standing army and to pay her soldiers, instead of relying on the occasional service of farmer-soldiers. Veii fell in 396 before the great M. Furius Camillus, and was destroyed; [1] a few years later the Romans placed two Latin colonies at Sutrium and Nepete to guard the gates of Etruria; but it was not for another hundred years that Rome could claim lordship over the whole of Etruria to the river Arnus (the modern Arno). And however much Etruria became Romanized as the centuries passed, the Etruscan stock remained dominant; nor is it fanciful to trace to it much of the fierce warfare of mediaeval Tuscany, and the grim conceptions of an after-life that appear in the paintings in the Campo Santo at Pisa, and even in not a few pages of Dante's "Inferno." [2]

Meanwhile the Romans had wars to fight nearer home. The Latins, long suspicious of Rome's increasing power, and perhaps thinking that the new Republic was likely to be

---

[1] Veii is to-day a most interesting site to visit; a walled crag above a stream, such as Virgil describes among the ancient glories of Italy:
"   tot egregias urbes operumque laborem,
tot congesta manu praeruptis oppida saxis,
fluminaque antiquos subterlabentia muros."
                                        Georg. II, 155-157.
[2] See further D. Randall-MacIver, *The Etruscans* (Oxford, 1927), and R. A. L. Fell, *Etruria and Rome* (Cambridge, 1924).

weaker than the Monarchy, tried with some success to assert their independence. But Rome, for the first time resorting to the desperate expedient of appointing a dictator, partly crushed the revolt at Lake Regillus (501); and the Latin League first treated with Rome on equal terms and then acknowledged her leadership, till the League was dissolved (338).[1] But the dissolution did not take place till Rome, aided by the Latins, had nearly won her supremacy over the other Italic tribes.

Rome's strength, at the beginning of the Republic, extended over the Latin plain and a few vantage points in the foothills of the mountains. Behind the hills, amid the wild moors and the plateaus of the Apennines, lurked the fierce Italic tribes, separated by ravines and valleys. They could raid the plain, and they did raid it many times in the course of the early years of the Republic. But they lacked cavalry, and could not follow up an advantage, while the broken character of their country made it difficult for them to combine their forces in a common campaign. Up the valleys the Romans could press, deal separately with each tribe, and leave garrison-colonies to hold back the army, till in due time the enemy could be incorporated in some manner in the Roman state, and could be used in the Roman armies against other foes. Thus the Sabines in their hills to the northeast of Rome were assimilated, and a proud Roman family of later days traced its descent from the Sabine Attus Clausus, or Appius Claudius, as he was known at Rome. The Aequi, to the east, the Volsci, further south, and the Hernici, wedged between them, became subjects or dependents of the Romans. It was a characteristic piece of Roman strategy that the Hernici were defeated first, and that it was with their aid that the Romans defeated the Aequi and the

[1] Cf. p. 38.

Volsci. During these wars individual Romans began to emerge from the throng: the proud exile Coriolanus, relentlessly leading the Volsci against his fatherland, till at the last he was so moved by the embassy of Roman women, led by his mother and his wife, that he withdrew;[1] and Cincinnatus, called from the plough to the dictatorship and the war against the Aequi, and returning to the plough sixteen days later, when danger was past.[2] By 400, the Latin plain was ringed about by tribes which, if not altogether friendly, at least served as a buffer against the formidable Samnites in the mountains beyond.

Before the Romans were compelled to meet the Samnites, however, they passed through a new peril. Already the Gauls had swarmed down past the Alps into the Po valley, had driven back its Etruscan inhabitants and poured into the marches of Etruria itself. Some of them forced their way further south, and in 390, after a battle at the Allia, a tributary of the Tiber, they captured and burned the inadequately walled city of Rome. Possibly the Capitol itself escaped capture; Livy tells of the awakening of the garrison by the cackling of the sacred geese, kept in the Temple of Juno.[3] But the Gauls, weary with the seven months' siege of the Capitol, were willing to be bought off with gold; and weakened by fever they retreated, though not immediately, to the Po valley, which was long known as Gallia Cisalpina. From time to time, for another two hundred years, the Gauls flung themselves against the Roman territory; at Telamon, in Etruria, forty thousand Gauls fell in battle in

---

[1] Livy, II, 33–39.   [2] Livy, III, 26–29.
[3] Livy, V, 47. He tells also of the great impression made on the rude barbarians by the white-bearded senators sitting impassively in the Senate House. One Gaul ventured to stroke the beard of an aged senator, as a sign of respect; the Roman indignantly struck him with his staff, and carnage followed.

225; a few years later Hannibal found Gallic allies during his invasion of Italy; at the beginning of the first century B.C. the great Marius routed the hordes of their kinsmen, the Teutons and the Cimbri, in southern Gaul and in the Po valley. The campaigns of Julius Caesar and his successors finally built a northern bulwark against the Celts and the Germans that lasted until the fabric of the Roman Empire had begun to crumble, and the barbarians again pressed down on Italy. But it must never be forgotten that many Gauls remained in Italy, and were absorbed in the civilization of Rome; and none of the Romans born in the city of Rome were more Italian or even Roman than Catullus of Verona, than Virgil of Mantua, than Livy of Padua, all, it may be believed, with at least some Celtic blood in their veins.

The burning of Rome by the Gauls probably destroyed few buildings of great beauty; it may have deprived us of many records of early Roman history, and compelled us to depend in part on the inventions and surmises of later Roman historians. But the city rapidly revived; the walls long called "Servian" date chiefly from this period of recovery;[1] and the army was fundamentally reorganized in efficient tactical units, and equipped with better armor. The Etruscans were being curbed; the Latins were compelled to give up their League; and now Rome faced the Samnites. Some of these hardy mountaineers had already descended into the rich plain of Campania, where the Etruscans had been weakened by the defeat of their navy by the Syracusans a hundred years before, and where the Greek cities kept up too jealous a rivalry to present a common front. The Etruscan fortress of Capua fell to the Samnites in 424, the Greek city of Cumae in 420. Rome tried by alliance and by force of

[1] Cf. p. 21.

arms to prevent further encroachment on the part of the
Samnites, for there was a real danger that they would flood
the Latin plain, and their rude ways and the Oscan tongue
would dominate Italy. And now that the Latin League was
no more, the great struggle with the Samnites began, to last
for two generations. Indeed the struggle had begun a few
years before the last war against the Latins, when the Romans, having a prudent eye on the control of fertile Campania, saw occasion to defend the somewhat softened Samnite inhabitants of the opulent city of Capua against the
encroachments of the more hardy Samnites of the hills. The
Romans took possession of Capua, and presently hurled
army after army through the mountain passes, built the Via
Appia from Rome to Capua as a military road (312 B.C.),
and planted fortresses in the mountains and in the plain.
Once, in 321, both Roman consuls and their armies were entangled at the narrow Caudine Forks, and were compelled
to assent to harsh terms and to suffer the humiliation of passing under the "yoke." But the right of the consuls to assent
to such terms was denied by the Senate, and the war went
on. The Romans gained a foothold in Apulia, to the east of
the Apennines, from which they could attack the Samnites
from the rear. Valiant warriors though the Samnites were,
they lacked the political capacity and the discipline of the
Romans, and theirs was a losing struggle. They were failing
in their several efforts; they made one last desperate attempt by joining forces in the north with the Umbrians,
Etruscans, and Gauls. It was in vain; the Romans diverted
the Etruscans, and with their main army defeated the rest of
the confederates in Umbria at Sentinum (295 B.C.).[1] The
battle marks a landmark in Roman expansion; for it broke

---

[1] In this battle another Decius Mus "devoted himself to death," as his
father had done in the Latin War (cf. p. 38, n. 1).

the back of Samnite resistance, and thus drove a wedge of Roman territory from the western to the eastern coast of Italy, separating the chief remaining alien inhabitants of the peninsula, the Greeks in the south and the Gauls in the north. The Samnites did again, to be sure, take advantage of the dangers of Rome to rebel: once after the battle of Cannae (216 B.C.), when Hannibal was a walking terror in central Italy, again in the general revolt of the Italian allies (*socii*) in the "Social War" (90–88),[1] and once more during the civil wars between Marius and Sulla, till Sulla cut them to pieces at the Colline Gate of Rome (82 B.C.). But in the main the Roman fortress colonies in the mountains, Beneventum, and Luceria, and Venusia, and the great Via Appia, which had now been extended from Capua through the mountains eastward to Tarentum, served to hold the Samnites in subjugation; and the Roman policy continued to incorporate the new subjects in the state with partial civil rights, and to use them in the army.

Nothing now stood in the way of the Roman domination over all Italy except the Greek cities. The Greeks of Campania had been weakened by the luxuriance of the land, as well as by Etruscan and Samnite invaders; and Neapolis (Naples) fell to the Romans in the Samnite War in 326. But the cities of Magna Graecia, though not united and though in conflict with Italic tribes, were still strong, and the Greeks of Sicily disputed with the Carthaginians the control of the island. The men of Tarentum, the strongest city of Magna Graecia, saw with anxiety the approach of the Roman power; and when the Roman democracy, newly enthroned, decided to occupy Thurii and to defend it against the Samnites, the Tarentines seized a favorable opportunity to make war on Rome. From Epirus, just across the sea in western

---

[1] Cf. pp. 66 f, 203–206.

Greece, they brought the brilliant young king Pyrrhus, with his phalanx and elephants, as the champion of a united Greek cause. But his victories at Heraclea (280 B.C.), southwest of Tarentum, and in other parts of southern Italy were so costly that a "Pyrrhic victory" has always meant a defeat. Though he reached the borders of Latium, the Romans, with the moral support of the Carthaginians, would not treat with him unless he left Italy. Finding both his Greek and his Samnite allies lukewarm, and being remote from his base in Epirus, he attempted a new campaign in Sicily against the Carthaginians, which proved to be another defeat in victory. On his return to the Samnite country he suffered a severe defeat at the hands of a Roman army at Beneventum (276 B.C.), and left Italy. The cities of Magna Graecia could but submit to the Roman rule, which now reached from the Po valley to the heel and the toe of the peninsula. Fortresses, colonies, land allotments, and towns, roads,[1] harbors, and ships, above all the Roman system of political organization, completed the work of conquest. And Rome was coming to be known abroad as a great power receiving delegations and forming alliances with Massilia

---

[1] Of the more important roads, a few may be mentioned: the Appian Way (312 B.C.), from Rome to Capua, extended eventually via Beneventum, Venusia, and Tarentum to Brundisium. This, the "queen of roads" (Statius, *Silvae* II, 2, 12), is the route followed by Horace in his "Journey to Brundisium" (*Sat.* I, 5). The Latin Way, begun in the fifth or the fourth century, pursued a more inland route than the Appian, from Rome to Capua. The Flaminian (300–220), the northern highway, running through part of the Tiber valley, then through the Apennines to the east coast near the Metaurus River, and along the coast to Ariminum (Rimini); the Aemilian (187), from Ariminum through the southern part of the Po valley, through Bononia (Bolognia), Mutina (Modena), and Parma, to Placentia (Piacenza), — the railroad follows its course to-day; the two roads through Etruria, one, the Aurelian, along the coast to Pisa, the other, the Cassian, inland by Clusium (Chiusi), Arretium (Arezzo), and Florentia (Florence) to Luca; the Popilia (about 132), from Capua to Rhegium (Reggio) at the toe of Italy. For the construction of these roads, see pp. 150 f.

(Marseilles), with Carthage, and even with Alexandria in Egypt. She was already the strongest single Indo-European power in the world; only the Carthaginians, a Semitic people, remained as her rivals in the western Mediterranean.

Before proceeding, however, to watch the stages by which Rome, already the mistress of Italy, won her empire overseas, let us pause to note how lacking in calculation or farsighted design was the Roman expansion in Italy. The Romans were only to a slight extent a commercial people; it would be idle to seek in economic motives a sufficient explanation of the conquest. Nor did individuals, greedy or ambitious, urge the state to go to war. Still less did Romans generally, then or even later, justify conquest on the ground of the blessings of Roman rule, however real the advantages might be in some respects. So far as there was any militaristic party interested in territorial expansion it was apt to be the popular party, rather than the more cautious Senate.[1] In the main Rome was merely looking out in the most practical way for her own immediate safety, as the other peoples of Italy were struggling to protect theirs, apparently with equal prospects of success. But Rome, partly because of her geographical position, gained an initial advantage; this she enhanced by her early adoption of the policy of making her recent foes her allies and citizens, and of building up a centralized power whose authority was absolute. To this *imperium*, the right to command, not only Romans but all whom the Romans conquered learned the habit of yielding implicit obedience, so that Italy did not remain, like Greece, a country divided into a chessboard of sovereign petty states. From the early days one village, now become a city-

---

[1] Cf. T. Frank, *Roman Imperialism*, pp. 64–67. J. W. Spaeth, Jr., in *A Study of the Causes of Rome's Wars from 343 to 265 B.C.* (Princeton, 1926), finds more political consciousness and more aggressiveness in Rome's attitude during this period, in all except the Gallic Wars.

state, seemed to later generations to have been singled out by manifest destiny to rule. With the inevitability of any healthy organic growth, families grew into clans, clans into a nation, drawing new blood and vigor from the peoples that were absorbed into the nation.

We must observe, moreover, that this growth was the result of an attitude that seldom looked beyond the next step. Romans met their problems only when they had become acute; they invented or adapted reasons and principles afterwards. In their political conflicts and in their wars they generally "muddled through," though at terrible cost in human lives. Especially is this true in the matter of territorial expansion; one step at a time was enough, and the Romans were seldom aware of what might lie beyond the present step. Furthermore, there seemed to be no natural limit to expansion, except when natural geographical boundaries were reached; for behind a conquered people always lay other peoples yet unconquered. Reasoning after the event, it is possible to formulate the course of expansion somewhat as follows: "Raids and acts of pillage must be put down. To do this the tribes on the frontier must be reduced to a state of submission. This result once attained, these tribes take to more peaceful habits, but are in turn exposed to the attacks of the more distant tribes against whom the State is bound to protect them. If, the robbers once punished, the expedition is withdrawn, the lesson is soon forgotten. In order to put a stop to this state of permanent disorder, fortified posts are established in the midst of these hostile tribes, and an influence is brought to bear on them which reduces them by degrees to a state of submission. But other, more distant tribes beyond this outer line come in turn to threaten the same dangers, and necessitate the same measures of repression. The State is thus forced to choose between alternatives — either to give up this endless labor and abandon its frontier to perpetual disturbance, or to plunge deeper and deeper into barbarous countries. Such has been the fate of every country which has found itself in a similar position. All have been forced by imperious necessity into this onward march, where the greatest difficulty is to know where to stop." These words happen to have been written by a Russian,[1] in 1864; but they may well serve to describe the blind course of Roman expansion to the limits of Italy, and we may well keep them in mind as we follow the growth of Roman territory outside of the peninsula until something like natural geographical limits are reached.

2. FROM CITY-STATE TO WORLD-EMPIRE

Until the Romans won the whole of Italy to the Po valley, and indeed for many years after, they remained chiefly an agricultural people. Their wars had been fought for the protection of lands against marauding Etruscans and Gauls and Samnites or for the repulse of Greek invaders. Their lands had produced sufficient food for their population; they had no extensive foreign trade. The waters of the western Mediterranean had been sailed by Greek traders and Etruscan corsairs; more recently they had become the exclusive province of the merchants of Carthage, a city now reaching the height of her power. From their excellent harbors on the coast of Africa (modern Tunis), opposite western Sicily, the Carthaginians plied a trade to the east and to the west; much of northern Africa was theirs, and the coast of Spain; they held ports in Corsica and Sardinia, over against Italy; in Sicily only the waning power of Syracuse was left to pre-

---

[1] Prince Gortchakoff, quoted by H. H. Powers, in "Independence or Civilization?" (*Atlantic Monthly*, February, 1925), as "the classic statement of [the] compulsory forward policy."

vent the island from becoming wholly Carthaginian. Silver
from Spain, tin from Britain, textiles from the Orient, filled
the Carthaginian ships, while the rich lands south of the city
of Carthage were worked in great estates by slave gangs for
their merchant owners. But Carthage lacked the citizen-
farmers who were the strength of Rome. In culture she had
much in common with some of her Semitic cousins in the
east; but despite her material opulence, she originated nothing in religion, art, science, or politics. Her religion permitted brutal human sacrifice; her political system allowed
magistrates and people to fall under the control of wealthy
families, and bribery was rife; her army consisted largely of
mercenaries. No attempt was made to consolidate subject
peoples; perhaps the fusion of widely separated and alien
peoples would have been impossible. And if the goal of Roman expansion was assimilation and political consolidation,
that of Carthage was purely commercial exploitation.

As early as 348 B.C. the Romans had made a commercial
treaty with Carthage, being content to divide the seas with
her; under pressure of the Samnite wars, they made another
treaty (306), by which they were excluded from the harbors
of Sicily and the Carthaginians were excluded from Italian
ports. During the invasion of Pyrrhus, Rome and Carthage
made a temporary alliance against their common enemy;
after his defeat the two powers must have realized that their
interests in the Mediterranean would soon conflict. Rome
had just won the control of Italy; yet her ships were forbidden the ports of Sicily, and could not reach the eastern
harbors of Italy without passing through the straits of Sicily,
toward which the Punic power was steadily advancing. Unless Rome were content to face the possibility of the western
Mediterranean becoming a Carthaginian sea, a *mare clau-
sum*, and of suffering constant interference with the coasts of

Italy, she must be ready to check further encroachments. War was imminent.

In 265 B.C. a band of Campanian soldiers calling themselves Mamertines ("Sons of Mars"), who had captured Messana (Messina), the Greek city at the corner of Sicily nearest to Italy, found themselves at odds with Syracuse, a few miles to the south. Divided in counsel, one party called for aid upon Carthage, the other upon Rome. Carthage immediately responded, and seized Messana. The Roman Senate was reluctant to embark on a policy of war or conquest overseas; moreover Syracuse had recently helped Rome, and Carthage was formally a Roman ally. But the Roman Assembly, led by Appius Claudius, clamored for war; and in 264 Roman soldiers for the first time left the soil of Italy to fight across seas.

Although Syracuse soon joined the Romans, it was not until 241 that the Carthaginians were vanquished. The Romans had to build a navy and to learn the art of naval warfare, aided by the advice of Greek allies. They achieved the unexpected, and won two great victories at sea by boarding tactics. A thrust at Carthage itself would doubtless have succeeded, had the two consuls been allowed to pursue their advantage; but the old custom of brief summer campaigning recalled one consul with much of the army at the end of the summer; his colleague, Regulus, after temporary successes, was captured.[1] Bad weather and lack of nautical skill lost one Roman fleet after another; but the will of the Romans was not broken. New fleets were built and

[1] He demanded such impossible terms after his successes that the Carthaginians rejected them, and were fortunately reinforced by Greek mercenaries, who turned the table on Regulus. Roman tradition made of Regulus a hero who, when allowed to return to Rome and to submit the Carthaginian terms to his fellow countrymen, advised against them and honorably returned to Carthage to receive the torture that he knew must await him. (See Horace, *Odes* III, 5.)

manned, though Rome's resources in money and in men were becoming exhausted. As the years wore away, the Romans gained most of Sicily by dogged fighting on land; yet two great fortresses in the west held out against them. At last a Roman fleet built by voluntary contributions from wealthy men, if the tradition may be trusted, won a decisive victory in 241; and Carthage had to accept severe terms. All Sicily, except the small part held by Syracuse, was ceded to Rome, together with an indemnity of 3200 talents (the equivalent of over three million dollars). The western Mediterranean was no longer a closed sea, the exclusive possession of a Semitic power, but lay open to Roman influence; it soon became wholly Roman. Since the great Egyptian navy and the Macedonian navy had recently weakened each other, Rome was left with the strongest fleet in the Mediterranean. Carthage was crippled for twenty years, during which Rome seized Corsica and Sardinia and, after repelling a Gallic attack, pushed her frontier to the Alps.

But the most momentous consequence of the war for Rome was the acquisition of Sicily, which was organized as the first Roman province; its people did not become, like the conquered peoples of Italy, partial members of the Roman state, fighting in the Roman armies. A few favored communities, to be sure, were given independence or were made allied states; but the rest became Roman subjects, paying annual tribute in money and in grain, and governed by magistrates sent out yearly from Rome. The grave political and economic results of this system, which was applied, with local differences, to each of the new provinces as they were added to the growing empire, we must consider later. At present it is enough to notice that Rome was now committed, largely through circumstances not of her own seeking, to responsibilities outside of Italy for which her experience had not prepared her; and she was subject to the temptation to extend her territory in the hope of increasing her wealth. It was the jingoist Assembly of the people, not the Senate, who had shown a desire to go to war with Carthage; and it is interesting to read in the Greek historian of the war that the people rejected the first terms made by the victorious consul, and sent to Sicily commissioners who imposed more severe terms.[1] Carthage could not resist, and was crippled for twenty years; but when the Senate assumed control of affairs, it showed a still more cynical foreign policy.

The new Roman spirit of confidence and of aggressive empire-building appeared again a few years after the war. Convenient pretexts were seized to add Corsica and Sardinia to the empire (238 B.C.). After some of the Gauls in the Po valley had been ejected, the popular leader G. Flaminius proposed, against senatorial opposition, the distribution of considerable land among Roman citizens (but not among their allies); and the Romans had to fight a serious war against the Gauls (232–222)[2] before they could control the region and secure it by colonies and by the Flaminian Road (220),[3] pushing the frontier to the foot of the Alps, but not enrolling the Gauls as allies. An invitation from Greeks across the Adriatic enabled the Romans to suppress for a time the Illyrian pirates (228), and some years later Illyricum became a province (167). Rome was already beginning to take part in the affairs of the eastern Mediterranean and to establish friendly relations with some of the Greek states. Before she became very active in this quarter, however, she was to undergo another terrible war with Carthage.

Balked in her aims in Sicily, and no longer being the mis-

---

[1] Polybius I, 63. [2] Cf. pp. 43 f.
[3] Cf. p. 47, n. 1.

tress of the sea, Carthage had to some extent made good her losses by building up in Spain an empire that reached as far north as the river Ebro. At this frontier Rome bade her halt her advance; but to the brilliant young Hannibal, from his childhood the sworn foe of Rome,[1] the command was a challenge. His answer was given by his siege and capture of the Greek city of Saguntum, an ally of Rome (219 B.C.). The Roman ambassador sent to demand satisfaction of the Carthaginians "folded up his toga, and said, 'Here we bring you peace and war. Take whichever you please.' To that they cried out no less grimly, 'You can give whichever you choose!' Whereupon he shook out the toga. 'I give war,' he said; and they all cried out, 'We take it, and will wage it just as fiercely as we have received it.'"[2] They spoke truly; for never did the Romans have a more implacable or a more resourceful enemy than Hannibal.

To the amazement of Rome, Hannibal staked everything on the desperate chance of an invasion of Italy from the north. He reasoned, correctly enough, that his small but seasoned army of forty thousand men was more than a match for the far larger armies of Rome, with their divided command and successions of generals, provided that he could strike before Rome could muster her forces; he knew that he could not safely transport his army, and especially his Numidian cavalry and elephants, across the sea to southern Italy, so weak was the Carthaginian navy; and he counted on finding the Greeks and the Italic peoples ready to rise against Rome. Before the Romans realized what he was about, he slipped out of Spain and through southern Gaul, evaded a Roman army at the Rhone, crossed the steeps of the Alps amid snows and hostile natives, and descended, with scarcely thirty thousand men, into Italy. Victories at

[1] Nepos, *Hann.*, Ch. 2. [2] Livy, XXXI, 18.

the Ticinus and the Trebia brought him many Gallic allies; but a Gallic invasion was just what the Italic peoples least desired, and Hannibal's hope of a general Italic rising was disappointed. Even after a Roman army had been caught and cut to pieces one misty morning at the Trasimene Lake in Etruria (217 B.C.), the Italian allies remained loyal to Rome; not in vain had Rome given them a share in the state and become the champion of Italian security. Hannibal moved in 217 toward the fertile southeast, where his cavalry was more useful and supplies could be found, hoping moreover to shake the loyalty of the Greeks and the recent Samnite allies. Since the cautious dictator Q. Fabius, nicknamed Cunctator ("The Delayer") because of his dilatory tactics,[1] avoided a decisive battle, impatient leaders at Rome caused him to be superseded; the commanders of the year 216 put into the field an army of some eighty thousand, but Hannibal, with little more than half as many men, chose his ground and met them at Cannae, in Apulia. The prevailing wind blew dust in the eyes of the Romans; and Hannibal, whose greatest strength lay in his cavalry, succeeded in surrounding them and so cut them to pieces. Seventy thousand Romans, including half the nobility, were killed. It was one of the darkest moments in Roman history. Hannibal was now the master of southern Italy, and was joined by many Samnites and by some of the Greek cities; he received the promise of help from Macedon. Capua soon fell into his hands, and Syracuse went over to him not much later.

Nevertheless Rome never faltered. New armies were raised; striplings and slaves were armed; and the Fabian tactics were resumed. Diplomacy succeeded in fomenting Greek rebellion against Macedon, so that Hannibal never

---

[1] He gave a name to the "Fabian" group of socialists, whose purpose is educational, rather than revolutionary.

received the help that he had expected; and Syracuse was besieged by Marcellus and was finally betrayed to Rome. Hannibal, unable to raise the Roman siege of Capua, marched along the Latin Way to the very gate of Rome; but no Roman allies deserted, no offers of peace were made to him, nor did the Romans abandon the siege of Capua in order to oppose him. Indeed, they sent off a detachment of troops, with flags flying, bound for Spain, and sold at auction at its full value the very field on which Hannibal was encamped. We are not told that his counter-offer to sell the shops about the Forum found any takers. At any rate, he withdrew again in discouragement to southern Italy and stormed Tarentum, while Capua was recovered for Rome, and was made a terrible example to warn other cities against yielding to Hannibal. The war dragged on; both sides were nearing exhaustion, but time and the losses of men favored Rome, with her far greater resources, and Carthage failed to give proper support to Hannibal. Tarentum was again won for Rome. Meanwhile the war had been waged vigorously in Spain, with which country the Roman lines of communication were kept open by sea and by land. Two Scipios were slain in a great Roman defeat, but the son of one of them, young P. Cornelius Scipio, succeeded in turning the tide of war in Spain. Hannibal's brother, Hasdrubal, succeeded in escaping from him with an army; but before he could join Hannibal in southern Italy his army was crushed by the Romans at the river Metaurus in Umbria (207).[1] His head, tossed into Hannibal's camp, brought Hannibal his first news of the battle. For a few years more Hannibal stood at bay in Italy; but young Scipio's success in driving the Carthagians from Spain had won for him from the Roman people, against the judgment of the Senate, the consulship

[1] Horace, *Odes* IV, 7.

and the opportunity to carry the war into Africa. Continued successes resulted in a continued command, — a new departure in Roman military policy, and one destined to make and mar the fortunes of the Republic. Hannibal was recalled to Carthage; but his hastily gathered forces were no match for the "division tactics" of Scipio's army. At Zama, a few miles inland from Carthage, he was decisively defeated (202), and Scipio, now honored with the cognomen Africanus, dictated the terms of peace. Carthage had to give up all her navy except ten triremes, and to pay a tribute of ten thousand talents. Although her land in Africa was not yet annexed as a province, and soon became the source of a reviving prosperity, she lost Spain, and she gave up the right to make wars outside of Africa; she was to wage wars in Africa only with the consent of Rome. Her national independence was gone. Rome profited by the tribute, and still more by the lands of Spain, soon to be organized as two provinces, Hither and Further Spain (197). Though not fully pacified for many years, Spain became thoroughly Romanized during the early Empire, and gave Rome writers, officials, and emperors.

The second Punic War thus left Rome supreme in the western Mediterranean, without a military rival, and with a complicated system of political relations. Each part of her growing empire was in a different status, — Roman citizens, "Latin towns," Italic allies, the province of Sicily, and the conquered but hardly organized territories of Sardinia and Corsica, of Carthage and Spain. Each part, however, was connected solely with Rome; government and foreign policy were derived from the city-state, which was perforce fast becoming an empire. Scarcely fifty years after Zama the reviving prosperity of Carthage, which was now based on intensive agriculture rather than on trade, aroused such apprehension at Rome that the Romans, egged on by the famous words of Cato, the spokesman of the land-owing class, clamored for war. A pretext was found in the fact that Carthage, forbidden by the terms of peace to make war without Roman consent, and yet not defended by Roman arms, had been compelled to defend herself against the encroachments of the Numidian chieftain Masinissa, in which Rome had connived. In 146 B.C. the Romans, commanded by another Scipio Africanus (grandson by adoption of the former Africanus), destroyed the city of Carthage and made her territory, known as Africa, a Roman province, with Numidia as an allied state under Roman suzerainty to guard the hinterland.[1] Less than a hundred years saw the whole of the Carthaginian power pass under the rule of Roman magistrates. The same year that Carthage was destroyed, the Romans were busy in destroying the Greek city of Corinth. How did Rome come to enter the eastern Mediterranean?

Before the first Punic War Rome was too much engaged in winning Italy to turn to the east, even if she had cared to do so. Perhaps it was a common fear of Carthage that caused a treaty to be made (273 B.C.) between Rome and Ptolemy II Philadelphus of Egypt, who was also threatened by a coalition of Macedon and Syria. After the first Punic War, as we have seen, the influence of Rome spread across the Adriatic at the invitation of Greek cities. During the

[1] Although it is ordinarily assumed that Rome's motive in destroying Carthage and Corinth was jealousy of their commercial greatness, and that the commercial classes at Rome dictated the policy, it must be noted that Rome's foreign trade at this time was far less important than her agriculture, and was carried on chiefly by Greeks and other foreigners, as is shown by inscriptions in Delos. Even after the destruction of Carthage, Rome allowed the city of Utica to take over the trade formerly enjoyed by Carthage, instead of seizing it herself. Only after the Gracchan legislation do we find the commercial classes of Rome greatly interested in foreign policy or able to influence it. See further T. Frank, *Roman Imperialism*, Ch. XIV.

second Punic War, Hannibal's alliance with Philip V of
Macedon (215) kept Rome in constant fear; but she was able
to renew the Egyptian alliance and to stir up opposition to
Macedon in Greece. The great empire of Alexander had long
since broken apart into three smaller empires, — of the
Ptolemies in Egypt, of the Seleucids in Syria and Mesopotamia and southeastern Asia Minor, and of the Antig-
onids in Macedonia, — together with smaller independent
kingdoms and city-states, such as Pergamum and Rhodes;
and the Achaean and the Aetolian Leagues in Greece were
struggling to build up, against the old Greek tradition, some
degree of solidarity among the little states. Even while
Hannibal was terrorizing Italy, Rome initiated the policy
that eventually won her eastern empire and consolidated her
African empire. At first the policy was one of temporizing,
without any realization of the extent to which circumstances
were to lead from alliance to conquest, from overlordship to
annexation. By keeping the balance of power among jealous states and letting them wear each other out; by making
alliances with friendly states, which gradually became more
and more dependent, and at last were reduced to the condition of vassalage or of subjection; and by erecting buffer
states on the frontiers, with client princes recognized by
Rome, great territories were won with the loss of fewer
Roman lives than would have been required by deliberate
Roman conquest. Until the end of the Macedonian Wars, or
even later, the Senate was very reluctant to create new
provinces in the east and to assume the heavy responsibilities of provincial administration and defense; but after the
rich and ancient communities of Greece and the east fell to
Rome to be exploited, the commercial classes at Rome
forced the Senate to undertake a greater measure of responsibility. And once the feet of the Romans were set on the

road to empire, there seemed to be no turning backwards without incalculable danger.[1]

The humiliation of Carthage at the end of the second Punic War gave Rome the opportunity to reckon with Macedon. Not only had Philip promised to aid Hannibal, but he was now (203) preparing to divide Egypt with the Seleucid king Antiochus III. Unless Rome were willing to allow the eastern Mediterranean to be closed to her ships as the western Mediterranean had been closed by Carthage, she could hardly refuse to meet Philip with firm resistance, even though the war meant a departure from the old Roman tradition of fetial law which permitted only wars in defense of Rome herself and of those who were technically her allies (*socii*). But hatred and fear of Philip were enhanced by a growing pride of empire and by a rising desire to be the champion of Hellenic civilization against the tyranny of Philip. It was the Senate, formerly, at the outset of the first Punic War, the champion of peace against the jingoist Assembly, that now had to persuade the Assembly to go to war. The chief Greek states came to the support of Rome. On a foggy day at Cynoscephalae (197) the rigid phalanx of Philip was routed by the more flexible legions and the Aetolian cavalry under T. Quinctius Flamininus. Philip, shorn of his outlying possessions, was allowed to remain king of Macedon and a nominal Roman ally. Greece was proclaimed "free," but soon plunged into her normal career of civic animosities and feuds; and Rome's insistence on dealing with cities, and not with the proud young leagues, taught the Greeks the limited meaning of "freedom." Roman opinion was divided between the philhellenism of the Scipionic circle and the jealousy of Cato and his party, who would have either abandoned Greece or exacted from her a real material

[1] Cf. pp. 49 f.

and political return for Rome's efforts. In the aftermath,
Philip's son and successor Perseus surpassed his father in his
intrigues for the restoration of Macedonian power, till he
was defeated by L. Aemilius Paullus at Pydna (168); and
Macedon, after being constituted for a few stormy years as a
protectorate, became a province (146). The troublesome
Achaean League was crushed, and the confederacies were
dissolved; many leading Greeks, including the historian of
Rome, Polybius, were carried to Rome, and many thousands
of others were enslaved. Though the prestige of Athens
caused her to be left "free," the city of Corinth was destroyed (146) by vote of the Senate, as a warning against
further disorder. The other cities were given new charters;
but Greece did not become a province for more than a hundred years. The Romans had little reason to be proud of
their treatment of Greece, even if the worst acts of pillage
and violence were unauthorized. To be sure, the incessant
bickerings of the Greeks tried the patience of the Romans
sorely, and the Romans were fully occupied in other quarters. Yet the system of provincial government that served
well enough in the less civilized western Mediterranean, —
disarmament, isolation, and taxation, — was in many ways
ill adapted to the older communities of the east, which always remained more Greek or Oriental than Roman; nor
did the Romans often make any real effort to deal under-
standingly with local differences. And it is significant that
from the victory of Pydna till the reign of Diocletian, a
period of nearly five hundred years, the citizens of Rome
were exempted from paying direct taxes (the *tributum*);
Rome was learning to live on her empire, and imperialism
had acquired a new motive.[1]

Meanwhile, Rome was expanding further east. Antiochus

[1] Cf. pp. 84, 214–216, 259.

III of Syria had failed to help Philip against Rome, and had profited by Philip's difficulties to take some of his Greek possessions in Asia. After the Macedonian War, the Romans, who were now the protectors of Greek interests, turned to meet this new danger. Though the king's power was more apparent than real, he was not without an adviser; for the dread Hannibal, who had escaped from Carthage a few years after Zama, had embraced this last opportunity to oppose Rome, and had urged the invasion of Italy. But Antiochus had let the chance, if it was a chance, go by, and wasted his strength in Greece; and it was L. Scipio who, accompanied by his brother, the great Africanus, finally defeated Antiochus in Asia Minor at Magnesia (190). For the first time Rome had pitted her legions against an Oriental army. Hannibal, a great and a tragic figure, once more escaped, only to be hunted to a pitiful death a few years later. The battle gave to Rome the rich lands of Asia Minor, as far as the river Halys, with buffer states to the east. Again the Senate hesitated long before organizing provinces; but Pergamum and Rhodes, at first favored allies, were soon reduced to dependency; the island of Delos was established as a free port, with an enormous slave trade, to injure their commercial prosperity (166); and the pirates that infested the eastern Mediterranean went unpunished for many years. When Attalus III of Pergamum bequeathed his kingdom to Rome (133), it was organized as a province, though with characteristic senatorial caution.[1]

[1] The democratic reformer G. Gracchus contrived, with the best of intentions, to exploit it for the benefit of indigent Romans by introducing the contract system of tax-collecting, much to the demoralization both of the business classes of Rome and of the provincials. It was in a similar spirit of expansion and exploitation that his successors overrode the opposition of the Senate and converted the narrow strip of land on the southern coast of Gaul, hitherto held for purely military purposes, into the productive province of Gallia Narbonensis (i.e., "Provence").

And already Egypt, long a friendly ally of Rome, had acknowledged the protectorate of Rome (168). Thus within a century Rome had fallen heir to all the empire of Carthage in the west, and to much of the empire of Alexander in the east. But the work of consolidation was far from complete; and Rome was further than ever from having reached natural boundaries in her conquests. Buffer states were insecure; invading Celts and Germans, and Oriental and African tribes were still to be repelled and kept beyond defensible frontiers. And Rome's own house must be set in order before there could be any question of achieving a truly Roman empire overseas.

3. Growth, Defense, and Retreat

So rapid had been the expansion of Roman territory during the hundred years that ended in 146 B.C., and so pressing had been the dangers of the Punic Wars, that many economic and political abuses of long standing and not a few anomalies arising during the wars had to wait for attention till a more peaceful era. Democracy had seemed to arrive in Rome when the Hortensian Law was passed (287);[1] but during the following century and a half of wars and expansion the Senate had been allowed to direct military, financial, and foreign policies. Toward the end of this period the Senate had been much less efficient and patriotic, and the younger Gracchus succeeded in restoring some of the former power of the Assembly, which jealously watched the rights of the people. Rome had two masters, and foreign policy suffered accordingly. The century that followed is important chiefly for the political struggles that grew from these conditions; these matters will be considered in a later chap-

[1] See p. 197.

ter. But the forward march of empire was not halted, though new motives began to appear.

Three wars must be mentioned here, not because they added much new territory, but because from them grew a new use of Roman armies. Numidia had fallen into the hands of the shrewd prince Jugurtha, who found that he could defy Roman rule as much by bribing the aristocratic officers as by fighting, — a sad commentary on the changing character of much of the aristocracy since the days of the Punic Wars. And apart from any question of honesty, the Senate was clearly reluctant to press the war to a conclusion, and hoped rather to patch up some sort of understanding with Jugurtha and use him as a client prince. The angry Roman populace demanded a change of command; they would not even leave in command the honest and moderately successful aristocrat Metellus, but defied the Senate and sent instead the democrat Marius, who was ignorant and politically incapable, but a soldier to the marrow. Jugurtha was captured and put to death in Rome (105). Yet only a small part of Numidia was actually incorporated in the Roman Empire, from which it may be inferred that Marius and his democratic and business friends were perhaps less interested in territorial expansion than in damaging the prestige of the Senate.

Hardly had Marius enjoyed his triumph when he was sent to cope with the barbarians of the north, who were pressing down as of old on both sides of the Alps, and had already defeated six Roman armies in succession. Marius annihilated the Teutons at Aquae Sextiae (102) and the Cimbri at Vercellae (101). He had proved himself to be the indispensable man in Rome's need, and had already held the consulship five times. To his army, no longer restricted to substantial farmer-soldiers, he welcomed all free-born citizens who could fight, including even paupers; and he had increased the tactical efficiency of the legions by subdividing them into cohorts. The usual weapons of the legionary were now the pair of javelins (*pila*) for hurling, and the short two-edged sword (*gladius*) for stabbing. Efficient though the Roman infantry had become, in the use of cavalry the Romans were always weak. Like the first Scipio Africanus, whose success had continued him in the command, Marius was a professional general; but his army, attached to him by a personal allegiance, not only was a professional army but was quite as much the army of Marius as it was the army of Rome. To his soldiers, largely landless city-bred men, he held out hopes of land allotments as the prize of service; here was a new incentive to territorial expansion for generals with a career to make and for the city proletariat with a living to seek. The army was becoming the weapon of political parties; and a series of indispensable men, — Marius, Sulla, Pompey, and Caesar, — given armies and a free hand, carried laws and won empire. The failure of the Roman system to draw a clear line between military and civil government gave successful generals, when continued in office, a dominating power in politics; and the dangerous appeal to armed force as a political weapon in the days of the Gracchi was a thousand times intensified in the civil wars of Marius and Sulla, of Pompey and Caesar, of Antony and Octavian, — to mention only three of the dozen [1] civil wars to which Italy was subjected within less than a hundred years.

Two wars of defense, against Jugurtha and against the Teutons and Cimbri, had made the greatness of Marius; a third, the Social War (90–88), against the revolting Italian allies (*socii*), brought to the fore both the veteran Marius

[1] Cf. R. S. Conway, in *Virgil's Messianic Eclogue*, by J. B. Mayor, W. W. Fowler, and R. S. Conway (London, 1907), pp. 33 f.

and the younger aristocrat Sulla, who had already won a
great reputation as an officer under Marius and as a commander in border warfare in Asia Minor. The tremendous
political importance of the Social War will concern us later;
the increasing personal rivalry between the people's general,
Marius, and the rising hope of the Senate, Sulla, bore bitter
fruit in their struggle for the command in the new eastern
war against Mithradates, and recoiled on Rome in proscriptions and massacres.

The failure of Rome to accept full responsibility for the
protection and government of Asia Minor, as well as her
difficulties nearer home, had enabled young Mithradates
Eupator ("the Great"), king of Pontus, to come near realizing his ambition of driving the Romans from Asia Minor
and Greece, and of creating an Asiatic empire that should
revive the greatness of Persia and that should protect the
Greeks from their Roman oppressors. A lineal descendant
of the Persian royal house, and by education a Greek, he
seemed likely to unite the greatness of a Cyrus and of an
Alexander. His power grew along the Black Sea, in Armenia
and Parthia, and among the Greek cities of Asia; Roman
arms and Roman diplomacy checked him only temporarily.
Even Athens became his ally. Instigated by him, the Greek
cities massacred eighty thousand Romans and Italians (88).
But it was not till the Social War was over that Rome was
to able deal effectively with Mithradates. Sulla, the choice
of the Senate, after marching on Rome to assert his claim
over Marius, the people's choice, assumed the command. He
took Athens and European Greece, and drove Mithradates
back to Asia Minor. Knowing that in his absence the party
of Marius had seized control of the government and declared him an outlaw, he made terms with Mithradates as
harsh and as immediate as possible, so as to be able to re-

turn to Rome at once with the prestige of a great conquest (84). Mithradates was sent back to Pontus; on the Greek cities was saddled an impossible burden of taxation and indemnity, aggravated by the exactions of Roman money-lenders and the unchecked raids of Cilician pirates; [1] and so little was Sulla interested in a lasting settlement that no measures were taken to defend Asia Minor and Rome's client princes from a revival of Mithradates' power.

Soon after Sulla left the east, Mithradates began to recover his influence and power, while his son-in-law Tigranes was building up a mighty kingdom in Armenia, and was advancing into Mesopotamia, Syria, and southern Asia Minor. Rome was for a time unable to stay their progress, until the great L. Lucullus was sent out (74), who by his brilliant strategy defeated both kings in succession, and by his humane measures alleviated the plight of the province of Asia, thus offending the Roman tax-gatherers and their friends. In 68, when he was ready to invade Parthia, his legions mutinied, and he could hardly hold his own against Mithradates; the next year he learned that the Senate had removed him from the command, and he returned to Rome to enjoy his famous gardens and banquets.

The successor of Lucullus, Gnaeus Pompeius, had already won from his superior Sulla the surname of Magnus for his soldierly qualities shown in the campaigns against the Marian party. But he had since then become the champion of the popular party in the political compromises of the years following the supremacy of the Sullan constitution. To him the people had turned in 67, when a commander was needed

---

[1] Sulla's exactions were alleviated only by his assessing the districts for fixed amounts and ousting the *publicani* (cf. p. 214), as Caesar and Augustus later did; but his scheme lasted only till Pompey partially restored the Gracchan system of tax-farming.

to clear the Mediterranean of the pirates,[1] whose raids, long unchecked, reached the mouth of the Tiber, and cut off the supplies of grain coming from Egypt and Africa. In forty days Pompey swept them from the western seas; in another seven weeks he crushed them in their lurking places in Cilicia, colonized them in Cilicia and Greece and Italy, and received as a reward the supreme command not only in the war against Mithradates but over the east generally. Such absolute powers had been intrusted to no Roman before Pompey; and it was not the Senate who bestowed them on him but the popular party and the capitalists, who saw in him the man who would deal firmly with the enemy and add new provinces and protect their investments and tax-gathering interests.

The task of defeating Mithradates had been all but completed by Lucullus, the fruits of whose campaigns Pompey reaped. Mithradates was easily crushed; Tigranes surrendered without a blow; Pompey marched eastward to the Caucasus Mountains and the Caspian Sea, reducing the barbarian tribes to submission, and then south into Syria, capturing Jerusalem, and to the borders of Arabia. Pompey gathered in the fruits of victory. Bithynia was already a province, to which western Pontus was now added; of Syria, including Judaea, another province was made;[2] cities, the natural type of political unit in the east, were founded or re-

[1] The command against the pirates was conferred by the *Lex Gabinia*; that in the Mithradatic war by the *Lex Manilia*, supported by Cicero in his extant speech.

[2] Judaea was always a troublesome land for the Roman rule. At first a part of the province of Syria, it was later (40–4 B.C.) a dependent principality under Herod the Great; then divided for some forty years into parts, ruled by "tetrarchs." Herod Agrippa became king of the united country between 37 and 41 A.D.; but in 44 A.D. Judaea proper was again given to a procurator responsible to the emperor. A rebellion was crushed by Vespasian before he became emperor; Jerusalem was captured and destroyed by his son Titus (70 A.D.); and Judaea remained an imperial province.

founded; Roman overlordship was asserted over the tribes on the frontier; tribute was regularly exacted. Only the Parthians, in the Mesopotamian valley, remained to dispute Roman sovereignty in the east. With rich booty and princely captives Pompey returned in 61 B.C. to dazzle the populace of Rome.

Such power as Pompey held was more akin to monarchy than to republican government; yet Pompey had no ambition to become a king. And in order to gain the Senate's approval of his "acts" and the distribution of lands for his veterans that they expected, he found it necessary to form a coalition with the rising young politician of the popular party, Gaius Julius Caesar, and the wealthy M. Licinius Crassus, — the "First Triumvirate" (60).[1] Crassus, ambitious of a success like Pompey's, endeavored to push the Roman frontier from the Euphrates to the Tigris, but perished wretchedly in Mesopotamia at Carrhae (53).[2] Caesar, an aristocrat with democratic traditions, entertained a shrewd realization of the fact that Rome was destined to be ruled, if not by a monarch, by one armed with extraordinary powers. Already balked more than once in his ambitions, he was ready enough to accept the opportunity of using Pompey as his catspaw; he supported Pompey's modest claims, and received not only the consulship, but, far more important, the command for five years (later extended to ten years) in Illyricum and in Gaul on both sides of the Alps. He was to be responsible for the military and civil admin-

---

[1] This name for the coalition must have been a later invention. See H. A. Sanders, "The So-Called First Triumvirate," in *Mem. Am. Acad. Rome*, Vol. X (1932).

[2] The hard-riding Parthian archers, with their sudden pretended flights and as sudden attacks, continued to be the terror of the Roman imagination. Cf. Horace, *Odes* I, 19, 11; II, 13, 17. The standards lost by Crassus were restored to Tiberius (the future emperor) in 20 B.C.

istration of the region extending from the frontiers of Macedonia to the Pyrenees. Until he received this command, nothing in his career showed him to be the sober, responsible statesman that he appeared in his last years; and it was a purely self-seeking ambition, not any deliberate Roman policy of expansion, that led to his Gallic campaigns. He hoped to carve out a Roman territory in the west no less important than Pompey's conquests in the east, and in the process to forge an army of his own and a base of support that would make him Rome's indispensable man. Never was so bold a scheme so successful.

Cisalpine Gaul was already largely Romanized, though not yet politically a part of Italy. Roads, colonies, and *fora*, or trading posts and centres of administration, had prepared the country to become a province in 81 B.C. The inhabitants south of the Po held the Roman citizenship, while those north of the river had only "Latin rights," till given the full Roman franchise by Caesar (49). Beyond the Alps, Rome had long had friendly relations with the Greek city of Massilia (Marseilles), and when she added Spain to her territory she found it necessary to control the land route through southern Gaul; but it was not till about 121 that Rome broke the power of the native tribes along the coast and annexed the province presently known as Gallia Narbonensis (the modern Provence).[1] The northern border, however, was troubled by the descents of the terrible Teutons and Cimbri till the rugged Marius put an end to the peril. Transalpine Gaul was now disturbed only by occasional rebellions among the Celtic tribes, especially among the Allobroges, along the Rhone. But in the spring of 58 Caesar learned in Rome that Orgetorix and his Helvetii, once the allies of the Teutons and the Cimbri, were leaving their home northeast of Lake

[1] Cf. p. 63, n. 1.

Geneva, and were determined to seek, along with neighboring tribes, more than three hundred thousand strong, a new home in the rich plains of Gaul.

Within eight days Caesar reached the Rhone with his single legion and such Gallic recruits as he could muster on the way. He destroyed the bridge across the river, so that the Helvetii must find another and more arduous route through the mountains. With fresh troops from Italy he met them again, cut to pieces their rear guard, pursued their main force, turned aside to provision his army, chose his ground, and met their onset. After a decisive victory, he ordered those who were left of the Helvetii (less than a third of their original number) to return to their homes, as a defense against German invasions.

This opening campaign was characteristic of Caesar's method during the nine years of his wars in Gaul. His aim from the beginning was to conquer the whole of Gaul to the Rhine. His method was to defend the small province of southern Gaul against invasions, whether of Gauls or of Germans; to reduce defeated Gauls to the status of allies, so that they must be defended, if loyal, or punished, if rebellious; to use partially Romanized Gauls, and finally even Germans, as far as possible, against less civilized Gauls and Germans; to build up a hardy and versatile army devoted to himself; in his tactics, to divide the enemy and defeat their forces piecemeal, and to keep his lines of communication open, so that his food supplies could always reach him, whereas the enemy could not feed their multitudes except by spreading out over scattered areas. Thus Caesar's final victory was won no more by his skilful tactics on the field of battle and by his personal courage and determination than by his matchless use of the quartermaster's art. Most of his winters were spent in Cisalpine Gaul in supervising the details of civil administration, and in keeping closely in touch with his agents in Rome; *supplicationes* (thanksgivings) at Rome served to remind the people of the great deeds that Caesar and his armies were doing across the Alps, and young aristocrats were glad to gain staff appointments with him.

Caesar's nine years in Gaul (58–50) were filled with endless campaigning. No sooner had he defeated the Helvetii than he had to defend his Gallic allies, the Aedui, against the encroachments of Ariovistus and his Germans, and to drive the invaders back across the Rhine. The Belgae, the fiercest of the Gallic tribes, interpreted the continued presence of the legions in their neighborhood as a threat to their own independence, and took up arms; of them, the Remi at once submitted, and after the Nervii had been defeated in a desperate battle, Belgian Gaul acknowledged Roman sovereignty. Insurgent tribes along the Atlantic coast were subjugated by the creation of an impromptu Roman fleet at the mouth of the Loire. Gauls and Germans on either side of the Rhine made common cause against Caesar; one battle routed them, and the Rhine became the Roman frontier. In order to strike fear into the hearts of the Germans, Caesar built a trestle bridge over the Rhine, and made a display of force on the further side. Not yet, however, was Rome to attempt the conquest of Germany; Caesar withdrew his legions and destroyed the bridge. A similar motive of intimidation led to two brief reconnaissances in southern Britain, but the conquest of the island was prevented by a series of scattered Gallic revolts, suppressed only by persistent marching and countermarching and surprise attacks. Far more dangerous was the great uprising of the tribes of central Gaul under the gallant and able chief Vercingetorix, who succeeded for a time in holding together the tribes in a confederacy. The rebellion became general; even the faithful Aedui revolted.

Vercingetorix hoped to hold Caesar in check by guerilla warfare, while three simultaneous attacks were to be made on the province in the south of Gaul. But Caesar beat off the attack of Vercingetorix, who took refuge with a great force in the stronghold of Alesia. The legions invested the fortress with siegeworks ten miles long, and were meanwhile surrounded by hordes of Gauls who many times outnumbered them. Three times they beat back the assaults from both sides, and in the end Vercingetorix surrendered. The rebellion was now easily crushed, and no very serious resistance thereafter prevented Gaul from being pacified. The natives were enrolled as allies; the exaction of hostages and tribute and military contingents for the Roman army was directed by Caesar, and later by the governor of Gallia Narbonensis; only in 27 B.C., after the Civil War, was Gaul beyond the old province divided by Augustus into three parts, each with a separate provincial government. Thus the famous words with which Caesar began his *Commentaries on the Gallic War* recorded the natural geographical division of Gaul which Augustus preserved in the political division. For Caesar's pen was busy during his last years in Gaul with the composition of a great political pamphlet interpreting his wars. Behind its rapid narrative, devoid of rhetorical flourishes, and its restrained impersonal style, men in Rome must have perceived the greatness of Caesar's achievement; here was another indispensable man! And those who could not read the *Commentaries* could not fail to be thrilled by the sight of Vercingetorix marching in Caesar's triumph in Rome (46), only to be put to death in the Mamertine Prison.

Pompey in the east, Caesar in the west, each had proved indispensable to Rome; but their friendship had cooled, and Rome could not hold them both. The story of their civil war does not belong to the record of Roman expansion, but rather to political history. And the few years left to Caesar after his defeat of Pompey were too short to permit him to carry out his schemes of extending the empire to natural limits, — on the east to the Euphrates (with the subjugation of the Parthians) and to the Caucasus Mountains; no the north to the Danube and the Rhine, or even the Elbe; on the west to the Atlantic. Even in his brief dictatorship, however, he improved the provincial system of government within the frontiers, and extended the franchise more readily than did most of his successors. The civil wars that followed his death (44) delayed the execution of Caesar's plans. Antony, indeed, made spectacular but fruitless attempts to invade Parthia, and played the rôle of king-maker among the states of the east; and his rival Octavian made a beginning of the conquest of Pannonia that was necessary if the Danube frontier was to be secured.

The victory of Actium (31 B.C.) not only gave Octavian, who was soon to be known as Augustus, the supreme military and political power within the empire, but compelled him to conceive a deliberate policy of frontier defense, if not of expansion. For the first time the frontiers of the empire were not a prey to the ambitions of rival generals but were considered as a single problem; the conditions of the several provinces, the attitudes of the peoples beyond them, the geographical difficulties involved, the military strength available, — all were weighed. And the policy of Augustus was continued, with few exceptions, by his successors.

In the year after Actium, Octavian (Augustus) had taken over the rule of Egypt, long a client state, from the last of the Ptolemies; but he did not make it a province in the usual sense. Too valuable a granary and too promising a base for the machinations of some future Antony to be allowed to fall into the hands of any senatorial governor, Augustus kept most of it as his private domain, administered through a prefect of equestrian rank. All the coast of northern Africa was now Roman except Mauretania, which was added a few years later (40 A.D.). In central Asia Minor, Augustus annexed the province of Galatia, to which Tiberius added Cappadocia toward the east; so that the eastern frontier was then formed by Syria and the river Euphrates, with only Armenia and Parthia and the Arabian desert as outlying spheres of influence. On the west and north, Spain, which was now still further subdued, and Gaul, now comprising four provinces, touched the natural limit of the Atlantic; but the long northeastern frontier, from the English Channel to the Black Sea, caused the greatest difficulty to Augustus and his successors. Caesar had planned the conquest of Germany, but had died before he could push the frontier beyond the Rhine; and he had left unconquered a deep wedge of territory in what is now Switzerland and the strip of land to the east between the Danube and the provinces of Illyricum and Macedonia. The generals of Augustus subjugated the Alpine highlanders, completed the conquest, begun by himself, of Pannonia, and added to the empire the provinces of Rhaetia and Noricum (eastern Switzerland [1] and Austria), Pannonia and Moesia (roughly corresponding to Jugo-Slavia and Bulgaria). Thus when Claudius annexed Thrace (46 A.D.), the frontier from the North Sea to the Black Sea ran along the courses of the Rhine and the Danube, and only a small wedge of land between the headwaters of the two rivers remained to be added to the empire by the Flavian emperors and Hadrian in order to rectify this part of the frontier. Germany itself remained unconquered. Augustus at first hoped to realize Caesar's plan, and to shorten the

---

[1] The Romansch and the Ladin dialects, still spoken in the eastern cantons of Switzerland, are persistent reminders of the Roman occupation.

northeastern frontier by advancing from the Rhine to the Elbe. For a time his stepsons, Drusus and Tiberius, were successful in the invasion of Germany; but the terrible defeat of the legions under P. Quintilius Varus by the German Arminius (Herman) in the Teutoburg Forest [1] (9 A.D.) compelled the elderly Augustus to adopt, and to commend to his successors, the policy of regarding the Rhine as the frontier.[2] The campaigns of Germanicus beyond the Rhine (14–16 A.D.) recovered the lost standards of Varus and something of Roman prestige; but no attempt was made to conquer the country. The empire was reaching its greatest extent; consolidation was replacing conquest.

In only three directions did Roman arms add more territory. Caesar had made two brief expeditions of reconnaissance in Britain (55 and 54 B.C.), and had declared a protectorate over some of the tribes that had submitted to him; Augustus had planned the conquest of the island; the mad Caligula proclaimed that he was going to invade it, but contented himself with "the spoils of the sea," — the shells gathered on the coast of Normandy. It was Claudius who actually sent four legions to Britain (43 A.D.); whether his motive was desire of glory, or of commercial gain from British mines, or, as appears most probable, of security for Gaul, is uncertain. Claudius himself spent only sixteen days in the island; but his generals were occupied for many years in driving back the British tribes and suppressing rebellions. Though the capture of the valiant Caratacus in Wales marked a momentary success,[3] insurrections flared up anew. The Queen Boudicca (Boadicea) several years later led a great rebellion in eastern Britain, but was at last defeated.[4]

---

[1] The site of the battle has been discovered recently near Osnabruck, in the province of Hanover.   [2] Tacitus, *Ann.* I, 11.
[3] Tacitus, *Ann.* XII, 33–37.   [4] *Ibid.*, XIV, 29–37.

Southern Britain was made a province as early as 43 A.D., with camps, forts, and military roads; yet the advance of the Romans was gradual. Agricola indeed reached the northern part of the island in 85; but the great walls of defense claimed for Rome only the part south of the Forth-Clyde line (the thirty-six mile Wall of Antoninus) and after about 180 the smaller area south of the Tyne-Solway line (the seventy-three mile Wall of Hadrian, built in 120 and rebuilt by Severus in 208).

The two remaining additions to the Roman territory were made in the reign of Trajan, a warrior of heroic mould, who revived the forward policy of Julius Caesar. Since the days of Augustus the wars of defense along the Rhine had become less grave; those on the Danube had become serious. The great column of Trajan in Rome [1] records his crossing of the lower Danube and his conquest, beyond the river, of the Dacians (101–106 A.D.), a people dangerous to the southern provinces, with lands rich enough in minerals to be worth conquering. For a time Dacia was a fully organized province, and its modern name, Roumania, and the Roumanian language are reminders of the Roman occupation; but in the absence of any defensible northern frontier it seemed too costly for the hard-pressed emperors of the next century to hold, and Aurelian gave it up (270–275). Still less lasting and far less wise were Trajan's conquests in the east. The Parthians, to be sure, had continued to be troublesome neighbors since they had defeated Crassus at Carrhae,[2] and had seized Armenia; but the brilliant conquest of the Parthians and the nominal addition of Armenia, Mesopotamia, and "Rocky Arabia" to the empire (105–114) was less costly than would have been the attempt to hold all this new territory beyond the Euphrates; and Trajan's successor Hadrian

[1] Cf. pp. 170, 181.   [2] Cf. p. 70.

immediately relinquished Armenia and Mesopotamia, which never again became, except for short periods, parts of the empire. The year 117 A.D., in which Trajan died, may therefore be regarded as having witnessed the greatest extent to which the Roman Empire ever expanded.

Long before the empire reached its greatest extent, the Roman army had changed in character and in mobility. The old citizen militia of farmer-soldiers, who had sallied out with their Italian allies for a season's campaigning and had dispersed in the autumn, had been transformed by Marius into a professional army, whose members served for twenty years or more, moving about as frontier wars or civil wars demanded. It was Marius who gave each legion its silver eagle as a standard, and who divided its strength, numbering between three and six thousand men, into ten cohorts, fighting under seasoned centurions and military tribunes; from Julius Caesar's time each legion was commanded by an experienced *legatus* of senatorial rank. On the return of peace to the Roman world soon after the battle of Actium, Augustus reorganized the legions as a standing army with a fixed system of enlistment, service, and veterans' retiring allowance, and concentrated them at a few important posts near dangerous frontiers. For two hundred years the army, excepting the special bodies of guards, — the Praetorian and the City cohorts, and the watchmen who policed Rome and Italy, — was seldom to be seen in the peninsula. Nothing testifies more impressively to the completeness of the *Pax Romana* and the economy with which it was administered than the small number of troops needed to patrol the empire and to defend its frontiers. Under Augustus and his successors usually not more than about twenty or twenty-five legions were required, — a force, including native auxiliaries (cavalry and archers and light-armed infantry) in numbers about equal to the legionaries, that comprised a total of perhaps a quarter of a million men. One legion sufficed for Spain, so thoroughly Romanized had it become; Britain generally had two or three legions; the dangerous Rhine-Danube frontier required from twelve to sixteen; the eastern frontier was controlled by four legions; and one or two occupied Egypt and Roman Africa. Each legion acquired a distinct name and maintained a continuous history and traditions.

The camps of the legions, or *castra*, were still laid out after the four-sided pattern of the ancient pile-dwellings of the "terramara" inhabitants of the Po valley,[1] with ditch and rampart and palisade, and main streets intersecting at the headquarters and the granary not far from the middle. The name of many an English town, like Lancaster and Rochester and Gloucester, records the site of a Roman camp;[2] and many another town, like Pompeii in Campania and Lambaesis in Africa, shows a plan similar to the camp, whether by imitation or by actual growth from military to civilian uses.[3] The emperor Hadrian began the policy of spreading the legions more thinly behind the frontiers, with permanent

[1] Cf. pp. 11 f.

[2] The remains of some of these camps and fortifications, still to be seen in the English countryside, are impressive: e.g. at Hardknot Castle, Cumberland; at Ambleside, Westmorland; at Caerleon-on-Usk (= Castra Legionis), Monmouthshire, now in process of excavation; and, best of all, at Chesters and at Housesteads, in Northumberland, on Hadrian's Wall. See R. G. Collingwood, *Roman Britain*; the same author's *The Archaeology of Roman Britain*; and F. Haverfield, *The Roman Occupation of Britain*.

[3] In Pompeii may be traced in "Stabian Street" the *cardo maximus*, or north and south line, of a camp; and, crossing it approximately at right angles, streets ("Nola Street" and the "Strada dell' Abbondanza," with their continuations) corresponding to the *decumanus maior* and the *decumanus minor*. Recently an earlier town plan has been discovered, underlying the present one, with smaller lots and a different orientation. (See A. Ippel, *Pertica Pompeiorum*, Mitteilungen des Deutschen Archaeologischen Instituts, Römische Abteilung, Band 46 [1931], 34.)

fortresses (*castella*) and long walls and entrenchments at the actual frontier. Between the Rhine and the Danube [1] and across Northumberland may be seen not a few fragments of these great walls, with fosse and rampart, and parallel to them another ditch, or *vallum*, and at intervals the forts, "mile-castles," and turrets in which patrols and sentries were housed.[2] Just inside the wall ran a road, by which troops could be rapidly moved to any point that was threatened by raiders or smugglers. In the pacified interior of a province like Britain or Gaul a network of hard, straight roads (often following older tracks) served armies and traders alike.[3] Camps became towns; veterans were settled in *coloniae*, as the modern Cologne (Köln, the ancient Colonia Agrippinensis) and Lincoln (Lindum Colonia) still remind us. The provincial countryside was dotted with the villas or castles of the gentry.

By the reign of Septimius Severus (193–211) the distribution of the legions along the frontier was fixed, and soldiers would be quartered during most of their lives in some camp, some miniature Rome. Public baths, theatres, and other substantial buildings sprang up. More important still, the legionaries naturally found their wives among the native women of the provinces, and their sons naturally entered the Roman army. Though Augustus had allowed natives to

[1] In the "Devil's Wall."

[2] There is a good brief account in R. G. Collingwood, *A Guide to the Roman Wall* [2] (Newcastle-upon-Tyne, 1932).

[3] For convenient maps showing roads see: for the Roman Empire generally, H. Stuart Jones, *Companion to Roman History*, opp. p. 44; for Gaul, in *The Legacy of Rome*, p. 149; for Britain, the *Ordnance Survey Map of Roman Britain*, the maps in T. Codrington, *Roman Roads in Britain*[2], and in R. G. Collingwood, *Roman Britain*, front flyleaf. Many of these roads are still highways, others provide the foundation for railroads, while still others, no longer used, but clearly marked, tempt the pedestrian to follow their march over hill and fen (e.g. in England over parts of Watling Street, Ermine Street, Akeman Street, the Fosse Way, and the Iknild Way).

serve in the Roman army only as auxiliaries, the difficulty of levying sufficiently large armies from the Roman citizen body caused his immediate successors to bestow the citizenship on native recruits; and the edict of Caracalla that bestowed the Roman citizenship on all freemen within the empire (212 A.D.), while seeming to make the army all Roman, barely concealed the fact that it was chiefly barbarian. Few Italians now served in the legions; and the "German army" now meant not a hostile army of Germans but a Roman garrison on the German frontier that included many soldiers of German blood. Thus the ancient militia system, long abandoned in Italy, was revived on the frontiers.

Within the frontiers the Romans rapidly achieved their lasting work of building up communities, of spreading Roman law and administration, of diffusing the culture that they had forged from the legacy of their fathers and of the Greeks. The task must be accomplished rapidly or not at all; for outside the frontiers the barbarians were still threatening the empire or were already penetrating the outlying provinces; and the Roman armies themselves, as we have just seen, were becoming foreign, in some evil day to crumble under the pressure of stronger barbarians. The philosopher-emperor Marcus Aurelius (161–180) had to spend many weary years campaigning against the Parthians and against the Germanic tribes on the Danube, — the Boii, the Quadi, and the Marcomanni; indeed his partial victory over these tribes was purchased only by allowing large numbers of them to settle within the empire. The economic decline and the political revolutions of the following hundred years further weakened the defenses of the empire. Though Septimius Severus restored order for a time and checked the barbarians, the scarcity of coined money compelled him to pay his troops by settling them near the frontier and allowing them to marry and rear families.   The militia thus formed soon felt more closely attached to the region that it inhabited than to the remote and feeble authority of Rome; and it was not long before Roman "emperors" were made, as in the year following the death of Nero, by the various provincial armies, or parts of the empire, as Gaul and Palmyra, even asserted a large measure of independence for some years, and took care of their own frontiers. Septimius Severus, a rude African soldier by birth, had no special pride in the privileges of Rome and Italy, and actually quartered a legion on the Alban Mount, once the centre of the Latin League. Once more, as in her earliest days, Rome was under a military domination and was ruled from Alba. It was Caracalla, the son of Septimius Severus, whose edict, by raising the provincial freemen to the status of Romans, reduced proud Italy to the level of the provinces; [1] and it was henceforth governed as but one unit among many.

The third century saw the barbarian peril threaten Rome more dangerously: Germanic tribes, — Alemanni, Goths, and Franks, — crossed the Rhine and the Danube, and ravaged Gaul, Spain, and the Balkan provinces, including Greece, and were only with the greatest difficulty driven back to the two rivers. Dacia was given up. In Parthia, the new Persian Empire, under the Sassanid dynasty, likewise burst through the Roman defenses and for years defied Rome, though checked by the buffer state of Palmyra. Only the vigor of Aurelian (270–275) kept the empire from falling into fragments; but the great wall with which he engirdled Rome [2] as a defense against barbarian raids was a sign of weakness rather than of strength, for it indicated that the distant frontiers were no longer secure.

[1] Cf. pp. 82, 257 f.
[2] Cf. p. 21.

Still more than the monarchy of Aurelian, the strong despotism of Diocletian (284–305) by force of arms and by administrative machinery postponed the inevitable dissolution; but the inhabitants of Italy now for the first time in nearly five hundred years were compelled to pay taxes like the provincials,[1] and Rome was no longer even nominally the capital of the elaborately subdivided empire. The actual separation of the empire into its eastern and western halves, begun by the joint emperorship instituted by Diocletian, and hastened by Constantine's refounding of Byzantium as an oriental capital (330), was only the natural result of the fact that the empire, bulky and soft as an overripe fruit, was falling apart because there was no longer strength enough to resist economic ruin and barbarian invasion. Several times divided and reunited, the empire was finally divided between the sons of Theodosius (395).

The long struggle between Rome and the northern barbarians continued. Though she had been able in the days of Marius and of Caesar to overcome superior numbers and superior physical vigor by the discipline of her army and by the organization of her food supply, both of these advantages had now been lost. The morale of the army had been undermined by civil wars and by the barbarization of the provincial garrisons; the commissariat was crippled by the general economic decline of the empire. During the fifth century, invasion, migration, and plunder became increasingly common. The Franks and the Alemanni, to be sure, were checked by Constantine's nephew Julian (later emperor) at Strassburg (357), but the West Goths (Visigoths), hard pressed by the Huns, had been permitted by the Romans to take refuge south of the Danube. They presently revolted against Rome, and defeated the Roman army at

[1] Cf. pp. 62, 259.

Adrianople (378). Theodosius pacified them both by allowing them to remain in the Balkan peninsula and by using their leading men, along with other Germans, like the Vandal Stilicho, as generals and ministers of state. But their ambitious leader, Alaric, saw his opportunity in the dissensions of the sons of Theodosius, now emperors of the divided halves of the empire; he captured Athens, seized Illyricum, and after the death of Stilicho made his way into Italy and plundered Rome (410). After his death, his people marched into southwestern Gaul and Spain, where they established a Visigothic kingdom.

How seriously the resources of Rome were crippled may be seen from the fact that she now relinquished her control of Britain. Picts and Scots had been driven into the highlands; Saxon invaders on the east coast had been repulsed by the legions under the "Count of the Saxon Shore"; and Roman Britain had survived the adventures of several pretenders to the emperorship who had drained off her defenders to fight their battles. But now the legions were needed in Italy, and Watling Street and the Fosse Way heard their tramp no more; it was not long before Britain became less Roman than Saxon.

Meanwhile the plight of the empire was serious. Vandals and other Germanic tribes had crossed the Rhine and pushed through Gaul into Spain and the province of Africa, where they set up their kingdoms. Later, under Genseric, they raided Rome (455) with such ruthlessness as to leave their name as a byword for all time. By this time another Germanic people, the Burgundians, had also migrated into southeastern Gaul, and the western Roman empire had shrunk, except for the nominal allegiance of some barbarian states, to the confines of Italy. More terrible, however, than any of the Germanic invasions, was Attila and his great Hunnish empire in central and eastern Europe. Already levying tribute from the eastern Empire, he threatened Italy and the west with utter ruin. Fortunately for Rome, the Visigoths joined the western emperor at Châlons-sur-Marne, in Gaul, and dealt the Huns a decisive blow (456). Before Attila could carry out his intended invasion of Italy, he died, and the Hunnish peril disappeared. At Rome, shadowy emperors continued to be made and unmade by the Germanic chieftains, till 476, when such a figurehead, young Romulus Augustulus, was deposed, and the eastern emperor was informed that there was to be henceforth no emperor of the west. Italy, like Spain and Gaul and Africa, was now a kingdom under barbarian domination, though acknowledging for a few years the sovereignty of the eastern emperor. Change followed change. The East Goths (Ostrogoths) migrated from beyond the Danube into Italy; and in 493 their leader Theodoric established himself as king of an Ostrogothic kingdom that finally embraced parts of Gaul and Spain. Though uneducated, he became in many ways a truly beneficent ruler and patron of literature. Before the western empire could be revived, however, by any successor of Theodoric, the eastern emperor Justinian attempted to reconquer the western empire. His general Belisarius succeeded, indeed, in conquering the Vandal power in Africa and the Ostrogothic kingdom in Italy; but no strong civil government was established in Italy, and its inhabitants, weakened by successive invasions, could not prevent the Germanic "Longbeards" (Langobardi, or Lombards) from seizing the Po valley. No civil or military power was left in Italy strong enough to build up anew a single state; and only the growing influence of the bishops of Rome was able to make terms with the barbarians, already partly converted to Christianity. It was a bishop of Rome, or pope, who in 800 crowned as Roman emperor Charles the Great, king of the powerful Frankish kingdom, and thus gave to the new empire some semblance of continuity with the old Roman empire. But in its rulers and in its character the new empire was truly a mixture of Roman and German elements; and from this fusion many of the nations of modern Europe were to spring.[1] Rome had done her task not only by conquest but by diffusing organization and law and language among many races.

There were conquering nations before Rome; but mere conquest, without a civilization, is not lasting. It is hardly interesting. The ideals of imperialism and chauvinistic nationalism have less appeal to-day than ever before, in an age when the claims both of cosmopolitanism and of individuality are strong. Epics are seldom written now; they are perhaps less than ever read. But the expansion of Rome meant more than mere conquest: it meant that for a time men of many races, with all their differences, learned to live in one great society, to speak a common language, to share a common fund of ideas. And when Rome ceased visibly to rule over a great territorial empire, she did not cease to assert a predominating influence over men's habits and minds; the Latin language remained a *lingua franca* for diverse peoples, and the social experience of Rome gave them a common heritage, the *lingua franca* of civilization. As the nations of the modern world come to have closer dealings with each other, their Latin heritage becomes more and more a guarantee of mutual understanding. From the chronicle of Roman expansion we must turn, therefore, to consider what manner of men the Romans were.

[1] To the Latin nations of Europe should be added the countries of Latin-America, Africa, and Asia colonized by Spaniards and Portuguese. The Latin-speaking population of the world to-day amounts to about 200,000,000, considerably exceeding the English-speaking population (about 160,000,000).

CHAPTER III

HEARTH AND HOME

Sic enim mihi perspicere videor, ita natos esse nos, ut inter omnis esse societas quaedam, maior autem ut quisque proxime accederet.

Cicero, *De Amicitia* 19.

1. THE FAMILY

IF WE would learn what is most characteristic of Roman politics, we must not begin by asking about the inalienable rights of the individual citizen or about the views of the great statesmen; if we would understand Roman law, we must not study first the opinions of the great jurisconsults; if we would enter into the heart of Roman religion we must not ask how the Roman hoped to save his immortal soul. In each case we must realize that the Roman was first of all a member of a social group, whose habits and traditions he expressed, and was only secondarily, if at all, a free agent expressing his own personality. If great Romans towered above their fellows, it is none the less true that in every field except literature the greatest part of the Roman achievement was all but anonymous; hence the solidity and the conservatism of their work. And although the state bulks large in Roman history, it is not in the state but in the family that we must find the seeds of Roman politics and law, of Roman religion and character. For the state itself was only the more efficient expression of the social life of its component clans (*gentes*); and each clan, in turn, was a group of families with a common ancestor. It was in the family that the Roman found his first and most lasting discipline, those habits of obedience and the religious attitude and the family traditions and ideals that he generally carried through life.[1]

The Roman family (*familia*) embraced more than we ordinarily include in a "family." Beside the father and the mother and those of their descendants who had not been emancipated in some formal manner from the authority of the father, it included also the dependents of the household, both the free *clientes* and the slaves.[2] In a real sense, too, it included also its dead members and its gods. Of all its members, only the head, the *pater familias*, was legally his own master (*sui iuris*); over his wife he held the authority known as the "hand" (*manus*); over his descendants he exercised the *patria potestas*; and as master of his property, together with such chattels as slaves, he enjoyed the *dominica potestas*. A son, even if full grown and with children of his own, remained in private matters, though not in public relations, subject to the *patria potestas*, unless he were specially emancipated; a daughter would leave her father's authority only if she were thus emancipated or if she were married by a rite that placed her under the *manus* of her husband or of the head of his family. By this patriarchal custom, only the *pater familias* held property;[3] and his authority over his dependents was absolute. Legally he might even put to death a disobedient son or slave, and a few cases of such ex-

---

[1] The French still preserve to a large extent the Roman attitude. Charles Wagner writes: "The spirit of family is a spirit of cohesion, but of cohesion tending to extend itself endlessly. It reaches from our immediate contemporaries to our predecessors, from whence come our traditions, our inheritance, our customs and ideas; it binds us to posterity, whose interests are in our care."

[2] *Famuli*, whence the very word *familia*. In this larger sense, "household" is a better translation of *familia*.

[3] The property of a descendant or of a slave was held only by consent of the *pater familias* and was called *peculium*; the English "peculiar" therefore emphasizes the idea of separateness of ownership.

treme severity are known to us. But cruelty and unreasonable severity were effectively checked by custom and the force of public opinion. The Roman father, though severe, was not often tyrannical. And so anxious was he to leave sons to continue the family name and to pay due offerings of food and drink to its dead that if he was childless he was apt to adopt a son to continue the line.

The three names that a Roman ordinarily bore likewise testify to the priority of the family; for his *nomen* or name *par excellence*, standing second in order, always told to which clan (*gens*) he belonged, — Claudian, or Julian, or Tullian, or whatever it might be. His personal name (*praenomen*, or forename), usually given him on his ninth day, was chosen from a rather restricted list; only thirty are known to us, and among patrician families a small number of these sufficed, such as Marcus, Titus, or Quintus. In the Julian *gens* only three names are found, — Gaius, Lucius, and Sextus. In formal inscriptions, the *praenomen* of a man's father and grandfather sometimes followed his own *nomen*. Third in order usually stood the *cognomen*, an added name or nickname that sometimes told of the occupation or physical traits or character of some ancestor (as *Piso*, "one who grew peas"; *Dentatus*, "one with prominent teeth"; *Severus*, "the severe"); it now served to tell to what branch of his *gens* its bearer belonged. Some *cognomina*, moreover, were acquired by adoption; when, for example, Gaius Octavius Caepias was adopted by Gaius Julius Caesar, he took the name of the latter, with the addition of his own *nomen* and the suffix *-anus*, thus becoming Gaius Julius Caesar Octavianus. Still another form of *cognomen* was such an honorary name as that borne by Publius Cornelius Scipio Africanus, whose last name was acquired after his defeat of Hannibal; or Pompey's "Magnus," given him by Sulla; or the religious title of "Augustus," chosen for reasons of state. Sometimes an honorary *cognomen* was handed down like the title of an hereditary peer, to the winner's eldest son, but it apparently died with him. Women's names were oftenest simply the family *nomen* in the feminine form, sometimes with the father's or the husband's name added in the genitive; thus the name of Cicero's daughter might be written as Tullia M[arci]f[ilia]. A slave, at first referred to merely as the "boy" of his master (Marcipor, the *puer* of Marcus), might later be distinguished by his nationality (Davus, from Dacia), or given a *praenomen* followed by the *nomen* and *praenomen* of his master (Felix Popil[ii] L[ucii] S[ervus]); if given his freedom, he kept his personal name as a *cognomen*, and took his master's *nomen*, and his master's or some other *praenomen* (as Cicero's amanuensis Tiro became Marcus Tullius Tiro). Every time that a Roman was addressed, therefore, he was reminded of the closely-knit social group of which he was a member.

"Marriage," writes Cicero, is "the seed of society, which is developed in the possession of children and which flowers in the unity and community of the home. This is the origin of the State, too: homes are the seed-bed of social life." [1] Such was the typical Roman view, neither sentimental nor on the other hand precluding the possibility of real sentiment, but dwelling chiefly on the union from which were to come new citizens, new toilers, new members of the family to carry on the family cult.

Marriages were arranged, as often in France to-day, by the families concerned, sometimes when the parties were hardly in their 'teens; the wedding might take place several years before the girl reached the age of twenty, and when the man was not much over twenty, though he might post-

[1] Cicero, *De Off*. I, 17.

pone marriage till thirty or even forty. Marriage was therefore chiefly a matter of prudence, not the flowering of a romantic love at first sight. The advantage of the families and of the state outweighed private feelings, though there is reason to believe that a real and lasting affection between husband and wife as often grew up under the Roman system as under the more emotional method of American marriages. But it is also true that human nature will not be denied; and the Roman system in not recognizing love as the necessary precursor of marriage naturally brought forth both loveless marriages and lovers' intrigues and irregular attachments. Romans disapproved, as we may find it hard to do, the passion of Aeneas for Dido, because it was incompatible with his duty to family and nation; and Catullus found that for him love and unhappiness were one.

The marriage customs, formal as they sometimes appear, emphasized the solemnity of the step by which the bride left her own home and joined in the establishment of a new home, bringing a dowry as a sign that the union was expected to be permanent. Plebeians, to be sure, who at first were hardly considered citizens at all, were denied the forms of patrician marriage. They might practise marriage by "use" (*usus*), which was considered complete when husband and wife had dwelt together for a year; if the wife wished to remain a member of her father's household, she need only absent herself from her husband for a period of three nights each year. The plebeians might also use a form symbolizing marriage by sale (*coemptio*), the bride's father or guardian going through a fiction of selling her, in the presence of five witnesses and a person holding a pair of scales, into the "hand" of the husband. A marriage contracted under either of these forms was considered a regular and binding union, and in time was fully legal; but it lacked altogether the solemn religious character of the exclusive patrician ceremony of the confarreate marriage.

From the earliest times the patricians had felt that in marriage a bride was not only leaving her own family but entering another family, comprising members both human and divine; the sanction of the divine members must therefore be sought. This initiation they symbolized by the use of a cake, always made of spelt (*far*),[1] which was first offered to Jupiter Farreus, and then eaten sacramentally by the bridal couple. Henceforth the bride was completely a member of her husband's family, and subject to his *manus*; she was fully qualified to take part in the family religious rites, and her children, unlike those born of mothers not married by *confarreatio*, might hold certain of the major priesthoods on whose functions the welfare of the state was supposed to depend. Several motives conspired, however, to cause the confarreate marriage, and indeed any form of marriage by which the wife and her property passed from the *patria potestas* of her father into her husband's *manus* to become rare during the later Republic and the Empire. The woman herself was gaining in independence and in influence; moreover her family was often reluctant to allow that part of its property that stood in her name to pass beyond recall into the absolute control of another family. Thus marriage contracted *sine manu* became a simple compact between the parties, which could be dissolved as easily as it was made, and divorce, rare if not unknown in early Rome, became very common.

Whatever form of marriage was used, the wedding was

---

[1] Cf. p. 9. *Confarreatio* means simply the partaking together of the *far*. The wedding cake of modern times seems to be an inheritance from the cake of *far*, of which, however, none but the wedding couple partook. The guests ate squares of another kind of cake.

apt to include many symbolic ceremonies reminiscent of earlier days. The betrothal, which occurred usually some time before the wedding, consisted of the simple pledge on the part of the heads of the two families. "Spondesne?" asked the young man's father. ("Do you pledge your daughter in marriage to my son?") "Di bene vortant! Spondeo!" was the reply of the girl's father. ("So may the gods help us, I do pledge her.") And the other father echoed the solemn words of the prayer: "Di bene vortant!" Gifts were made to the girl, including an iron ring to be worn on the third finger of the left hand, from which a nerve was supposed to run directly to her heart; these gifts could never be recovered, even if the young man chose, as he legally could, to break the engagement in favor of some other girl. On the eve of the wedding day, the bride dedicated to the Lares of her father's house her childish playthings and the fringed toga that she had worn as a girl; and on the wedding day itself, — a lucky day, chosen with care, — she was dressed in her bridal attire: a tunic of an old-fashioned weave, bound about the waist, for good luck, with a woolen cord tied in the "knot of Hercules," that only her husband might untie; yellow slippers (*socci lutei*); and a large veil of the same color (*flammeum*) that covered her head. To "take the veil" (*nubere*) for a Roman girl therefore meant the vows not of the vestal but of the matron.[1] Over her hair, which had been divided into six locks by a spear-shaped comb (symbolizing primitive marriage by capture), she wore a chaplet of flowers plucked by her own hands. The bridegroom of course wore the toga, the conventional dress of

---

[1] In recent years, by edicts of the Pope and of the Fascist government, an attempt has been made to require brides to wear a nun-like wedding dress, with high neck, long sleeves, long skirt, and veil enveloping the head and part of the face.

formal occasions. So far we have been concerned with matters important, doubtless, in the eyes of the bridal pair and their friends, but not essential to a legal marriage; what followed was vital. The auspices were taken, to make sure of the approval of the gods. If these were favorable, the marriage contract was signed, and a matron (the *pronuba*) formally introduced to each other the bridal couple, who symbolized their mutual consent to the marriage by joining their right hands (*dextrarum iunctio*). This essential act was followed by prayers to Jupiter, Juno, and other divinities associated with marriage and by a sacrifice to Jupiter. "Feliciter!" ("Good luck!"), cried the guests, and joined in a feast provided by the bride's father.

Toward dusk, as the evening star rose, began the formal procession (*deductio*) that escorted the bride from her old home to her husband's house. Sometimes the bride was figuratively "torn" from her mother's arms, again in reminiscence of an older marriage by capture. Torches and flutes gave entertainment to the bystanders, who sang ribald verses (*versus Fescennini*) to insure the good luck of the happy pair, and shouted the mysterious wedding cry "Talassio!" [1] Boys scrambled for the nuts that were scattered, as rice is thrown to-day. The bride was accompanied by pages, one of whom carried a torch of white thorn, which she later tossed to the guests as a modern bride tosses her bouquet; other attendants carried a distaff and spindle, emblems of domestic pursuits. She herself bore three coins, of which she offered one to the gods of the nearest crossroad, another to the gods of her new home, and a third, symboliz-

---

[1] The meaning of the word had long since been forgotten; but Livy tells (I, 9) the ancient legend that attributed it to the henchmen of one Talassius for whom an especially beautiful girl was being carried off. "For whom?" asked others. "Talassio!" ("For Talassius!"), they answered.

ing her dowry, to her husband. Arrived at her husband's
house, she paused to deck its doorposts with woolen fillets,
and anointed the door with oil and fat. Her husband now
lifted her over the threshold, whether once more as an act of
pretended capture or in order to avert the ill omen of a possible stumble. At the door she repeated the words that she
had already used in her father's house, if she was married by
confarreatio or by *coemptio*, "Ubi tu Gaius, ego Gaia.") ("So
long as you are John Doe, I am Mrs. John Doe.") The
names, originally chosen probably for their propitious character,[1] never varied; and legal as the formula may sound,
who knows with what shy tenderness the bride may have
pronounced a pledge of union that should last "till death us
do part"? Once inside his house with the guests, the husband presented his wife with fire and water, the essentials of
domestic life.[2] Before throwing the torch to the guests, the
bride lit with it a fire from fuel that lay on the hearth. After
a prayer before the marriage couch that stood on this occasion in the atrium, the guests departed, though many of
them returned on the following evening to the feast at
which the wife, now a matron, made her first sacrifice to
the gods.

No more beautiful poems were ever written in the Latin
tongue than the pair of marriage songs of Catullus, who was
himself never the partner in a Roman marriage. In them
the hard legalisms and the quaint symbolic survivals are
absorbed in the eager, half-amused sympathy with which he
follows the course of the ceremonies. In the first of the pair
(the sixty-first poem) he invokes Hymen, the Greek god of
marriage, for the wedding of his friend Manlius Torquatus

---

[1] Gaius may be related to *gaudere*, "to rejoice."

[2] The formula of exile against a Roman citizen simply denied him the use
of these elements in Rome.

and Vinia Aurunculeia, a goodly maiden, with goodly auspices, bidding him bind his temples with the blossoms of sweet-smelling marjoram, and don the flame-colored veil and yellow slippers and lead the mystical song and dance. Through stanza after stanza of lyric music the poem dwells on the sweet gravity of this Roman marriage and the loveliness of the modest bride, looking forward to their happy years of harmonious married life and the little Torquatus who may, he hopes, some day stretch forth tender hands from his mother's bosom and with half-parted lips laugh toward his father. The second poem of the pair (the sixty-second), in hexameters full of delightful refrains and echoing or contrasting phrases, reminds one more of a Greek epithalamium. The evening star has risen while the bands of the young men and girls have lingered over the feast; now they vie with each other in singing the sadness of the bride's loss of her old home, and the gladness of her new life. Once a shy flower in a walled garden, now she will be cherished by her lord as the vine is cherished by its husband the elm.

The poet's picture is no sentimental exaggeration, for the Roman matron enjoyed a greater freedom and respect than fell to the lot of women in any other ancient society. Though legally still either in her father's *potestas* or in her husband's *manus*, actually she was the mistress (*domina*) of her home, and went abroad dressed in the distinctive matron's *stola*, with her retinue of servants. Hers was a privileged position at the theatre, at the public games, and at the public religious rites. There were no separate women's quarters in the house, as in Greece and the Orient; and the matron sat at table when her husband's guests came to dinner, — sat, we must observe, for good form required that she should not recline, in the usual manner of fashionable Roman diners, when guests were present, and that she should abstain from wine. Cooking was considered a menial task, to be done by slaves; but the matron not only presided over the spinning and weaving of her maids but took part in the work herself. We are told that Augustus, in his attempt to revive the pristine virtues of earlier Rome, would wear only garments woven by the imperial fingers of the ladies of his household.[1] Like the ideal woman of the Bible, who "seeketh wool and flax and worketh willingly with her hands; she layeth her hands to the spindle and her hands hold the distaff," so the Roman matron is often praised in her epitaph for her excellence as a *lanifica* (worker in wool). Thus one stone of the second century B.C. inscribed in quaintly old-fashioned Latin, reads as follows: "Stranger, stand and read the little that I tell. Here is the homely tomb of a fair woman; her parents named her Claudia. She loved her husband with all her heart. She bore two sons; one of these she leaves on earth, the other she buried. Cheerful in speech, dignified in mien, she kept house; she made wool. I have told my tale. Depart." [2]

If the education of Roman women seems to have been confined during most of the Republic to their A B C's and to domestic lore, it must be remembered that their early schooling was just what most boys received, and that the primary schools were often mixed. Greek women had fewer opportunities; and Roman men, till late in the Republic, lacked a "higher education" as much as did their wives. The matron, moreover, joined in the family councils on all matters of importance; old Cato declared that she actually ruled her husband. Though it is the famous Cornelia, mother of the Gracchi, and such figures as the matrons in Shakspere's Roman plays who are the most familiar and

[1] Suetonius, *Aug.*, 73.
[2] *C. I. L.* I, 1007 (= VI, 15346).

conspicuous examples of Roman womanhood of the earlier period, they must not cause us to forget the countless obscure mothers whose indirect influence on home and society powerfully moulded the Roman character. It was the nameless mother at whose stern bidding the boys learned to carry in the firewood who bred the race of warriors that defeated Pyrrhus and Hannibal.[1] She and her sisters received their due homage not only on their birthdays in the privacy of the home, but on the first of March at the "Mothers' Day" (*Matronalia*), a great public festival.

Customs changed, and with them something of the sanctity of the home. As early as the second Punic War, legislation began to try, though with imperfect success, to curb the growing luxury and independence of women. A war measure limiting the amount of jewelry that they might wear was actually repealed a few years later, despite the vehement opposition of Cato, when the women flocked to the Forum and browbeat the legislators.[2] Laws intended to prevent women from accumulating large fortunes by inheritance were more effective. But the increasing tendency toward marriages without *manus* and toward divorce more than compensated for the restriction, and the freedom of women to live their own lives became a favorite subject of the satirists of the late Republic and the Empire. Their invectives and innuendoes must be taken with more than a grain of salt; yet it appears certain that the new freedom was gained without compensating responsibilities in careers private or public. Women sometimes acquired a smattering of literary education and engaged in a dilettante pursuit of the arts. Debarred from politics, the matron, especially if she were an

[1] Horace, *Odes* III, 6, 38 ff.

[2] Livy, XXXIV, 1-8. Cato's speech, as given by Livy, is very entertaining. Plutarch also records his complaint: "Men usually command women; but we command all men, and the women command us" (*Cato Maior*, 8).

empress, sometimes engaged in political intrigue; debarred from business, she was the prey of the legacy-hunter; and in the decline of the older Roman religion she found a new emotional outlet in the foreign cults of Bacchus, Cybele, and Isis, sometimes with scandalous consequences.[1] If Roman divorces were less often than American divorces the result of romantic marriages made in haste, both marriages and divorces were more often the convenient means of advancing or remedying the economic and the political exigencies of a Cicero or an Augustus or of men far less worthy than they.[2] And still later, when Christianity revolted against the unbridled license of women in which the Roman tradition had ended, it was driven at first to offer as a substitute the theory of the naturally evil character of woman and her necessary subjection to her husband. Only when this teaching had been tempered by social traditions from northern Europe did a more exalted ideal of womanhood emerge, to be expressed in terms of chivalry and of respect for the Virgin Mary. These ideals dominated the conception of womanhood till recent times, when the further economic and social emancipation of women led to a more rational view of the equality of the sexes.

However gravely Rome may have suffered in many cases, and these not the least conspicuous or the least interesting to the satirist, from the legal emancipation of women, it would be wrong to suppose that the change was all disastrous, and

[1] Cf. p. 330.

[2] Cicero, after living for some thirty years with his wife, the *difficile* Terentia, chose to divorce her for reasons that reflect little credit on either party, and married the young and wealthy Publilia; but this marriage was no more happy. Augustus both in his own case and in dealing with members of his family made and unmade marriages with a cynical and heartless freedom. A convenient summary of his accomplishments in this field is given by R. S. Conway in "The Place of Dido in History" (in *New Studies of a Great Inheritance*, pp. 155 f.).

that the majority of women, apart from the feverish life of the capital, did not remain with their husbands and live busy and contented lives. Many a tombstone tells us of a couple who dwelt together during many years S. V. Q. (*sine ulla querela*), "without any complaint." And luck has preserved the long inscription in which a Roman husband, probably Q. Lucretius Vespillo by name, recorded his devotion to his wife Turia, who had recently died (about 8 B.C.); it seems to represent, though in the form of a direct address to her, what he may have said in the *laudatio*, or funeral eulogy.[1] They had lived in the dangerous years of the Civil War, passing through almost incredible adventures both before and during their forty-one years of married life. In every emergency Turia showed her resourcefulness and courage and her utter devotion to her husband, coping successfully with ruffians and assassins, with unscrupulous relations and a brutal triumvir, concealing her husband when his life was in danger and sending him help when he was absent. Tranquil years followed; and Turia, who was still childless, horrified her husband by innocently proposing that he divorce her so that he might have a son and heir by another wife. Though he appreciated her unselfish motive, his love for her would not for a moment tolerate the suggestion, and they lived together till her death. Nor is Turia a solitary example of affection among Roman wives during periods when the satirists were crying out against decadence. For a picture of a happy couple, we need only read the letters of the younger Pliny, whose Calpurnia doted on him to the extent of listening greedily to his recitations from the concealment

---

[1] *C. I. L.* VI, 1527. The Latin text appears also in Rogers and Harley, *Roman Home Life and Religion*, pp. 102–106; there is an interesting discussion of the whole inscription by W. Warde Fowler, in *Social Life at Rome in the Age of Cicero*, pp. 158–167 (reprinted almost in full by Rogers and Harley, 97–101), and in *Roman Essays and Interpretations*.

of a curtain, and of memorizing his speeches and setting his lame verses to music. Pliny himself was equally devoted to her: when she was absent he read and reread her letters, and begged her to write twice a day; his feet found their way to her room as when she was present, and her illness filled him with anxiety.[1] More heroic and more famous was Arria. When her husband and their son lay sick, and the latter, an unusually handsome and modest lad, died, she concealed his death from her husband, pretending that he was regaining his health. When her grief was too much to bear, she would leave the sick-room and burst into tears. Then, drying her eyes, she returned to the room, as if she had left her bereavement outside. Later, during the reign of Claudius, when her husband had been caught in a revolt and was being taken to Rome in a ship, she resolutely followed him in a fishing smack. He was condemned to death; she led the way by stabbing herself and handing him the dagger with the words, "Paete, non dolet." ("It doesn't hurt, Paetus.") [2] Their daughter Fannia carried on the family tradition by twice following her husband into exile and finally suffering banishment for helping in the publication of his life.

In early Rome, as among most vigorous farming and fighting peoples, large families were common; sons were needed for the army and the farm, as well as to carry on the family cults, and daughters were hardly less desired, to spin and weave. Such common names as Quintus and Sextus, though later handed down and used without any regard for their meaning, were originally given to a fifth or a sixth son. But that families must have become gradually smaller and that marriage was not universal we may infer from the fact that as early as 463 B.C. a law was enacted imposing a bach-

[1] Pliny, *Epist.* VI, 4 and 7.
[2] *Ibid.* III, 16. Cf. Martial, I, 13.

elor's tax (called "wife money," *aes uxorium*) on all Romans who reached old age without marrying. Cicero, the father of two children, praised Metellus for the size of his family; and Augustus, alarmed at the "race suicide" caused by the decline and the instability of marriage in his day, attempted to remedy the situation by penalizing the unmarried and the childless, and by granting to the father of three children the privilege (*ius trium liberorum*) of inheriting freely from distant kinsmen and of priority in candidacy for offices and governorships. These measures seem, however, to have been of small effect; and the *ius trium liberorum* was bestowed by later emperors on many who had by no means qualified for it.[1]

The absolute right of the *pater familias* might be exercised on the day when his child was born; for the infant was placed on the ground at his feet, near the hearth, and he must decide whether to acknowledge it as his own and to rear it. Occasionally a deformed child, or a girl that seemed too great a liability for its poverty-stricken parents, might be "exposed" in some public place, to die or to find its way into slavery or beggary;[2] ordinarily, of course, he would "lift up" the child in his arms (*tollere*, or *suscipere*), as a sign that he received it into his family. Nine days later (or eight, if it were a girl), the child was solemnly purified, and received its *praenomen*. Numerous divinities watched over its every need and deed, — divinities of sucking, drinking, crying, speaking, toddling, home-leaving and home-coming. Little trinkets and images of various implements, strung together

---

[1] E.g., the younger Pliny, who had no children, received it from Trajan (*Epist.* X, 2); and Martial, who was not even married, received it from Domitian (II, 41, 42).

[2] Very rarely, however, either in Athens (cf. L. Van Hook, in *T. A. P. A.*, Vol. LI [1920] or in Rome (cf. H. Bennett, in *C. J.*, Vol. XVIII, No. 6 [March, 1923]; and M. Radin, in *C. J.*, Vol. XX, No. 6 [March, 1925]).

as a necklace (*crepundia*), were given the child both as a plaything and as a safeguard against evil influences, and especially as a charm against the malignant power now known as the "evil eye" (*fascinatio*).[1] The child wore, hung from his neck, a small amulet enclosed in a receptacle shaped like a watchcase, and called the *bulla*. This charm, made of metal or of leather, was not laid aside by a girl till the eve of her wedding, or by a boy till he donned the *toga virilis* and was registered as a full-fledged citizen.

Childhood was doubtless as happy a time among Romans as among modern peoples, if dolls and gocarts, tops and balls and marbles (or rather nuts), and all sorts of games could make happiness. Pets, — especially birds and dogs, — were treasured members of the household. The mother shared with the nurse (a Greek, if possible) the early care of the children. At the mother's knee they began to receive that discipline in habit which was always the most important element in Roman education. Stories and songs of old Roman worthies, and especially of their ancestors, inculcated as an ideal for imitation the "custom of the ancients" (*mos maiorum*); industry and thrift and obedience were the rule of the home. Meanwhile the conversation at the table, at which they were present, might accustom their ears to the best of Latin. By constant companionship with the father the boys learned much of practical value about the farm or about public affairs. Horace's father gave the future poet no little initiation into his understanding of human nature by drawing his attention to the characters of people about him.[2] Education of a more bookish sort was not wholly lacking even in childhood; in early Rome it was apt to be the father who would, if possible, launch his children among the

[1] Cf. p. 303.
[2] Horace, *Sat.* I, 4, 105-126.

rudiments of "the three R's"; but this task was presently handed over to well educated slaves, usually Greeks. The elder Cato, to be sure, persisted in the older custom, though one of his slaves acted as tutor to other children. "As soon as the dawn of intelligence began in his son, he decided to give his personal attention to his education. For, he tells us, if his son's progress happened to be slow, he had no intention of having him reprimanded, or pulled by the ear, by a servant; nor did he wish him to be indebted to a mean person for his education. So he taught him literature and law himself, and also the necessary sports, — javelin-throwing, fighting hand to hand, riding, boxing, and swimming, even in rapid rivers, and the endurance of heat and cold. He also tells us that he wrote out stories for him, in large hand, to acquaint him with the romance and the traditions of his country. He was as careful not to utter an indecent word before his son as he would have been in the presence of a vestal virgin." [1]

Since fathers were of necessity more and more away from home, fighting in the wars or engaged in public and private business, schooling in the home was gradually replaced by private schools in conveniently situated houses or colonnades. The boys, and often for a few years the girls also, were escorted daily to and from school by the *paedagogus*, the slave who, though he did not actually teach them, as the English derivative would imply, faithfully looked out for their welfare. As the schools developed, largely under Greek influence, they came toward the end of the Republic to have three distinct stages. At about the age of seven the young Roman went to what we should call a primary school, named less often a *schola*, or place of leisure, after the Greek

---

[1] Plutarch, *Cato Major*, 20. It is pleasant to read later in the chapter, after an account of the younger Cato's subsequent career, that "Cato's care of his education was thus justified by results."

name, than a *ludus*, or place of play, — whether as a snare of youth or as an indication that methods of training ordinarily accounted modern actually prevailed. From the *ludi magister*, or *litterator*, children learned their letters, — that is, both reading and writing, — and simple processes in arithmetic. They also memorized, as late as Cicero's boyhood, the archaic formulas of the Twelve Tables, as our forefathers recited by rote their catechism and the verses of the *New England Primer*. Unfortunately the schoolmaster was ordinarily a slave or a freedman, who could seldom arouse any real respect; for discipline he therefore depended on corporal punishment. For the lazy and the stupid the rod was seldom spared. Never did Horace forget the schoolmaster of his childhood, Orbilius, "the man of blows"; [1] and when Martial wished the *ludi magister* of his acquaintance to give his tender charges a vacation in the dog days, he begged him to let the cat-o'-nine-tails slumber: "in summer if boys enjoy good health they are learning quite enough." [2]

After half a dozen years under the *litterator*, promising boys would pass on to the instruction of the *grammaticus*, who taught them, well or ill, not merely grammar, in the narrow sense, but literature, both Greek and Latin, and all the miscellaneous lore, — history, geography, mythology, and ethics, — that literature involves. Such training would continue till the age of our college students, when a small number of the young men of the better families would become pupils of the *rhetor*, in anticipation of their entry into public life. Public speaking was now the all-important subject of study; practice in composition and in delivery aimed at producing the fluency and the plausible show of reason that should some day sway the minds of jury or Senate.

[1] Horace, *Epist.* II, 1, 70; *plagosus*.
[2] Martial, X, 62.

Much of this training was of real value, even if pursued from a narrowly vocational motive; yet an air of unreality gradually invaded the rhetorical schools during the Empire, as the treatment of flimsy, hypothetical themes and a striving for clever effects occupied men's minds, with literary consequences that were on the whole unfortunate.[1] The curriculum of Roman schools became somewhat enriched with such subjects as geometry and astronomy, music and dancing (of a very sober sort), and technical subjects like architecture and medicine; but the practise of the latter professions tended to be restricted to foreigners, and training in science was never highly developed. And perhaps the most surprising feature of Roman education is the failure of the state to control it for moral and patriotic ends, as Plato and Aristotle, though not the average Greek state, would have controlled it. There was never, during the Republic, anything corresponding to a state-supported public school system, although some of the emperors and some citizens (like the younger Pliny) endowed schools and scholarships to some extent, or gave salaries and privileges to the notoriously underpaid teachers. The explanation is perhaps simple. The early type of Roman education was primarily a discipline in character, which seemed to fall within the sacred duty and privilege of the *pater familias*, and with which the state therefore did not presume to interfere. The laissez faire attitude continued; but education had lost its strong ethical quality with the decay of family life, and had become chiefly literary and rhetorical when economic motives impelled emperors to endow education as they were coming to endow orphanages. Teachers now took their place in a state bureaucracy, and education was state-controlled. But though Roman schools were late in coming under state support and management, the

[1] Cf. p. 424.

elementary schools were always open to the children of all classes, and the fees were small and discipline severe for rich and poor alike. Rudimentary education was more general in Roman society than among any other ancient people.

By the time that the Roman boy was ready to leave the *grammaticus*, at about the age of seventeen, he was usually considered to have ended his boyhood, and to be ready for full citizenship. The change was symbolized by his putting aside with due solemnity, usually on the festival of Liber ("the freer"), the *bulla* and the *toga praetexta*, with its crimson border, and his assuming the pure white *toga virilis*; and his were now the liabilities and the privileges of citizenship, both civil and military. Physical and military training, always an important part of Roman education, continued during these years. The more promising scions of noble and wealthy families were apt to supplement their rhetorical training by a year or more of study and travel in Greece or the east, — study of oratory and perhaps of philosophy in the university town of Athens or in Rhodes (Cicero studied in both places), and a *grand tour* probably of the famous cities of Greece and Asia Minor and Egypt, with whose works of art and ancient culture nothing in Italy could vie. If a boy showed a greater bent for a military career, he went at once, on attaining the *toga virilis*, into the army; and many with political ambitions, like Cicero, served for a short time on the staff of some commander, thus gaining experience of military and practical afiairs. Such an apprenticeship with lawyers and statesmen, moreover, was the accepted method of gaining an entrance into a legal and political career, for there was no formal system of legal education. Lucky were those who, like Cicero, absorbed their law from so great a jurist as Q. Mucius Scaevola. Doubtless the method had its advantages, in that example is often more effective than precept, especially when not only information but moral integrity is concerned. Most physicians and lawyers, until something like a hundred years ago, picked up a great part of their knowledge by spending a few years in the office of a veteran practitioner and accompanying him on his professional errands. Personal influence, sometimes of an almost parental sort, thus continued the earlier training of the *pater familias* in the Roman home.

The critical events of birth and marriage were closely bound, as we have seen, to the continuity of the family; and when a Roman breathed his last and joined his fathers, the traditions of the family were invoked in no less significant manner. For among the Greeks and the Romans death was no mere personal incident, and the manner of burial was not a matter of indifference. If the deceased did not receive his proper due, — at least the symbolic "three handfuls of dust" thrown upon his body, and reverent offerings of food and drink from his descendants, — not only would his soul suffer in its dark abode but it would haunt the survivors and bring them misfortunes.[1] Two of the extant plays of Sophocles turn on the tragic necessity of the dead, Ajax and Polyneices, finding burial. Even if the bodies of soldiers or sailors were lost, the obligation remained of erecting a cenotaph and of giving them due offerings.

If a Roman died at home, some near kinsman would endeavor to catch his last breath, and would lead those present in loudly calling upon him by name, whether originally to recall the departing spirit, or merely to find out if he were really dead. One is reminded of this cry (the *conclamatio*) to-day when a Pope dies, and a cardinal calls upon him

---

[1] "Licebit iniecto ter pulvere curras," cries the hapless mariner to the wayfarer, in an ode of Horace (I, 28, 36). A mysterious house in Athens is no longer haunted when a skeleton in the garden is found and given due burial; for the ghost is laid. (Pliny, *Epist.* VII, 27.)

thrice by his Christian name before pronouncing him dead. The eyes were then closed, and the body was prepared to lie in state on its funeral bier in the *atrium*, dressed for the last time in the toga, and with feet pointed toward the door through which it was soon to depart. If the deceased were a man of distinction, the insignia of his rank or honors would be displayed, and a death mask of his features would be taken. Except during the classical period, a coin was placed in his mouth, to serve as his fare in Charon's bark when he should cross the Styx. To warn passers-by that the house was under pollution of death, a branch of pine or of cypress (still the characteristic tree in Italian cemeteries) was set at the door.

There is no evidence that the dead were ever buried within the house, or indeed very near it; in fact the Twelve Tables (450 B.C.) forbade interment within the city. Nevertheless, a noisome "potter's field" on the Esquiline continued to receive the bodies of paupers together with all manner of refuse, till Augustus put an end to the nuisance by requiring it to be covered with earth, and it became a part of the Gardens of Maecenas. All burial thereafter, like the burial of all but the most friendless long since, took place outside the city, chiefly beside the roads, as the impressive lines of tombs along the Appian Way and the "Street of Tombs" outside Pompeii still bear witness. To such a place the funeral procession made its way from the house of the deceased, originally at night, in later times by day, except in the case of children and of the very poor, whose pathetic funerals were still conducted as inconspicuously as possible in the obscurity of night.[1] Roman conservatism, however,

---

[1] Nero, after poisoning his half-brother Britannicus, aged thirteen, explained the hurried nocturnal funeral by observing cynically that a child's funeral was considered by the ancients too tragic to be exposed to the light of day (Tacitus, *Ann.* XIII, 17).

caused torches to be carried even by day; and to-day a
funeral attended by the shrouded *fratres misericordiae* (the
confraternità) marches through the streets of an Italian town
with tall candles in broad daylight.

The funeral of a distinguished Roman was a great public
spectacle, to which citizens were invited by a crier in the archaic words of an ancient formula: "Ollus Quiris leto datus.
Exsequias quibus commodum, ire iam tempus est. Ollus ex
aedibus effertur." ("Such a one, a citizen, has been surrendered to death. For them who find it convenient it is
now time to attend the obsequies. He is being carried forth
from his house.") The procession formed and issued forth:
the musicians with their blaring trumpets, and the hired
mourners; the death masks (*imagines*) of illustrious ancestors removed from the wall to be worn by actors, as if the
whole family line had come to life again; the trophies won
by the deceased, carried as if in a triumph; the dead man
himself on his bier, with face uncovered; the family, with
freedmen and slaves, and the friends, dressed in the dark
togas of mourning; and the noisy cortege was followed by the
torch-bearers. At the Forum the procession paused for some
near kinsman to pronounce the *laudatio*, a eulogy resonant
with fulsome praise of the virtues and deeds, real or imaginary, of the deceased. It must be admitted that the exag-
gerated praise of many of the heroes whom we meet in the
pages of Roman historians is derived from the memory of
such panegyrics. Political capital might be made of the
occasion, as when the murdered Caesar's body, on its way to
be buried with pomp in the Campus Martius, halted in the
Forum, and "instead of a *laudatio* the consul Antonius
(Mark Antony) had proclaimed by a herald the decree of the
Senate by which it had voted him every honor divine and
human, and likewise the oath by which all had pledged

themselves on behalf of his safety; and then he added a very few remarks of his own." [1] The minds of the populace were so inflamed, egged on, it was believed, by the supernatural appearance of two young men, that benches and clothing, arms and jewels, were heaped upon an impromptu pyre, and Caesar's body was burned on the spot.

Ordinarily the procession would pass on through a city gate to the place of burial. Both burial in the ground and cremation are represented in the early graves in the Forum; and we have seen reason to believe that burial was the practise of the earliest inhabitants of Italy as well as of the Etruscans, and was continued by many of the plebeians of Rome; while cremation, preferred on hygienic grounds, was the rule with the Italic invaders, and became the custom with all Romans who could afford to practise this more costly method. [2] Some conservative Roman families of the aristocracy always buried their dead: of the Cornelii, only the dictator Sulla directed that his body be burned, lest it be desecrated as he had dishonored the bones of Marius. Even when cremation was all but universal it was customary to preserve the ancient method to the extent of burying some small part of the body, usually a finger-bone. The Christians, moreover, buried their dead, whether because of the smaller expense or because they hoped for a resurrection of the body. [3]

The tombs varied greatly in size and shape, from the small altar-shaped memorials of individuals, to the larger chamber-

---

[1] Suetonius, *Jul.*, 84. On the suggestion of these "very few remarks," Shakspere invented Mark Antony's masterpiece of innuendo. (Dio Cassius gives a long and elaborate version of Antony's speech [*Hist. Rom.* XLIV, 36 ff.]; the account in Appian's *Civil Wars*, II, 143 ff., is somewhat nearer to Shakspere's.)   [2] Cf. pp. 16 and 20.

[3] A change from cremation to burial was general also among pagans during the early Empire; the reasons, however, are not religious, but merely those of fashion. (See A. D. Nock, "Cremation and Burial in the Roman Empire," *Harvard Theological Review*, Vol. XXV, No. 4 [October, 1932], pp. 321-359.)

sepulchres in which successive generations of a family were laid to rest, and the still larger *columbaria*, or "dove-cotes," with niches in which were placed the numerous cinerary urns of humbler folk, each with its inscription, under the care of burial societies, or guilds (*collegia*).[1] When the funeral procession reached the tomb, the tomb was first consecrated; then the body either was placed in its sarcophagus at once, or more commonly was placed on the funeral pyre with spices and perfumes and gifts, to be lighted with a torch by a kinsman with face averted. The embers of the fire were finally quenched with water or wine; and all present called upon the dead for the last time, *Ave atque vale*, "Hail and farewell." When they had been sprinkled thrice with water, to be purified from the pollution of death, all but the family were dismissed with the last words of the ritual, *ilicet*, "You may go." [2] After the remains had been gathered together, to be dried and buried later, a pig was sacrificed, the mourners partook of a meal, and then returned to the house to purify it by a solemn feast and to sacrifice to the Lares. After a nine days' interval of mourning, during which the ashes were laid away in their urn in the tomb, the mourners revisited the tomb and made a sacrifice; in early times this day was marked also by funeral games or even plays. The anniversary of the birth and of the death was celebrated with offerings of water, wine, and milk, poured through the open-

[1] Occasionally an individual would have a large tomb, like the pyramid of Cestius, at the Wall of Aurelian near its southwestern corner (about the beginning of the Christian era), or the tower-like mausoleum of Caecilia Metella, by the Appian Way (of the Ciceronian age), or the still larger mausoleum of Hadrian, by the Tiber (now the Castel di St. Angelo). Many tombs not only are inscribed with the names of their occupants but bear sculpture depicting their callings — that of soldier, baker, etc.

[2] The *novissima verba*, "the last words." (But see Servius, commenting on Virgil, *Aen.* VI, 231; there is some uncertainty as to the order of the phrases *"vale"* and *"ilicet."*)

ings in the slab that covered the urn.[1] A public festival of
eight days, the *Parentalia*, each February commemorated all
the dead, a pagan All Souls' Day.[2] And when violets blossomed in March, and roses in May, the living shared their
beauty with the dead by decking the tombs. On any such
occasion, offerings to the gods in their temples were not forgotten; little lamps were lit at the tombs in honor of the
hallowed dead, — that they were hallowed, the inscribed
stones, with the letters D. M. (*Di[i]s Manibus Sacrum*,
"sacred to the hallowed shades"), reminded the living, even
if they did not record offices held and substantial deeds
done.[3] And the offerings given the dead, like the objects
buried or burned with them, represent the affectionate effort
of the survivors to bring them a little cheer in their gloomy
abode, to share with them the feasting which they themselves enjoyed.

Behind all the formality, and the antiquarian survivals of
the Roman funeral ceremonies, reflected for example in Virgil's story of the funeral of Misenus,[4] one can detect the more
universal human note of pity for the dead, of sympathy for
the bereaved survivors. The dead somehow lived on in another world, but endured a cheerless existence, most Romans
held, and not a blessed eternal life, however much the
learned few, with Cicero [5] and Virgil,[6] might philosophize

---

[1] Cf. Walter Pater, *Marius the Epicurean*, Ch. I.

[2] See W. Warde Fowler, *The Roman Festivals*, pp. 306–310. Virgil's account of the rites for Anchises, *Aen.* V, 42–603, combines the private analogue
of the *Parentalia*, the cheerful anniversary observances of the dead, with the
funeral games suggested by the games held by Achilles for Patroclus. The
Romans also had a more primitive and more gloomy festival in May, the
Lemuria, at which hostile ghosts were laid (Fowler, *op. cit.*, pp. 106–109).

[3] Like the famous inscriptions of the Scipio family (conveniently printed
in J. C. Egbert, *Introduction to the Study of Latin Inscriptions*, pp. 232, 294–
297).   [4] *Aen.* VI, 156–184, 212–235.

[5] Especially in the first book of the *Tusculan Disputations*.

[6] *Aen.* VI, 868–892, esp. 637–751.

(and Platonize) man's instinctive craving for immortality and blessedness for the righteous. The manly Lucretius, hostile to even so moderate a hope, bade men leave the feast of life, without repining, like guests well sated; [1] Propertius trifled, in a sweet luxuriance of sorrow, with the thought of his own obsequies; [2] and the gentle melancholy of Horace, pained at the thought of Death's impartial knock at the doors of castle and of hovel, and at the ending of this good life, could find no wiser counsel than the prudent enjoyment of the fleeting hour. But a special sadness colored the grief of the Romans for the untimely death of children; [3] of young men and maidens unwedded laid on the funeral pyre before their parents' eyes; [4] of a Marcellus dead ere his prime; [5] of a young wife torn from a husband, [6] of brother torn from brother. Catullus was not present when his brother died in the Troad, and could not till a later occasion visit his grave there and mingle offerings with tears.

"Over the mighty world's highway,
    City by city, sea by sea,
Brother, thy brother comes to pay
    Pitiful offerings unto thee.

I only ask to grace thy bier
    With gifts that only give farewell,
To tell to ears that cannot hear
    The things that it is vain to tell.

---

[1] Lucretius, III, 938 f.

[2] Propertius, II, 13.

[3]   Continuae auditae voces vagitus et ingens
       infantesque animae flentes, in limine primo
       quos dulcis vitae exsortis et ab ubere raptos
       abstulit atra dies et funere mersit acerbo.
                                        Aen. VI, 426–429.

[4] *Georg.* IV, 476 f.; *Aen.* VI, 307 f. The sadness was enhanced by the reversal of the natural order; old men expected to be buried by their sons, not to bury them. (Note, too, in *Aen.* II, 238, the ominousness of the phrase "pueri innuptaeque puellae," echoed from its context in the *Georgics.*)

[5] *Aen.* VI, 854–886.   [6] Catullus, 96.

And, idly communing with dust,
   To know thy presence still denied,
And ever mourn forever lost
   A soul that never should have died.

Yet think not wholly vain to-day
   This fashion that our fathers gave
That hither brings me, here to lay
   Some gift of sorrow on thy grave.

Take, brother, gifts a brother's tears
   Bedewed with sorrow as thy fell,
And 'Greeting' to the end of years,
   And to the end of years 'Farewell.'" [1]

2. THE DEPENDENTS

The Roman *familia*, we have already seen, included the
dependents of the household. Not all of these were necessarily slaves; for influential Romans were apt to have a number of "clients" [2] who voluntarily attached themselves to
their "patrons" in the expectation of receiving help of various kinds, legal and financial, and of bestowing in return
their respectful attendance at the patrons' morning levee and
their public appearances; perhaps also, in earlier times, of
doing honest work for them on their farms and in the field of
war. The relationship was hereditary, and dated from the
time when the members of the patrician *gentes* enjoyed a
privileged status, and newcomers to Rome, including artisans and farmers and conquered foes who had not been enslaved, had to put themselves under the protection of citizens. Descendants of the original patrons were under almost
sacred obligations to befriend the descendants of the original
clients and of the other clients that had flocked to their re-

---

[1] Catullus, 101, tr. Garrod. These lines, and Catullus' greeting to his villa
at Sirmio (the 31st poem), are called to mind by Tennyson in his "Frater Ave
atque Vale."

[2] *Clientes*, or *cluentes*, those who heeded or gave ear (*cluere*) to others.

spective houses. In theory a natural and even admirable institution, clientship inevitably brought forth arrogance in the patron and servility in the client. But when the plebeians won political rights almost equal to those of the patricians, clients no longer felt so dependent on patrons as before; and the growing number of slaves meanwhile made superfluous to the patrons the expensive services of their clients. Toward the end of the Republic the old institution of clientship disappeared. During the Empire, however, wealthy men played the patron to a new class of itinerant parasites who also claimed the name of client. Attentive, expert in adulation, these hangers-on were bound to their patrons by no ties save those of their own hunger and their patrons' vanity. Especially demoralizing was the *sportula*, or dole, at first food shared with the patron at his board or given out in a "little basket" (as the Latin word indicates), and later converted into a daily gift of money sufficient to support the client. It is no wonder that the lazy preferred to win *sportulae* from one, or if possible from several, clients by flattery rather than engage in productive work.

During the early days of Rome, when farms were small and men's fortunes differed but little, there were few slaves. We are told that in the fifth century B.C. they comprised about one-eighth of the population. But as Italy and the rest of the Mediterranean world was conquered, and captives of war were enslaved, the proportion grew rapidly. After the first and the second Punic Wars, when farmers had left the plough for the sword and returned to find the grain that they could raise on their impoverished farms undersold by the grain of Sicily, many of them became slaves for debt. Some slaves, too, and these often the most faithful, were born and reared in the homes of Roman slave-owners; but this means of recruiting the supply was more expensive than purchase in the slave market where both captives of war and victims of brigands and pirates were exposed for sale. From the newly conquered territories of Sardinia and the Po valley, from Spain and Greece, captives were carried off by fifty thousands and hundred thousands. Of the Gauls, Caesar was said to have killed a million, enslaved a million, and left a million. The great slave markets in Delos and Puteoli and Rome were flooded with the unfortunate victims of slave hunts on the frontiers; a single day, in the reign of Augustus, might see the sale of ten thousand slaves in Delos. At this time the slaves in the city of Rome may have comprised nearly half of the total population of about one million. After the great wars of conquest were over, by the beginning of the second century A.D., it was chiefly organized kidnapping that kept up the supply. Prices naturally varied with the nature of the slave and the condition of the market: we hear of prices running below the equivalent of a dollar apiece, on the battlefield, and again of an educated slave who fetched a price equivalent to twenty-eight thousand dollars. Farm laborers brought usually from one hundred to two hundred and fifty dollars (the elder Cato thought the latter price the maximum that should be paid); the more accomplished and handsome slaves employed in the home came rather higher. Fancy prices were commanded by unusual specimens: for example, by Mark Antony's pair of handsome boys supposed to be twins, but actually born one in Gaul and the other in Asia Minor, and therefore a more valuable pair, according to the clever dealer, than if they had been really twins! [1]

For a long time almost the only important use of slaves was in the labor of the farm. In Cato's day the ideal farm of about sixty acres of vineyards could be worked by sixteen

[1] Pliny, *N. H.* VII, 12.

slaves; or, if it extended to about one hundred and fifty acres of vineyards and olive yards together, by thirteen slaves. In either case the slaves would be under the control of a *vilicus*, or bailiff, probably himself a slave who would work them like domestic animals in the hope of showing his master such a handsome profit as would some day win his own liberty. Gradually, and after the Punic Wars more rapidly, the small farms were apt to accumulate in the hands of a few great landlords, and their vast estates (*latifundia*) were worked by gangs of slaves.[1] The most profitable form of farming, now that Italian grain was undersold by imported grain, was the culture of the vine and the olive and the raising of flocks and herds. Meanwhile, as trades and industries grew up, there was no form of labor known to freemen in which slave labor was not also used; and during the empire slave labor largely replaced free labor. The state, too, had its public slaves, employed as caretakers and attendants. Before the end of the Republic the number of slaves to be found in the homes of even ordinary citizens was surprising; the throngs employed in those of wealthy men were sometimes enormous. Every need and every luxury was met by a retinue assigned to minutely subdivided duties. Most of these house-slaves performed no productive service, and merely satisfied the vanity of their masters and the expectations of the fashionable world.

In no time or place have slaves been really happy, and the slaves of the Romans were ordinarily treated with severity. In theory the power of their masters over them, as over sons, was absolute and without redress. The masters might command them to do anything, might punish or torture them, might even put them to death. For reasons which will be

---

[1] Another form of servitude, that of the *coloni*, who were equivalent to serfs bound to the land, will be explained later (pp. 264–266, 267 f., 274).

apparent, these extreme rights were seldom exercised. Nevertheless, the slave was in the eyes of the law chiefly a thing and only to a very minor extent a person.[1] Punishments were harsh: floggings and fetters, the *furca* (a forked log to which the arms were bound), removal from the lighter work of the city household to the tasks of the farm, or to the harder task of grinding at the mill, or to the still more disheartening labor of the quarries. Some desperate characters were sold off for gladiators. Runaways, when captured, were branded with the letter F (for *fugitivus*); and slaves who murdered their masters were crucified. If the culprit could not be detected, the whole *familia* of slaves of the murdered man might be crucified. It is no wonder that the fear of such penalties led to the insurrection of thousands of slaves on several occasions; on the other hand, the fear of such dangerous insurrections as that led by Spartacus (73–71 B.C.) caused the masters to be all the more ruthless in punishing guilty slaves.

Not all slaves, however, were guilty, nor were all masters cruel. We have evidence of kindness, even of intimate friendships between master and slave, particularly when the slave was educated and able to enter into his master's interests. Tiro, who was Cicero's secretary and edited his letters after his death, and who invented a system of shorthand, was a trusted confidant of his master, who wrote to him most affectionately and familiarly; once, when Tiro was ill, he wrote him three letters in one day. The younger Pliny likewise showed his affection for his talented freedman Zosimus, and arranged for him to have treatment, when ill, in Egypt and on the Riviera.[2] Moreover the lot of the slave

[1] It is often stated that slaves had no legal personality. But that this is an overstatement, especially for the condition of slaves during the Empire, is shown by W. W. Buckland, in *The Roman Law of Slavery* (Cambridge, 1908).

[2] Pliny, *Epist.* V, 19.

was gradually improved somewhat by custom and by law. He was often allowed as a matter of fact to hold property, although in theory such property belonged to his master. A law enacted in the reign of Augustus took from the master and gave to the prefect of the city the right to condemn a slave to the arena; under Hadrian the master's right to put a slave to death was removed, and Constantine dealt with such action simply as murder. At all times sensible masters realized that, even on the lowest grounds of economy, it did not pay to treat their slaves cruelly. When Cato advised that farm slaves be worked hard, like the animals on the farm, and be sold off when they had passed their usefulness, he was rather more inhumane than most Romans; but even he would not counsel wanton cruelty. Under the Empire, as the position of the emperor was exalted, freemen and slaves differed less than before; all were subjects of a common lord (*dominus*). Meanwhile the Stoic philosophers, without attacking the institution of slavery as immoral, were urging that all men, whether slave or free, partake to some extent in the divine reason, and are to that extent brothers. Christianity was still more effective in wiping out any natural distinction between bond and free, though it accepted the institution of slavery as a fact. And the great legal codes, drawn up by lawyers who were often Stoics, recognized the natural equality of slaves with freemen.

The greatest amelioration of the slave's lot, however, which also served as the strongest motive to secure his loyalty and industry, was the hope of winning his freedom. In this respect the Roman slave, though in general more severely treated than the Greek slave, had more to hope for. His master might manumit him outright, as the reward for faithful service, either during his own lifetime or (as did George Washington) in his will; the slave then became, not, to be sure, a freeman (*ingenuus*), but a freedman (*libertus*), and enjoyed the protection of his former master or of his master's heir, who was now his *patronus* and who often provided him with the means of starting a business of his own. But freedom was probably more commonly won by purchase; the slave was permitted to save as his *peculium* [1] such small sums of money as he could earn by thrift or industry, until he had accumulated enough to buy his own freedom. A clever slave might be put by his master in charge of a small trade or business, receiving a proportion of the profits. The arrangement was to the advantage of both parties. Yet the constant emancipation of slaves was not altogether to the advantage of the state; for freedmen were apt to prove unsatisfactory citizens, with slave habits and instincts and ideals which mere emancipation could not transform. And the fact that most of them were originally foreigners, and that much of the best Roman stock was killed off in the wars, meant that by the end of the Republic the population of Rome consisted largely of the descendants of enfranchised alien slaves. Augustus attempted by law to check manumission and to curb the political power of freedmen, while giving some of them social recognition and municipal responsibilities in the *ordo Augustalium*. As in the United States, so in Rome, justice to the slaves required emancipation; but grave difficulties remained after emancipation, leaving no doubt in either case that the only happy condition would have existed if there had been no slaves to be set free. In one important particular, however, Roman slaves differed from American slaves: comparatively few slaves in the Roman Empire were not either Aryan or Semitic, whereas hardly any slaves in America in the nineteenth century were other than black. The slaves emancipated by the Romans were

[1] Cf. p. 89, n. 3.

therefore more easily absorbed into the political and social organization than the negroes in America; indeed, so intelligent and well trained were many of the Greek slaves and freedmen at Rome that they were used for the most important secretarial and financial positions not only by individuals but even by emperors, sometimes amounting practically to ministers of state.

To appraise accurately the various effects of slavery at Rome is not easy. Doubtless in the earliest times it was more humane to enslave captives of war than to butcher them; doubtless, too, the protracted absence of free-born Romans during wars of defense and of conquest required the existence of an agricultural and industrial class who should work under compulsion. Yet the economic unsoundness of the system is obvious; it undersold the labor of freemen, hastening the abandonment of small farms and the increase of the city rabble that eked out casual labor by doles of food. On the other hand slave labor was seldom as efficient as the free labor that it practically drove out, and in the end it was not so cheap; furthermore, as we have noticed, most of the slaves in the homes by catering to the love of luxury and by confining themselves to minutely subdivided duties performed unproductive services. If the economist must condemn the system, the statesman must condemn its political results no less. Not only were slave uprisings a constant terror, but Marius used slaves in his army on occasion; and nothing in the plan of the desperate Catiline was more dreaded than his intention of arming the slaves. Another political consequence of slavery, already noted, is the changing character of the Roman population when diluted with alien freedmen, and its waning capacity for statesmanship. But the worst effect of slavery was its moral effect on slave and on master. The slave was a man without a country, without family (except as he was allowed to mate with another slave), and save in rare cases without social ties. His acts, if good, were not those of a free moral agent; his vices were his own, unless, to be sure, he was compelled by his master to act against his own better nature. His greatest hope was of ceasing to be what he was, a slave. The master, for his part, had the most demoralizing of all opportunities, absolute power without responsibility; only a humane man could exercise it without having his moral fibre coarsened. Even poor freemen who had been thrown out of work by slave labor suffered from idleness and the pauperizing influence of the dole, while rich slave-owners living on the toil of others were in danger of becoming lazy and effeminate. Such were some of the baleful influences of slavery that came to imperil the ancient strength and beauty of the Roman home.

3. LIFE IN THE HOME

The Romans dwelt in several different kinds of habitation. Families of the poorer classes huddled together in cramped quarters in *insulae*, blocks of tenements that in many ways anticipated the modern apartment house. The very rich had palatial dwellings sometimes set, even in the city, amid extensive gardens. Though the country folk lived in simple huts, there were to be found also in the country, especially among the hills near Rome, the luxurious villas of the wealthy classes with their scores of rooms and with libraries, gardens, and parks designed to meet every need of hospitality and pleasure.[1] But the ordinary resident of Rome,

---

[1] For a description of such a country villa, this time at the seashore, see Pliny's *Epist.* II, 17; translation in Rogers and Harley, *Roman Home Life and Religion*, pp. 25 ff. The absence of satisfactory country hotels and summer resorts made it customary for those who could afford it to own at least one country place, and if possible several villas in different regions, as did both Cicero and the younger Pliny, for example.

if he was in comfortable circumstances, lived in a simple house of a peculiar type. Of its primitive shape we can gain some idea from the hut-shaped urns, made in Latium, as well as at other "Villanovan" sites, in the early Iron Age, in which the Italians placed the ashes of their dead; these represent an attempt to provide the dead with a home like that to which they were accustomed during their lifetime. Some are round, like the House of Vesta in the Roman Forum, and preserve for us an early pre-Italic wigwam type of structure which was probably thatched like the shepherds' huts (*capanne*) still to be seen here and there in the Campagna; others are rectangular, and show vent-holes in the roofs through which smoke might pass. This kind of house seems to be the ancestor of the characteristic Roman house. But to some early Roman there occurred a method of improving its utility. Whereas the venthole had been intended to let the smoke out, it had also let in a certain amount of rain, perhaps to the discomfort of the inhabitants; but to some enterprising householder occurred the thought that a water-supply within the house would be an advantage. He therefore not only enlarged the opening but built the roof so that it sloped toward the middle of the house, and gathered the rain in a cistern below; he had built the first *atrium*.

Whether the *atrium*, always the heart of the Roman house, was named from the smoke-blackened rafters, is not certain;[1] there can be no doubt that even after other parts began to be added to the house it was still here that the hearth was situated and the shrine of the household gods was to be found and the cooking and other household work continued for a long time to be done. But convenience and increasing wealth suggested that another room be added be-

[1] *Ater* = black. Other derivations are less plausible.

hind the *atrium*, and that alcoves or small rooms be divided from the *atrium*, thus providing greater privacy for bedrooms and dining rooms. To this Roman form of house was later added at the rear the *peristylium*, a court or small garden enclosed by columns and surrounding rooms; this delightful feature was borrowed from the Greeks. Much of the life of the home, except formal occasions, tended to be transferred from the *atrium* to the greater quiet and privacy of the *peristylium* and the rooms that opened on it. Here were bedrooms, dining rooms, library, chapel, and kitchen. Frequently a second story, or even three or four stories, were built over a part of the house, and the bedrooms were transferred to them.

Such was the Graeco-Roman house that prevailed at the end of the Republic and during the Empire, and that is familiar to the visitor to Pompeii. Unlike modern houses in more northern climates, it derived practically all its light from the central opening in the roof of the *atrium* and from the larger central opening in the *peristylium*; for if there were any windows at all on the outside walls, they were very small. The house was turned inwards, therefore, as in its descendants the mediaeval cloister and the college quadrangle. And since Romans did not expect to look streetwards from house windows, they often found it convenient and lucrative to build rooms or even small houses at the front or on the sides of their homes, opening directly on the street and walled off from their own houses. These they could let for shops or homes to other families, without diminishing the privacy of their own homes. In Rome or Pompeii the houses would be built out to the line of the street, and would show a row of shops on the ground floor, with here and there a doorway leading by a narrow passage to a comfortable house within. Sometimes instead of having the shops directly on the street they would be placed behind an arcade or covered sidewalk beneath the second story, as in the Doges' Palace in Venice and in many modern Italian towns, and as in the "Rows" in the English town of Chester. Small windows might appear in the second story, if there were one; but the façades of houses were usually rather blank and lacking in charm and variety; all the interest and all the effort to beautify the home were spent on the interior where the life of the home went on. And if the Roman house was almost wholly lacking in windows, it was as inadequately provided with a chimney to carry off the smoke and the odor of cooking from the kitchen; a small hole or flue in the wall had to serve this purpose. Nor were the rooms, except perhaps the bathroom, often heated except by portable braziers containing burning charcoal; the bathrooms, and in Roman villas in Gaul and Britain sometimes other rooms, might be warmed by a central furnace that sent hot air through pipes of hollow tile in the floor and walls. Most city houses were well provided with water carried in by pipes from the mains.[1]

The houses recently excavated at Ostia are rather different from most Roman and Pompeiian houses. They very rarely have an *atrium*; the right comes from numerous windows opening on the street or on a courtyard. There are often two or more stories, sometimes arranged as apartments with separate entrances. Seen from the inside, the courts remind one of Renaissance houses; and the street façades, of red brick not coated with stucco, with frequent windows and evidence of many balconies, present a very modern appearance. Most of what may be seen at Ostia belongs, indeed, to the second century A.D., and represents a later style and technique than that of Republican Rome and than that

[1] Cf. p. 153.

of most of the remains at Pompeii. Nevertheless, there are at Pompeii and Herculaneum and Rome not a few traces of experiments in the new style, with brick construction, with porticoes and rows of shops on the façades, and with *insulae* (tenement houses) replacing the earlier *atrium* type of house. It was in this new style, beyond doubt, that Rome was largely rebuilt after the fire of 64 A.D.; the most impressive example now visible is the "Market of Trajan." [1]

Humble indeed was the Roman house that did not attempt to adorn the walls of its rooms with paint; floors and ceilings, too, were often decorated. [2] The furniture was rather scanty, and was more often beautiful than comfortable. The *lectus*, or couch, used both as a bed at night and as a sofa by day, was so poorly devised for the purposes of sleep as to go far to explain the notorious prevalence of insomnia among the Romans. Nor were the chairs much more comfortable: the *sella*, or stool, the high-backed *solium*, or armchair, and the almost comfortable *cathedra*, which at least did not always require a rigidly erect attitude of its occupant. Tables of many sizes and shapes afforded their makers a chance to display costly materials and cunning workmanship, and were a favorite article for the collectors; chests and wardrobes, cases for the care of books, oil lamps and bronze lamp stands were abundant. The visitor to Pompeii, who sees bronze and marble used profusely in household furniture, may think of the houses as having been colder and more metallic than they really were; he must remember that most of the wooden articles, the cushions, and the hangings have perished. Nevertheless, there were

---

[1] See the illustration opposite. See further, Axel Boëthius, "The Neronian *Nova Urbs*," in *Corolla Archaeologica* (Lund, Sweden, and Oxford, 1932), pp. 84–97.

[2] For the kinds of decoration, by painting, mosaic, and stucco, see further pp. 155 ff.

HEMICYCLE OF TRAJAN'S MARKET

(Photo by Alinari)

no rugs on the concrete floors; the houses were airy and not stuffed with many things. In a warm climate this was, on the whole, an advantage.

Equally well adapted to the climate was the dress of the Romans, except on formal occasions. Over the loin-cloth worn by the primitive Italians, and still worn by old-fashioned Romans, was pulled on a short-sleeved shirt reaching just below the knee, ordinarily woven of wool, and known as the *tunica*. For greater freedom of movement the Roman pulled up part of the tunic through a belt; for greater warmth he might put on another tunic. No trousers, we must notice, were any part of the Roman dress; they were characteristic of Persian and of Gallic costume.[1] No buttons were used; no pockets, except the folds of garments; no stockings, except a sort of leggings permitted in cold weather to invalids; even safety pins (*fibulae*) were sparingly used as fastenings for some kinds of garments. In ordinary weather the tunic was all that the citizen wore about the house or when engaged in any vigorous activity; when he received callers, however, and when he went about his business, and of course when he was present at any formal occasion, he invariably wore over the tunic the somewhat uncomfortable though dignified toga. This was the national garb of the Roman, worn by him *de rigueur* on such occasions and by him only; it is perhaps the earliest distinctively racial garment known to us.[2] At first it was simply a large woolen

[1] Hence the designation of Gallia Narbonensis as Gallia Bracata, "Gaul in breeches." Similarly, Transalpine Gaul was often known as Gallia Comata, "Long-haired Gaul"; for it was characteristic of the Gauls to wear long hair (and moustaches), while the Romans of the upper classes during historic times were always close-cropped and generally clean-shaven. Beards were worn by most of the poorer classes and by many others after the time of Hadrian (117–138 A.D.).

[2] See Lillian M. Wilson, *The Roman Toga* (Baltimore, 1924), p. 20. This is an indispensable book for those who wish to reconcile the literary with the archaeological evidence for the form of the toga.

shawl draped so that one end fell in front over the left shoulder nearly to the feet; then the rest was carried around the back, under the right arm, across the chest, again over the left shoulder, and fell almost to the left heel. The right arm was thus unimpeded; but it could be tucked inside if it were cold. Gradually the toga was made of wider and wider materials, tapered toward the ends, which when worn fell in ever more voluminous folds. What it gained in dignity and grace it lost in convenience and comfort, especially in hot weather. But as the badge of Roman citizenship it was more and more prized. We hear that Nero's court painter, being a Roman, wore his toga even when at work, doubtless to distinguish himself from his Greek assistants. The satirists might affect a disdain for this stuffy conventional dress; but Virgil expressed the pride of Rome when he wrote of "the Romans, the masters of the world, the race that wears the toga." [1]

The tunics and togas of ordinary folk retained the natural color of the wool, white or grey or brown. Some men in mourning, for personal or for political reasons, might wear a toga of dingy hue. Those who aspired to public office, on the other hand, made themselves conspicuous by having their togas whitened with chalk; they were thus *candidati*. But the most important rôle that color played in men's dress was in the narrow and the broad stripes that distinguished respectively the middle of the tunics of members of the equestrian and the senatorial orders; these stripes (the angusticlave and the laticlave) were of "purple," that is, of what we should call crimson or magenta. Of the same color was the border of the "fringed" toga (the *toga praetexta*) worn by

---

[1] *Aen.* I, 282. Horace also writes of Romans who were so cowardly as to surrender to the enemy, "forgetful of the toga." (*Odes* III, 5, 10 f.)

lads till they put on the *toga virilis*, and also by the higher magistrates and priests.[1]

Against the cold and the rain and dust the Romans wore various forms of cloaks, some provided with hoods that could be pulled over the head (like that of Little Red Ridinghood, or like mediaeval and modern academic hoods). Shoes varied from the light slippers worn in the home to the brogues of soldiers and the distinctive red footgear of senators. Hats were seldom worn except on long journeys.

The dress of Roman women differed less from that of the men than is the case to-day. But instead of the toga they wore an outer tunic (*stola*), reaching to the feet, but usually pulled up somewhat through a girdle. If the wearer was a matron, the lower edge had a flounce. An outer shawl or wrap might be worn for additional warmth, or might be pulled over the head; hats were not worn. The chief opportunity for individuality and display in women's dress was in the variety of materials, — wool and linen and silk of different colors, — and in the arrangement of the hair, which was often extremely elaborate. Roman women, like Italian women of all times, were very fond of jewelry, and sometimes spent fabulous sums on a coveted gem. On warm and sunny days, fans and parasols were as commonly used as to-day.

For most Romans, the day began early. Artificial light was so poor that most kinds of work could not easily be done in the evening; it was only a few scholars who burned the midnight oil and a somewhat more numerous class of revellers who caroused till the small hours and then slept as late as they could. Most humble folk rose before dawn, paid their respects to the gods and had a bite of breakfast, and

[1] The original purpose of the stripe may have been to avert the "evil eye" (cf. p. 303).

were very noisily about their work by sunrise; [1] for them the labor of the farm and the shop continued till nearly sunset, broken only by a pause of an hour or so about noon, when the chief meal was eaten, and they retired not long after sunset. Members of the upper classes of course managed their day somewhat differently. Breakfast (*ientaculum*) was, even for them, ordinarily a simple and an early affair, consisting chiefly of bread dipped in wine or eaten with raisins, olives, or cheese. A man of letters might then begin his literary work, and a man of affairs would attend to his private business and give orders to his slaves and freedmen, before proceeding to the *atrium*, where his clients were already cooling their heels. The *salutatio* followed; some of the clients had come to obtain advice, others merely to pay their respects. From a cabinet in the recess at one side of the *atrium* looked down the waxen *imagines* of the patron's ancestors, who in past centuries had received the visits of these clients' ancestors. After the *salutatio* was over, the master of the household would go forth to his various engagements, perhaps walking with a retinue of clients and slaves, perhaps riding in a litter; the use of carriages in the crowded streets of Rome was severely restricted. The rest of the morning and perhaps the early afternoon would in many cases be spent in the Forum, in the business of the law courts, at the Senate, or in attendance at a literary recitation; [2] but in any

---

[1] The *Moretum*, attributed probably wrongly to the youthful Virgil, gives in realistic verse an account of a peasant thus rising betimes, groping his way to the hearth, stirring the fire, and setting about the preparation of bread and a salad for the morning meal. It was at this hour that the early Christians, most of whom were humble folk, had the opportunity to hold their meetings without being disturbed by their social betters. Their secrecy was naturally misunderstood. (See pp. 360–362.)

[2] The younger Pliny enumerates among the time-consuming occupations of a day in Rome attendance at a young man's "coming of age" (" officio togae virilis interfui "), at a betrothal or a wedding, at the witnessing of a will, and legal aid given in court or in private counsel. *Epist.* I, 9.

case all work stopped toward noon for a simple lunch (*prandium*), usually of bread, vegetables, fruit, and nuts, and for the noontide *siesta* that invariably followed in ancient as in modern Italy. An important session of the Senate might last till sunset, but never later; other kinds of business ordinarily claimed but little time of the man of affairs in the afternoon, so that he was free after the siesta to take his exercise and his bath at one of the great public establishments, and to linger there to chat with his friends as in a modern club. In the late afternoon he would return to his home and prepare for dinner (*cena*); immediately after dinner he would go to bed. Holidays would bring him a respite from public business and leisure to attend the theatre or the circus and other public amusements,[1] or to visit his estate in the country. But the average day might pass somewhat in the manner described, and a poem of Martial reviews the day for us. "The first and the second hour exhausts those who pay their morning calls; the third busies the hoarse advocates; Rome extends her varied labors into the fifth hour; the sixth hour brings rest to the weary; the seventh will make an end of business; the eighth is for the wrestling-ground, where the oil glistens; the ninth bids men to crush the high-piled cushions of the banquet room; the tenth is the hour for my booklets. . . ."[2]

To a far greater extent than is easy for us to understand without reflection, the dinner was the important social event of the aristocratic Roman's day. In early times, when all men toiled with their hands, the chief meal was naturally at noon; and this custom continued among the laboring classes. But with the growth of a class of Romans whose chief occu-

---

[1] Cf. pp. 163–168.
[2] Martial, IV, 8. The Romans divided the day from sunrise to sunset into twelve "hours," which of course varied in length according to the season.

pations were legal and administrative and commercial, and of others who had leisure to enjoy the amenities of life, the tendency was for the substantial *cena* to be postponed till the middle or the end of the afternoon, and for the simple *prandium* to be eaten in the middle of the day. Thus business need not be seriously interrupted at noon, and the diners could prolong the enjoyment of the *cena* into the evening without feeling hurried. If we remember that the Romans lacked most of the other forms of evening entertainment familiar to us, — receptions and dances, theatrical performances and concerts and moving pictures, — and that conversation took the place of newspapers and of much other literature, it becomes easier for us to realize the importance of the *cena* as the chief form of relaxation and entertainment among the Romans. On few evenings did a Roman in comfortable circumstances fail either to have guests at dinner or to dine out at a friend's house. Of course the dinner-party sometimes became an occasion of vulgar display for the nouveau riche, despite repeated sumptuary legislation; but it was also of incalculable value among Romans of a better class for the ripening of friendships and the exchange of ideas. Usually the *mater familias* and the older children were present when guests came to dinner; this was a refining influence unknown to Greek dinner-parties. And when we seek for standards by which to appraise the value of Roman civilization, we must not forget that the Romans developed the primitive satisfaction of hunger till they made of dining a fine art; indeed, in the value that they set on the unhurried intercourse of the table they surpassed many of us of a later day who cannot find time fully to enjoy such pleasures, or to break the afternoon by the amenities and the revivifying powers of tea.

Till about the beginning of the first century B.C., Roman

meals were still eaten in the *atrium*, and were comparatively frugal. The staple articles were the "Mediterranean triad," [1] — the products of grain, the olive tree and the vine, the latter consisting chiefly of native wines always mixed with a larger amount of water,[2] or occasionally sweetened with a little honey. Variety was secured by the use of eggs and milk and cheese (but not butter), many kinds of fruits and vegetables (but not oranges, tomatoes, or potatoes), and now and then a little meat. On the whole, the Romans were vegetarians, whether by the necessity of poverty or by the preference of a simple taste like that of Horace, who professed to find contentment in a fare of olives, endives, and mallows.[3] Yet the Romans were also fond of meat, when they could get it, especially of pork, which they learned how to prepare for the table in fifty ways; beef and mutton, which would not keep so long as pork, were less used. Chickens and game were welcome additions to the menu; fish, at first little appreciated, came to be greatly enjoyed, and certain rare kinds were imported from great distances at enormous expense, or bred in fish pools on country estates. Of oysters the Romans came to be so fond that it is said that some of them, when exiled from Rome, took care to choose an abode where the oysters were especially good.

These luxurious tastes belong, however, to the age when the Romans had given up dining in the *atrium* and had set apart one or more special dining rooms usually opening on the peristyle, or even open to the sky save for perhaps

---

[1] Cf. p. 7.

[2] Martial complains of the innkeeper of Ravenna, where fresh water was scarce; the poet asked for wine and water mixed, and the rascal gave him wine! (III, 57.)

[3] *Odes* I, 31, 15 ff. Probably the earliest Italians in Latium, being herdsmen and shepherds, had eaten much more meat; in historic times, however, the Romans led an agricultural life, and even the army lived chiefly on grain.

an arbor.[1] Like the peristyle, the dining-room (*triclinium*), was borrowed from the Greeks; as the name suggests, the room contained three sloping couches arranged about three sides of a central table, one side being left open for the convenience of the servants.[2] Instead of sitting at tables, as in former days, the diners now reclined on the couches, Greek fashion, their left arms being supported on cushions and their right arms being free. The host's wife still sat, however, if guests were present; and children, if present, regularly sat at the open side of the table or at a separate children's table.[3] Each of the three couches was divided into three parts, so that as many as nine persons could dine together with comfort; more were seldom crowded into these spaces. The ideal dinner-party, according to a Roman saying, comprised persons in number "not more than the Muses nor fewer than the Graces." A very small party might therefore use a single curved couch about a round table, and a larger party might overflow into another *triclinium*; such a case was the more common since Roman etiquette gave the invited guest the privilege of bringing with him unexpectedly friends or dependents described as his "shadows" (*umbrae*).[4] The places of honor on the couches were care-

---

[1] See Horace's picture of himself, attended by a single slave, drinking beneath a thick-grown vine (*Odes* I, 38).

[2] The kitchen was now usually in the rear part of the house, not far from the *triclinium*. The stove was still a primitive affair — merely a brick hearth, with "hobs" for pots and pans to stew or fry over a charcoal fire. Baking, though sometimes done at home, was more often the task of central bakeries. Large dinner-parties, placing too great a strain on the domestic kitchen, sometimes called in caterers from outside.

[3] Cf. Tacitus, *Ann.* XIII, 16.

[4] When Cicero entertained Julius Caesar at Puteoli, the visitor's staff dined in three rooms, the freedmen and slaves received liberal entertainment elsewhere; the superior guests dined sumptuously on "fare well cooked and seasoned with good talk." Cicero "showed that he was somebody" (*homines visi sumus*). The conversation avoided politics, and was wholly literary. (*Epist. ad Att.* XIII, 52.)

fully assigned with due regard both for convenience and for social distinction, the principal guest being at the "lower" corner of the middle couch, next to the host, who was at the "higher" corner of the "lowest" couch.

When the guests had arrived in the *triclinium* and the gods had been invoked, they took their places on the couches, and allowed their sandals to be removed by their slaves. Water and towels were provided for the washing of hands, and dinner began. Slaves brought in the successive courses on trays and placed them on the table; but there were no individual plates and little in the way of utensils,[1] so that fingers were much in use, and water and towels made their appearance after each course. Napkins were provided not by the host but by the guests, who sometimes had to guard them against playful thefts on the part of fellow-guests, if we may believe Catullus.[2] On the table there stood a plate, for offerings to the gods, and a salt-cellar. These were of silver, if the means of the family permitted; and Horace, in commending the "golden mean" betwixt wealth and poverty as the ideal life, writes: "He lives well on little on whose modest board shines his fathers' salt-cellar."[3]

---

[1] Fortunately the carving of meat was well done by a slave, whose rhythmical gestures won him the title of *saltator* ("dancer"). Carving has always been an art, and was long considered to be one of the accomplishments of a gentleman; thus Chaucer's Squier "carf biforn his fader at the table."

[2] Carmen 12.

[3] *Odes* II, 16, 13 f. Why, it may be asked, the salt-cellar of all possible articles? The answer to this question leads us among interesting byways. In the first place, of course, salt is an absolute essential for the digestion of food. "Salting the cattle" is a familiar task of the herdsmen; to deny prisoners salt in their food was once a subtle form of torture. Hence the importance of supplies of salt in determining early frontiers. We have seen that a regular trade route ran from the salt-works at Ostia up the Tiber valley into the Sabine hills; the part of it leading inland from Rome is still known as the Via Salaria, the "Salt Way" (cf. p. 19). Early settlers in the interior of New Hampshire would sometimes walk eighty or ninety miles to the coast and return with a fifty-pound bag of salt on their shoulders; and the settling of sev-

In the historic period dinners were divided into three parts. The first consisted of eggs, oysters, a bit of fish, or raw vegetables, intended to whet the appetite. The *cena*, or dinner proper, might include one course, or a number of courses, and comprised the substantial fare, the meats and vegetables, together with a little wine. A pause ensued, during which wine, salt, and meal were offered silently to the Lares. The *secunda mensa*, or dessert, was apt to consist of fruits, nuts, and cakes, accompanied by more wine. The phrase "ab ovo ad mala" ("from the egg to the apples") was thus traditionally used to describe the whole range of the dinner.[1]

Doubtless on most occasions it was not long after the conclusion of the last course that the guests would "ask for their sandals," as the phrase ran, thus indicating their readiness to take their leave. But the evening's enjoyment might be

eral parts of the Middle West was determined by the discovery of inland deposits of salt or of salt springs. In many countries to-day the sale of salt is a government monopoly and source of revenue; hence the act of Gandhi and his followers in British India in making their own salt was chosen as a symbol of defiance to the government. The money paid to Roman soldiers for their salt has given us our word "salary." It is no wonder, then, that salt was regarded as a typical article of food and was one of the articles which was, therefore, regularly offered to the gods, sometimes in a cake of spelt (cf. p. 9). (Cf. Horace, *Odes* III, 23, 20; clean hands and a pure heart together with the salt cake will win the favor of the Penates.) The salt-cellar therefore took its place on the table as the symbol of food and of hospitality. (In some societies the social equals of the host and his inferiors were distinguished at table according as they sat "above" or "below" the salt.) Laelius, in Cicero's *De Amicitia*, 67, cites a proverb (found also in Aristotle) to the effect that friendship must be seasoned by time, and "many pecks of salt must be eaten together." An oriental proverb, on the other hand, bids us "Never betray a man you have eaten salt with." Finally, salt has its metaphorical uses. The righteous are the "salt of the earth"; a knave is "not worth his salt." And as salt on the table is the seasoning of food, so wit is the seasoning of conversation; and it was especially "Attic salt," the wit of the most brilliant people of Greece, that became a byword at Rome. So Catullus, inviting a friend to dinner, bids him bring with him a good big meal, not forgetting a pretty music girl, "and wine, and salt and every sort of laughter." (Carmen 13.)

[1] E.g. Horace, *Sat.* I, 3, 6.

prolonged in several different ways.[1] Toward the end of the Republic it became fashionable to imitate the Greek *symposium*, or drinking party following a dinner, with its elaborate ritual of drinking wine mixed with water in proportions fixed by the toastmaster (*arbiter bibendi*). Perfumes and garlands of roses and other flowers not only added to the beauty of the occasion but were supposed to delay intoxication. Music girls and dancers and jugglers provided entertainment more or less refined. Diners of greater education would often be entertained by the recitations or readings of talented slaves. Pliny writes, to a friend who accepted his invitation to dinner but failed to appear, an amusing account of the meal that the friend missed, and the entertainment provided by a reciter of comedy, a reader, and a lyre-player. But he implies at the end of the letter that the chief delight had been the frank and carefree conversation, both serious and jolly. This, we need not doubt, was indeed what most appealed to many Romans of the better sort who lingered over their wine; and Cicero represents the elder Cato as finding the Roman term *convivium*, a "living together," a better word to describe such social life than the Greek term *symposium*, with its emphasis on drinking.[2] He chose to ignore, perhaps, the high level of conversation reached at such Greek banquets, even if Plato's *Symposium* is an idealization; nor could he guess that we should use the word "symposium" to signify a group of essays by different persons on a common theme. But at any rate the Romans did value conversation as a fine art, and did not fail to appre-

[1] If it was intended to lengthen the dinner, a common practice was to begin fashionably early, stealing an hour or two from the business day (cf. Horace, *Odes* I, 1, 20). But some banqueters probably burned the candle at both ends.

[2] Cicero, *De Sen.*, 44–46. (The passage is translated in Rogers and Hardy, *Roman Home Life and Religion*, pp. 187 f.) Of course Cicero is really using "Cato" (an idealized figure) as a mouthpiece for his own ideas.

ciate the dinner as conducive to good talk. "It has always been my way," observes the Cato of Cicero's dialogue, "to measure the enjoyment of banquets as much by sociability and the delights of conversation as by its physical attractions. . . . I love the good old-fashioned toasts and speeches; the discussions introduced by the head of the table over the wine; the delicate liqueur-glasses mentioned in Xenophon's *Symposium*; iced wine in summer; the summer sunshine too, and a jolly fire in winter no less. These pleasures I regularly seek at my Sabine farm, and every day I fill my table with my neighbors; and we protract our meal talking far into the night on every possible subject." Cato (or Cicero) had learned, then, that men might be really interesting to themselves and to their friends, without falling back on professional entertainment; and that is a very important mark of progress in civilization.

Even the elder Pliny, an indefatigable student, devoted three hours to dinner, and was thought to be niggardly of his time. How he contrived to write his encyclopaedic works, his nephew the younger Pliny explains at length to a friend.

You wonder at a busy man having completed such a number of books, — books, too, containing much abstruse matter; you will wonder more when I tell you that for some time he was a pleader, that he died at the age of fifty-six, and that meantime he was much hindered and distracted by important state business, and by his intimacy with our emperors. But his intellect was quick, his industry perfectly marvellous, his power of remaining awake remarkable. From the 23rd of August he began to study at midnight, and through the winter he continued to rise at one, or at the latest at two in the morning, often at twelve. Sleep he could always command. Often it used to come upon him and leave him in the midst of his books. Before daybreak he would go to the Emperor, Vespasian, who also worked at night, and thence to his official duties. On returning home he gave what time remained to study. After taking a light meal, as our forefathers used to do, he would often in summer, if he had leisure, recline in the sun, and have a book read to him, on which he wrote notes, or from which he made extracts. He read nothing without making extracts, for he used to say that you could get some good from the worst book. After reading in the sun he generally had a cold bath, then a light meal and a very short nap, after which, as if he was beginning another day, he would study till dinner-time. During dinner a book was read to him, and he made notes upon it as it went on. I remember one of his friends stopping the reader, who had pronounced a word incorrectly, and making him repeat it. My uncle said to him, "Did you not understand the word?" "Yes," he replied. "Why then did you stop him? We have lost more than ten lines by this interruption." So parsimonious was he of his time. He rose from dinner in the summer by daylight, in winter before seven, as regularly as if constrained by law. Thus he lived in the midst of his work and in the bustle of Rome. In the country, he exempted only his bathing-time from study; I mean, the actual time of his immersion in the water, for while he was being rubbed or dried, he would hear something read or would dictate something. While travelling, he threw aside every other care, and gave himself up to study; he always had a scribe at his side with a book and writing tablet, whose hands in winter were protected by gloves, so that the cold weather might not rob him of a single moment. Even at Rome, he used to be carried in a litter with this in view. I remember his rebuking me for taking a walk. "You might have managed," he said, "not to lose these hours." In fact, he thought all time lost which was not given to study. It was by this intense application that he completed so great a number of books, and left me, besides, a hundred and sixty volumes of extracts, written on both sides of the leaf, and in the minutest hand.[1]

The uncle, whose industry the nephew chronicles with such gusto, was a bookworm of a sort uncommon among Romans,

[1] Pliny, *Epist.* III, 5; translated by Church and Brodribb. Horace ordered his days more carelessly, but accomplished more that the world still prizes; see his account of a typical day (*Sat.* I, 6, 111–131).

and it does not surprise us to find that his writings are mere compilations of no particular literary value. Nevertheless the account of his way of living serves to show us something of the place of books and writing in Rome during the first century A.D. In Rome of an earlier day it was the custom to scribble on bits of wood or bark [1] or broken pottery, or to inscribe important matters on stone. More convenient then, and in later times as well, were found to be the hinged sets of thin waxed boards or slabs of ivory, protected by raised edges from rubbing against each other, on which the pointed metal *stilus* scratched the words; these are the tablets that the elder Pliny's scribe used, and that the younger Pliny took with him even when he went boar hunting. They lent themselves readily to rapid writing and to easy correction or erasure, the wax surface being smoothed over by the blunt end of the *stilus*, and were extensively used for memoranda; when wound about with thread and sealed they were dispatched as letters. For longer writings, such as lengthy letters and works of literature, the Romans, like the Greeks, learned from the Egyptians to use the "paper" prepared from the fibrous pith of the papyrus plant, writing on it with a pen of split reed and ink made of soot. The strips of papyrus were spread in two layers at right angles to each other, and joined with a thin paste; a number of sheets thus formed, after being dried, smoothed with pumice, and trimmed, were joined together in a larger sheet perhaps twenty or thirty feet long, which was rolled up on a central rod when not in use, and was therefore called a roll, or "volume" (*volumen*). The outside of the roll might be protected by a parchment cover; and from the end projected a small tag on which were written the author's name and the title (*titulus*) of the work. A number of rolls were kept in a

[1] *Liber*, "bark," thus became the usual Latin word for a book.

cylindrical case, or on the shelves of a cabinet. The yellow-brown color of papyrus was pleasing to the eye; but the material was fragile, and a still greater inconvenience was the form. To read a papyrus volume meant to unroll it, a column or two at a time, with one hand, and to reroll it with the other hand on another rod; to find a certain passage in it was a tedious matter, even if the whole work was divided into a number of shorter "books." A more durable writing material was found in the skins of animals (*membrana*, or *pergamena*),[1] which could, moreover, be folded, as the brittle papyrus could not, into leaves like those of the tablets and of modern books, — a far more convenient form than the *volumen* for the use of the reader. Since the tablets, consisting of several wooden leaves, resembled a block of wood (*caudex* or *codex*), the term *codex* continued to be used of the book of folded parchment leaves. We know that booklets of this sort were made in the first century A.D., or even earlier; but parchment was not commonly used at Rome till about the fourth century A.D., when it tended to become the regular material for the preservation of all important literary works, which were thus "codified," like the laws. Whether parchment was cheaper than papyrus, as Martial seems to imply, remains uncertain.

Such were the materials at the disposal of the man of letters or of affairs; but we have seen in the cases of the elder Pliny and of Cicero that it was customary for busy men to dictate to trained scribes, and to employ skilled readers. Even poets did not always scorn such aids to composition. When the time came for publication, the author would have copies of the autograph manuscript made by the educated

---

[1] From Pergamum, in Asia Minor, where such skins were said to have been used first; our "parchment" (a derivative), "sheepskin," and "vellum" are modern equivalents.

slaves in his own household, or would avail himself of the
services of his friends' scribes, as Cicero employed the scribes
of his friend Atticus. It was in a similar manner that he secured copies of the works of other authors. Within his lifetime, however, began the commercial copying and publication of books. Since there was no law of copyright or system
of royalty, the Roman author had no control over the text of
his works when they had once been made public; and unless
he had private means he was dependent on patronage for his
living. That Horace, thus dependent on Maecenas, preserved his independence of spirit, speaks well for both patron
and poet. The author's words, for their part, fell a prey to
all the inaccuracies and stupidities of which copyists were
capable, new errors creeping in every time that they were
recopied, to be the vexation and the delight of later scholars
whose task it is to trace the pedigrees of manuscripts and to
recover the words of the autograph copy. For nearly a
hundred years before Cicero's day, Roman generals returning from the East had brought back libraries of Greek
books; and in his day it was fashionable for Romans of
wealth and education to have libraries in their homes both
in the city and in the country. Public libraries began to appear a few years later; the first was founded by G. Asinius
Pollio,[1] and others by Augustus and later emperors.

We must leave the Roman home and its activities, but not
without a backward glance at its real strength and beauty.
The Englishman's home, we say, is his castle; and he is slow
to say all that he feels about it. The Roman's home was also
a place of privacy, though the Italian climate and his own

---

[1] Soldier, orator, poet, historian, friend of Horace and of Virgil (who dedi-
cates to him the fourth or "Messianic" Bucolic), and founder also of the
recitatio, or author's reading, the source both of sound criticism and of much
boredom, as the younger Pliny's letters unintentionally make evident. Cf.
p. 424.

habits impelled him to spend much of his time out of doors, generally in public places; the Roman nevertheless expressed freely his love of home. The same underlying human instincts may be supposed to operate in either case, whether near the surface or more deep-seated. Attachment to a familiar spot, hallowed by memories of childhood, and the growing associations of family life, — these are for all fortunate men a common experience. But for the Roman there was also a peculiar bond inherent in the feeling that the home was the abode not only of its present living occupants, but also in a sense of the dead, even if they were not actually buried under the hearth of the *atrium*; [1] still more was it the abode of the divine members of the family, the family deities. Here dwelt Vesta, goddess of the hearth and its fire; here the Penates, divinities of the larder, along with the family Lar, the spirit of the farm brought into the house to share its life; even the *pater familias*, in whose body was incarnate the continuing life of the family, of generations past and generations yet to be born, had his personal representative or second self, his "Genius." Visible symbols of these divine powers met the eye as the Roman entered his *atrium*: the little bronze image of the Lar in its shrine, which he greeted on entering and on leaving the house for a journey, and honored daily with wine and frankincense and garlands; the *lectus genialis*, or marriage couch; and the *imagines*, if he had noble ancestors, reminding him what manner of men had begotten him.

Much of the active faith in the ancient religion of the home, of course, had been laid aside by the sophisticated city-dwellers of the late Republic and the Empire, even if the

---

[1] Walter Pater has dealt sympathetically, in the second chapter of *Marius the Epicurean*, with this "intensely realized memory of the dead," a "subjective immortality."

ancient ritual was carried on. Yet the power of even a waning faith may easily be underestimated, especially where
man's deepest needs and feelings are at stake. Latin literature is permeated with the love of home. Catullus, returning from the East to his beloved Sirmio, greets not only the
laughing waters of the lake but "the Lar that is his very
own," and is overjoyed to lay himself to rest on his longed-
for couch.[1] Horace welcomes home a friend to his "ances-
tral gods and the sky of Italy." [2] Ovid, no sentimentalist,
pictures in exile the night when he left Rome, — his distracted wife, the deserted Penates, — and prays at least to
be buried in Roman earth.[3] Livy puts into the mouth of
Camillus, pleading against the proposed migration to Veii,
the question: "Were it not better to dwell in huts, like shepherds and country folk, amid our religious rites and our own
Penates, than to go as a people into exile?" [4] Cicero, urging
the restoration of his own house, which has been destroyed
by Clodius during the orator's exile and replaced by a
shrine dedicated to Liberty, is of course engaged in special
pleading, and his words have a rhetorical ring; yet they voice
what the average Roman felt: "That wonderful Liberty you
invoke overthrew the shrine of my Home, outraged its most
sacred associations, and established herself therein like a
victorious chief. There is nothing more holy, nothing more
securely guarded by every religious instinct, than each individual Roman's home. His altars, his fireside, his shrine,
his worship, his conscience, his ceremonies — all are centred
here. Here he has a refuge and a stronghold so sacred that it

---

[1] Carmen 31. This and most of the following passages cited are collected
in Rogers and Harley, *op. cit.*, pp. 1 ff.
[2] Horace, *Odes* II, 7.
[3] *Trist.* I, 3; III, 3.
[4] V, 53. With what a fierce devotion the Romans regarded the very site
of Rome, we have already noted (pp. 23 f.).

is a crime to use violence against it or to deprive him of it." [1]
And Horace, though but the son of a freedman, and less
dceply rooted than many Romans in any special spot, is
most himself in the bosom of his Sabine farm. Amid the dis-
traction of the city he breathes his prayer: "O country,
when shall I behold thee? When may I drink sweet oblivion
of life's anxieties, now from the books of old sages, now from
sleep and idle hours? O when shall the beans (those kinsmen
of Pythagoras!) and the garden mess, well larded, be set
before me? O nights and banquets fit for the gods, when my
friends and I feast before my own fireside (*ante larem pro-
prium*), and feed my saucy home-born slaves on what is
left!" [2] The country, after all, more than the city, is the
place of beloved homes. And the same Sabine mountains
that Horace loved looked down on the birthplace of the emperor Vespasian. His family were plain people, and could
boast no *imagines*; his boyhood was spent under the tutelage
of his grandmother on a farm. "Wherefore," writes his
biographer, "even when emperor he constantly visited the
place that had cradled him, keeping the villa as it had been
of old, so that nothing of its familiar aspect should be lost to
his eyes; and so greatly did he cherish the memory of his
grandmother that on holy days and festivals he was ever
careful to drink from her small silver cup." [3]

[1] *De Domo Sua*, 108–109 (tr. Rogers and Harley).
[2] *Sat.* II, 6, 60–67. Elsewhere, in a description of country life ironically
put in the mouth of a money-lender, Horace pictures these favored slaves in
their places at supper about the Lares that gleam in the firelight (Epode 2,
65 f.).
[3] Suetonius, *Vesp.*, 2. Devotion to the family homestead is not rare
among American city-dwellers; nor are we unacquainted with a President
whose vacations were spent by preference on his father's Vermont farm,
"kept as it had been of old."

CHAPTER IV

UTILITY AND ADORNMENT

The early Romans made but little account of the beauty of Rome, because they were occupied with other, greater and more necessary matters; whereas the later Romans, and more particularly those of to-day and in my time, have not fallen short in this respect either, — indeed, they have filled the city with many beautiful structures.

Strabo, *Geog.* V, 3, 8 (written in Greek in the Augustan Age).

1. THE MOTHER OF INVENTION

Labor omnia vicit
improbus et duris urgens in rebus egestas.

Virgil, *Georg.* I, 145 f.

WHEN there was work to be done, the Roman could usually find a way to accomplish it. Whether he would do it with tact and consideration for other people, whether he would foresee all the conditions to be met and would deal with them with economy, above all whether he would add to his work the zest and the grace of gesture that makes of work a fine art, is quite another question. It is at this point that the Roman stands most clearly contrasted with the Greek. For Greek art is nothing superficial or foreign, but is rather the flowering of the native life; it is the handcraft, the tale, the thought made perfect by the joy and interest of the individual craftsman or thinker. Greek art therefore lives and gives life, even though the jealousies of the little city-states made havoc of the political life of Greece. Rome's most characteristic achievement consists in her practical work of social and legal organization, a work of slow accommodation and compromise, based on a sober

sense of reality and immediate need, and related so inti-
mately to the social expression of man that much of Rome's
organization and way of thinking is wrought into the fibre of
modern society. Roman art, on the other hand, like much of
Roman letters, often seems to be something alien, something
added to the main fabric of Roman life; and the most typical
arts of Rome are perhaps indeed those practical arts that
grew from the immediate necessities of the national life.
Thus the roads and walls and bridges, the viaducts and
aqueducts, the sewers and drains and military siege works,
and the great public buildings of the Empire are on the
whole more typical than the private houses or even than
the temples; and Roman painting and sculpture are, except
in a few significant respects, hardly Roman.

How the territorial expansion of Rome throughout Italy
and the provinces called for military roads, and how the political consolidation of the new territories stimulated the
building of a network of commercial roads, we have already
noticed.[1] If we city-dwellers to-day are inclined to take for
granted the existence of roads, we need to realize the difficulties of warfare in broken country without roads for the
rapid movement of troops, and the enormous difference that
the building of good roads makes to a backward country district to-day. Even the penetration of the western part of the
United States by the railroad was of less importance. The
Romans would deserve to be remembered as a race of road-
builders, if for nothing else. Often, to be sure, they made use
of still earlier routes, — a prehistoric trail, the trade route
up the Tiber valley (the Via Salaria), the Persian "Royal
Road," the native road in Gaul and Britain. But in at least
four respects they dealt in a masterful fashion with these
roads. By cutting through hills, and building causeways and

[1] Cf. p. 47.

viaducts and bridges, they straightened the most important roads and gave them the business-like brevity, the steady march across and through all obstacles, that we associate with "the Roman Road." Again, they selected for improvement chiefly the routes that were of military and of administrative, rather than of commercial, importance, and left to chance or further convenience the building of new trade routes. Furthermore, during the early Roman Empire the roads were better patrolled and safer for travel than any roads in the world have been since then until a hundred years ago.

Not the least important phase of Roman road-building is the great thoroughness with which the roads were constructed. The highways were excavated to a depth of nearly a yard, and then fitted with successive layers (varying in different localities) of stones, gravel, and cement, or chalk and earth pounded to a firm consistency. Sometimes, as along the Rhine, the surface was of rammed gravel, somewhat like our "macadam" roads; but for hard use the Romans preferred to finish the road with a paving of large blocks of stone carefully fitted together. Near Rome these stones were of hard basaltic lava quarried from volcanoes. Such roads had sufficient solidity to stand the traffic of many centuries with practically no repairs; and the use of layers of different materials provided sufficient resilience to resist the attacks of the weather. Indeed, the conditions of modern traffic have in some regions required a return to something like Roman methods of road-building. The Roman roads had enough "crown" to carry off the rain, and were generally far better drained than all but the most modern roads.

Although Roman roads were usually not more than ten feet wide, the main roads were apt to have beside them other roads for local traffic, as well as raised sidewalks, in the

vicinity of large towns, for pedestrians. Even in Rome the
most important streets might be only from fifteen to twenty-
four feet wide; and with the crowded conditions of the late
Republic and the Empire it became necessary to close the
streets to vehicles during the first ten hours of every day,
except for certain necessary or privileged classes of persons.
All others walked or rode in litters; and at night a light
sleeper's slumber was disturbed by the rattle of market
wagons. But travel in the country could be rapid, and, except for the absence of good inns, reasonably comfortable.
The poor walked; for the well-to-do there were horses and
mules, coaches for seven or eight persons, and light carriages
for two, as well as litters for seated or reclining passengers.
Despite the fairly effective policing of the roads, important
personages would travel with a large retinue; a busy highway like the Appian Way was doubtless thronged most of
the day with wayfarers, equipages of rich men, and legions
marching to and from distant frontiers. Every now and
then a more rapid traveller would pass by; he would be one
of the public couriers taking messages between Rome and
some provincial magistrate. Under the Republic the governors had used their own orderlies or the messengers of the
publicani for such business; but a regular state posting system was established by Augustus, with relays of mounted
couriers, or with a single messenger travelling in a carriage
and changing horses at the posting stations. Whereas the
ordinary traveller might average, at the most, some fifty
miles a day, a state courier could easily cover a hundred;
Julius Caesar once travelled eight hundred miles in eight
days; and there is a record of a courier in Spain taking the
news of Nero's death to Galba a distance of 332 miles in
thirty-six hours. Private citizens, however, could not take
advantage of these rapid methods of travel; even for the

sending of letters they had to depend either on the kindness
of travellers whose route lay in the desired direction, or, if
they were wealthy, on their own servants. Milestones, recording (in Italy) the distance from Rome or (in the provinces) to the nearest large town, served to beguile the weari-
ness of the traveller, and now help us to understand many
points of Roman provincial policy.[1]

Modern architects and engineers are filled with admiration for the courage and the technical skill with which the
Romans bridged rivers and crossed valleys by viaducts consisting of a succession of semicircular arches. Several of the
bridges over the Tiber at Rome, as well as bridges and viaducts elsewhere in Italy and the provinces still remain to
speak eloquently for their builders. The rapidly constructed
fieldworks of the military engineers, — ramparts and
ditches, towers and terraces, — were less remarkable than
the impromptu bridges, of which Caesar's timber bridge
across the Rhine is the best-known example. Great difficulties were skilfully surmounted by the builders of bridges and
of harbors who had to lay foundations under water. Another
very characteristic achievement of the Romans consists in
their control of water-supply and drainage. From very early
times the Romans, in imitation of the Etruscans, learned
how to carry off by underground channels the excessive
rains that might otherwise wash away the precious top-soil
that farmers needed, and to drain swamps (such as the Pon-
tine marshes) by ditches, or marshy regions by subterranean
channels; the Cloaca Maxima (first built, according to tradition, under the kings, but probably actually built in the
fourth century and reconstructed under Augustus) still

---

[1] Statius celebrates in one of the poems of his *Silvae* (IV, 3) the reconstruction of the Appian Way under Domitian, and the boon that it is destined
to confer on the world.

drains the Forum Romanum and the hills about it. Still
greater skill was required for the drainage of lakes and the
diversion of their waters, permitting the irrigation of the
neighborhood and in some cases the cultivation of the fertile
lake bottoms. As early as the fourth century B.C., the Alban
Lake was thus controlled by a system still in operation. The
large Fucine Lake was imperfectly drained, under the emperor Claudius, by a tunnel more than three miles long; the
drainage was completed in the nineteenth century. Most
important of all was the carrying of pure water from distant
springs and reservoirs to Rome and other cities. The water
was gathered by dams in reservoirs among the hills, and
allowed to flow through tunnels or over aqueducts supported
on arches for many miles across the plain, into a reservoir
from which it was distributed by lead pipes to fountains in
public baths and private houses throughout the city. Little
use was made of the knowledge that "water will seek its own
level"; the aqueducts therefore had to be graded with the
greatest care throughout their course so as to provide for a
gentle but steady flow of water. Nothing in the Roman
landscape is more impressive than the march of the Claudian Aqueduct [1] as it approaches the city; nothing in Rome

[1] It is curious that the Claudian *gens* gave Rome both Appius Claudius,
the builder of the Appian Way and the Appian Aqueduct (312 B.C.), the
earliest aqueduct, and the emperor Claudius, whose aqueduct was one of the
last to be completed (38–52 A.D.). During the Empire Rome had eleven principal aqueducts, from which flowed a supply of water but slightly less in
proportion to the population than that of the most favored modern cities.
(M. H. Morgan, "The Water Supply of Ancient Rome," *T.A.P.A.*, XXXIII
[1902], 30 ff.) There is still interest for the modern reader in the *Treatise on
Aqueducts* of Frontinus, who was water commissioner in 97 A.D. The barbarians broke the aqueducts in the sixth century A.D., so that the Campagna
became a marsh, and the inhabitants of Rome again had to drink Tiber
water. Not for many centuries were the aqueducts repaired. The control of
the Tiber banks against floods, it may be added, was attempted by Augustus;
but not till the nineteenth century was a partially effective embankment
built.

itself is more charming than the cool and sparkling fountains [1] gushing with water still flowing from the Sabine hills by the same ancient channels, in some cases, as in ancient times.

For the building of these works and of other edifices, both private and public, the Romans were abundantly provided by nature with various kinds of excellent material: timber, from the mountains; stone, quarried near Rome; bricks, either sun-dried [2] or kiln-baked; and cement, the wonderfully strong and durable product of lime and the volcanic ashes found at Puteoli (near Naples) and near Rome. The visitor in Rome soon becomes acquainted with the native varieties of stone: the coarse, grey, volcanic *peperino*, with its tiny pebbles imbedded in it, a stone easily quarried, but apt to crumble; the dun-colored volcanic tufa (a mechanical conglomerate of sand and ashes), also coarse and fairly soft, and proof against fire; the hard black lava; and the creamy-hued limestone deposited by the river Anio at Tibur (Tivoli) in the Sabine hills, known as travertine (*lapis Tiburtinus*), with its characteristic lines of stratification.[3] He learns to distinguish the white marbles of Carrara, and the many beautiful colored marbles [4] of Africa and Greece and Asia Minor that were used as columns or in thin slabs as a decora-

---

[1] These belong to the period of the Renaissance, and are well described by Mrs. Charles MacVeagh, *Fountains of Papal Rome*, with woodcuts by R. Ruzicka (New York, 1915). The lover of Rome enjoys also Respighi's orchestral suite "The Fountains of Rome."

[2] Such bricks, known in Spanish America as "adobe," were the usual material of Roman houses till late in the Republic. But they were apt to dissolve under persistent rains; to "wash a brick" is the Greek and the Roman phrase for wasted effort (cf. Terence, *Phormio*, 186).

[3] Travertine was used for facing parts of buildings, and is often imitated to-day. Fire reduces it to lime.

[4] Such as the variously streaked golden *giallo antico*, and the ruddy *rosso antico*; the plum-colored porphyry; the ringed green "onion-stone" (*cipollino*); the bluish or rosy-veined *pavonazetto*.

tive veneer over the walls of public buildings or, more rarely, of private houses. Mamurra, one of Caesar's friends, is said to have been the first Roman to use marble slabs in his house; and the wealthy Crassus, who introduced columns of Greek marble into his *atrium*, was nicknamed "Venus Palatina," as such columns had been used hitherto only for temples. Most of the marbles, however, were removed from the buildings, as we have seen,[1] by the barbarians or by Christian builders in search of materials, so that the construction beneath is now exposed. The many types of construction, too, the visitor learns to distinguish. Primitive walls of "Cyclopean" boulders or rudely quarried rock were succeeded by walls in which the stones were squared and well fitted (*opus quadratum*). The characteristic Roman type of construction began when the Romans learned to use cement (*opus caementicium*), ordinarily interlarded with pieces of rock and known to us as concrete, and usually faced with the thin edges of bricks (*opus testaceum*) or with tufa stones set irregularly (*opus incertum*) or in regular lozenge patterns (*opus reticulatum*). The surface was then covered with stucco, or with marble; in most cases the stucco, like the marble, has disappeared. Doorways and other important parts of a building might be built or faced with travertine or with more costly stone, and might be carved.

2. ADORNMENT

Horace, always ready to contrast the extravagant luxury of his day with the simplicity of Rome's more wholesome days, remarks that in Cato's age private incomes were small and that only in the temples of the gods was marble to be

[1] P. 29.

found.[1] Since we have already noted the development of the Roman house from the thatched wigwam or hut to its typical form with Italian atrium and Greek peristyle,[2] it will be sufficient here to observe how the Romans of the late Republic and the Empire added adornment to utility in building their houses. Nothing was done to beautify the plain stucco exterior of the house. Thatched roofs had long since been replaced by roofs of tiles supported by rafters. Floors of pounded clay tended if possible to give way to floors of cement or of slabs of stone, or even of mosaic, consisting of small pieces of stone of various colors, set in geometrical designs and in exquisite pictures.[3] Ceilings might exhibit the open rafters or might have panelled or coffered surfaces elaborately decorated, — no protection against anxiety, as Horace reminds us.[4] Occasionally in large buildings they were vaulted and finished in stucco moulded in beautiful designs. But it was the walls of their houses that the Romans cared most to decorate. Only a few wealthy persons could afford to veneer their walls with marble; but many painted them in imitation of marble incrustation, suggesting structural relief, with divisions in different colors, and ordinarily with dado and frieze. In the course of time, other styles of decoration in painting were developed, well rep-

---

[1] Horace, Odes II, 15.

[2] Pp. 124–128.

[3] Pompeii (with the Naples Museum) is, of course, a familiar storehouse of examples of the art of mosaic making (*opus musivum*), including the famous depiction of Alexander at the battle of Issus, from the "House of the Faun," probably the finest ancient mosaic in existence; and quaint mottoes, such as the "HAVE" (= Ave, "welcome") and the "CAVE CANEM" ("Beware of the Dog!") mosaic door mats. There are thousands of other mosaic floors throughout the Empire: for example, elaborate Egyptian scenes, at Palestrina; a portrait of Virgil writing the *Aeneid* (from Hadrumetum, now in Tunis); good geometric designs and figures in several parts of England. The finer specimens required sometimes 100 pieces to the square inch and reflect not only opulence but refined taste on the part of their owners.

[4] *Odes* II, 16, 11 f.: "curas loqueata circum | tecta volantis."

resented at Pompeii, to which it is customary to give the names "Architectural," "Ornate," and "Intricate." As these names indicate, the surface of the wall was treated in such a way as to represent in perspective doors, windows, columns, architraves, and other architectural members, framing spaces or panels in which pictures were painted. The architectural elements, especially in the last two styles, tended to become more and more refined and attenuated, or even fantastic. The pictures, like the rest of the decorations, were executed in fresco, that is, painted in water-colors while the plaster was still moist ("fresh").

Painting, though appreciated by the Romans, never became to any great extent a Roman art. The wall paintings found in Etruscan tombs show a certain instinct for decoration, and betray strong Greek influence; some of the paintings in the tombs at Tarquinia (Corneto) are striking in color and in composition; but Etruscan draughtsmanship is often poor.[1] The Romans engaged the services of Greeks and Etruscans at an early period, though a few native Romans tried their hand at painting. We hear of realistic paintings of battles and other events, anticipating the similar later sculptures in relief; but curiously enough no example of such paintings has survived. Nor have we any examples of the easel-paintings, which would show more careful technique. Most of the thousands of "Roman" paintings that we can see are of the Augustan age or of the first century A.D., and are quite in the tradition of Greek Alexandrine painting. They were frankly intended to be primarily the

---

[1] For excellent renderings in color of paintings in the Tomba del Triclinio at Tarquinia, by P. Duell, see *Mem. Am. Acad. Rome*, Vol. VI (1927). Important paintings from Vulci, depicting Gneve Tarchu: Rumach (= Gnaeus Tarquinius of Rome), Mastarna (= Servius Tullius?), Etruscan deities, etc., are in the Torlonia Gallery in Rome (usually inaccessible); copy in the Vatican. Discussion of their historical bearing by Inez Scott, in *Mem. Am. Acad. Rome*, VII (1929), 71–80.

decorations of houses, and only secondarily to be regarded
as independent works of art. Among the finest are some
illustrations of scenes from the *Odyssey*, found in a house on
the Esquiline and now in the Vatican, showing a real feeling
for landscape. Many of the wall-paintings at Pompeii have
no little charm, but few of them can have been the work of
painters of more than fair ability, as their use in this provincial town would in itself suggest. Furthermore, the very
haste in which the painter had to work, before the plaster
dried, often resulted in poor draughtsmanship and brush-
work; and the coloring, intended to harmonize with the rest
of the decorations, and sometimes used to brighten an ill-
lighted room, is frequently gaudy rather than delicate.
Greek myths supplied many of the subjects, whether serious
and pathetic or, as frequently at Pompeii, more trivial and
dainty in conception. Landscape is usually merely incidental; but figures from legend or from daily life or from the
theatre present themselves in infinitely varied and graceful
poses, with here and there a realistic portrait or a pleasant
bit of still life. Among the newer excavations may be seen
in the "House of the Mysteries" a superb series of paintings depicting initiation into the mysteries of Dionysus.[1]
Especially familiar are the engaging series of pictures in the
"House of the Vettii" depicting lively bands of Cupids
and Psyches in various serious or sportive occupations, —
as vinedressers and goldsmiths and makers of oil, as flower
dealers, and as contestants in races riding curious animals or
in the games of the Circus. Considered as decorations and
as background for social life, corresponding to the wall-
paper and the hangings of a modern home, the Pompeian
paintings are more than adequate; they create an atmosphere of gaiety or relaxation or reverie.

[1] Cf. p. 333

From the private house, however, we must now turn to the much more significant achievement of the Romans in public buildings; for deep-rooted though their interests were in their homes and their families, both the temperateness of their climate and their social activities impelled the Romans, like the Greeks, to spend most of their waking hours away from home. The traditional Roman respect for the state caused the religion of the state to be enshrined in dignified structures; the sagacity of Augustus and his successors realized how the splendor and convenience of every sort of public building could enhance the prestige of their rule and could make the city populace contented even if most families had only a room or two in a humble *insula* for their homes.

Until nearly the end of the Republic, Rome could boast of little in the way of beautiful architecture, and what she had showed considerable borrowing from Etruria and the Italiote Greeks. Till the year 494 B.C., we are told, "all things in Roman temples were Etruscan";[1] the tradition ran that Tarquin brought Etruscan builders to erect the Temple of Jupiter Capitolinus in Rome.[2] If the Etruscans did not invent the arch, but brought it from the East, where it was occasionally used underground in crude forms, the Etruscans at least used it freely in gates, bridges, culverts, and tombs, and transmitted it to the Romans, who made it their own. From the Greeks the Romans borrowed, either through the Etruscans or directly, the use of the three "orders" of column, Doric, Ionic, and Corinthian, each modified in minor ways; and they came to exhibit a great fondness for the Corinthian and for the rather sumptuous

---

[1] According to Varro, quoted by the elder Pliny, *N. H.* XXXV, 154.

[2] Livy, I, 56. The tradition is credible enough; and early Roman temples seem to have shown Etruscan traits. See below, pp. 160 f.

"composite" capitals that combined Ionic volutes with Corinthian acanthus leaves. But whereas the Greek architect
had used columns as strictly useful, though also very beautiful, members of a building, all supporting their share of the
structure, the Romans tended to treat columns as something
to be added as an adornment to a building already structurally complete. The subdivision of the Roman building
trade, which gave different guilds the control of different
parts, further accentuated the division of construction from
decoration, so that an edifice might be built by one set of
workmen, and have a shell of decoration added later by
marble facing or columnar façade.[1] This tendency manifested itself especially, to be sure, after the peculiarly Roman features of Roman architecture were established, with
the steady use of brick and concrete construction. By this
time columns or pilasters might mask a building whose real
structure rested on arches and vaulting. Roman architects
excelled, then, in adapting the Etruscan arch and the Greek
orders to their own concrete and brick method of construction; and this, as we shall see, was just what the social needs
of the Empire demanded.

During most of the Republic, the important public
buildings were temples; of these few traces remain. Nevertheless a few foundations and other fragments, representations on coins of the restored Temple of Jupiter Capitolinus,
and the extant later temples (such as the well preserved late
Republican Temple of Fortuna Virilis in Rome, near the
Forum Boarium,[2] and the "Maison Carrée" at Nîmes, in
southern France, dating from Hadrian's time), show us
certain characteristics: Etruscan high base, approached by

[1] G. Giovannoni, "Building and Engineering," pp. 431–433, in *The Legacy
of Rome.*
[2] This temple is well illustrated, with a restoration, in M. Rostovtzeff,
History of the Ancient World, II, 96, Plates XIX–XX.

steps at one end, rectangular ground plan, columns at the ends, and often an imitation of a colonnade made by half-columns or pilasters attached to the sides. The construction was at first of wood, with terra cotta revetments and decorations. The "Etruscan column" was apparently a clumsy imitation of Greek Doric columns, with a base; later the Roman modifications of all the Greek orders were used. A single roof might shelter three divinities, each with a separate chamber. Another common type of Roman temple was circular, with surrounding columns. This may be derived from the primitive Italian wigwam hut; at any rate the few Greek circular temples or shrines are all of a late period, and the Roman circular temples tended, rightly or wrongly, to be connected with the name of Vesta, goddess of the hearth. The round base of the Temple of Vesta in the Forum Romanum is still visible, and also the fairly well preserved Temple of Mater Matuta or of Hercules in the Forum Boarium (once known as the Temple of Vesta), and parts of the charming Temple, various called "of Vesta" and "of the Sibyl" at Tibur (Tivoli).

Most famous of round Roman temples, and best preserved, is the great Pantheon in the Campus Martius, which represents the temple dedicated by Agrippa in 25 B.C. to the divine ancestors of Augustus, several times burnt, and restored by Domitian, Hadrian, and later emperors. Not only in its impressive proportions but in its peculiar construction, it is an admirable example of truly Roman architecture. The façade consists of a deep portico 109 feet wide, of eight columns in the front and three columns at the sides, of red and grey Egyptian granite, with Corinthian capitals of Pentelic marble surmounted by a gable or pediment. This portico is extended by masonry, adorned on the outside by pilasters, and flanking a great vestibule through which one enters the round main chamber of the temple, 142 feet in diameter, canopied by a dome or rotunda which soars to an equal number of feet. The walls, 20 feet thick, are of brick and concrete, designed with consummate skill by a complicated system of recesses and relieving arches to sustain the weight of the dome.[1] The dome itself is in effect a solid inverted bowl of masonry, unlike much other Roman vaulting whose ribs anticipated the groined vaulting of Gothic architecture. At the top there is an opening 27 feet wide through which the blue sky is visible, and the whole building is fully lighted by the shaft of light that falls through it. Tiles of gilt bronze once covered the roof, and the external walls were partly encrusted with white marble, partly coated with stucco. The internal walls are broken by niches and columns and entablatures; the ceiling is broken by deep-sunk panels, once richly decorated. The temple has been used as a Christian church, and contains the tombs of Raphael and of the first two kings of reunited Italy.[2]

Most Roman temples, to be sure, were far smaller than the Pantheon; and Christian churches found the inspiration for their buildings chiefly in other quarters. For the temples of the Greeks and the Romans were intended primarily to be the abode of divinities and to house the cult-images and the treasures, rather than to provide shelter for large congregations of worshipers. Indeed, it was only the happy discovery of cement construction and of the vault that made possible the spanning of great areas without the necessity of breaking them up with columns or piers. Apparently the early Christian churches in Italy were modelled on private houses

---

[1] On the technique of this and similar systems, see G. Giovannoni, "Building and Engineering," pp. 441–457, in *The Legacy of Rome*.

[2] The Library of Columbia University, in New York City, in general imitates the form of the Pantheon.

and on the chapels of the mystery religions,[1] of which
a subterranean example has been found near the Porta
Maggiore in Rome, with nave, aisles, and at one end, where
the ritual was conducted, a bay, or apse, which became the
Christian chancel. But in a sense the mystery-chapels were
only a variety of the secular buildings known as *basilicae*,[2]
which were often of great size; accordingly it was under the
influence of these *basilicae*, and later of the great public
baths, that the larger Christian churches came to be built.
These *basilicae* were the equivalent of law courts and bank-
ers' offices, and opened on the *fora*.[3] At first they were nothing more than halls (sometimes open at the sides), with aisles
divided by colonnades, supporting a roof of rafters, with a
tribunal at one or at both ends for the presiding magistrate;
later, the central aisle was raised and vaulted and pierced by
windows in the upper part, which became the clerestories of
Christian churches.

It is not necessary to suppose that the Romans were more
cleanly in their habits than the Greeks; in fact, the Greeks
taught them to bathe regularly. But certain it is that the
great public baths of the Romans are among the most striking remains of antiquity, and that they were patronized
as clubs by citizens of every degree. For this they were
indebted to the plentiful supply of water, denied to the
Greeks, which the aqueducts brought to the cities, and again
to the new type of construction that enabled them to give

[1] Cf. pp. 333.

[2] The Greek name "basilica" is connected with the idea of a royal palace;
but the Roman building has no such association. Something like the basilica,
with its system of aisles and clerestory windows, had been known in Egypt
and Greece; see the illustration in J. H. Breasted, *Ancient Times*, p. 703.

[3] E.g. the Basilica Julia, begun by Julius Caesar and completed by Augustus, of which the ground-plan is visible at the southwestern corner of the
Forum Romanum, and the Basilica of Maxentius or of Constantine, still
standing in parts at the northeastern corner.

shelter to thousands of bathers. They learned how to heat some of the rooms and pools by piping hot air from furnaces through hollow tiles under the floors; they arranged successions of baths, tepid, hot, and cold (to be used in the order given), with swimming-pools and rubbing-rooms, dressing-rooms and lounging-rooms, a *palaestra* or exercise ground, and even lecture halls and libraries. No provincial town was too small to boast one or more public baths; and fine examples are to be found in Pompeii, in Paris, in Bath, and in Caerwent (England). The walls and ceilings were decorated with frescos and moulded stucco, the floors often with mosaic. But of course the most impressive remains of Roman baths are to be seen in Rome itself, where there were hundreds of establishments. The Baths of Dioletian, now known as the *Terme* (*Thermae*), cared for 3,200 bathers at once; the building is so large that parts of it now house a church and a museum and other offices. The enormous Baths of Caracalla still show great walls and broken mountains of brick and concrete masonry, with here and there enough of marble facing and mosaic left to suggest their former splendor, when marble columns helped to support great vaults and panelled ceilings. The complex ground-plan of such baths, and of the great semi-public buildings on the Palatine ("palaces" that were both residences for emperors and offices for the administration of the various departments of state), served in more modern times as the ultimate model of such large groups of public buildings as the Vatican and the Bank of England. The way in which the architects of these baths spanned by bold vaults the areas needed by enormous crowds was the direct inspiration for the Pennsylvania Station in New York City.

On other buildings designed for public amusement the Romans left their mark. The Greek theatre had been scooped out of a hillside, with seats for the spectators rising in tiers and filling about two-thirds of a circle; they had left in the centre the round level dancing-place (*orchestra*), empty except for an altar, for the evolutions of the chorus; behind it they had placed the stage, raised very slightly, if at all, and the simple buildings, representing palace or temple, that served both as scenery and as actors' dressing-rooms. When the Romans began to build permanent theatres, almost at the end of the Republic, they borrowed these ideas in general, but often built up their theatres with masonry from the level ground, finishing the exteriors with arches and cornices and successive tiers of engaged columns and entablatures. The auditorium filled only half a circle, unless it was elongated into the shape of a horseshoe; since the chorus was no longer used, the *orchestra* was filled with seats for members of the senatorial order, while the fourteen rows of seats just behind were reserved for the *equites*. The entrance passageways were covered with vaults, having tribunals, or boxes, over them for privileged personages; awnings sometimes covered part of the auditorium. A narrow, raised stage was used, and behind it rose a high and ornate back-wall, the ends of which met the corners of the auditorium. Curtains were raised from a slot in the bottom, instead of being lowered, to conceal the stage. In Rome itself not much remains of the various theatres that stood in the southern part of the Campus Martius; but the Theatre of Marcellus, still standing, was converted into a mediaeval *palazzo*, and has recently been liberated from the grimy shops and tenements that invaded parts of it. Pompeii can show a fairly well preserved theatre of a type partly Greek and partly Roman; there is also a small theatre, or music-hall, once roofed over. At Taormina, in Sicily, the Greek theatre was remodelled by the Romans; but however handsome the brick and stone back-wall may have been, one is glad that only part of it remains to cut the superb view of distant Mt. Aetna and the coast. Still more accessible and well preserved is the splendid theatre at Orange, in southern France, which is quite Roman in all its features.

The theatre never won the hearts of the Romans so completely as did the games that were held in the amphitheatre. As the name implies, this is a round or elliptical structure, equivalent to two theatres facing each other, and is a purely Roman development. Although good examples may be seen in Verona and Pompeii and Syracuse, and in many other towns in the provinces, it is the Flavian Amphitheatre, or Colosseum, that is largest and most famous, and is also typical of the rest. Surrounding an area whose axes are 287 and 180 feet, it covers an area of six acres and rises to a height of 160 feet. The construction is of concrete, faced with brick or (on the outside) with travertine and stucco; internally it contains well arranged passageways and stairs leading to seats at different levels, as in American stadiums and "bowls," and beneath the arena are substructures containing dens for the wild beasts and mechanical contrivances for scenic effects and for flooding the arena. The exterior, formerly covered with stucco, shows four stories, the lower three consisting of series of arches framed by engaged columns, Doric, Ionic, and Corinthian (in rising order), and entablatures; the fourth story, apparently built later than the rest, is broken only by windows, and is adorned by Corinthian pilasters supporting a coping pierced by holes in which were set the masts that once held awnings to protect the spectators. Estimates of the seating capacity of the Colosseum vary from 45,000 to 80,000; and if gladiators of special note or outlandish beasts were to be shown in the arena, some thousands more could find standing room.

For track athletics the Romans cared less than did the Greeks, though they made some use of them to supplement military training. More than one emperor built a stadium in the Greek style; the general plan of that of Domitian, in the Campus Martius, may still be seen in the Piazza Navona. But the chariot races, held in the Circus, were immensely popular; as many as six circuses were built in or near Rome. Best preserved to-day is the Circus of Maxentius, on the Appian Way three miles from Rome. The earliest and largest, the Circus Maximus, which once filled the valley between the Palatine and the Aventine, can be traced in its outline, and its eastern end has recently been excavated; its appearance is known from coins that show it in its heyday. Perhaps the circus was once round, as the name indicates; but the circus as we know it was always in the form of a stadium with certain features added for the needs of chariot racing. Along the middle of the circus, for some two-thirds of its length, extended a wall, the *spina* ("backbone") round which the race was run, the ends marked by pillars (*metae*), or turning posts. By an ingenious system of stalls or "prisons" (*carceres*), the chariots were all equidistant from the actual start of the race. On the *spina* were placed various statues and trophies, and at either end the seven marble eggs and dolphins that were taken down, one with each lap of a race, to indicate the number of laps still to be run. Another trophy placed on the *spina* might be an Egyptian obelisk; the one set up in the Circus Maximus by Augustus now stands in the Piazza del Popolo, where the Flaminian Way leaves the city, and obelisks from other circuses stand in similar positions. In the time of Augustus the Circus Maximus provided seats for 60,000 spectators; later emperors enlarged it till 150,000 or even 200,000 spectators could find seats in it. On a gala day the Circus must have been a brilliant spectacle. It began with a stately procession of presiding magistrates in triumphal garb, guests, contestants, priests, and musicians, moving from the Capitol to the Circus. The chariots were drawn most frequently by four horses, and from four to eight or sometimes twelve teams raced in a single heat of about three miles; in a day's racing there were from half a score to a score of heats. The expenses were borne by the magistrate who gave the games; but the teams and the drivers were organized in four or five commercialized clubs, distinguished by as many colors (red, white, blue, green, and purple and gold). Enormous amounts were spent in breeding and training the horses and securing skilful drivers; the populace bet on their favorites with feverish excitement. The races themselves were exciting enough, especially as the turns about the *metae* had to be executed sharply, so as to avoid adding to the distance, yet not too sharply, so as to avoid collision either with the *metae* or with rival chariots. Accidents occurred very frequently; nor were they at all deplored by the spectators, who found in them merely additional thrills. No record was kept of the time in the races.

In yet another type of construction, with several phases, a dominant trait of the Romans manifested itself. Despite the Roman's willingness to sink himself in the state, and despite the haziness of his views or his scepticism with regard to a future life, he was very anxious to leave a permanent record of his personal achievements, his *res gestae*, and to provide for a continuing reverence to his spirit. We have already noticed some of the characteristic forms of burial, and among them the monumental tombs that perpetuated a family cult.[1] Some of them were large enough and solid enough to serve in the Middle Ages as fortresses. Still more closely

[1] Pp. 109–114.

connected with the idea of the individual's personal achievement are the triumphal arch and the column, also products of the Roman love of pomp and magnificence. Though something like a triumphal arch is to be found in the ruins of Assyrian and Parthian royal palaces, it appears that the Roman triumphal arch was a native development replacing the temporary wooden structures used in early time.[1] The simplest form is represented by the Arch of Titus, at the eastern end of the Forum Romanum, and by Trajan's Arch, at Benevento,— a single arch piercing a massive block of masonry, with decoration of engaged columns and entablature and coping, several of the flat surfaces (inside the arch, as well as outside) being adorned with sculpture in relief. More elaborate, but not better executed, are the arches of Septimius Severus, at the western end of the Forum, and of Constantine (remodelled from an earlier arch), between the Palatine and the Colosseum, with a great central arch flanked by two smaller side-arches. In scale and in adaptation of means to end, these structures served their purposes most admirably and still invite the imagination to follow the triumphal processions of generals and legionaries that once filed through them. Not quite so much can be said of the columns. Granted that the single column used for a purely monumental purpose was a happy invention of the Romans, it was not so happy a thought to surround it with a spiral band of relief sculpture, the details of which cannot be seen

[1] Cf. J. H. Breasted, *Ancient Times*, Fig. 248, p. 611, for oriental arches. Roman triumphal arches probably represented at first a form of ritual purification for a general and his army who had shed blood on the battlefield; the glory of an individual was a later phase. See also C. D. Curtis, "Roman Triumphal Arches," *Supplementary Papers of the American School of Classical Studies in Rome*, II (1908), 26–83. Martin P. Nilsson holds that the origin of the triumphal arch is to be found in the elaborated basis of statues, pierced for convenience by a passage. *Corolla Archaeologica* (Lund, Sweden, and Oxford, 1932), pp. 132–139.

easily from the ground (or even from surrounding buildings);
nor on the whole does it enhance the dignity of an emperor
to ensky him on so tenuous a pedestal as a column. The
Column of Trajan, erected in his magnificent new Forum in
the level space between the Capitoline and the Esquiline,
formerly supposed to measure with its hundred feet of height
the amount of earth cut away, is now thought by some to
have been erected on "made" land over the sepulchre of the
emperor.[1] Its spiral reliefs, depicting the Dacian campaigns
of Trajan, are of no common interest both historic and artistic; the statue of the emperor has been replaced by one of St.
Peter. The total impression is one of strength, perhaps even
of grace; but the Column of Marcus Aurelius in the Campus
Martius is inferior in proportions and in execution. How
much depends on very minor details, in monuments of this
kind, one may discover by the study of modern columns and
monuments; the simplest are the most pleasing, and if decorated the figures or the reliefs must have some justification in
conception and in style for their use and their position.[2]

[1] G. Boni excavated the site. The last two lines of the inscription run: AD
DECLARANDVM QVANTAE ALTITVDINIS MONS ET LOCVS TANTIS OPERIBVS SIT
EGESTVS. Boni interprets them (Proceedings of the British Academy [1907–
08], p. 98) as follows: "In order to make visible [that is, from the summit of
the column, one hundred feet above the sepulchre of Trajan] how much in
elevation the hill [Slope of Quirinal] and the site [of the Forum Ulpium] had
been raised up by such noble works of art." The hillside was doubtless also
scarped for the new buildings now again visible.

[2] Compare, for example, in Paris the well-proportioned column in the
Place Vendôme, surmounted by an insignificant figure, and the more squat
July Column in the Place de la Bastille, with its incomparably graceful
archer; or the well-conceived Nelson's Monument in Trafalgar Square, Lon-
don, the figure dwarfed by the capital just below it; or again the Washington
Monument in Baltimore, a fine Doric shaft supporting an awkward statue.
In some ways the most satisfactory monuments are those that are simple
obelisks, like the Bunker Hill Monument (Boston), and the Washington
Monument in Washington. The latter gains also by its superior setting. The
Romans spoiled some of their finest effects by huddling together structures
that need a spacious environment. The French have placed the Arc de

To trace in detail the influence of Roman architecture and building on the work of later times would fall outside the scope of these pages. A bare enumeration of some of the kinds of buildings would be impressive, including arched bridges, churches roofed by vaults or by great domes, cloisters and similarly conceived groups of buildings such as collegiate edifices and mediaeval inns built round courtyards, houses built over arcades, and houses with slightly overhanging second stories, common in Europe and in early New England,[1] construction in stone and brick and concrete, the central heating of houses (possibly suggested by the heating of Roman baths), the use of glass windows, and of mosaic in decoration (replaced in northern climates by stained glass windows).[2] But such enumeration would not convey any impression of the effect that the original Roman work still conveys to the eye. That is an impression of the Roman character itself, deliberately working out in the most durable of materials a far-reaching purpose, appropriating ideas and methods at will, halting at no technical difficulty. Utilitarian and political in the main, Roman architecture has justly been described as "the first social architecture," for it showed how the builder's art may be used for the needs of a great organized society. Deliberate in investing itself with a garment of magnificent external adornment, it re-

Triomphe, which in itself is inferior in design to several of the Roman arches, in such a commanding site that it gives greater pleasure. The last word in such matters was spoken by the Greeks, who, without much of the gift for city-planning that the French have developed, instinctively placed their temples in settings of great natural beauty; and they also, unlike the Romans, knew how to leave the structural lines of their buildings exposed nakedly to the eye, reserving decoration for the unstressed parts.

[1] For these last three points and others besides, see J. Bellows, "Survivals of Roman Architecture in Britain," *Proceedings of the Cotteswold Naturalists' Field Club*, Vol. XIII, Part 3.

[2] See further G. McN. Rushforth, "Architecture and Art," in *The Legacy of Rome*.

mains no less magnificent now that much of the marble facing and the chiselled detail have perished. The very ruins speak, and speak perhaps more truly than the perfect structures, of Rome's will to achieve. Others, indeed, might draw from bronze and marble a more living and graceful expression of humanity than the Romans; their will to command, to spare, to make a world of peace and order, was above dispute. Yet in spite of the great lines spoken by Virgil's Anchises,[1] something must be said of the Roman's use of the sculptor's art; for if sculpture was not a peculiarly Roman art, it was, nevertheless, compelled in time to serve for the expression of the Roman genius in a peculiar sense.

3. The Record and the Ideal

Long before the Romans themselves endeavored to create sculpture, they were familiar with the work of the Etruscans and of the Greeks in southern Italy. The greater part of Etruscan sculpture has perished, for the work executed in terra cotta was easily broken, and the bronzes were apt to be melted for other purposes; yet enough has been preserved to show us its character. Some works, like the fine sixth-century terra cotta "Apollo" found at Veii, show archaic Greek traits in their conventional treatment of eyes and hair and drapery. A life-size figure in bronze, known as the "Arringatore" ("the haranguer") and dating perhaps from the time of the Punic Wars, shows an orator dressed in a robe something like a toga, with arm extended; finished in technique, it exhibits nevertheless the prevalent Etruscan carelessness in

[1]   Excudent alii spirantia mollius aera
credo equidem, vivos ducent de marmore vultus.
Tu regere imperio populos, Romane, memento
(hae tibi erunt artes) pacique imponere morem,
parcere subiectis et debellare superbos.
                              Aen. 847–848, 851–853.

anatomy.[1] Very common are the figures on Etruscan sarcophagi, in terra cotta or in stone, of men reclining as at a banquet, or recumbent as in sleep, and the reliefs cut on the sides of stone sarcophagi, depicting processions and combats. There is sometimes an attempt at portraiture in the figures, and less often a tendency toward idealization that suggests Greek influence. In the main, however, Etruscan artists were content to bring to sculpture the same skilful technique that they manifested in their decorative work in metal, — bronze cauldrons and candelabra, mirrors and boxes, and elaborate jewelry; as for ideas, and as for the perfect treatment of the human form or of gods in idealized human form, they were lacking. Their religion, indeed, presented evil powers, rather than gods to be admired; and their social life was a compound of luxury and gluttony and cruelty and a pessimism that brooded much on death and the evils of an after life;[2] at best, they could borrow for their cinerary urns and sarcophagi and their tomb paintings the Greek myths that served to illustrate or to instigate the terrors of death. Some of these qualities, infinitely refined in spirit and in expression, were destined to flower in the great art and literature of Tuscany in the late Middle Ages and the Renaissance. Not from the ancient Etruscans, however, could the Romans learn much that could ennoble or beautify their city by plastic forms.

From early times, however, the Romans had acquired the habit of recording the features of their distinguished men by making wax *imagines*, or death masks, which were kept in the *atrium*, as family portraits, except when they were borne in the triumphal or the funeral processions of their descend-

---

[1] The "Apollo" is now in the Villa Giulia, Rome; the "Arringatore" is in the Archaeological Museum, Florence.

[2] Cf. pp. 13, 39–41.

ants. From them, transmuted into marble and bronze, and developed by the greater skill of Etruscan and Greek artists, were derived the Roman portrait heads and busts that are one of the two chief and most characteristic glories of Roman sculpture. Moreover, we know that the early Romans erected portrait statues of their national heroes in public places; in 158 B.C. those statues about the Forum which had not been legally authorized were removed. Though Etruscan and Greek artists were probably employed, the works were doubtless more valuable for their historic or patriotic associations than for any great artistic merit. Nevertheless, the surviving heads and figures that represent this tradition as it developed during the later Republic and the Empire have great interest, if not always great beauty, because they so often show us the kind of men and women who moulded Roman civilization. Doubtless the earlier examples are wrongly named; but the strong features, whether bearded (a "Brutus") or clean-shaven (a "Scipio"), present not merely types but real persons; some of the numerous busts of Caesar and Cicero and of members of the household of the various emperors have not been surpassed in their skilful characterization by any artists of later times until the full Renaissance; even the realistic portrait heads of obscure or unknown citizens of provincial towns appeal to us because of a faithfulness that is not so much photographic as sympathetic and interpretive. Even when they represent persons who are far from beautiful, their very homeliness disarms contempt and sometimes even fascinates.[1]

Meanwhile, of course, a new era had arisen from the greater contact with Greek art and the greater wealth that

[1] Vernon Lee well speaks of "the beautiful portraits of ugly old men." See further A. B. Hawes, "Similitudo non Pulchritudo," *C. J.*, Vol. XX, No. 7 (April, 1926).

had sprung from Rome's adventures east of the Adriatic. Not only did Mummius set the fashion for other Roman generals when he carried off Greek works of art from Corinth (146 B.C.), but Greek artists found a public in Rome who had at least the collector's interest. A certain natural acquisitiveness, combined with a love of outward splendor, manifested itself both in the private houses and country villas of wealthy Romans and in the decoration of public buildings. Cicero's letters to his friends travelling in Greece contain frequent commissions to them to pick up appropriate bits of sculpture for his library. In Italy itself, during the century and a half between the Macedonian Wars and the end of the Republic, Greek sculptors worked to supply the Roman market with original works and with copies, influenced but little by their environment. Greek myths and legendary heroes, Roman gods in Greek forms, were the staple subjects, and the technique sometimes showed an archaizing tendency, but more often, as was natural, imitated the style of the late Hellenistic period. Pasiteles, an Italiote Greek honored with Roman citizenship early in the first century B.C., was the great name, and belonged to the archaizing school, while Arcesilaus led the followers of the Hellenistic school; in the surviving works of their pupils one can discover little that might not have been produced in Greece. Native Romans rarely became sculptors, partly, it is easy to suppose, because of an instinct against so temperamental, and at the same time almost servile, a form of activity. Cicero, though a connoisseur, was shrewd enough, in the presence of Roman auditors (real or imaginary), to praise the poet Archias especially for his patriotic services in commemorating the deeds of illustrious Romans, and to feign imperfect acquaintance with the very names of the Greek sculptors.[1] Achilles quite

---

[1] Cicero, *Pro Archia Poeta*, 19; *In Verrem, Actio Secunda* IV, 2, 4 f.

naturally sang to the lyre; Julius Caesar probably would not; and one of the greatest reproaches against Nero was not his viciousness, but his fondness for dabbling in Greek arts. The Roman sense of dignity, then, would tolerate the collection of Greek works of art, or the employment of Greeks to record the faces of Romans; self-expression was another matter.

The founding of the Empire revealed a new use for sculpture in the recording of the national achievement: the return of peace within the state, conquests abroad, and the sense of the mission of Rome in the world. There were still heroes to be represented in busts and statues; but above all there were deeds to be chronicled in relief sculptures, and great public buildings and monuments to be adorned with such forms as should remind both Romans and foreigners of the greatness and destiny of Rome. Within the two centuries that followed the accession of Augustus to the principate, the Romans not only borrowed anew from Greece but adopted new methods, probably derived from the East, for her own purposes; nevertheless, this period is the most important and the most typically Roman of all.

In the age of Augustus, it was the most serene and perfect phase of Greek sculpture that influenced the portrait sculpture done at Rome; yet the ideas were Roman. Thus, in the statue of Augustus discovered at Prima Porta, near Rome, and now in the Vatican, we see the emperor addressing his troops with outstretched arm; pose and proportions remind one of the Doryphoros of Polycleitus; the use of Cupid riding a dolphin to symbolize the descent of Augustus from Aphrodite recalls other Greek works; the treatment of the breastplate, the tunic, and the cloak, is realistic, and the decoration of the breastplate actually includes a scene depicting the recovery of the Roman standards from the Parthians; while the expression of the face is at once a fairly realistic representation of the actual Augustus and an idealized expression of his confident, masterful reign comparable to the Augustus of the *Aeneid*. During the succeeding reigns, portrait sculpture became again increasingly realistic, culminating in the remarkable series of busts belonging to the period of the Flavian dynasty (69–96). A compromise with idealization was made, however, by the curious expedient of representing actual persons, realistically portrayed, in the guise of mythological personages; thus we find portrait heads on athletic figures, or, as incongruously, on divinities, — a "Livia as Ceres," a "Claudius as Zeus," and (later) a "Commodus as Hercules." Under Hadrian, a traveller and lover of Greek art, was fostered a revival of Hellenizing sculpture at Rome, of which good examples are found in the numerous representations of the emperor's young favorite, Antinoüs, sometimes portrayed as Dionysus or Silvanus or some other young god. Nevertheless, faithful portraits continued to be produced. Hadrian himself wore a beard, which set the fashion for many of his successors; and sculptors found a new interest in treating the hair and beard, by undercutting the marble, so as to present strong shadows and a contrast with the smooth skin. For two centuries or more after the Hadrianic revival, there were made respectable or even excellent portrait heads and figures, including equestrian figures, — of Marcus Aurelius and others, — practically a new departure in art. Moreover the Roman love of abstraction that appears in the worship of divinities like Fides ("Good Faith") and Concordia found constant expression in the representation not only of such divinities but of Fortuna and of allegorical embodiments of cities and nations.

Even more than in sculptures in the round, however, the Roman symbolized or idealized the achievement of Rome by the use of sculpture in relief, applied to triumphal arches and columns and public buildings. The pediments of early Roman temples had been decorated with groups of figures by Etruscan and Greek artists, as later representations of them bear witness; but of relief sculpture in the strict sense nothing of importance has survived that is older than the Augustan age. In the Ara Pacis Augustae we meet one of the noblest monuments of Roman art, and the most significant embodiment of the new age. Voted by the Senate, on his return from Spain and Gaul in 13 B.C., in honor of the Emperor and the peace restored by him, and dedicated in 9 B.C., this structure stood in the Campus Martius; parts of it are now preserved in various museums in Rome and elsewhere. The altar itself stood in a paved area surrounded by a marble wall about twenty feet high, and measuring thirty-five by thirty-seven feet on the sides, with openings on the east and on the west. The decoration of the wall included pilasters, carvings of garlands and ox-skulls, panels with scrolls of foliage, and a narrow frieze with figures. The garlands and scrolls, though in the tradition of Hellenistic art, are treated in higher relief and with the addition of more realistic details, — fruits, buds and blossoms, birds and insects, — and are of great beauty. The figures, however much they may owe to Greek sculpture, are Roman in conception. A fair comparison would be with the sculptures of the Parthenon, a temple built as a thank-offering for the deliverance of Greece from the Persian wars. The Parthenon sculptures nowhere deal directly with the Persian wars, and merely suggest them by presenting legendary conflicts of Centaurs and Lapiths; the Roman work depicts in part not, to be sure, a scene from an actual battle, — like the Alexander sarcophagus from Sidon, and like many Roman friezes of later times, — yet nevertheless an actual moment in a sacrificial procession consisting of real Romans, dressed in the national garb, and showing the serious, rather stolid features of individual persons. No successful attempt has been made to identify these persons; but it has been thought that the Emperor himself, as Pontifex Maximus, his consort Livia, and his son-in-law Agrippa, can be distinguished, as well as other figures who must be members of the imperial family. Priests and consuls, lictors and other attendants, sacrificial victims, senators and citizens, complete the procession. Interesting from the point of view of technical skill is the attempt of the artists to suggest depth by carving the figures on two planes, those nearest the spectator being treated in high relief, the others in low relief. This device, probably borrowed from the Hellenistic sculptors, and ultimately from the Orient, is now commonly known as the "illusionist" method; here used somewhat experimentally, it came to be a characteristic Roman method, and certainly succeeds in conveying an impression of figures moving in a world of three dimensions with light and air playing about them. The general composition of the figures comprising the friezes is less well conceived than is the Parthenon frieze; on the other hand, in several of the groups the figures are well related to each other, especially in the turn of their heads and the expressions of their eyes, which contribute to a superior dramatic or spiritual effect. The composition is completed by the inclusion of sacrificial scenes with background of landscape and architecture, and of graceful allegorical figures of a matron who has traditionally been identified as *Tellus*, Mother Earth,[1] the opulent source of the blessings of peace, with the attendant spirits of Air and Water, but

---

[1] "Fertilis frugum pecorisque Tellus | Spicea donet Cererem corona; | Nutriant fetus et aquae salubres | Et Jovis aurae." Horace, *Carmen Saeculare*, 29 ff. (sung in 17 B.C.). Cf. Tibullus, I, 10, 45 ff.

who is perhaps better interpreted as the embodiment of the Saturnian land, the goddess Italia.[1] These symbolic figures, like the songs of the Augustan poets, celebrate the restoration of prosperity and the ancient Roman art of agriculture under the new regime. The Ara Pacis is both a record of achievement and the evidence of aspiration toward an ideal.

Commemorative of actual events are the reliefs on the inside walls of the Arch of Titus;[2] but these, unlike the reliefs of the Ara Pacis, record the *res gestae* directly. The Arch was dedicated in 81 A.D., just after the death of Titus, in honor of the conquest of Judaea by Vespasian and his son Titus (71 A.D.); the interior reliefs represent on one side the procession of soldiers carrying off the sacred utensils from Jerusalem, — the table for the shewbread, the trumpets, and the seven-branched candlestick, — and on the other side the Emperor in his triumphal chariot attended by allegorical figures of Victory and the Genius of the Roman People and Roma and by throngs of citizens. Admirable is the suggestion of life and motion and the impression of depth secured by the "illusionist" method; the figures, carved in many different planes and sharply silhouetted, seem to be viewed as through a window; the background is no longer a flat wall, but is itself moulded by the chisel as the painter seeks by line and shadow to create the illusion of depth. It is no wonder that these reliefs have been compared with the work of Velasquez. Despite the success of this bold experiment, however, there are almost childish faults in perspective and arrangement, — the placing of the arch through which the soldiers are to march, the direction in which chariot and horses respectively face.

[1] Cf. Virgil, *Georg.* II, 136–176 (quoted in part on p. 3). Cf. A. W. Van Buren ("The Ara Pacis Augustae," *J. R. S.*, III [1913], 134–141). See the illustration opposite.

[2] Cf. p. 169.

"ITALIA, AIR, AND WATER," FROM THE ARA PACIS

The reliefs on the Column of Trajan [1] not only record actual events in the war against the Dacians across the Danube and make use with some skill of a controlled "illusionist" method, but illustrate as well what has been called the "continuous" method, by depicting successive scenes as parts of a single long scroll, and representing the leading personage many times.[2] The method is one not unknown to Egyptian and Assyrian sculptors, and was even used in the picture-chronicles of Roman generals on the occasion of their triumphs; but it is a method which the Greeks "had almost civilized off the face of the earth." [3] Certainly it has its disadvantages; so large and complicated a design cannot be taken in by the eye at once, even if the details could in ancient times be surveyed from the buildings that surrounded the column; and what unity it has depends on the recurrence of its chief personage in diverse situations, somewhat like that of the hero in an epic poem. That is almost equivalent to saying that it is attempting what sculpture had better leave to the sister art of poetry, which deals naturally with events and feelings that succeed each other in time, rather than in space.[4] On the other hand the sculptures, when viewed patiently, do achieve an accumulative effect as the expression of the Roman will to conquer; and many parts, like the pages of Livy, are of great interest because they present dramatic episodes, exciting, pathetic, even humorous. Landscape and architecture, reduced to a miniature scale, provide a semi-realistic setting; and everywhere the figure of Trajan dominates the scene, as in the Christian art of later centuries the central figure dominates the surrounding

[1] Cf. p. 170.

[2] In the 660 feet of the relief Trajan appears more than 90 times, and there are in all some 2,500 figures.

[3] P. Gardner, *Principles of Greek Art*, p. 259, n. 3.

[4] This is in general the point made by Lessing in his *Laokoon*.

group. Similar in interest to Trajan's Column, if not quite
equal in execution, is the Column of Marcus Aurelius;[1] the
spiral reliefs showing the campaigns of the Emperor are in
the "continuous" method, but are more episodic in subject
and cruder in workmanship, though not without pathetic or
even tragic appeal.

If the Column of Trajan succeeds, in spite of obstacles, in
conveying an idea, still more successful is his Triumphal
Arch at Benevento, on the Appian Way, newly rebuilt by
him, where it enters the Apennines. Not unfolding their
message in one continuous scroll, the carved panels nevertheless supplement each other so as to convey a single impression of Trajan's greatness, to be studied in detail by the
spectator. The various panels on the side toward Rome
show the superb forms of the Capitoline gods and the Emperor as Princeps Optimus of the Roman people; he receives
the thunderbolt from Jupiter and is exhibited in kindly relations with veterans and with merchants. On the outer side
of the arch, the sculptures represent phases of the Emper-
or's provincial policy: the gods that safeguarded the newly
conquered province of Dacia, the submission of Mesopotamia, the Emperor receiving embassies of Germans and
Parthians, and figures symbolizing the benefits of Roman
discipline and the growth of prosperity in the provinces, now
raised to the level of Rome. Scenes of greater local interest
adorn the inner walls of the arch: the sacrifice offered by the
Emperor at the time when he set forth for the East by the
very road later spanned by this arch, and the charities of
Trajan to Beneventum and other cities, with throngs of
parents and children and the symbolic figure of the cities
with their mural crowns. Thus a great idea is set forth in
manifold scenes, some requiring the intellectual grasp of a

[1] Cf. p. 170.

student, others so simple that the wayfarer could hardly fail to read their significance. Athenians were reminded in the sculptures of the Parthenon of the gratitude that they owed to the gods for deliverance from Persia; the citizens of Amiens in the thirteenth century, even if they were ignorant of the alphabet, could read their Bible in the carvings of their cathedral;[1] and the Florentines were taught by Ghiberti to read Biblical history from the ranged reliefs on the doors of the Baptistery. So the Roman sculptors used their art to inculcate and to glorify a political idea: the order and dignity and prosperity brought through the imperial system, and the devotion due to the several emperors.

Of later sculpture in relief not much need be said. The Arch of Constantine,[2] which is a finely proportioned triple arch of the first century A.D. reconstructed in 312 A.D. as a tribute to Constantine, is decorated with some excellent medallions (hunting and sacrificial scenes) of the Flavian period, some of the heads being replaced by those of later emperors including Constantine, and with panels carved in the days of Trajan and of Marcus Aurelius. But the friezes dating from the time of Constantine exhibit a curious decadence; they are filled with clumsily carved, squat figures, crowded yet detached from each other, ranged in rows like wooden dolls in boxes, with little attempt to convey any impression of motion or to relate the figures to each other. A similar crowding of figures is found in the reliefs on the sides of sarcophagi carved during this period, though the execution is often finer and the composition is better conceived; and in all these reliefs the figures are apt to be on the same plane, considerably raised from the deeply chiselled background, so that heavy shadows gather between them. The

---

[1] Cf. J. Ruskin, *The Bible of Amiens.*
[2] Cf. p. 169.

best that can be said of such sculpture is that the regular patterns of heads and feet, the alternations of light and shade, produce when viewed at a distance a decorative effect somewhat like geometric or conventional floral designs; but human interest and significance are wanting. This is the more strange because good portrait heads continued to be made throughout this period.

The sculpture of more recent centuries naturally has learned more from the Greeks than from the Romans, whenever Greek works have been available. Of sheer beauty, and especially of the beauty of individual human figures, the Greeks remain the greatest masters. Nevertheless, in certain fields it is the Romans rather than the Greeks who have served as models: for the sculptured portals of mediaeval cathedrals, for recumbent effigies and recessed tomb figures, for equestrian statues, for the terra cotta work of the Della Robbias, for decorative scroll work and festoons of flowers and fruits, and ornate pilasters, and indeed for most types of relief sculpture.[1] Though Greek temples in their noble simplicity, and Gothic cathedrals with their aspiring lines and their flaming windows, and towering feudal castles and ivy-mantled manor houses have a greater spiritual appeal or a more intimate charm than most of the monuments built by the Romans, we must not forget who taught later generations how to build for all kinds of social purposes structures of dignity and solidity, and how to commemorate people and events in sculptured forms. The city of Rome, and the works of the Romans in other places, may strike us in different moods as inviting, impressive, overwhelming; they seldom fail to convey to us an idea. And the idea is not

---

[1] Examples of these types will occur readily enough, especially in Italian art; but it is well not to overlook so Roman a work as the Shaw Monument, by St. Gaudens, on the Boston Common. See also G. McN. Rushforth, in *The Legacy of Rome*, esp. pp. 414-427.

one of mere size or mechanical efficiency or brute strength, but rather of the deliberately calculated adaptation of means to end, of material to form, of individual wills and personalities to the organized and enduring needs of society. From the arts of the Romans we must now turn to consider the Roman achievement in dealing with social relations and citizenship.

CHAPTER V

CIVIS ROMANUS

Si tu apud Persas aut in extrema India deprehensus, Verres, ad sup-plicium ducerere, quid aliud clamitares, nisi te esse Romanum?
Cicero, *In Verrem, Actio Secunda*, V, 64.

I. THE STRUGGLE FOR FREEDOM

ON A famous day, when a riot in Jerusalem had been quelled by the Roman soldiers, St. Paul was taken captive, and was about to be scourged and cross-examined. "And as they bound him with thongs," the narrative runs, "Paul said unto the centurion that stood by, 'Is it lawful for you to scourge a man that is a Roman, and uncondemned?' When the centurion heard that, he went, and told the chief captain, saying, 'Take heed what thou doest: for this man is a Roman.' Then the chief captain came, and said unto him, 'Tell me, art thou a Roman?' He said, 'Yea.' And the chief captain answered, 'With a great sum obtained I this freedom.' And Paul said, 'But I was free born.' Then straightway they departed from him which should have examined him: and the chief captain also was afraid, after he knew that he was a Roman, and because he had bound him." [1] To be a Roman citizen, then, meant at this time to hold a position of especial privilege. But "this freedom" (or more accurately, "citizenship") had not always been enjoyed even by all of Roman birth; and it was a recent thing for members of an alien race, like the Jew Saul of Tarsus, to be able to claim the citizenship as an hereditary right. How had the Romans

[1] *Acts*, xxii, 25-29.

built up this conception of citizenship, for themselves and for others? Of what degrees and relationships did it admit? What privileges did it confer?

We have learned little of the Roman character if we suppose that the Romans began with a theory and applied it to the facts. As usual, they dealt with facts, and "muddled through," inventing theories afterwards. Indeed, we sometimes exaggerate the Roman political genius, forgetting the costliness of their struggles and blindnesses, and their utter failure to solve not a few problems. But let us be careful to give them their just due; to recognize that if they, like other vigorous peoples of their age, conquered with the sword, they differed from most other early peoples, Oriental and Greek, in what has been well described as their "power of inclusiveness, of reconciliation, of sympathy." [1] However tardily, however reluctantly, they did at last assimilate and incorporate old foes as citizens in a common republic; and after the simple machinery that sufficed for the government of a village or for a city-state broke down when used to govern a far-flung empire, Romans sacrificed freedom to efficiency, submitting themselves and their provincials alike to the centralized authority of the state and even to the worship of its first citizen, and tolerating or establishing free towns throughout the empire. When Christianity displaced Caesar-worship as the state religion, and proved to be too individualistic and too cosmopolitan to serve as political cement, the Romans and their former subjects, now equals, split apart under pressure from without. The political experience of the Romans thus has the continuity not of a logical system but rather of a river of events. At every stage we shall see them inclined to pretend that no change has been made, — convenient precedents, compromises that

[1] B. W. Henderson, *The Study of Roman History* (London, 1921), p. 15.

saved their faces, the stretching or accommodation of institutions and laws, the invention of legal fictions, all convinced the Romans, to their own satisfaction and sometimes to our amusement, that they were really true to their old traditions.

If we seek to pierce the mist of legend and to discover the organization of the earliest Romans, we find them living under a monarchy and gathered into communities on the hills by the River. At least this consolidation of villages into the town of Rome, what the Greeks described as *synoikismos*, we may plausibly attribute to the kings, as well as leadership in war, in religion, and in the settling of disputes. The *rex* holds the *imperium*, the right to say *"impero"* ("I command"); he, like his republican successor, the general in command of an army, and like every *pater familias*, is, at least in theory, absolute in his authority. As judge, the *rex* is perhaps less important than the heads of the families, who are already developing a law based on precedent. As chief priest, he inquires the will of heaven on behalf of the state before all important undertakings, and may be assisted by technical advisers, augurs and *haruspices*, who obsevre respectively the flight of birds and the organs of sacrificial victims; but their functions are quite limited, and there is nothing like a theocracy at Rome. The king, though accompanied by the *fasces*, the bundles of rods and two-headed axes that symbolize absolute authority,[1] is not hedged with divinity like the Homeric monarch. His rule is not even hereditary (except perhaps among the Tarquins), but depends on the nomination of a predecessor, the confirmation

---

[1] The two-headed axes were doubtless brought by the Etruscans from the coast of the Aegean Sea, where such axes had long symbolized divinity. The *fasces* were conveniently adopted by the strongly centralized government of Mussolini in 1922 as the sign of discipline and authority, giving the name to the Fascist movement.

of a council of Elders, and the acclamation of the people; and he is expected to consult these Elders, the Senate, a body nominated by himself from among the *patres*, or chiefs of the *gentes* (clans). The people themselves are variously organized, partly on a basis of birth, partly in local divisions, and are summoned to meet in assemblies (*comitia*) to give their assent to the proposals of their leaders. Already a distinction is appearing between the members of the families included in the patrician [1] *gentes* and those other Romans who are not so included, and who are called *plebeii*. The members of the *gentes* claim descent from a common ancestor, common religious rites, and possibly a joint piece of territory; except in primitive times, new patrician *gentes* are seldom formed. Nor are captives of war often admitted to the *gentes* even if they were nobles in their own towns; most newcomers must go to swell the plebeian population, being added to some territorial division, such as the *tribus* (tribe) either as clients or as independent citizens. The plebs is further enlarged by the decay of patrician families, by the growing independence of clients from their patrons, and by the immigration of traders and artisans. Rome is a feudal state, then, with king, nobles, and a citizen body consisting primarily of land-holders, and acknowledging the superiority of "The Families" over those who can boast no ancestors. But all the citizens together, as warriors, are known as *Quirites*, ("spearmen"). [2]

There is every reason to accept the tradition that there were kings at Rome; the tales of the individual kings handed down in the legends show, however, besides a plausible

---

[1] The Romans themselves wrongly explained *patricii* as equivalent to *patres*; whereas the *patres*, as Senators, were selected from the heads of families, and the *patricii* were all who belonged to their blood.

[2] Probably a Sabine word. In later times it curiously changed its meaning, in Cicero's day denoting the civil, not the military aspect of citizenship.

enough account of what must have happened at some time, almost too artistic an arrangement to be altogether acceptable. Thus we have in Romulus a shepherd-founder, who is divine in origin and in the manner of his departure, succeeded by a contrasting pair of kings: Numa Pompilius, the gentle law-giver and dispenser of religious institutions, and the warlike Tullus Hostilius, the destroyer of Alba Longa. The fourth king, Ancus Martius, can present no strikingly new character, and is portrayed as the ideally balanced figure, soldier and builder, too. With Tarquinius Priscus the Etruscans enter Rome. His heir, Servius Tullius (identified by the Etruscans with Mastarna, whose name has been found in Etruria[1]), is credited with the building of walls, perhaps not wholly wrongly, and with the political and economic reorganization of the army that we shall consider presently. To account for the expulsion of the kings, the legends present the last Tarquin (Superbus) as the villain of the piece, a builder but a cruel taskmaster, who strained the *imperium* to the breaking-point. Throughout Roman history the very word *rex* was the most odious of words: men as patriotic as Spurius Maelius, the Gracchi, the younger Livius Drusus, and Julius Caesar, when suspected of aiming at royal power, fell by the assassin's hand. Almost the only reminiscences of the kings were the title of the priest, the *rex* (*sacrorum*) who carried on part of the king's duties and lived in the *regia*, and the name (*interregnum*) that continued to be used for the brief period that elapsed between the death of a magistrate and the election of his successor.

The end of the monarchy by no means spelled the end of the *imperium*; it merely caused the *imperium* to be limited to an annual magistracy, and to be divided between two colleagues. So far is Mommsen right in declaring that "the

---

[1] Cf. p. 157.

king stands in the background of Roman history." In fact, he has disappeared; but in theory his prerogatives are vested in the magistrates, whose office is by a fiction unrestricted, so that at the end of the term they have to pretend to abdicate. Probably the first magistrates chosen, on the overthrow of the monarchy in 509, were known as praetors; [1] but they soon received the name that is more familiar to us, consuls; and the praetors, who for a time had the same military and judicial functions as the consuls, presently were distinguished from the consuls, and held purely judicial duties, while the consuls were chiefly generals. In theory each consul was supreme, and might be checkmated by his colleague; in practice such a contingency seems to have been avoided by the drawing of lots for spheres of action, or by alternation in command. The distinction between the command *domi* (at home, i.e. in Rome) and the command *militiae* (in the field of war) was scrupulously observed: the two were never again united until Julius Caesar's day. Not only did the intercession of a colleague serve to check a possibly tyrannical magistrate, but from the very beginning of the Republic there was provision for an appeal (*provocatio*), on the part of a citizen who thought he was wronged, to one of the popular assemblies. Nevertheless, the divided authority of the magistrates sometimes proved inefficient, especially in war: in emergencies a dictator was sometimes given sole authority, and during the second Punic War Rome learned the advantage of continuing the command of a really great general.

The expanding Republic presently required other magistrates, besides the two consuls and the one praetor (later two praetors). Quaestors, at first charged with the duty of

---

[1] *Praetor* (*prae-itor*), "leader." A general's headquarters were always called the *praetorium*.

hunting out murderers,[1] became the financial assistants of the praetors, hunting out sources of revenue, and increased in number from two to four (in 421) and later to considerably larger numbers. Greater financial responsibility, required in the preparation of the budget and in the award of state contracts, was vested in the two censors,[2] elected for a term of five years, who were also given the very important duty of supervising the muster-rolls and the registration of citizens in their proper classifications as members of the Senate, of the *Equites*, or of the various divisions of the citizen body. Since the censor's *nota*, or check against a citizen's name, might imply moral disapproval, as well as a mere query about his financial rating, the modern associations of "censorship" and "censure" began to gather about the office, which was one of great dignity. The four aediles [3] had charge of temples, streets, and public works and amusements in general, and came to be responsible for the administration of the food supply of the city. A regular sequence of offices, the *cursus honorum*, lay before the ambitious young aristocrat, who might become successively aedile or quaestor, praetor, and consul, holding perhaps also membership in one of the priestly boards (such as the board of augurs, or the "Board of Fifteen" that cared for the Sibylline oracles), or the sacred office of *rex sacrorum*, or (later) that of *pontifex maximus* (chief priest), and in some cases reaching the culminating dignity of the censorship.

From the men who gained political experience in the higher annual magistracies was recruited the membership of the Senate, once the advisory council chosen by the kings, and now the body into which magistrates at first almost

---

[1] *Quaestores parricidii*; cf. *quaero*, "seek."
[2] Cf. *censeo*, "think, vote."
[3] Cf. *aedes*, "building."

automatically, and later quite automatically, graduated and remained for the rest of their lives, unless removed by a censor's *nota*. Practically all legislation originated in this body, and all legislation was discussed in it. Aristocratic and elderly in its composition, it was naturally conservative if not reactionary in its leanings, and was of all Roman institutions the most Roman. Cautious, resolute, dogged, vigorous in emergencies, it could save the state from its foes; but it was not imaginative enough to recognize dangers long before they were imminent. Above all, it was not a body calculated to perceive or to sympathize with the needs and the distresses of humbler people, whether Roman or foreign. The expulsion of the kings at Rome, as in the Greek states, was less a democratic than an aristocratic movement; and the purpose of Rome was not so much to broaden the basis of government as to get rid of an alien dynasty. The *imperium* was as absolute as before, and was simply shared by members of the Roman aristocracy. The patricians considered themselves to be the real Romans; plebeians were tolerated, or even encouraged to live at Rome (and to work, and presently to fight for Rome). Clients they might become, or citizens in a limited sense, with their own religious cults on the Aventine, but they had arrived too late to be numbered among the patrician *gentes*, to hold land, or to hold office. If they were oppressed by their landlords, and their patrons could not or would not help them, it was not from the Senate that they could hope for redress. Accordingly the first two centuries and a half of the Republic are marked by a series of struggles between the patricians, who were interested in preserving the *status quo*, and the plebeians, who finally succeeded in wresting from the patricians most of their peculiar privileges. But it was chiefly the richer plebeians whose political ambitions benefited by the victory; the poorer plebeians gained little economic relief. The patricians yielded with bad grace, and every concession was made only after a bitter conflict, sometimes stained with bloodshed. It is not a little curious that the patricians, who were so heroic in war, were in peace so selfish and blind to the just claims of the new citizens; yet a similar trait has been noticeable among modern aristocracies.

The landmarks in the struggle will be noted presently. But first we should notice the various ways in which the people were organized for different purposes. The *gentes*, we have observed, were all but exclusively patrician, and were significant chiefly of the continuity of the old families, their religion, and their lands. The *tribus* (tribes), on the other hand, admitted new members; and though the three tribes at Rome itself (the Ramnes, Tities, and Luceres, — later reorganized as four tribes with local names) were all patrician, the increasing number of country tribes, 35 in all, in 241 B.C. also becoming local in character, admitted men who were not patricians. The tribes were further subdivided, originally territorially, into *curiae*, of which there were 30 at Rome; these functioned as groups of households organized for political purposes, but lost territorial significance. The *comitia*, or assemblies of the people, might meet organized either by tribes (the *comitia tributa*) or by *curiae* (the *comitia curiata*), in either case consisting chiefly of small farmers living in or near Rome, whose votes were counted not individually but by the tribe or the *curia*. According to tradition it was King Servius Tullius who not only built the "Servian" walls but reorganized the army; but probably it was the capture of Rome by the Gauls (390) that showed the need both of stronger walls and of an army consisting no longer chiefly of patricians but of all the more substantial citizens. Accordingly, the assemblies were for

most purposes superseded by a new organization, the *comitia
centuriata*, which was based on the army divided into 98
"centuries" classified according to wealth. Since wealth was
reckoned chiefly in land, and the centuries voted as units,
those containing the more wealthy citizens being given the
predominance in the voting, it appears that the centurial
organization was intended to increase the army by the inclusion of plebeians, who were perhaps rewarded by small
gifts of land,[1] the real political power remaining with the
substantial land-holders, who were still in most cases the
members of the old *gentes*. None of the assemblies could
meet, however, unless summoned by a magistrate; none
could initiate, discuss, or amend legislation. Their whole
function consisted in the election of magistrates and in voting "Yes" or "No" when proposals were laid before them
by the magistrates.

Although the need of new soldiers to curb Rome's neighbors caused the grudging admission of the new population to
the limited, plebeian form of citizenship and the granting of
the right of appeal to the Assembly, they were long debarred
from the magistracies. The first step toward greater freedom came in 494 B.C., when the plebeians, overwhelmed by
poverty and by laws of debt controlled by the patricians,
seceded in a body to a point a few miles from Rome, returning only when they were allowed to have officers of their
own, called tribunes, who could come to the rescue of any
oppressed citizen, veto the acts of the magistrates, and lay
proposals before the plebeian corporation. They were not
magistrates, and were responsible only to the plebeians;
their persons, however, were sacrosanct. How they were

---

[1] The public lands were, however, seldom distributed among the plebeians; "colonies," amounting to military garrisons in the Roman territory,
with small farms for the soldiers, were the usual response to plebeian demands
for land.

first elected is unknown; from 471 they were elected by the *comitia tributa*, which became henceforth in practice identical with the *concilium plebis*, the plebeian corporation. Their number increased (in 471) from two to four, later to ten. The aediles were their assistants, as the quaestors were the assistants of the consuls. In theory the tribunes were given impossibly wide powers, without any real province of action, and their powers were wholly negative. A tribune could do nothing, but could stop anything, including the veto of a colleague. All the tribunes must therefore act together, if they were to accomplish anything; and this clever patricians learned to prevent by securing the support of at least one tribune. In practice, however, the tribunate served temporarily to check the worse tyranny of the patricians, and in time the tribunes forced their way into the Senate.

Continued economic distress and uncertainty as to the bearing of the laws, still unwritten and preserved as the sacred lore of the *gentes*, brought about the appointment in 451 B.C. of a Commission of Ten Men (the *Decemviri*), who drew up the famous code known as the Twelve Tables. Though this document was treasured as the "source of all law, both public and private"[1] and was studied by Roman schoolboys even in Cicero's time, the actual content of the code shows little that is not conservative, the stabilized custom of an agricultural society which has not developed industry or commerce. Nevertheless, the clear statement of disputed points and the publication of the whole code was a gain for freedom. Unfortunately Appius Claudius and the other Decemvirs refused to retire when their task was done; the plebs again seceded, this time to the Janiculum, until laws (the Valerio-Horatian Laws, 449 B.C.) were passed reaffirming the right of appeal and the inviolability of the

[1] Livy, III, 34.

tribunes, and possibly providing also that the resolutions passed by the plebeians in their tribal assembly should bind the whole people.[1] This last measure, if actually carried at this time, was a notable victory for the people; but it is to be observed that similar measures are recorded for two other occasions: in 339 B.C. a Publilian Law provided that the sanction of the Senate (*patrum auctoritas*), hitherto required after a vote of the Assembly, must now be given beforehand, and was thus reduced to a merely formal assent; and in 287 B.C. the Hortensian Law removed the necessity of even this formality, by stating that the plebiscites passed by the plebeians in the *comitia tributa*, when proposed by a tribune, should differ only in form, not in force, from the laws (*leges*) passed in the *comitia centuriata* on the proposal of a magistrate.[2] Why the triple record should exist is not clear. Conceivably an early measure may have fallen into disuse or have been nullified by the patricians, and have been reaffirmed, as Livy would imply. More probably it was only the Hortensian Law that for the first time made the self-regarding ordinances of the plebeian corporation binding on the whole people, and Livy has confused this measure with the partial privileges given in earlier centuries. In any case, the plebeians had by 287 B.C. wrested from the patricians an enormous concession in establishing the sovereign power of the assembly which the tribunes dominated; and it seems clear that the Romans believed their plebeian institutions to be the result of "a revolutionary act which set up a State within the State." [3]

[1] Livy, III, 55. "Ut quod tributim plebes iussisset, populum teneret."
[2] "Ita factum est ut inter plebiscita et legem species constituendi interesset, potestas autem eadem esset" (Pomponius, *Digest*, I, ii, 2, 8). Cf. the common phrase, "sive haec lex est, sive plebiscitum."
[3] This illuminating phrase I borrow from H. Stuart Jones (*C. A. H.*, VII, 455), who remarks further (p. 458) that these institutions, looked at from

Meanwhile the plebeians had won other victories hardly less important, by compelling the patricians to open to them some of the great magistracies. The first proposals to allow plebeians to hold the consulship, in 445 B.C., were side-tracked by a masterpiece of compromise, in the institution of the "military tribuneship with consular power," an office open to plebeians. Between 445 and 367, consuls were elected in 28 years and "military tribunes" in 50 years. Only a few years later, plebeians were admitted to the consulship, the dictatorship, the censorship, and the praetorship; by 342 it was ordered that both consuls might, and one consul must, be plebeian. Various priesthoods were also opened to the people; and marriages between patricians and plebeians had been sanctioned in 445.

Superficially it might seem, then, that the struggle for freedom had been won; plebeians could legislate for Rome, and so far as eligibility for office is concerned their opportunities were theoretically better than those of the patricians. Indeed, it may well be maintained that the year 287 B.C. marks the high tide of democracy at Rome; and the Greek Polybius, living at Rome only a hundred years later, when the external forms of government were practically unchanged, was full of admiration for the balance of power between magistrates, Senate, and people.[1] In fact, however, the forces of oligarchy were deeply intrenched. The ple-

---

one point of view, "were revolution made permanent," but that because of the Roman habit of finding a *modus vivendi* among apparently discordant institutions, they became "revolution domesticated."

[1] Polybius, VI, 11–18. Similarly Cicero (*De Rep.* I, 45) points out that the Roman constitution combines democracy, aristocracy and monarchy. (See further, G. H. Sabine and S. B. Smith, *Cicero, On The Commonwealth*, Introduction, esp. pp. 39–99.) Tacitus, writing in a more disillusioned age, remarks (*Ann.* IV, 33) that "a constitution formed by selection of these elements it is easy to commend, but not to produce; or, if it is produced, it cannot be lasting."

beians had sought political power, partly, at least, as a means of remedying economic abuses; now that the prizes of office were within their grasp they found that they were apt to fall, if to plebeians at all, to those plebeians who had become wealthy and whose economic interests were not very different from those of the patricians. Thus aristocracy had come to consist as much in wealth as in birth; the real struggle was no longer between patricians and plebeians, as such, but between rich and poor. If plebeians won office, and passed into the Senate, they were apt to acquire the conservative attitude of their fellow-senators; even if they persisted as champions of democracy, they were a small minority in a powerfully conservative body. The office-holding aristocracy, both patrician and plebeian, was not greatly interested in helping the small farmers, who were more than ever in distress, and were being absorbed by the *latifundia*, the great estates. Even if the Assembly had nominally won its freedom to legislate, its members were mostly men who could not afford to devote much time to practical politics; hence power rested with the magistrates, men almost always chosen from the great families, whether patrician or plebeian, which had already achieved office, and still more with the Senate, the body which was at once the flywheel of the state and the almost exclusive domain of the hereditary office-holding class.[1]

[1] Cf. Viscount Bryce, *Modern Democracies*, II, 602. "Nature is always tending to throw power into the hands of the Few, and the Few always tend by a like natural process to solidify into a class, as the vapours rising from the earth gather into clouds. Fortunately the Class, by a like process is always tending to dissolve. . . . Thus Free Government cannot but be, and has in reality always been, an Oligarchy within a Democracy." See also the figures, prepared by H. J. Laski, in *Publications of the Fabian Society* (1928), showing that in the century and a quarter preceding the Labor Government of 1924 60 per cent (182 out of 306) of all the men who reached Cabinet rank in Great Britain were hereditary titled aristocrats; 209 of them had gone either to Oxford or to Cambridge; 119 came from Eton or Harrow.

The character of the Senate goes far to explain why Rome never proceeded further on the road to democracy. It was the only truly deliberative body at Rome. The members of the assemblies were now scattered throughout central Italy, and would not come to Rome to vote except on very important occasions; they could meet only when summoned by their magistrates, and even then they had no opportunity to discuss the proposals laid before them. And as the various classes of citizens were levelled, the differently organized assemblies, whose provinces of action differed little, seemed to have lost significance. The Senate, on the other hand, was almost continuously in session, and provided for full discussion. The large increase in the number of magistrates and the subdivision of their functions weakened the influence of the individual magistrates, even if they did not actually check one another; whereas the Senate gained by the influx of these magistrates, and became in effect the permanent reservoir of all Roman political talent and experience. Even if the Senate could not force its advice on a magistrate, as a matter of custom it was always consulted. The crucial dangers of the Samnite and still more of the Punic Wars imposed new burdens on the only institution at Rome that had a sufficient fund of experience in military and financial matters. If a general of tested ability was to be continued in his command; if new revenues were to be raised to carry on a war; if negotiations were to be made with a foreign state or terms with a conquered foe; finally, if a conquered territory was to be organized as a province, the only competent body to undertake the responsibility was the Senate. Indeed, the Senate was more truly representative of the interests of the people than were the assemblies, with their scattered memberships, or than any "representative" body (in the modern sense) that might have been devised to include members of

the new Roman subjects. During the stress of the second
Punic War and afterwards, to be sure, the Senate assumed
many powers which legally, as a merely advisory council, it
did not possess. No magistrate, whose office would expire
within a year, was likely to lead an effective opposition; least
of all those few members of the Senate, the *novi homines*,
none of whose ancestors had held office, and who were
usually debarred from speaking by the procedure of that
body. Nor was the tribunate any longer a strong instrument of opposition: it was chiefly wealthy plebeians who
held the office, and they were normally on good terms with
the nobility of hereditary office-holders. At least one tribune
could ordinarily be found to veto legislation disliked by the
Senate, or to propose to the people measures favored by the
Senate. Legislation and continuing policies, then, were controlled by the Senate, and the magistrates were chiefly the
executors of the measures approved by the Senate. Even
the procedure of the Senate was so hedged with restrictions
as to play into the hands of the conservatives. A meeting
could be held only when called by a magistrate, only on one
of the permitted days, and only in a consecrated place: it began at daybreak, and could not be prolonged after sunset;
the business to be transacted was not necessarily known in
advance, and remained secret until the *acta* (proceedings)
were published by Julius Caesar. The finding of unfavor-
able omens might vitiate a meeting: as late as Cicero's day it
was possible for an obstructionist to block the proceedings in
an important political investigation by announcing that he
was engaged in observing the heavens.

The result of the extraordinary growth of the Senate's
power from the fourth to the second century B.C. was that
the people were nominally and theoretically sovereign, but
did not actually rule. They were primarily farmers and

soldiers, interested in politics only as a means of economic reform, and ordinarily content to leave administration and legislation to their betters. The direct democracy of Athens would not have been feasible at Rome because the voters were too widely scattered, and the Assembly would have been impossibly large, not to mention differences of temperament. Nor was there any system of public education which would have taken the place at Rome of the Greeks' greater leisure and their adroit if amateurish democratic statesmanship. For better or for worse, the Roman farmers had to elect their rulers and trust them to govern well; this was in effect, though not in form, something like representative government. Their loyalty and their trust were on the whole justified as long as the Senate's patriotism and efficiency remained unquestioned, or during the Samnite and the Punic Wars. But with peace and greater prosperity the nobility became more selfish and short-sighted. "What will become of Rome when she will have no longer any state to fear?" asked the elder Cato, noting the ominous signs of relaxed discipline. The populace was thronging Rome, equipped with votes but without political experience; grievances that dated from the years before the great wars, but that had been endured with patriotic fortitude during the national danger, now cried for sympathetic attention under skilful leadership. Rome was coming to the end of an age; [1] mere average ability and honesty could no longer cope with the complex problems that followed the Punic Wars: problems of foreign policy, of landless farmers and hungry city-folk, of provincial administration, of dishonest officials. Too many classes of people had axes to grind, and compromises

[1] Cf. Mommsen: "500 years of extraordinary deeds and ordinary men between the Tarquins and Caesar." Note how few names of statesmen appear in Roman history before the Gracchi.

had become distasteful; the time had come for brilliant leadership, for autocratic control, for revolution. And the last hundred years of the Republic (roughly 133–31 B.C.) are a century of revolution, the background of which we must now consider in three important phases.

Most of the struggles of the revolutionary age arose from differences among Roman citizens; one problem remained from earlier days that concerned other people as well, — the relation of Rome to the conquered peoples of Italy. And here we may see once more two conflicting tendencies which we may call respectively the narrow and the far-sighted policies. As the patricians held the plebeians aloof till they were forced to share political privileges with them, so the Romans in general treated the Italians as aliens, till they were compelled to adopt the wiser and really more characteristically Roman policy of inclusion and incorporation. About 385 B.C. the Latin League was closed against new members; in 338 it was broken up, and Rome henceforth dealt with other towns separately. Citizenship meant the possession of a complex of public and private "rights"; and Rome found it convenient to classify her allies in various ways, admitting some to what were now called "Latin rights" or to other partial privileges, and keeping full Roman citizenship for the inhabitants of Rome, of "colonies," of allotted public lands, and of a few incorporated communities. Italy was becoming a checkerboard of carefully graded political units, all contributing in various ways to Rome's army, and sharing unequally in Rome's growing power; [1] most of them kept a considerable measure of local self-government. In early times there was no general desire on the part of these allied communities to claim full Roman

---

[1] Cf. Beloch, *Der Italische Bund*, map at the end; *C. A. H.*, VII, 820 (maps); and T. Frank, *Roman Imperialism*, pp. 33–40.

citizenship: it was forced on Tusculum in 381 and on revolting Privernum in 330;[1] Praeneste declined it during the second Punic War. Yet Hannibal found, to his dismay, that his invitations to Rome's Italian allies to revolt were seldom accepted; for there was security and some dignity in membership in a *municipium*, an allied town incorporated in the Roman state, even if the burdens of military service were considerable and the "rights" were wholly private, without votes or offices at Rome. And although the political value of citizenship decreased, especially for those who lived at a distance from Rome, the economic advantages of land-allotments to full citizens increased often at the expense of non-citizens.[2] Meanwhile the burdens of military service remained, and the arrogance and the requisitions of Roman officials were sometimes oppressive to mere subjects.[3] It is not surprising that the Italian allies became more eager for full membership in the Roman state, or that the old citizens of Rome became more jealous of their privileges.

The narrow policy triumphed in 187 B.C., when 12,000 Latins were ejected from Rome; ten years later, when booty was to be distributed, a law expressly forbade the allies from receiving equal shares with the citizens. There were not lacking a few Roman statesmen of sufficient breadth of view to champion the Italian allies; but all who successively proposed to enfranchise them were assassinated, so bitter was the opposition of land-holding senators, and even of the landless poor, who were not eager to share with new citizens whatever land was to be distributed. When such a proposal,

---

[1] Livy, VIII, 21. Many in the Roman Senate admired the speech of a frank Privernate who on this occasion pointed out that a lasting peace must be based on fair-play and good will; the consul himself commended him, remarking that only those who think of nothing but liberty are worthy of becoming Romans.

[2] E.g. the distributions in Cisalpine Gaul and Picenum, in 232.

[3] Cf. Livy, XLII, 1.

made by M. Fulvius Flaccus (125), was defeated, the town of
Fregellae promptly revolted, and was treacherously reduced;
a similar proposal from so good a friend of the Roman democracy as Gaius Gracchus (122), cost him much of their
support; and it was a renewal of the same proposal by M.
Livius Drusus (91) that caused his murder. The immediate
result was the terrible Social War.[1] Rome would have been
far wiser if she had done justice to the allies at once; for after
two years of fighting it was not Roman victory that brought
peace, but the enactment of two laws giving full Roman
franchise to Italian states not in rebellion and to individual
Italians who applied for citizenship within sixty days.
Henceforth the distinction between colonies and *municipia*
in the old sense vanished; a *municipium* now meant simply
a country town enjoying full Roman citizenship, with local
self-government. As such it developed during the next two
hundred years a vigorous life, within the larger organism of
the Empire, that is not the least important political achievement of Rome.

In the Social War, Rome stooped to conquer. She gained
immeasurably by making Romans of the allies; within a generation she could claim the Volscian Cicero and the Transpadane Gaul Virgil as true Romans.[2] But she might well
feel that the Social War was a tribute to her prestige. Other
empires had fought wars against rebellious or seceding subjects; only she had fought a war against those who wished
closer relations. So, too, the plebeians had sought not free-

---

[1] Social, because waged by the *socii*, "allies"; there is no suggestion in the
name of class warfare. On the whole, the trading coast towns of Italy, bene-
fiting by the expansion of Rome across seas, had reason to remain loyal to
Rome; it was the allies in the interior, farmers and military auxiliaries of
Rome, who revolted.

[2] Cisalpine Gaul south of the Po became part of Italy in 89; the rest of it
in 49, thanks to Julius Caesar.

dom from Roman rule, but full participation in the government. And, with rare exceptions, this remains true of her later history: "men do not seek to get rid of Rome as their ruler; they wish to become Romans, and, in that character, to help to rule both themselves and others." [1] Even during the Social War the allies paid Rome the compliment of imitating the Roman state as a city-state with consuls, senate, and assembly, and adopted the name of "Italia" for their capital (previously called Corfinium), the name thus being used for the first time in a political rather than a racial, sense. The idea was not wasted when Virgil came to write, less than two generations afterwards, the later books of the *Aeneid*. But for the Romans generally the question remained whether the narrow or the far-sighted policy was to prevail, as the *imperium* was extended over still wider territory. Were provincials to become full citizens, magistrates, senators, emperors? We shall see that opinions varied among citizens and among emperors, but that in the end Caracalla's Edict (212 A.D.) made Roman citizens of all free inhabitants of the Roman world.[2]

The Italian allies, we have just observed, had struggled for equal political privileges largely because of the economic opportunities attaching to them; the struggles at Rome itself during the century of revolution were also precipitated by acute economic conditions. The earlier struggles of the plebeians had grown partly from unjust laws of debt and still more from their difficulty in gaining access to the land. Several early reformers, notably C. Licinius Stolo (367 B.C.), had sought, like the Athenian Solon, to impose a limit on the amount of land that any individual might hold; but such laws were always evaded. Large estates grew larger; "squat-

---

[1] E. A. Freeman, Introduction to English translation of Mommsen's *History of Rome*, I, xviii.   [2] Cf. p. 257.

ters" quickly learned that possession was as good as a legal
title to the land, and small farmers facing ruin were apt to
sell out to those who had sufficient surplus to stand a bad
year. The Hannibalic War greatly aggravated the situation,
and also drained from the countryside the best of the farmer-
soldiers, many of them never to return, or, if they survived, only to find their farms desolate. Colonization in Italy
was no longer a military necessity, and actually stopped
in 157 B.C.; colonization across seas had not yet begun.
The governing class, though still unwilling to give political
status to the Italian "squatters" on the Roman public domain, was unwilling to provoke a conflict with them by
assigning the land occupied by them to individual Romans.
Nor were they willing to relinquish any of the land held by
members of their own class. For the senatorial order was
debarred, by the Lex Claudia (218 B.C.) from foreign trade,
lest foreign policy should be dictated by the interests of the
governing class. True it is that ways were found of evading
this legislation; for example, the nobles could hold shares in
commercial companies, and could engage in trade by the
agency of their slaves and freedmen. Nevertheless, the general result of the legislation was to drive the nobles into exploiting the land as their source of income, at the same time
that the introduction of new manners and oriental standards
of luxury and the demands of political life, of canvassing and
election-exhibitions, made a modest income seem like poverty.[1]

[1] The Lex Cincia (204), forbidding clients to make presents to their patrons, attempted to prevent the legal profession from being commercialized;
the nobles were to give their services. Already debarred from foreign trade,
and now cut off from making a living by the law, the senatorial class was the
more dependent on investments in land. As a matter of fact, however, the
Lex Cincia was evaded in various ways (e.g. by legacies; cf. G. Boissier,
Ciceron et ses Amis, pp. 86–90), in spite of frequent reënactments, till under
the Emperor Claudius legal fees, within a limit, were permitted. (Tacitus,
Ann. XI, 5–7.)

The new system of agriculture bore very hard on the freeman farmers. The Licinian limit of the size of farms had seldom, if ever, been enforced; now estates were bought up, seized, and in every way thrown into the *latifundia*, owned and managed by the nobles. Their motives are not in all cases to be condemned; for the state had shirked the division of newly conquered domain land, except to confirm "squatters" in possession; furthermore, it was far easier, even more economical, for the large holder with surplus capital, than for a pauper, to reclaim wild land for cultivation. Even so, the small peasant proprietors might have hoped to continue to win their bread from the soil but for a second and more serious matter. The large owners, who regarded their landed property simply as investment, took care to work it by the cheapest labor obtainable, and that meant usually slave labor.[1] Against this cheap labor, the freeman farmer found it hard to compete: he, unlike the slave and the freedman, must serve in the army; and if he were evicted from his farm he could seldom find employment as a hireling. Of course slave labor, though cheap, was inefficient and relatively unproductive, so that with the growing demand for wine and oil the great landlords found that their land made a better investment if turned into vineyards and olive yards; and many an abandoned farm afforded profitable pasturage. But all these forms of farming required less free labor; and the freemen trudged to Rome to live, in crowded *insulae*, the lives of paupers. Thus there were more mouths to be fed somehow, more votes to be angled for by the politicians, more grievances to be appeased. Yet the land could have been managed justly and productively without great difficulty if merely agricultural problems had been involved; it was the complication of the agrarian question by political

[1] Cf. p. 119.

considerations and by personalities that led to tragic consequences.

The commercial disabilities of the senatorial class were not shared by the order still known as the *equites* (though their military service as cavalry was no longer significant); on the contrary, they were a favored class, allowed to bid for government contracts and to farm the public revenues. Organized into societies with the financial support of large numbers of shareholders, and even of incognito senators, they acted as the middlemen of the state. They undertook contracts for the building, maintenance, and repair of public works, roads, and supplies; they leased the fisheries, salt works, mines, forests, and occasionally even public domains of tilled land. In an increasing degree they assumed the collection of all debts owed by individuals or by states to the public treasury, and as *publicani* they farmed out the revenues to subordinate collectors. They learned from the Italiote Greeks the methods of banking, and managed all kinds of exchange, money-lending, and the transfer of property. Not unnaturally their financial interests caused them to enter into politics, in order to secure favorable terms for their contracts. In opening up new territory for exploitation and in increasing the volume of business at Rome, the *equites* served a useful purpose; but they were not always either efficient or honest. The state-owned mines in Macedonia had to be closed, so demoralizing were their methods; and the revenues from the provinces suffered a shrinkage from the handling of dishonest officials. After allowance has been made for the considerable expenditures in the provinces for police and defense, — and here Rome usually did less rather than more than her duty, — it is doubtful whether any province except Sicily at this period produced for the state a net gain of any great amount. It is worth noting, too, that the Roman economy was in the main unproductive. Given by nature a central position in the Mediterranean, her functions became in an ever-increasing degree those of middlemen, of distributing agents, of carriers and brokers. Even her home industries were becoming no longer the concern of guilds of freemen, but were being managed by slaves and freedmen for the profit of their masters. Thus at the beginning of the century of revolution the line of cleavage between capitalists and proletariat had been drawn so distinctly that even those who were traditional rivals in political matters were, perhaps unconsciously, allied in economic opposition to the proletariat. Public policies were dictated largely by the motives of an oligarchy.

If the weaker Romans suffered from the oligarchy, the provincials suffered as much, with even less opportunity for redress. The provincial policy of Rome was not, to be sure, wantonly oppressive, but was rather the result of *laissez faire*. Most of the provinces had been reluctantly organized by the Senate from the territory acquired in the course of an unsought war of defense;[1] they had been surveyed by senatorial commissions of ten *legati*, and given charters which recognized local differences and preserved some measure of local autonomy.[2] More and more, especially after 146 B.C., the commercial classes brought pressure on the Senate to assume more freely the responsibilities of provincial government. The governors were simply ex-consuls or ex-praetors, sent out for a year with full powers, military and civil. But the fact that they were remote from the supervision of the Senate gave them the chance to be in effect kings for a year, an anomaly in the Roman system; the fact that their office

---

[1] Cf. pp. 48–50.
[2] Note that the discriminations shown among communities stamped full Roman citizenship as a privilege worth seeking.

lasted for only a year prevented them from seeking a real career in the office and from inaugurating far-sighted policies; and the fact that their office carried no salary tempted them to practice extortion in various crooked ways, whether to recoup themselves for previous political or personal expenses or to lay by a fortune for the future. The provinces were the absolute property of the Roman people, for the use of which their native inhabitants must pay taxes or tithes. This meant the gradual adoption of a theory new to the Romans, in which the ownership of a subject empire was substituted for leadership of a confederation. In amount the taxes were at first generally not excessive, — tithes (*decumae*) in most of Sicily (according to the plan of Hiero of Syracuse) and (after G. Gracchus [1]) in Asia; elsewhere a fixed tribute (*stipendium*) which in Macedonia was only half of the sum previously demanded by the kings. The governors were supposed to be bound by the charters of their provinces, and by the edicts which they promulgated on assuming office, — edicts which usually reaffirmed most of those of their predecessors; yet the legal rights of the provincials were absolutely within the discretion of the governors, and only those who had somehow acquired Roman citizenship, like St. Paul, had a right to the protection of the Roman law. No one pretended that the provinces were governed for their own good; it was well understood that they were being exploited for the benefit of the Roman state and of Roman provincial officials and men of business,[2] curbed slightly, if at all, by the permanent court of trial for cases of extortion tardily set up in 149 B.C. (by the Lex Calpurnia de Repetundis). Even the best Romans were curi-

---

[1] For the abuses that arose from the Gracchan system, see pp. 214, n.2; 216.

[2] Cf. W. Warde Fowler, *Social Life at Rome in the Age of Cicero*, pp. 60–96.

ously callous to the just claims of the provincials; ordinary Romans, like the worst, regarded provincial posts as stepping-stones in political or military careers amid the rough-and-tumble of party politics, or as especially attractive opportunities for commercial exploitation. Though it cannot be maintained that the failure of the republican government to deal fairly with the provinces had much to do with the actual fall of the Republic, it is no exaggeration to hold that the immeasurably improved condition of the provinces under the Empire is enough to justify the fall.[1] And of course it was not the provincials themselves who overthrew the Republic, but rather the vicissitudes of party politics at Rome and the need of controlling provincial governors commanding great armies. Within the century of revolution the constitution of the little Roman city-state, like its physical boundaries, had been quite outgrown; the empire and its resources were swamping the state; a master must be found.

In dealing with the claims of the Italian allies, the Roman farmers, and the provincials, we have sketched some of the background of the revolution, but without reckoning with the great personalities who emerged from the struggle and who successively dominated it.[2] We have space here to give brief mention to only a few of the greatest; but as they pass before us we must notice how curiously, how tragically, patriotism had to bow to circumstances, and how the constitution itself was warped and finally all but destroyed as men of iron will carved their careers amid the ruins of the old Roman city-state and the growing empire.

Plutarch tells us that it was the sight of the desolation in Etruria that moved the young Tiberius Gracchus to assume

[1] Cf. B. W. Henderson, *The Study of Roman History* (London, 1921), pp. 90–91.

[2] Mr. Henderson has a spirited page (*op. cit.*, p. 64) characterizing the deeds of these figures.

the championship of the democracy and to strike at the root of the oligarchical system and the economic evils engendered by it. As tribune (133 B.C.) he proposed at first a moderate measure, — the distribution of those state lands held by "squatters" in excess of the Licinian limit, with compensation to the present occupants. When the government, in response to the objections of the land-holders (among them some non-Roman Italians), opposed him, he retaliated, rather unfairly, by withdrawing the offer of compensation; when his colleague vetoed his proposal, he deposed his colleague and forced his bill through. This bold act, though contrary to precedent, was quite in keeping with the original theory that the tribunate was to be the expression of the sovereign people's will, rather than the tool of the Senate. In order to secure continued control, so as to carry out this measure and further benefits for the people, including the division of the new legacy of Attalus of Pergamum, he sought reëlection to the tribuneship. It was this, his second irregular act, that provoked a riot and his own death; for the first time blood had been shed at Rome in a civil disorder. From the failure of Tiberius Gracchus several political lessons were to be drawn. It was clear that any attempt to deal with the economic situation must rest on a broader political basis than he had at his command; it was necessary to break up the alliance of the Senate and the capitalists, and at the same time to acquire a more enduring position for the popular leader. The right of reëlection to the tribuneship was secured soon after his death; the other task was left to his younger brother. At the same time, the Italian problem was becoming acute, as the revolt of Fregellae showed (125). The next proposal for the benefit of the Romans must be undertaken in such a way as to make the Italians at least not the losers.

Gaius Gracchus succeeded in attaching to himself the support of the city populace by distributions of cheap grain,[1] and by granting them certain legal rights, as well as by his agrarian and colonial schemes (never realized except in small areas, and later overturned by senatorial legislation). At the same time he detached the *equites* from the Senate in two ways: by making them the jurors in the courts that tried formerly cases of extortion and now capital cases also; and by giving them the new province of Asia to pillage by a system of tithes replacing the older fixed tribute, for the collection of which the business men of Rome were invited to bid at auction.[2] Hitherto only a social and economic class, the *equites* now became a political order. In other ways, too, the younger Gracchus took occasion to humble the Senate, by usurping functions which they had arrogated to themselves (the management of the state grain-supply, colonization, etc.); and he freely used the tribunician initiative, foreshadowing the day when one-man rule was to supplant the oligarchy. It was when he undertook to deal with the Italians that he met with his defeat and death. That his proposal to extend the franchise to them should have been bitterly opposed by the Senate was to be expected, for it

---

[1] F. B. Marsh argues, "In Defense of the Corn-Dole," *Classical Journal*, XXII (1926), 10 ff., that Gracchus had to use grain distributions in order to relieve the city mob from their dependence on the aristocracy; the occasion was as pressing, and the result was as bad, as in the case of unemployment doles after the recent war. But Gracchus had also in mind schemes of road-building, etc., to employ idle labor, as have certain British and American and Italian economists, to tide over periods of depression.

[2] The tithes were increased for the provincials by the system of tax farming by the *publicani*, who extracted as much more as they could. Tax gathering had existed, of course, in the various countries before the Romans came; but the Gracchan system magnified the possibilities of abuse. Of the bad influence of the *publicani*, it could be said as early as 167 B.C. (Livy, XLV, 18): "Ubi publicanus esset, ibi aut ius publicanum vanum, aut libertatem nullam esse." Not altogether without reason did the Jews group together "publicans and sinners."

tended to decentralize the government. But the jealous opposition of the Roman populace showed how much more self-interest had weighed with them in their former support of Gracchus than any pure sense of justice. The Senate, supported by this mass of prejudice, contrived to out-manoeuvre him; an armed struggle in Rome resulted in his suicide and the summary execution of several thousands of his supporters, with the formal approval of the Senate. That he should have been cut off before his task was done is one of the greatest tragedies of Roman history, for it prevented him from testing his socialistic schemes and from remedying the abuses to which some of his measures immediately led. It therefore makes it difficult for us to appraise his statesmanship fairly.

From the point of view of economic reforms, the careers of the Gracchi must be considered comparative failures. The land distributions were in most cases blocked; and the importation of cheap food from Sicily and Sardinia for the city populace was anything but helpful to the farmers near Rome. Indeed, the Gracchi were quite unable, both through lack of understanding and because of the treachery of their supporters and their foes, to deal with the fundamental economic abuses. Moreover, the absence of any provision in the Roman constitution for continuous leadership on the part of reforming or democratic statesmen had compelled them to commit the rash experiment of straining the powers of the tribunate and of the assembly, long recognized by custom, and even to set a precedent for holding office illegally. The personal prestige of the two brothers cannot disguise the fact that their violent deaths brought the tribunate into disrepute; on the other hand, their attacks on the Senate weakened that body, just when it needed to be purged and strengthened, and stung it into committing the deeds of vio-

lence and corruption that launched the revolution. From a
political point of view their achievement must be considered
a failure, except that they left behind them possibilities of
democratic reform under responsible leadership.

Now in effect, if not in intent, the younger Gracchus was
achieving the position of a king, or of a tyrant. Yet, it was
not till Marius based his power on an efficient and devoted
army that tyranny became a fact. And however tyrannical
Gracchus may have been, he left a popular party (the
populares) but no personal successor, so that power returned to the oligarchy (who posed as the *optimates*, the
"best men"). But the conditions were changed; the aristocracy was compelled to govern with the instruments which
the democracy had forged. From this time, the mob was a
force to be reckoned with, and to be pampered with largesses
of grain. The rivalry of Senate and *equites* bred corruption
in the provinces. Scandalous cases occurred where just and
distinguished governors were prosecuted before an equestrian jury, and suffered the confiscation of their property as a
penalty for maintaining justice among the capitalists. "It
requires divine virtue to satisfy the *publicani* and yet to preserve the allies from ruin," wrote Cicero to his brother.[1] Not
falsely had Gaius Gracchus boasted that with the dagger of
his law (i.e. the equestrian juries) the nobility would stab
itself. Most galling of all was the circumstance that the
execution of the agrarian and colonial laws of the democracy
was left to be accomplished by the aristocracy, until by stages
they contrived to nullify the agrarian laws, and the *latifundia*
again spread across the countryside. An epoch of undisci-
plined misrule and social ruin ensued, attended by slave insurrections in Italy and the provinces, the outbreak abroad of
piracy, and the defeat of Roman armies under venal generals.

---

[1] Cicero, *ad Quint. Frat.* I, 1, 11.

The political experiments of Marius need not long detain us. He rose to power simply because he was a good disciplinarian and soldier, the one man who could finish the war against Jugurtha and check the barbarians on the northern frontier. But circumstances compelled him to become a party leader, the champion of the *equites*, who were impatient of senatorial mismanagement, and of the populace, who saw in him a new Gracchus. His loyal army, seasoned in many campaigns, and reorganized as an efficient fighting machine, was his chief asset; he was not only a novice in politics but a man of no political capacity. As a member of a coalition, with worthless demagogues for associates, he first attempted a programme not unlike that of the Gracchi; but in the hurly-burly of party strife he presently became the cat's-paw of the aristocracy, restoring order in a pitched battle in the Forum. After the Social War, in which the aristocrat Sulla (who had already received the formal surrender of Jugurtha) emerged with a brilliant reputation, Marius again became entangled in political intrigues, as a member of a reforming party, and invested with the supreme command in the Mithradatic War, though this identical command had already been given by the Senate to Sulla. The latter marched on Rome with his army (thus creating a precedent), reinstated the senatorial régime, and departed for the east. Marius, for a short time a fugitive, took advantage of the absence of Sulla and a new democratic revolution to return to Rome at the head of a motley army of rebels and slaves, and inaugurated a reign of terror; but he died the following year. Neither he nor his democratic associates had accomplished anything of lasting importance in the way of social or economic reform; but he had opened the eyes of all Romans to the single ominous fact that the future of Rome rested with the man who, by leading a loyal army, could command the continued confidence of whatever power, aristocratic or democratic, prevailed at Rome. The very principle of collegiate rule was crumbling. And more important than anything in the political struggles of the age is the change in temper of the Romans. After centuries of comparatively peaceful political development and schooling in self-government, they now were ready to draw the sword as the quickest, perhaps the only way to settle differences. The exploitation of subject peoples in Italy and the provinces had turned their heads, and had given their magistrates and generals irresponsible powers; the philosophy of the upper classes was becoming sceptical or cynical; the assembly and the armies were filled with men of servile, often of oriental, origin, whose respect for Roman traditions of discipline and liberty and self-control were slight. Could anything less than autocracy save Rome from ruin?

It was autocracy on the part of Sulla, at any rate, that restored order at Rome and that brought her rapidly nearer to the autocratic system of the Empire. During his brief intervention at Rome, in 88 B.C., after expelling Marius, he reënthroned the Senate, at the expense of the tribunate, his army overawing all opposition. On his return from the east, in 82, he fought his way into Rome, and made himself dictator, the first since the days of Hannibal. Though with rare self-denial he resigned his office as soon as his work was done, it was a reactionary constitution that he had established. Distributions of grain were abolished; the courts were taken from the *equites* and restored to the Senate, and other well organized courts were set up; the only assembly allowed important functions was the centuriate, in which tribunes were impotent, and the tribunes' wings were otherwise clipped; the enlarged Senate was to be recruited not by the censor but by the automatic inclusion of all men elected to the quaestorship; the number of magistrates was increased, and the order of the *cursus honorum* was fixed; [1] the functions of consuls and praetors, and the assignment and tenure of pro-magistrates in the provinces were regularized. The reform of the courts and the executive machinery was well conceived, and endured; the rest of the constitution, though consistent, was at least two hundred years behind the spirit of the times, and failed to reckon both with persistent economic abuses and with the new conditions created by the continued military commands of statesman-soldiers. Further seeds of discontent were sown by the Sullan proscriptions and the assignment of Italian lands to Sulla's soldiers; both the peasants thus dispossessed and his veterans, who were not suited by nature to farming, soon provided fuel for the attempted revolution of Catiline.

Such was the wooden constitution under which Cicero and Pompey and Julius Caesar grew up. In the absence of any organized democratic leadership, or of any single issue that could provide a rallying-point, senatorial mismanagement went on, as the career of the governor Verres in Sicily gives sufficient evidence. Pompey, though a former lieutenant of the aristocrat Sulla, was preëminently a soldier, and found, after rebuffs from the Senate, that his best prospects of advancement lay in such a command as the democratic party might bestow; accordingly he formed a coalition with Crassus and the democracy (71), and demolished much of the Sullan constitution, giving the *equites* a third share in the juries, and restoring most of the power of the tribunate; thus the *equites* once more became the rivals of the Senate, and the lower magistracies became the tools of the generals. Pompey's great opportunity came when he received from

---

[1] The magistracies now comprised 20 quaestors, 4 aediles, 8 praetors, and 2 consuls.

the Assembly the command against the pirates (by the Lex Gabinia, 67) and then against Mithradates (by the Lex Manilia, 66), with the support of democrats like Caesar, of the business interests, and of the cautious Cicero, who hoped for the best. The Senate was nominally in control of domestic affairs; nevertheless, every conservative in Rome, and not a few democrats, looked forward with anxiety to the day of Pompey's return, for never before had the people conferred such powers on a single man.

During Pompey's long absence in the East, when there was no considerable army in Italy, the times seemed ripe for one more attempt at revolution.[1] Though there was no single issue, there were the old grievances; and debtors, spendthrift Sullan veterans, ousted Italian peasants, and slaves had little to lose by striking a blow for a general overturn. It was on these elements that the disgruntled aristocrat M. Sergius Catilina depended; when balked of the consulship, he undertook to ride into power by leading a rebellion. His first attempt (66) was inchoate, and was discovered prematurely. Caesar was doubtless implicated; but he had designs on the control of Egypt, as a counterweight to Pompey's power, and was perhaps using Catiline as a cat's-paw. Even Cicero was not yet really hostile to Catiline,[2] and the next year thought of defending him against a charge of extortion, though with grave suspicions that he was guilty.[3] In 64, however, when Catiline again sought the consulship for the following year, Cicero, a *novus homo*, was put forward by the Senate and *equites* as the defender of law and order, and was elected. Catiline decided to make one more desperate attempt, and prepared arms and supplies in

---

[1] Sallust, *Cat.* XVI, 4.
[2] Sallust, *Cat.* XXII.
[3] Cicero, *ad Att.* I, 2. Catiline, though not defended by Cicero, as it turned out, was acquitted; but this proves little.

various places; he hoped to murder the consuls and his rivals at the elections and to force his own election as consul. Again Caesar was probably sympathetic. The conspiracy was defeated by the effectiveness of Cicero's secret service and his promptness and courage in denouncing Catiline, and as much by the blunders of Catiline's accomplices in Rome. The Senate, remembering the proscriptions of Marius, gave Cicero supreme authority, by what amounted to martial law,[1] to cope with the situation. Catiline tried to brazen out the matter, then betook himself to his army, and died fighting in Etruria. By every outward test, Cicero had saved the state, as the Senate declared, and as he was never weary of reminding the public. Yet it was only a few years later that his personal enemy Clodius was able to take up Cicero's summary execution of a handful of the Catilinarian conspirators as sufficient reason for exiling him. How was this possible? And how could Caesar have given even tacit support to the conspiracy? Was Catiline, after all, a martyr to the cause of democracy and was Cicero the ruthless tool of the oligarchy?

One need not "whitewash" Catiline completely, or pretend that "the plot was largely the fabrication of Cicero";[2] yet it is easy to overlook the real grievances of the men led by Catiline, grievances which Cicero hardly ever seems to mention, and for which he has no constructive remedy except the support of the old constitution and the conservative defenders of the *status quo*. The "republican" government was indeed a corrupt oligarchy, dominated by a caste; it had brutally assassinated all the democratic reformers, and proved that the only hope of the people lay in such reforms

---

[1] The words of this, the *senatus ultimum consultum*, passed only in times of grave danger, run: "Let the consuls see to it that the state suffer no harm."

[2] As E. S. Beesly contends, in *Catiline, Clodius, and Tiberius* (London, 1878).

as only a violent revolution could render possible. Catiline himself had tried every legitimate means of winning power. Nevertheless, there is no reason to suppose that he had the ability or the desire to carry out a genuine programme of reform such as Caesar, when sobered by experience and responsibility, carried out after his successful *coup*, fourteen years later. Catiline probably merely sought unscrupulously to capitalize the elements of discontent for his own aggrandizement. He failed; and Cicero's really brilliant success was great enough to excuse his vanity in after years, save only the odious line in his poem on his consulship: "O fortunatam natam me consule Romam!" What cannot be so easily forgiven is his blindness to the conditions that the Catilinarian conspiracy revealed, and that were no whit improved by the necessary achievement of the moment, the crushing of Catiline. Cicero's one programme, then and always, was the *concordia ordinum*, the harmony of Senate and *equites*, — in other words, a legalist's programme. Personally high-minded, and the philosophic exponent of republican principles against all autocracy, he was the personification of constitutionalism.[1] Even when he had to determine the fate of the Catilinarian conspirators, he hesitated to execute them summarily, as he could have done by virtue of the full authority already given him by the Senate to do whatever the situation might demand. He sought not merely to prove the gravity of the situation but to gain the special sanction of the Senate for inflicting the death

[1] A modern analogy might be the character of the Republican party in the United States, whose principles can be defined only as those of a coalition of natural conservatives, economic individualists, industrial but (generally) not agricultural protectionists, historic Federalists, Unionists, and Imperialists. Of course the Democratic party is also hybrid. Within a smaller sphere, an even better parallel would be such phenomena as the National Security League, the Sentinels of the Republic, and 100 per cent Americanism.

penalty. Nevertheless, Clodius did not fail, a few years later, to point out to the popular party the enemy who had executed a citizen without a trial. Neglected by the Senate and by Pompey, and at times safe only when protected by Caesar, whom he distrusted, it was not till the murder of Caesar that Cicero once more emerged from retirement as the leader of the Senate for one vigorous year. The age was not for the constitutionalist but for the man of action, for Pompey and Caesar.[1]

In 61 B.C. the great Pompey returned from his vast eastern conquests to Italy, disbanded his army, celebrated a triumph advertising his achievements, and asked the Senate to confirm his deeds and give land to his veterans. Now that his army was disbanded, the Senate let him bide his time, remembering his democratic aberrations during his consulship, and not forgetting that his great command had come from the Assembly. Cicero hoped to save Pompey for the Senate; but Crassus, chief of the *equites*, cleverly succeeded in completing the alienation, and Caesar induced Pompey and Crassus to pool their personal interests with his in the so-called "First Triumvirate" (60 B.C.). Pompey's demands were to be carried by the threat of Caesar's army; Crassus was to win certain concessions for the *equites*; Caesar, shrewdest of the three, claimed for himself the consulship, with the prospect of securing afterwards such a prominent governorship as would make him, he privately dared hope, as powerful as Pompey. A futile attempt was made to include Cicero in the scheme.

[1] Modern estimates of Cicero and Caesar vary significantly according to the political background of the critic. The Prussian Mommsen can see little good in the theorist Cicero, and eulogizes the efficient bureaucrat Caesar; liberals like Boissier and Fowler see more that is precious in Cicero's championship of republican principles, even in failure. How easy it is to be prophetic *after* the event, and yet how striking and illuminating are the disagreements of prophets!

Before he won the consulship (59 B.C.), at the age of forty-one, Caesar had shown few signs of his coming greatness. A patrician by birth, but a democrat by his marriage connections, he had tried his hand at prosecuting corruption and at democratic agitation; he had shown great courage and some skill as a soldier, especially in Spain; he had made high office, including that of Pontifex Maximus, contribute to political scheming. But he was thus far distinguished chiefly as a man about town with great debts and greater ambitions, a demagogue whose hopes had been bound up with unsuccessful plans of the popular party, — the opposition to the Sullan régime, Catiline's conspiracy, proposals to redivide public lands in Italy, and hopes of getting control of the food supply from Egypt. The consulship exhibited his decision in the ruthless way in which he overrode the Senate and his conservative colleague and dealt only with the Assembly. Thus Pompey's veterans were given land, senatorial opposition being cowed by Pompey's hints of violence; Pompey's acts were ratified, and the *equites* were given their concessions. Caesar's interests were now served by the passing of an agrarian bill in the interest of the populace, and by the assignment to himself of the governorship of Cisalpine Gaul (to which Transalpine Gaul was soon added) for five years. With an eye to the future, he married his daughter to Pompey, thus setting a precedent for the dynastic marriages of his successors. In all this he showed political adroitness, but hardly statesmanship. There is real statesmanship, however, in the law that he carried for the scientific control of provincial government, although his own record in Gaul violated several parts of it.

Caesar's campaigns in Gaul, undertaken for reasons of personal ambition, accomplished far more than Caesar himself had contemplated; and they witnessed an enormous growth in his sense of responsibility. During his nine years' absence from Rome he kept in close touch with the political situation, guarding lest either foes or associates take advantage of him. Cicero, to be sure, was no longer to be feared; his implacable attitude had caused Caesar before his departure to unleash Clodius, and Clodius had driven Cicero into an exile of a year (58–57), after which he was comparatively powerless. Pompey was becoming once more the hope of the Senate, and was given control of the food supply; but Caesar and Pompey, never good friends, were becoming estranged, and Pompey resented Caesar's having blocked his hopes of building up power by a commission in Egypt. Caesar effected a reconciliation of the triumvirate at the Conference of Luca (56); his command was lengthened by five years; Pompey and Crassus were to have the consulship in the next year, after which Pompey was to go for five years to Spain, and Crassus for as long to Syria. Crassus did go to Syria, and met an inglorious end at the hands of the Parthians (53). Pompey lingered in Rome, which was seething with brawls and corrupt politics, while his army was being trained in Spain. With the death of his wife Julia (Caesar's daughter) and of Crassus, he had few remaining bonds with Caesar. When the riots at Rome went past endurance, it was natural that the Senate at last turned to him for help; Pompey was therefore made "sole consul" in 52. He not only restored order but passed a law dealing with provincial commands in such a way as to embarrass Caesar very seriously at the end of his governorship. For two years, while Caesar completed the conquest of Gaul, the former associates and their agents engaged in proposals and counter-proposals intended to manoeuvre each other into disadvantageous positions. Finally the Senate virtually declared Caesar a public enemy, and Pompey became the official champion of the Senate and the constitution. Caesar crossed the Rubicon (49 B.C.) and began the war on the technical ground that violence had been offered to two tribunes who had vetoed a decree aimed at him. But matters had gone far beyond legal points of difference, and both leaders had cast the die for a struggle to the bitter end. Where both were concerned simply with personal advantage, not with genuine political or social issues, it is not profitable to debate the responsibility for the Civil War that followed. Both were tarred with the same brush. But Caesar, who had once sought to gratify personal ambition by leading the democratic party, and was about to prove himself as autocratic as any man who ever held power in Rome, had also a genius for bold and constructive statesmanship; whereas Pompey, who happened to have the sanction of the Senate and to seem to be the champion of republicanism (inconsistently enough, in view of his former autocratic powers and his debt to the Assembly), was bankrupt of ideas. Yet Pompey seemed also to control the real loyalty of most of Italy and most of the provinces, as well as the food supply of Italy.

Pompey's advantages melted away, however, before the rapid and determined attack of Caesar. While Pompey was training his raw recruits in Greece, Caesar was securing his own rear by crushing Pompey's army in Spain, and setting up a government in Rome and building a fleet. The duel between the armies, unwisely accepted by Pompey at the instance of his senatorial advisers, was fought on the plain of Pharsalus, in Thessaly (48 B.C.); Pompey's army was routed, and he fled to Egypt, where he was treacherously murdered. But opposition to Caesar was not yet crushed. He established, with unexpected difficulty, Cleopatra on the throne of Egypt, and restored order in Asia

Minor; after returning to Rome for a few months he subdued most of the remaining senatorial forces at Thapsus, in Africa (47 B.C.). The implacable Cato, great-grandson of the elder Cato, won fame and the epithet of Uticensis by his deliberate suicide at Utica after the battle had shown further resistance to be idle. Only one more rebellion against Caesar remained to be quelled in Spain a year later.

Decision, tireless activity, and personal courage had made Caesar supreme in Rome. Not his least important source of power, however, was his extraordinary clemency. He disappointed all fears of a renewal of the proscriptions of Marius; he regularly pardoned his captives, and even employed his recent adversaries as responsible officials. Thus he made the staunch republican Marcus Junius Brutus his governor of Cisalpine Gaul. His enfranchisement of the Transpadane Gauls at the beginning of the war had won him many soldiers. And his moderate policy in restoring credit at Rome had both created confidence and eased the difficulties of the debtors.

Caesar's personal supremacy was above dispute; the only question was what sort of position he would choose to assume. He saw clearly enough that the machinery of the republic could no longer govern the empire. Yet he was not ready at once to use the title of *rex* for his centralized power, but preferred such accumulations of republican titles, incompatible under the Republic, as made him in effect a despot. The consulship, the dictatorship, the tribunician power, the censorship, the office of *pontifex maximus*, the epithet of *pater patriae*, all enhanced his dignity and his growing popularity, though it was the command of the army that silenced all opposition. There were those who believed that he aimed at undisguised monarchy; and it is likely enough that if he had lived longer he would have dropped republican disguises. As it was, he established the cult of Venus Genetrix, claiming divine descent for his family, like any oriental despot, and regarded his dwelling as a *templum*; in the eastern half of the empire he was revered as "god," "savior," and "benefactor of the world." [1] So far as seemed practicable, he acted through the Senate and the Assembly; but the Senate was now greatly increased in numbers (to a total of 900) by the inclusion of large numbers of his retainers from all ranks and even from Gaul, and once more became a mere advisory body which regularly approved the carefully prepared bills submitted to it. Nor was the ex-democrat any longer dependent on the support of the popular party, though much of his legislation was for the benefit of the people.

Within the last two crowded years of his life, Caesar found time to carry out an amazing series of constructive measures, among them the reform of the calendar, the control of his veterans and of the city populace by colonization, sumptuary laws, and other measures intended to establish a more sound economy. Most valuable of all was the law (the Lex Julia Municipalis) establishing a "normal type of constitution, primarily for Italian towns, but applicable for extension to the provinces. . . . Each Italian town was, *mutatis mutandis*, a miniature Rome. They were self-governing municipalities, dependent of course in the last resort on the central sovereign authority, of which they were still in theory, though no longer in practice, participants. There were no vexatious interferences with local concerns. There was a respectable municipal career, with specific duties and privileges, open to all, and to the few the chances of imperial promotion." [2] Thus within the empire there grew up in-

---

[1] Cf. pp. 342–345.
[2] E. G. Hardy, *Six Roman Laws*, p. 140. This book contains a convenient translation, with introduction, of what remains of the law.

numerable municipalities with a large amount of home rule,
in which the citizens elected the magistrates, and the more
substantial citizens might hope to become magistrates and
then members (*decuriones*) of the city council, which enacted
statutes. This law, at once liberal and conservative, was
one of the strongest forces for Romanization throughout the
empire. Other measures, — the creation of frontiers on the
northeast and the east, and various ambitious engineering
projects, — Caesar had to leave to his successors; for in the
midst of his work, on the Ides of March, 44 B.C., he was
struck down by the daggers of a group of dissatisfied nobles.
Cassius was animated by personal spite; Brutus, by philosophical conceptions of liberty; the rest chiefly by resentment against Caesar's increase in the number of officials and
the consequent decline in power of a swollen senate.[1]

The assassins' daggers found the one weak point in Caesar's rule: he had had no time to provide for a successor to
his position. Was the *regnum* to perish with the *rex*? If not,
who was to be the new king? Over this question the state
was again plunged in civil war. Against the conspirators,
who commanded the support of the Senate, stood Mark
Antony, once Caesar's lieutenant and now the professed
avenger of his death. He cleverly capitalized the generosity
of his master and rose to power on the mounting tide of resentment against the murderers. But among the other
avengers was a stripling of nineteen, Gaius Octavianus,
great-nephew, heir, and adopted son of Caesar. His was a
delicate position. Slighted by Antony, whose ally he would
naturally have become, he enrolled a legion on his own account, and won over two more legions of Antony's. Surely
he did not wish to help Antony to climb higher at his own

---

[1] Cf. F. B. Marsh, "The Roman Aristocracy and the Death of Caesar,"
Classical Journal, Vol. XX (May, 1925).

expense; nor, on the other hand, was he ready to let the Senate use him without stint in curbing Antony. For a time he assisted in the rout of Antony and his associates, against whom Cicero was directing his fierce *Philippics*; when Antony was defeated, the Senate was ready to dispense with the services of Octavian, "a young man who was to be praised, given honor, and put out of the way." [1] Rebuffed by the Senate, and refused the consulship, he effected a reconciliation with Antony and Lepidus (who controlled the important province of Gallia Narbonensis), and formed the "Second Triumvirate" (43 B.C.). In the disgraceful proscriptions that followed, each member of the triumvirate pricked for slaughter the names of his enemies; and Octavian allowed Antony's assassins to still forever the fiery tongue of Cicero. A year later (42), at Philippi, the united avengers of Caesar defeated Cassius and Brutus; and the hopes of the senatorial party were practically at an end.

The triumvirs proceeded to divide the Roman world among themselves; but they and their retainers at once fell to wrangling and warfare. Again reconciled, they agreed that Antony was to command in the East, Octavian in the West, while Lepidus was to have Africa. The third member of the triumvirate, like Crassus in the first triumvirate, was presently eliminated from consideration, but by his own treachery; only two men were left to dispute the world. But Antony found the charms of Cleopatra absorbing, and the treasury of Egypt useful; and he enjoyed playing the king in Egypt and the king-maker among the petty principalities to the east. In effect, he was making Alexandria the capital of a new empire. Meanwhile, Octavian, with the aid of Agrippa, was suppressing the revolt of Pompey's son Sextus,

---

[1] "Laudandum adolescentem ornandum tollendum" (Cicero, *ad. Fam.* XI, 20).

pacifying the frontiers, invading Germany and the Danube regions, and restoring order in Italy. Antony grew more and more jealous of this cool, active youth. Charges and counter charges flew back and forth, till Octavian secured the abrogation of his rival's command, — the command of that slave of Cleopatra, — and the declaration of war against Cleopatra. At Actium, on the northwest coast of Greece, the fleets met on a fateful day in 31 B.C. Eastern luxury and despotism were vanquished by western discipline and the forces of ordered liberty; an Armada of heavy ships by light galleys; Cleopatra's misguided and misunderstood retreat-signal by Agrippa's resolution and watchfulness; the setting star of the worn-out adventurer Antony by the rising star of the clear-eyed young adventurer Octavian.[1] Before many months Antony had stabbed himself; and Cleopatra, who had won the hearts of Caesar and of Antony, found Octavian impassive, and put the poisonous asp to her breast.[2] Once more the Roman world had a single master.

[1] Well does Virgil (*Aen.* VIII, 675-713) picture the contrast of Italy, Senate, Roman people, and household gods, ranged against barbarian hordes, an alien queen, and monstrous alien gods. But the contrast, recent in Virgil's own experience, colors also his picture of another alien queen and the threat of domination by another oriental power; Dido is partly Cleopatra, and the Aeneas who denies her, in spite of all temptations to be an Antony, is partly Octavian.

[2] Cleopatra, the young Greek (not Egyptian, of course!) who sat on the throne of the Ptolemies, is a figure worth understanding. She captivated Julius Caesar (who gave her a son and a house in Rome) and Antony, but not Octavian. Horace gloats over her after Actium (Epode 5) but not after her death (*Odes* I, 37), and forebears naming Antony. Shakspere's *Antony and Cleopatra* contains superb poetry, and some fine scenes, but fails somehow to move one; G. B. Shaw's *Caesar and Cleopatra* contains delightful satire, but could have been written as well of any other hero and heroine. Not to be overlooked are the three sonnets of J. M. Heredia (the Cuban) in *Les Trophées*.

2. EFFICIENCY AND DECAY

The young victor of Philippi and of Actium had fought to avenge Caesar and to defend his personal privileges against a rival. For all his coldness and hardness, his heart would have kindled a little if he could have foreseen how different a light was to gather about his name and career after nearly half a century of power. But for the moment he had to decide what rôle to assume on his return to Rome, and all the world hung on his decision. Was he to proclaim himself a king? The example of Caesar warned him sufficiently against so great an offense to Roman feeling. Was he to restore the power of the people, and lead it like a Pericles or a Gracchus? Heir though he was of the democratic party, he knew how incompetent was the city rabble to govern the vast empire. Should he then restore the power of the aristocracy and retire, as Sulla had done? But the restored aristocracy of Sulla had been notoriously corrupt; and now, after two generations more of civil war, there were few remaining nobles of the old families on whom he could rely for honest and efficient government. He must exercise the real control; but he must show at least outward respect for the body that represented the great Roman tradition of public service, and he must use capable administrators wherever he could find them. For the old collegiate principle was substituted a new partnership, or "dyarchy,"[1] between the Senate on one hand and Octavian (and his successors) on the other. This was not genuine republicanism, and henceforth outspoken republicanism was the creed of only a minority of senators

---

[1] Mommsen's term. As a matter of fact, Italy was ruled more and more by the emperor, though Senate and consuls kept many of their functions; the dyarchy is characteristic chiefly of the provinces, which were divided between Senate and emperor.

and Stoic reactionaries, the official "opposition" party of
the Empire; but the rest hardly realized how completely the
Republic had ceased to exist, except in certain matters of
form. But what was Octavian's personal position to be?
In 29 B.C. Octavian returned to Rome and celebrated a
triple triumph.[1] The next year or the following, after holding a census and nominally restoring the dignity of the Senate, he laid down all his powers, — that is, the command
against Cleopatra formally conferred on him and all the
powers irregularly assumed, — and from the Senate and
People received instead the *imperium* in several concurrent
forms for definite periods. Over all the frontier provinces,
containing armies, he was given control; and even in the
older, more peaceful provinces, which were still governed by
magistrates responsible to the Senate, he came to hold
transcendent powers (*maius imperium*). These powers,
given for ten years, were later confirmed for periods of five
or ten years. For five years, beginning in 27 B.C., and twice
thereafter, he held the consulship. After 23 B.C. it was
chiefly by virtue of the tribunician power that he controlled
legislation; this office served also to mark him as champion of
the people. Other special privileges enabled him to enter the
pomoerium without giving up his military *imperium*, and defined his status as superior to that of all other magistrates except the consuls, whose dignity he shared; like them he could
summon the Senate and introduce business before it. The
dictatorship and a life consulship he refused. But in spite of
the avowedly limited and temporary nature of the republican offices that he held, and held for the most part only in
accordance with specified precedents, his prestige grew as

[1] The most important source for this and the following statements is the
autobiography known as the *Monumentum Ancyranum* (cf. above, p. 29).
See the edition by E. G. Hardy (Oxford, 1923), with introduction, translation,
and commentary.

the benefits of peace and renewed prosperity became evident. According to the point of view of the observer, his position was either an impossibly inconsistent one or the palpably successful establishment of a constitutional monarchy, the first in history.[1] At home he was a republican official, the foremost of the magistrates, further dignified by the term *princeps*, "chief," which had been used by Cicero of the first citizen in the state; [2] abroad he was seen to be a personal ruler, in effect a king. In Egypt, indeed, he was a king, the heir of the Ptolemies, as we shall see.[3] At home he refused formal worship, unlike Julius Caesar, but accepted in 27 the religious title Augustus, which became for him and some of his successors a proper name; [4] in the East it designated him as one of those autocrats or gods, like the kings of Persia or like Alexander the Great, to whom homage or worship were due.[5] Thus he strove to be all things to all men, and not without success. His ambiguous position suited local fashions everywhere; among the republicans of Rome he was a republican, and among the kings of the Orient he was a king. Caesar he was, as heir and adopted son of the dictator; *imperator* (whence our word "emperor"), as *generalissimo* of the Roman armies; [6] *princeps*, as the first citizen of the empire.

During the first eight years of his rule (27–19 B.C.) Augustus was concerned chiefly with the organization of the prov-

---

[1] F. F. Abbott, *Roman Politics*, p. 33, takes the latter view.

[2] So H. F. Pelham proves (*Outlines of Roman History*[4], p. 370; *Essays in Roman History*, pp. 49–60); another view derives the title from the holder's position as first in list of the Senate. For Cicero, see below, p. 294, n. 1.

[3] P. 237.

[4] One of the months was also given this name, in honor of him; Romans would not fail to observe that all the months that had proper names were named for gods. Cf. p. 345.

[5] See further pp. 345–347.

[6] He also employed the title *imperator* as a *praenomen*.

inces. Professing to continue the traditional policy of the
Senate, he showed a reluctance to annex new provinces, preferring to erect buffer kingdoms along the frontier and to
deal with client princes, like Herod in Judaea. Nevertheless,
he could not choose but take over the control of Egypt; and
the times were ripe for the organization as provinces of the
three Gauls beyond the Alps, of the still unsubdued western
part of Spain as Lusitania, and in Asia Minor of Cilicia,
Galatia, and Pamphylia; the provinces of the Danube region
he added later. If the centralized rule of the principate
needs any defense, a sufficient justification is to be found in
the transformed government of the imperial provinces.
Three-fourths of the Roman world, including all the regions
where armies were needed, was under the direct responsibility and control of the emperor; his considered policies,
based on a knowledge of the whole empire, continued over
long periods of time. No longer were these provinces at the
mercy of a succession of predatory governors who had no
knowledge of local conditions and who wished only to feather
their own nests within their brief year of office; of rival generals whose one desire was to prove themselves indispensable men by provoking unnecessary wars that might end in
booty and triumphs; of greedy *publicani* and tax-gatherers
without conscience. There was indeed little opportunity for
such tyranny. For in the emperor's provinces the governors were carefully selected with an eye to ability and character, and were kept in office long enough to become experts
in government and familiar with provincial problems. Since
they, unlike their republican predecessors, received generous
fixed salaries, and might be promoted to more responsible
positions, they were no longer tempted to be "on the make"
at the expense of their subjects; on the contrary, they had a
powerful incentive to make a real career as provincial gover-

nors by studying the welfare of their subjects. And since foreign relations were Caesar's affair, and practically all Roman armies were Caesar's armies, even triumphs being celebrated by him instead of by his generals, the only military glory that remained to be won was the glory of carrying out his commands with speed and resolution. To the more important provinces Augustus sent as governors senators of consular or praetorian rank; to some of the minor provinces he assigned equestrian governors; he regularly employed *equites* in the numerous financial positions throughout the empire. These equestrian officials, procurators, and the like, were directly responsible to him, and served as a powerful check on the governors. The *publicani* were gradually ousted from their control of tax-farming; provincial lands and their resources were leased to tenant proprietors who paid revenue directly to the state. Naturally the local organization differed in the various provinces; but some of the details were continued or borrowed from the systems that had long been in operation in Egypt and in Alexander's empire. Agriculture and industry, under capitalistic systems, flourished again.

In the comparatively few provinces still ruled by the Senate, the improvement was less obvious; but these were the provinces in which the absence of an army made abuses less dangerous. And even here the supervision of Augustus was considerable, especially through the presence of his financial officials.[1] The same social tendencies prevailed as in the emperor's provinces, — prosperity and the steady growth of municipalities that employed men's political propensities and went far to compensate for the policy of Augus-

---

[1] A senatorial court for expediting trials for extortion existed in Cyrene. In Tacitus and in Pliny's *Letters* only 27 trials for extortion are mentioned, of which 20 resulted in convictions.

tus and those of his successors who, unlike Julius Caesar, were very sparing in their extension of the Roman franchise to provincials. As a matter of fact, Augustus could not have found enough capable civil servants with whom to govern autocratically all the municipalities of the empire, or the necessary funds, even if such had been his desire.

One country Augustus had reason not to treat as a province in the ordinary sense. The example of Antony warned him against letting another Roman use Egypt to further his personal ambitions; moreover, he realized that it could be made the granary of Rome, and he could not afford to let it fall into another's hands.[1] Accordingly he claimed most of Egypt as his personal domain, appropriated the revenues for his private treasury, and made himself the political heir of the Ptolemies. The people were his tenants; he, and not Roma, was worshiped by them; the old autocratic organization was taken over, with the same local units (*nomes*) and officials (*nomarchs*, and over them three *epistrategoi*, or major generals).[2] No senator was allowed to set foot in Egypt without the express permission of the emperor; his personal representative, as viceroy, was called Prefect of Egypt, and was always to be of equestrian rank. One of the tragedies of Virgil's life was the end of his friend, the elegiac poet Gallus, whose head was so turned by his quasi-regal position as Prefect of Egypt that he accepted divine honors; the Senate referred his case to the courts recommending a sentence of exile and confiscation of property, and Augustus showed anger, whereupon Gallus committed suicide.[3]

---

[1] Cf. Tacitus, *Ann.* II, 59; *Hist.* I, 11.

[2] It is worth noting that he had some idea of imposing a similar system on the comparatively unorganized country of Gaul, subdividing it into districts under native chiefs, and compelling the population as serfs to carry the burden of the wars against Germany.

[3] Cf. R. S. Conway, "The Fall of Cornelius Gallus," in *New Studies of a Great Inheritance*, pp. 105–111.

The provincial municipalities, organized like miniature Romes, and filled with local civic pride, vied with one another in their zeal to become the "first city" or *metropolis* of their provinces. Paul of Tarsus boasted that he was "a citizen of no mean city." Ancient cities in the Levant, mushroom cities in the African desert, garrison towns in Gaul and Britain, show like Pompeii an approximation to the Roman type of city, with forum, amphitheatre, and baths, and political institutions like those of Rome.[1] But though the municipalities were almost autonomous, the provinces as such had practically no power of self-government. The *concilium provinciae*, or provincial assembly, seems to have included representatives of the communities, on the basis of population; but it was an honorary body whose functions were, in general, formal and religious. It did, however, initiate the impeachments of retiring governors, and later served as a link with the central government. At no period was there any real tendency to introduce a representative principle into the central government.[2] Between the provinces many bonds were forged. New roads, and the increasing security of travel and trade, greatly increased the exchange of goods between the various parts of the empire, and brought about an economic unity unhampered by any protective tariffs. Throughout the empire there sprang up a personal loyalty, partly semi-religious, partly political, to the emperor, binding together men of many races in a common sentiment. Later, when the political unity of the empire began to crumble, it was Christianity, a cosmopolitan religion, that bound together distant parts of the empire.

When the provinces had been pacified and their organization had been laid down, Augustus devoted himself for some

[1] Influenced by the Lex Julia Municipalis (p. 228).
[2] Cf. p. 278.

years, especially between 19 and 17 B.C., to domestic reforms. As he preserved a distinction between Romans and provincials, so among Romans he emphasized class distinctions and bestowed in honors and prosperity more than he took away of power. The Senate he purged several times of unworthy members, keeping its roster comparatively small.[1] Admission to it now depended on winning election to the quaestorship; this in turn came to depend on the nomination and commendation of the emperor, and was also limited to those men, possessed of at least 1,000,000 sesterces ($40,000), whose senatorial rank was indicated by the wearing of the laticlave (the broad stripe), an honor inherited by sons of senators and bestowed on certain others by favor of the emperor. Thus the senatorial order was a peerage, partly hereditary and partly selective; and the Senate was a House of Lords based both on heredity and on capabilities discovered by the emperor. It continued, at least under Augustus, to carry on a considerable amount of routine business, especially fundamental legislation and judicial work. But with the concentration of power in the hands of the emperor, the Senate became less a political or deliberative body and more a club, — a stately, honorable, and exclusive society.

The magistrates also enjoyed but a shadow of their former power. Shorn gradually of their control of provinces, legions, foreign policy, even of such administrative matters as food and water and roads, they made what they could of the social distinction of office. It was still an honor to be a praetor or a consul at Rome, perhaps even the emperor's colleague. Election to office came increasingly to be controlled by Augustus, who tended to nominate or commend candi-

---

[1] I.e. 600 members, as compared with Caesar's 1,000; he wished to reduce it still further, to 300.

dates; his successors went even further in this direction. Naturally the nomination or commendation of the emperor carried great weight. Nominally the magistrates were officials of the whole state, including the empire beyond the seas; actually they were on the way to becoming, what they later were, the officials of the municipality of Rome. Already Augustus had hit upon the idea of dividing Rome into fourteen wards (*vici*) presided over by *magistri*, and had opened these (largely honorary) offices to plebeians.

It was in the organization of the *equites* that Augustus made a most valuable innovation. Once the Roman cavalry, later the wealthy business class, the *equites* had been made by Gaius Gracchus a political order; Augustus used it as a reservoir for his civil service. He required of its members a financial rating of at least 400,000 sesterces ($16,000), and revived its military functions; but it was to be no longer merely a financial or hereditary class but, like the senatorial order, a selective class dependent on the definite choice of the emperor and attached to him and his family, and displaying as its insignia the narrow stripe (angusticlave). Membership in this order was the great ambition of the substantial middle class. From the *equites* the emperors drew not only the lower officers for the army but also the deputies and financial officials for the provinces and the staffs of many of the administrative departments in Rome. With the enormous increase of public business it was not the least of the achievements of Augustus to establish a civil service of able and usually patriotic middle-class Romans, especially when the scions of the senatorial class often seemed disinclined to enter upon such careers.

The holder of the tribunician power did not forget that he was thus designated as the protector of the plebeians. Their political power was destined to ebb, as they lost the opportunity to vote for any candidates save those favored by the emperor.[1] But their status as citizens was emphasized; the toga appeared in public as never before, and the emancipation of slaves was frowned upon. The solid rewards of peace and reviving prosperity were shared with the common people; and if the distribution of free food was limited to 200,000 Romans, the games were more lavish than before. Though a plebeian could not hold any military office above that of centurion, he might advance further if he was raised to equestrian rank. *Collegia* (guilds) of workmen were licensed, if they avoided politics, and served social and charitable purposes; political clubs were discouraged. Even wealthy freedmen at Rome, and more especially in the municipalities of Italy and the provinces, were admitted to the honorary but expensive priesthood of the *Augustales*, if they would contribute to certain public causes. Thus each class of Roman society, senatorial, equestrian, plebeian, and freedman, was kept in its prescribed place, organized for public service, and attached to the imperial house.

The administration of Rome and of Italy was organized with the same efficiency that characterized the provincial administration. For the first time a police system was instituted to patrol the City; a corps of guards, under a prefect, was on watch against fires and burglars; measures were taken against Tiber floods; some of the aqueducts were repaired at the personal expense of Augustus; the water-supply, managed by Agrippa till his death, was subsequently placed by Augustus under state control; and the enormous responsibility of safe-guarding the food supply in general (not merely the distribution of food to the poor) was con-

---

[1] Even this right, so far as the election of praetors is concerned, was transferred to the Senate under Tiberius. In a political sense the citizens of the *municipia* were now better off than the plebeians of Rome.

trolled by special guardians. Some of the heads of departments were elected by lot, some were elected by the Senate;
more and more, however, Augustus placed the departments
under his personal agents, who were generally *equites*. During absences from Rome, early in his reign, he had left in
charge of an armed guard a consular official, the Prefect of
the City; the holder of this office, like the Prefect of the
Praetorian Guard (concentrated by Tiberius in Rome) and
the Prefect of the Watchmen, came to be a very powerful
official, though his duties were municipal rather than imperial. Although the republic had already passed away, it is
interesting to note that the emperor dwelt in a simple house
on the Palatine, and was at pains to build for public use
splendid temples and basilicas and even a meeting-place in
the Campus Martius for the practically defunct Assembly.

Meanwhile, Italy was secured on the northern frontier by
the pacification of the Alpine tribes, and throughout by the
founding of colonies and the improvement of roads. When
Octavian settled a large number of his veterans on the land,
after Actium, he acted more wisely than he had done as
triumvir, and more wisely than Sulla and Pompey and
other generals had done; for he paid in full for any occupied
lands needed for this purpose. The rural parts of Italy began to revive somewhat.[1] The peninsula was divided into
fifteen administrative regions, each consisting of domain
land with a municipality at its heart; and the local self-

---

[1] Not fully, despite the impression conveyed by Horace and Virgil. See
W. E. Heitland, in *Agricola*, pp. 213–241; and in *The Legacy of Rome*, pp.
449–504. M. Rostovtzeff shows, however (*Social and Economic History of the
Roman Empire*, Ch. II), that Italy, with her thriving trade in wine, oil, pottery, and other industrial products, which she exchanged for grain and for
raw materials of all sorts, was still one of the most prosperous parts of the
empire. Augustus did not interfere with the Italian agrarian system, but followed here, as elsewhere, an economic policy of *laissez faire*; it was peace that
brought prosperity, or at least wealth for proprietors.

government, stimulated by Julius Caesar's charter, continued to develop in these towns.

For all these reforms money had to be found. Augustus had no idea of liberating the provinces from the chief burden, but he was a good enough business man to realize the advantage of knowing the resources of the various parts of the empire. He therefore held a census of the empire several times, and learned that it contained between four and five million persons, of whom about a million and a half were citizens. He made estimates of assets and liabilities, and devised something equivalent to a budget. For the complicated system of provincial taxation he substituted a simpler system based partly on the use of land and partly on personal property; the inhabitants of Italy paid small taxes on sales, auctions, and legacies, which served to meet the veterans' pensions after Augustus ceased to pay for them out of his private purse, and established a regular treasury, the *aerarium militare*, for this purpose in 6 A.D. But much of the expense of roads and public buildings he continued to meet. Over all the treasuries [1] he exercised a supervision and an increasingly close control.

In the interest of political unity and of the public morale Augustus fostered a deliberate policy of social and religious reform. Most of his measures seemed to aim at the revival of the social virtues and the practices of the old Republic. Thus some of his laws penalized celibacy and adultery, and encouraged, by the more rapid bestowal of political privilege, the rearing of large families of citizens; [2] others attempted to check intermarriages between members of dif-

---

[1] The old public treasury (*aerarium*), under prefects appointed by the emperor; the new treasury (*fiscus*), under his direct control, receiving the revenue of imperial provinces, confiscations, lapsed legacies, etc.; "Caesar's patrimony" (his official exchequer); his *res familiaris* ("personal estate").

[2] By the granting of the *ius trium liberorum*. Cf. p. 103.

ferent social orders. His rebuilding of eighty-two temples in Rome, his revival of the old cults and shrines and priestly colleges, and his opposition to alien gods, savored of antiquarianism; but he also sought to draw attention to other divinities which were associated with the fortunes of the imperial house, — Divus Julius (the deified dictator), Mars Ultor (the avenger of his death), Venus Genetrix (the divine ancestress of the Julian line), and Apollo, near whose shrine at Actium he had won his great victory. These cults appealed, more or less, to Romans; the worship of the emperor, on the other hand, was sanctioned chiefly as a unifying bond among the diverse races of the far-flung empire.[1]

Throughout his long reign, and especially during the last part, Augustus was concerned with the problem of frontiers. As a young man he led his army in person; afterwards he acted through his generals, Tiberius, Drusus, and others. We have already traced the steps by which he built up a frontier, consolidated previous gains within natural boundaries, and halted the expansion which Pompey and Caesar had so rapidly carried on.[2] He was not averse to the popularity that came from rumors of a war that he was to wage against the Parthians; but he recovered the standards that Crassus had lost by means of diplomacy instead of by fighting. Similarly he let it be understood that he intended some day to conquer Britain. But he gradually gained a shrewd idea of the cost of aggressive warfare, and gave to Rome the policy, only occasionally abandoned by his successors, of preserving the *Pax Romana* and avoiding foreign wars. He was able to reduce the army to a half of its former size; he stationed the legions as garrisons wherever the frontier might be threatened, and established fixed conditions for

[1] See further pp. 228, 339–348.
[2] Cf. pp. 75–77.

enlistment, service, and pension.[1] With the legions served "auxiliaries" of natives, who on completing their term of service received Roman citizenship. Seldom do we hear of the "Roman army" after this time; it is rather the "Gallic army," or the "Egyptian army," — that is, the army stationed temporarily in a given province and consisting partly of Romans, partly of provincials. This system, at first a source of new strength to Rome, later became a source of weakness and disruption, as the spirit of the army degenerated, or as, much later, the legions were filled with barbarians who had little reason to sacrifice themselves for the safety of the distant city of Rome. But that evil day was not yet to be feared.

Ten years after Augustus received his unique powers and honors, he held (17 B.C.) a solemn "Saecular" festival (supposedly held every century, or as was sometimes found more convenient, once in 110 years), with sacrifices, games, and the singing of a hymn to Apollo and Diana by a chorus of boys and girls. The poet Horace composed the hymn, as we are told by an inscribed stone still to be seen in Rome; the hymn itself, a stately and musical if not highly emotional poem, is preserved among his works as the *Carmen Saeculare*. The Augustan rule was recognized as the established order, the Augustan Age as an age of peace and returning prosperity and outward splendor. Virgil had died two years before, but not before leaving pastorals that paid graceful homage to the young Octavian, the *Georgics*, that celebrated the labors and the joys of the farmer's life even before there was an Augustus to attempt rural reconstruction, and, most significant of all, the *Aeneid*, that sounded the new note of Rome's imperial mission under a semi-divine prince. Virgil was dead; but Horace had taken up what amounted to a

[1] See further pp. 79–82.

poet-laureateship, and many of his odes lauded the blessings of the new age.[1] A court, in the strict sense, there was not yet; but the emperor received the salutation of senators and *equites*; foreign embassies from the ends of the earth came before him, as well as before the Senate; the doorway of his house was decked with laurel and with the "civic wreath" of oak leaves, by order of the Senate and People; Senate, *equites*, and People united in hailing him as *pater patriae* (2 B.C.).[2] Foreign powers were all but completely awed; domestic rebellion had died away in impotence; within the emperor's household the bitterness of early deaths and of a daughter's disgrace had been hard to bear, but otherwise the character of Augustus, once so cold and calculating, had mellowed in an Indian summer of achievement and appreciation. Full of honors as of years, he died in 14 A.D., and was laid in his Mausoleum near the Tiber. "Had he not well played his rôle in the comedy of life?" he asked those who stood by his death-bed.[3] Both they and posterity have agreed.

One problem Augustus had faced again and again; but the solution that he found was only a temporary or partial one. What was to happen when he died? In theory, supreme authority was shared by the Senate and the *princeps*; but it was quite obvious to Augustus, and doubtless to most other Romans as well, that the merely temporary character of the offices that he held was a fiction, and that the new system required a *princeps*. He himself had been the heir, both personal and political, of Julius Caesar; and it seemed likely that his personal heir would inherit the principate. Augustus, though several times married, was disappointed in his

---

[1] Cf. R. S. Conway, "Horace as Poet Laureate," in *New Studies of a Great Inheritance*, pp. 44–65. See also below, p. 339.

[2] *Monumentum Ancyranum* XXXII–XXXV.

[3] Suetonius, *Aug.*, 99.

hopes of a son. Yet his last marriage, to Livia, a cynical marriage of state, brought him in Tiberius a stepson of illustrious lineage. Though it was desirable that his heir should be clearly designated, to prevent rivalry,[1] he himself outlived several of those whom he considered for the succession. His sister's son, the young Marcellus, who died in 23 B.C., was immortalized in Virgil's picture of a young prince cut off in his prime.[2] The faithful Agrippa, his companion at Actium and in many a task and office thereafter, was of the same age as Augustus, and died long before him (12 B.C.). Augustus next considered his stepson Tiberius, an able general and administrator, though a reserved and morose person; soon, however, he allowed him to be eclipsed by the two young sons of Agrippa and his own daughter Julia, as they reached maturity. When these young Caesars died prematurely, he once more made Tiberius his heir-apparent, by adopting him and investing him with large powers and responsibilities. It was on Tiberius, an experienced public servant already fifty-six years old, that the burden of the principate fell at the death of Augustus.

The fortunes of the principate after Augustus we have space to consider only in broad outline, noting how the inevitable trend of circumstances and the ambition of certain emperors hastened the conversion of an outwardly constitutional, quasi-republican principate into an undisguised autocracy. Augustus had established the norm for a constitutional type of rule: the nominal sovereignty of the Senate, a superior position for Italy in comparison with the provinces within well-defined boundaries, and the avoidance of foreign wars. But another, earlier precedent had been set by the absolute rule of Caesar, the dictator, who had brushed

---

[1] Cf. p. 253, n. 1.
[2] *Aen.* VI, 860–886.

aside the Senate's privileges and treated the senators as his personal retainers; he had built his power on his democratic army and the expansion of the empire; and he had been willing to level the differences between classes of citizens, and between Italian Romans and provincials. Something like his rule was soon to emerge again. But the process of change was not steady; indeed, constitutional rulers appear sporadically, resisting the general trend. Let us review the procession.

The first four emperors that followed Augustus belong to the "Julio-Claudian" line, that descended from the union of the families of Augustus and Livia. Tiberius (14–37 A.D.) though able, conscientious, and thrifty, was never popular. From the beginning he controlled his army with decisive vigor; but his awkward attitude toward the Senate, from whom he derived his civil powers, showed at first a comic vacillation. Perhaps this was natural; for the unique career and the tact of Augustus had placed him in a position which it would have been hard for any successor to sustain. As it was, the aristocrats resented the continuance of the supposedly makeshift principate, inevitable though it obviously was; and nearly all the accounts of the early Empire, especially those of Tacitus, are colored by this hostility to the new system. Conspiracies had to be suppressed, and bred in turn a suspicious attitude on the part of Tiberius and his agents, the "informers." The populace of Rome, on the other hand, resented his economies and the lack of public entertainments. The treachery of his trusted Praetorian Prefect, Sejanus, was apparently the last straw; his declining years were spent in retirement, and, gossip whispered, in debauchery. That is one side of the picture; but we must not forget, what is to be read only between the lines of the ancient historians and in the inscribed records from the provinces, that Tiberius deserves an honored place among the Roman emperors who continued the constitutional policies of Augustus. And however black the historians may paint the crimes committed at Rome by a Caesar, however depraved Roman society may appear in the pages of the satirists, the provinces continued to flourish during this century and a half.

The sinister figure of Gaius (37–41 A.D.), nicknamed in childhood "Caligula" ("Little Shoes"), from the military boots that he wore in the camp of his father (Germanicus), does not matter so much personally except as a symptom of what was to come. Epileptic and a bit mad, he courted popularity, and essayed to ape the autocratic rule of Julius Caesar. But the weakness of his foreign policy, his extravagance at home, and the general irresponsibility and folly of his rule, led to his assassination only four years after his accession.

Tiberius and Gaius had been made emperors by the Senate and accepted by acclamation of the people; it was the Praetorian Guard that found Claudius (41–54) hiding in the Palace when his nephew Gaius was murdered, and made him emperor. The Senate perforce gave its consent. Boorish, learned, easily swayed by his wives and his freedmen, Claudius was nevertheless a capable, if unattractive, emperor. On the whole he carried on the Augustan tradition, but departed from it so far as to conquer and make a province of Britain, and to admit certain Gallic chieftains to the Senate. This last measure he justified in a considered speech, arguing that security was founded on a broad basis of political rights.[1] He also made the intelligent freedmen of his personal *familia* practically ministers of state, controlling the treasury and diplomatic correspondence. Public opinion

---

[1] Tacitus, *Ann.* XI, 23–25.

was offended; but the unified control was efficient, and the freedmen were presently replaced by *equites*.

When Claudius died, it was again the Praetorian Guard that proclaimed his stepson Nero as emperor; there were grave suspicions that Nero's mother, Agrippina, had poisoned her husband in order to hasten the succession; and Claudius' own son Britannicus, who was only a couple of years younger than Nero, was certainly poisoned by Nero the next year. The fatal game of intrigue, of dynastic marriages and divorces, of domestic murder as the regular tool of ambition, was being played for the stakes of empire.[1] Nero's reign (54–68 A.D.) began brightly enough to be sure, under the tutelage of the soldier Burrhus and the philosopher-statesman Seneca; but within five years he plunged into the career of bloodshed, profligacy, and extravagance that has made his name a byword. His personal vices, even his murder of his mother, might be tolerated. But it was hard for aristocratic Romans to endure his open indulgence of an artistic temperament and of sporting proclivities; still harder to endure his reckless neglect of public affairs and his contempt for the Senate, which he once threatened to remove from the state, in order to give the provinces and the armies to *equites* and freedmen. The official opposition, however, consisting largely of doctrinaire Stoics and disgruntled nobles, was more annoying than dangerous. The aristocratic Pisonian conspiracy at Rome failed, and brought down vengeance on the aristocracy. But even the armies in the provinces, on which the principate ultimately depended,

---

[1] See the readable works of S. Baring Gould, *The Tragedy of the Caesars: A Study of the Characters of the Caesars of the Julian and Claudian Houses*, 2 vols. (New York, 1902); and of S. Van Santvoord, *The House of Caesar and the Imperial Disease* (Troy, N. Y., 1902). (Note the tables on pp. 168 ff. and 195 ff. in the latter work showing the large number of members of the family who died by violence.)

could no longer put up with Nero's flippancy and neglect of the legions. In Gaul, Spain, and Africa, they revolted and marched on Rome, and Nero found a wretched death by his own hand (68 A.D.). The Julio-Claudian line of emperors came to an end.

The *princeps* was dead, but not the principate; for there was no question of restoring the republic. The armies had rebelled not against the principate, but against an inefficient *princeps*. Yet the provincial armies were not of one mind as to who should become emperor; within one year four successors to Nero had been proclaimed. The legions of Gaul and the praetorians accepted Galba, an honest drillmaster; the legions of Upper Germany refused to accept him, and hailed Vitellius as *imperator*, while the praetorians now recognized Otho. The brief ascendency of Otho was terminated by the legions of the northern provinces, who carried Vitellius into power. His reign began well; but the legions of the eastern provinces immediately put forward a new champion, T. Flavius Vespasianus, as the avenger of Galba; it was he and his sons Titus and Domitian who held supreme power at Rome for the next twenty-seven years.

Vespasian (69–79 A.D.) was an emperor of a novel stuff. Unlike the first Caesars, aristocrats boasting divine lineage, he claimed no *imagines* at Rome; he came from a simple middle-class business family in the Sabine hills. Yet he ruled with dignity and discretion; ruled, we must note, rather than reigned, though his constitutional powers were formulated by the special Lex de Imperio Vespasiani, which emphasized Augustan and other early imperial precedents.[1] To the Senate he welcomed members of the municipal aristocracy of Italy, especially since there were few members

---

[1] See the *Senatus consultum de imperio Vespasiani*, in C. G. Bruns, *Fontes Juris Romani Antiqui*[7], p. 202.

of the old Roman aristocracy left. He made no disguise of his Caesarian policies and his dynastic purposes, despite futile protests from Roman senators and provincial philosophers. He and his sons had frontier wars to fight in Germany and Judaea and later in Britain; but Vespasian's Temple of Peace testifies to the preference of at least the founder of the Flavian dynasty for a peaceful rule. The Flavians continued to break down the distinction between Italians and provincials. Vespasian, fearing the city rabble of Rome, excluded Italians from the legions, and converted the Roman army into an army of urbanized provincials fighting under Roman officers; later it was not the urbanized, but the rural, provincials (or barbarians) who took their places. Vespasian himself made vigorous reforms of the public finances, imposing taxes and otherwise replenishing the empty treasury, even at the expense of personal popularity. He favored the landholders at the expense of their tenants, who were beginning to become serfs. Of his sons, Titus was a popular and active young general, but survived his accession to the principate by only two years (79–81), during which he showed amiable qualities though little statesmanship. Not so his younger brother, Domitian (81–96), who had the cruelty and the autocratic temper of a Nero. Toward senators, philosophers, and Christians he displayed a vindictive attitude that caused him to be all but universally detested. His intentions may have been better than his tact; he could not brook interference. Though he had been distrusted by his father and his brother, who denied him military authority during their lifetime, he was, nevertheless, vigorous in his management of the frontiers.

The tyranny of Domitian, ended by assassination, was followed by the rule of five "good emperors" whose reigns bridged a period of more than fourscore years. Rome profited by the peaceful succession of heirs tested by responsibility and then designated by adoption.[1] Nerva (96–98), an elderly senator, had little time to do more than to give assurance of orderly, constitutional government, and to begin the important experiment of *alimenta*, loans to Italian farmers, the interest on which was not repaid to the treasury but was used by the municipalities to foster the children of needy parents.[2] This experiment, continued by Nerva's successors, throws light both on the plight in which many farmers must have been and on the declining birth rate. The city rabble had long had its dole; now the struggling Italian farmers, who were no longer recruited for the Roman armies, were given a helping hand; the burden, it must be noted, fell ultimately on the provincials, who were also assuming the bur-

---

[1] The civil wars fought over a doubtful succession in 68–69 A.D., and many times in the third century A.D., bear witness to the danger of having no designated and acceptable successor in readiness. If there is to be a monarchy, the best safeguard against bloodshed or against embroiling the crown in partisan politics is to have an hereditary monarchy. On the other hand, sons frequently lack their fathers' talents; if a king is to rule as well as reign, there is much to be said for succession by deliberate adoption. "To be born of royal blood," says a speaker quoted by Tacitus (*Hist.* I, 16), "is a matter of chance, before which all examination stops. On the other hand, he who adopts is judge of what he does; if he desires to choose the most worthy, he has only to listen to the voice of public opinion." And Boissier, commenting on this remark, adds: "What is certain is that adoption gave the world a succession of four great princes, and that Rome was quite happy until the time when M. Aurelius was so ill-fated as to have a son and leave him the Empire." (*Rome and Pompeii*, pp. 221 ff.) But if the claim to the succession be not respected, wretched is the claimant and his country, for civil war is almost certain to follow. (See further p. 272.) If, on the other hand, the claim to the succession be respected, whether on grounds of heredity or of adoption, the position of any body, like the Roman Senate, that is supposed to sanction it, is correspondingly depressed. That, and the bureaucracy of the principate, made the Senate a fifth wheel even before the principate became a military despotism. Safest of all monarchical systems, of course, are those in which the crown is lifted above party strife by being chiefly of decorative and sentimental value, other provision being made for the real work of government.

[2] Analogies may be found in such modern paternalistic undertakings of the government as farm banks and the Sheppard-Towner Act.

den of frontier defense. The provinces could doubtless well afford to undertake this new burden, and indeed might reasonably be expected to undertake it, especially as Rome was now giving them protection and an efficient government. But the day was not many centuries distant when Rome was to need Italians to stem the barbarian invasions where the frontier troops were weak or disloyal; eventually they were to defend the city of Rome itself.

In Trajan (98–117), a Roman born in Spain, the Empire received its first emperor from the provinces. He was a soldier by instinct and by training, and had already been associated with Nerva as "Caesar." The title was deserved, for in Trajan the Empire found a ruler possessed of the courage, the energy, the military aggressiveness, and the autocratic methods of Julius Caesar, with a strong vein of ostentation. He derived his authority, at least in form, from the Senate, for which he showed great respect, and broke the power of the troublesome and impudent Praetorian Guard. His conquests in Dacia and the East, and the Column and the Arch commemorating respectively the Dacian campaigns and the rule of Trajan, we have already discussed.[1] New roads, harbors, and an aqueduct showed his concern for the welfare of Italy. But the most interesting testimony to the character of this truly great emperor lies in the correspondence between him and the younger Pliny, who was his governor in Bithynia, — almost the only such evidence that we have, by the way, for the kind of problems that not only Trajan but many of his successors must have had to deal with. Pliny seems to refer to his master (*dominus*) every question that comes up in his administration, from petty economies in building to great instances of dishonesty or inefficiency, from the control of fire-brigades to the tremen-

[1] Pp. 78, 169 f., 181–183.

dous problem of the proper treatment of Christians.[1] If all provincial governors were as conscientious as Pliny in writing to their emperors, one wonders how the emperors had time for anything but their correspondence. But all Trajan's rescripts, or answers, show a patience, a common sense and willingness to cut through red tape in order to do justice, and a brevity, that are simply admirable.

Hardly less autocratic, but far less given to military ambition than Trajan, was Hadrian (117–138). A lover of literature and architecture and philosophy, a cosmopolitan traveller, he gave the Empire a breathing-space of peace. The thin-drawn garrisons of the frontier were placed along his massive walls; the civil service was reorganized with a largely equestrian personnel; the edicts of earlier praetors were codified, and a professional court of salaried jurists was constituted. Roman law became more and more a science, animated not merely by custom and formalism but by a concern for reason and justice. This codification and interpretation of law was faithfully continued during the tranquil reign of Hadrian's successor, the gentle Antoninus Pius (138–161), while the great Empire ran smoothly under its accumulated momentum.

Marcus Aurelius (161–180), who had been the colleague of Antoninus for fourteen years before succeeding him, was by temperament a philosopher, constrained by hard circumstances to wear himself out in thankless activities. Wars in the East, and the aftermath of plague brought back to Italy, campaigns against Germans and Sarmatians, disloyal officers, even faithlessness and profligacy in his own household, all must have sorely tried the temper of the Stoic saint, whose communings with himself we may read in the book now known as his *Meditations*. His reproaches, however,

---

[1] Cf. pp. 362–364.

are only sombre self-reproaches; his conscience is sensitive; his humanitarianism is almost Christian, except that his conscience compelled him to approve the persecution of Christians. But in his personal acts of charity, which exhausted his large private fortune, and in his public measures of relief and the legal aid of the humble and weak, he was the best example in his age of Roman tolerance and sympathy. And the administrative machinery which he perfected seemed at last to have found an equilibrium of forces nicely calculated to fulfill their tasks. Nevertheless, circumstances of which even the plague and the thunder of invasions along the Danube could give him little inkling were soon to make havoc of the Indian summer of comparative peace and prosperity that Rome and the empire enjoyed under the "good emperors."

The series of five "good emperors" succeeding by adoption ended with Marcus Aurelius; his son Commodus (180–192 A.D.), an irresponsible madman, demonstrated once more the danger of hereditary autocracy. Upon his assassination, the emperorship became the prize of rival armies and of the Praetorian Guard, whose candidates frankly depended on military support, and had frequently to crush the rebellion of pretenders to the title of "Caesar." Within ninety years after the death of Commodus, Rome had no less than eighty "emperors." The third to follow him within a few months was the well-meaning Septimius Severus, who succeeded in holding power for eighteen years (193–211). A native of Africa, speaking Punic, an energetic and usually successful soldier, though not a great general, he defeated his rivals and the Parthians with equal vigor. For Italy he had no reason to entertain any special tenderness; he replaced the Italian Praetorian Guard by one of provincials, and quartered a legion on the Alban Mount; he showed his contempt for the Senate by executing senators for "treason" and by re-placing them with provincials; and he was at no pains to disguise the military character of his monarchy. To his soldiers he felt it necessary to grant opportunities for marriage and homes near their barracks, and for the promotion of common soldiers to high rank; to his veterans, as well as to tenants of the imperial estates, he gave exemptions from municipal burdens. These privileged and greedy soldiers not only were becoming rapidly barbarized but were soon to become masters of the principate. In the East he encouraged municipalities by gifts of citizenship and autonomy. The rule of Septimius Severus thus continued the general levelling of differences within the empire, and at the same time hastened the coming of the day when the emperor was to be the tool of a democratic, barbarian army. Nevertheless, he emphasized the hereditary character of his rule, designating his sons as his successors, and attempting by religious cults and trumped-up titles to pose as the legitimate successor of the Antonines. In one sense he deserved to be so regarded; for he placed at the head of the Praetorian Guard, which now had important judicial functions, the great jurist Papinian. He, with his successors, did much to make Roman law humane.

Caracalla (212–217), the brutal son of Septimius Severus, is remembered chiefly for the great Baths that bear his name and for his Edict (212) bestowing Roman citizenship on all free-born persons within the empire, excluding only those who had no civic rights anywhere. This at least superficially democratic measure marks the last step in the gradual degradation of Italy by the elevation of the provinces. The immediate motive has generally been supposed to be the creation of a larger class of taxable persons, for the relief of the empty imperial treasury, which was already reduced

to the expedient of the debasing of the coinage. Nevertheless, it also brought practically all the Roman world under
the jurisdiction of Roman law, and stimulated anew the
studies of the jurists; and the advantages of Roman citizens
over non-citizens were still real.[1]

Assassination once more made away with the emperor,
this time (after a few months of civil war) for four years of
nominal rule by the fantastic figure of Elagabalus (218–222),
a Syrian sun-priest, cousin of Caracalla, thanks to the
machinations of ambitious dowagers of the imperial family.
He in turn gave place to his young cousin Alexander Severus,
(222–235), during whose reign there was some show of respect for the Senate and the old aristocracy. In the attempt
to encourage the lagging production of commodities, the old
trade organizations, once voluntary, were made compulsory,
and were bidden to deliver to the state their fixed amounts of
goods; and in the attempt to collect taxes the municipal
officials were bidden to deliver the proper amounts. The
first measure, like the later step taken by Diocletian regarding farm tenants, tended to make serfs of free laborers; the
second removed from the bourgeoisie the incentive to become prosperous by industry. Both were only partly successful; but they reflect the plight to which the empire was
now reduced. The military exigencies of the state and its
rulers were steadily drawing out of productive use the capital
without which civilized life could not continue. The armies
now consisted chiefly of provincial villagers, and did not re-
sent the change; they rather supported the military monarch of the moment. It was the city-dwellers who were now
the opponents of the peasantry and the monarchy alike.

The anarchy of the fifty years that followed the death of

---

[1] Cf. pp. 81 f.; and C. L. Sherman, "The Constitutio Antoniniana in the
light of the Γνώμων Τοῦ Ἰδίου Λόγου," in T. A. P. A., LIX (1928), 33–47.

the last Severus need not be described here. It was the
armies that made and unmade the twenty-six emperors with
amazing rapidity. All officials, from the emperors down,
came from the army; the pretense of constitutionality was
at last given up. Gallienus (253–268 A.D.), who held power
longest, reorganized the state on a purely military basis,
even excluding the senatorial class from the high command.
Aurelian (270–275) claimed the imperial power by divine
right, invoking the sanction of the *Sol Invictus* whom he
worshiped, and surrounded himself with the royal attributes
of an oriental despot. But his strongly centralized power
and his military discipline again saved the fabric of the state.

A few years later, Diocletian (284–305), facing the impending dissolution of the state, was compelled to make the
imperial authorities absolute, crushing national differences
and local government and organizing the whole empire as
mere administrative units of one system. Rome and Italy
finally lost their preëminence; Italy was once more taxed like
the provinces, and Rome ceased to be the capital, — the
capital of the empire moved with its emperor. The adoption
of royal insignia, the creation of a royal court, with titles for
the despot's favorites (*magistri, duces, comites*, — the last
two giving us the modern titles of "duke" and "count"), —
signified the final disappearance of constitutional government. Diocletian and a colleague assumed the title of
"Augustus" with two heirs apparent as "Caesars." A host
of officials constituted a minutely organized bureaucracy for
civil government throughout the four "prefectures," subdivided into 17 "dioceses" or 101 "provinces." In order to
enforce the productivity of the soil, Diocletian compelled the
payment (usually in kind) of a portion of the products of
each district to the state. This ancient system had been used
in many parts of the East as extraordinary or emergency

contributions (*munera* or "liturgies") for expenses of state; it was now made a permanent burden on the substantial citizens (the *decuriones*), who were responsible for the collection and payment of the produce in their districts. To prevent the wretched tenants from evading the burden, Diocletian forbade them to move, thus making universal the system of serfdom long familiar in Egypt; the result was the transformation of peasants into serfs. Similar restrictions were laid on the various industries, with similarly depressing effects. But the labor of all these classes was not more than enough to support the army on which the integrity of the Empire depended, a great new army recruited, of course, from the most barbarian frontiers. Thus Diocletian succeeded, at the cost of the distress of most of his subjects, in preserving the Empire as a political whole, and in giving it a new lease of life in its struggle against the barbarians. If the Empire was worth saving even at this cost, as it well may have been, Diocletian deserves to be remembered as an emperor who applied a desperate remedy to a desperate case. But his attempt to secure the succession by the principle of adoption resulted only in civil war between the heirs designate and other rivals; and Constantine (327–337), the final victor, abandoned the policy of succession by adoption in favor of an hereditary dynasty, and moved his capital to Byzantium, renamed for himself. The policy of a strongly unified Roman state was abandoned by the sons of Julian (361–363), who divided the empire between them, with courts in Milan and Constantinople. The only remaining force strong enough to bind together the Roman world was not political, nor even politics disguised as religion (as in the days of Augustus), but religion itself. This Constantine was shrewd enough to recognize when he tolerated and then patronized Christianity.

We cannot attempt here to recount the history of the later Roman Empire, — the temporary consolidation of the re-united Empire under Theodosius (379–395), and its final division by his sons; the new barbarian invasions, and the break-up of the Empire into national states; the continuation of many Roman institutions and laws throughout what had been the Empire, and the laws newly codified in the eastern Empire under Justinian (527–565); the increasing impotence of the western emperors, who in the fifth century could claim even a nominal sovereignty over nothing more than Italy; the deposing by the German soldiers, in 476, of the last of the western emperors, a stripling who labored under the name of Romulus Augustulus, uniting, in significantly diminutive form, to the name of the ancient founder of Rome the title of the founder of the principate; the rise of the Ostrogothic kingdom of Theodoric (493–526), with its capital at Ravenna, and of the Frankish (Germanic) kingdom, of which Italy became a part. These matters we need not pursue further, for Roman citizenship had so far degenerated that it now meant almost nothing. All persons had become the subjects of the reigning emperor, whether Roman or provincial or German, even if a caste system had grown up and Roman law favored the upper classes. During these centuries the important movements were not political, but were rather the growth of Christianity, its struggles with paganism, its gradual triumph, and the emergence of statesmanship and of temporal power among the prelates of the Church, especially among the bishops of Rome. Though barbarism was closing in, Greek and Roman and oriental civilizations were preserved here and there; noble architecture, both secular and Christian, continued to be produced; classical literature and Christian literature alike were preserved and copied by monkish hands; and Roman law, many times distilled, remained to be fused with the vigorous Germanic customs of western Europe.

But why, after all, should Roman civilization, so strong and proud in the days of the Republic, so efficient in the days of the early Empire, have suffered so rapid a decay? Shall we be content to admit that the barbarians battered away its vigor, and shall we repeat the familiar statement that Rome "fell" in 476 A.D.? In a sense, of course, Rome has never fallen; in another sense Rome began to fall long before the last "emperor" was deposed. The reasons for the decay have been many times discussed, though the wise Mommsen confessed, it is said, that he had never written on this subject because he had never been able to discover just why Rome fell. The secret of Rome's greatness, to be sure, presents a simpler problem, — granted that all such matters are highly speculative. A fortunate geographical position for the city itself; strength of character and discipline in her early citizens; good luck in that no two of her many great wars engaged her resources at once; sagacity in incorporating conquered peoples and assimilating their cultures; the solid advantages that she could bestow on the world, and thus gain acquiescence, if not gratitude,[1] in the Pax Romana, in Roman law and administration, and in the economic unity created by free trade and means of communication, — these were the chief factors in Rome's rise. The

---

[1] So even at the beginning of the fifth century Claudian, a native of Alexandria, writes of Rome as the only power that has taken the conquered to her bosom like a mother, and called them citizens, so that they who drink of the Rhone and they who drink of the Orontes are alike one people: "Cuncti gens una sumus" (*De Consulatu Stilichonis* III, 159); and the Gaul Rutilius Namatianus, forgetting the recent plunder of Rome by Alaric, apostrophizes her eloquently: "Thou hast made one fatherland of diverse peoples; it was to their advantage, even against their will, to become captive to thy rule; and in granting to the conquered a share in thine own law, thou hast made a city of what was a world" (*De Reditu Suo* I, 63–66).

Empire was not a deliberate creation, of course, but was the unexpected product of the will-to-live. But when a society discovers that slowly changing circumstances and a series of makeshifts, compromises, and well-meaning blunders have built up a massive human fabric on an insecure foundation, it is not possible to dismantle it at will and rebuild at convenience; the fabric disintegrates from pressure internal and external. So it was with Rome.

The insecurity of the foundation is implied by the fact of the decay, and has been analyzed in many ways: its exact nature remains uncertain, and will probably remain uncertain. Yet who can refrain from trying to form some opinion about it? We may dismiss as inadequate the attempt to explain everything in terms of any one simple factor.[1] The true explanation which an omniscient spectator of Rome's decline might be able to expound would surely consist in a proper evaluation of a large number of interwoven factors, aggravated by the pressure of the barbarians. But we may at least review rapidly the more important factors, noting why no single explanation is sufficient.[2]

The first group of factors might be described as physical and economic. As we have already remarked, the climate of Italy may have changed for the worse between 400 and 200 B.C., becoming warmer and more arid, with some improvement between the last century B.C. and 200 A.D., and other variations since then. During the less favorable periods the

---

[1] Some of these explanations are enumerated, and dismissed, by M. Rostovtzeff, *The Social and Economic History of the Roman Empire*, pp. 478–487.

[2] See in general T. Frank, *A History of Rome*, Ch. XXX ("The Causes of Rome's Decline"); M. Rostovtzeff, *op. cit.*, Ch. XII ("The Oriental Despotism and the Problem of the Decay of Ancient Civilization"); W. S. Davis, *The Influence of Wealth in Imperial Rome*, Ch. VIII ("Some Reasons why the Roman Empire Fell"); A. J. (Lord) Balfour, *Decadence* (Cambridge, 1908); and the other works mentioned in the following pages.

conditions were less stimulating to agriculture and industry, and to other human activities; and the changed conditions of drainage meant the invasion of Italy by the malaria-carrying mosquito, another cause of decreased energy and morale.[1] These forces, to be sure, operated unequally in different areas, and among different classes of Romans; and it cannot be assumed that the Romans as a people were lacking in energy at any time, however indolent the city paupers became late in the Republic, or however idle the nobles sometimes were during the empire, when their ambitions cooled under the encroachments of the principate.

Quite as important a factor was the decline of agriculture. For this decline one reason often stressed is the progressive exhaustion of the soil under excessive cultivation, first near Rome, then in the more remote parts of Italy, and at last even in some of the provinces (though never in Egypt, where the annual overflow of the Nile always replenished the top-soil).[2] The small farms (30 *iugera*, or 17 acres) that once were ample for the support of a Roman family no longer sufficed in the days of Tiberius Gracchus, who proposed to distribute to the landless allotments up to the Licinian limit of some 500 *iugera*; later distributions became progressively larger. Even in the elder Cato's day, toward the middle of the second century B.C., any kind of pasturage was more profitable than field crops; and it was worth while, even with fairly good prices for grain, to drain marshes rather than to reclaim exhausted soil. This exhaustion of the soil, it is argued, was the cause of the growth of the vast estates, or *latifundia*, which the elder Pliny held to be the ruin of

[1] Cf. p. 7, n. 1.
[2] Cf. V. Simkhovitch, "Hay and History," in *Political Science Quarterly*, Vol. XXVIII (September, 1913); and "Rome's Fall Reconsidered," *ibid.*, Vol. XXXI (June, 1916).

Rome.[1] And certain it is that the employment of slaves to tend the flocks and herds on the great pasture-lands that now absorbed more and more of the previously tilled land wiped out much of the old yeomanry and swelled the city population, who became less and less fit ever to return to farming. But granted that exhaustion of the soil began at an early period and had something to do with the growth of *latifundia* and therefore with other abuses, still it cannot have been the chief cause of decay. For one thing the soil recovered its fertility to some extent in various regions, either by lying fallow during periods of war or by being turned to pasturage; furthermore, it was the least exhausted provinces that were most burdened with the system of serfdom and that attempted, almost in vain, to provide a sufficient food supply for the empire;[2] and the system of serfdom itself led to desertions and rebellion.[3] Indeed, the whole problem of Roman agriculture,—its decline and the attempts to revive it,—is so much involved in political struggles that it is almost impossible to say whether such a factor as soil exhaustion was a cause or a symptom of the decline; we have a vicious circle. The growing use of slave labor on the farms, encouraged by proprietors perhaps primarily because it was free from military burdens, had permitted the growth of *latifundia*; the importation of foreign and provincial grain had further stimulated it. The Gracchan legislation had almost wholly failed to break up the *latifundia*; the settling of veterans on the land from the days of Sulla to the Augustan Age had disturbed the cultivation of the land without creating a large and successful peasant class; and throughout

[1] Pliny, *N. H.* XVIII, 7: "Latifundia perdidere Italiam, iam vero et provincias." Cf. pp. 206–209.

[2] Cf. pp. 259 f.

[3] Cf. W. L. Westermann, "The Economic Basis of the Decline of Ancient Culture," in *Am. Hist. Rev.*, XX (July, 1915), 723–743.

the principate it was the *latifundia* and country estates of the nobility, managed for their pleasure and profit, and the increasing imperial domain land, that absorbed most of Italy. Peasants still existed; but they were mostly tenants of the great absentee landowners, rather than freeholders. Wine was still exported, under protection of the state; but Italian agriculture as a whole suffered from the economic growth of the provinces, which raised sufficient food for their own needs.[1]

Nor did Roman industry ever develop large-scale production under a capitalistic system, probably because its market was restricted chiefly to the Roman empire, which had reached its full extent, and which was amply provided with the products of its own myriad small industries. Not being industrialized, Italy was less than ever self-supporting, and endeavored, for a time successfully, to live on the provinces. The system of *alimenta* introduced by Nerva and the Flavian emperors was an artificial and not a successful attempt to revive an Italian peasant class. At Rome the population had been accustomed to receive doles of food, for reasons partly humanitarian and partly political. The system begun by the Gracchi was many times revised, in the interest of party politics or of economy; the number of citizens entitled to cheap or free grain varied from 150,000 to 300,000; under Augustus only one-fifth of all the grain imported to Rome had ordinarily been needed for free distribution. But the general effect of such doles, as of the *alimenta*, had been to pauperize the Romans. They had become listless, without initiative, caring only for "bread and circuses." [2] The very

---

[1] The problem of our farmer is different: the competition of relatively unprotected farm products with protected industrial products; distance from markets; excessive middlemen's profits; overproduction of some crops; bad weather; long hours for farm labor in comparison with short hours for factory labor, and the lure of city life.   [2] Juvenal, *Sat.* X, 81.

efficiency of the bureaucracy deprived populace and aristocracy of political activity, if not of self-respect. Meanwhile a majority of the splendid public buildings that kept them contented diverted to unproductive purposes the revenues that should have been invested in productive industry and in imperial defense. Even these monuments were built wastefully, without scientific, labor-saving devices; Vespasian went so far as to reject a mechanism for the ready transportation of massive columns, with the words: "Let me find work for the maintenance of the poor people." More and more the imports of the Empire were luxuries, paid for not by the export of Roman goods but by the export of gold. Emperors sometimes even paid barbarian invaders to retreat. As early as the reign of Marcus Aurelius there was a scarcity of coinage, and the currency was depreciated by base metals. Thus both capital and coinage for circulation were drained away, and the scarcity of coinage and bullion encouraged hoarding, rather than the creation of new capital and therefore of increased production. Exchange was once more carried on largely by barter, and was naturally slowed down. Usury increased; and the state endeavored to extract by taxation what ready money there was.[1] It was in order to raise revenues for defense and the political machinery of the state that Diocletian launched his baleful schemes of taxation. Though the provinces had to contribute heavily to the treasury, they were on the whole better off than Italy. Innumerable small industries prospered in the provinces, though markets were no longer increasing. Moreover, provincial agriculture was still comparatively prosperous, especially in Africa and Egypt, thanks to elaborate schemes of reclamation and irrigation on *latifundia* of a feudal sort.

---

[1] W. Cunningham, *An Essay on Western Civilization in its Economic Aspects*, pp. 182–189; Rostovtzeff, *op. cit.*, pp. 417–421.

Nevertheless, as tenant farmers (*coloni*) became serfs, bound to the land (*adscripti glaebae*), skill and productivity declined.

A second group of factors in the decay of Rome is of a biological nature, and involves the character of the man power. Wars, both foreign and civil, killed off a large proportion of the best Romans. It was naturally the men of best physique who incurred the risks of war, and it was a point of pride in the scions of great families during the Republic to vie with their forefathers. Hence the bushel of senatorial rings gathered by Hannibal on the field of Cannae; hence, too, the decimation of the old nobility through the century of civil wars and political proscriptions, till few of the Empire could boast an ancient name. Even the survivors tended to have fewer children than of old, or actually to avoid the burdens of matrimony altogether, in spite of the attempts of Augustus and others to encourage large families;[1] babies flourish more on farms than in crowded *insulae* or even than in luxurious homes ruled by self-indulgence in an atmosphere of high nervous tension. The sturdy professional soldiers, who lived no longer on farms but in camps or on the march, begot illegitimate children by mothers often of bad character or feeble intelligence; and if they married after their retirement they were too old to have large families. In the time of Marcus Aurelius a great plague, brought back by the army from the East, cut a deep swath in the citizen body of Italy. The population of Italy grew, of course; but it was swollen to a great extent by alien blood, captives of war and the riffraff of oriental slave-raids, turbulent Gauls[2] and heroic Germans,[3] clever hucskstering

[1] Cf. pp. 102 f., 243.
[2] For a characterization, see Ammianus Marcellinus, XV, 12.
[3] Tacitus, *Germ.*, 4–20, doubtless stresses the nobility of the unspoiled Germans in order to satirize the corruptness of Rome.

Greeks, Syrians, and servile Egyptians, and others still more alien.[1] Now it is dangerous to attempt to rank races as superior and inferior; but it can hardly be doubted that the newer, largely oriental, population of Italy, which had become Roman not by immigration but through manumission after a generation or more of slavery, had less of Roman vigor and discipline and political genius than had the old Italic peoples. Long after slavery ceased to be an important factor in Roman industry, Rome continued to pay the penalty for having used slaves, in the altered character of her citizen body. Akin to this dilution of Roman blood through servile channels was the much later barbarization of the Roman armies on the frontiers.[2] Again the effect was to introduce, but this time into a more vital part of the population, an element lacking in discipline and in devotion to the old Roman traditions and in patriotism. Gibbon held that the fact that after the defeat of Valens the Goths never abandoned Roman territory was "the principal and immediate cause of the fall of the Western Empire."[3] Long before that, the vast majority of the Roman population ceased to be Roman in blood. The empire was "Romanized" only by a conscious effort, and principally in the interest of exploitation; the municipalities which were the chief instruments in the process were native to the eastern half of the empire, which therefore survived intact much longer than the western half, where municipalities were less congenial. It is partly true that the Roman Empire fell, as has often been remarked, because it ceased to be Roman.

[1] Cf. T. Frank, *An Economic History of Rome*[2], pp. 202–218; and "Race Mixture in the Roman Empire," in *Am. Hist. Rev.*, XXI (July, 1916), 689–708. The segregation of freedmen in the 4 city tribes (234 B.C.) long minimized their political influence, and was regarded by Cicero as a source of safety for Rome. Cf. *C. A. H.*, VII, 806.   [2] Cf. pp. 81–83, 245, 257.

[3] E. Gibbon, *The Decline and Fall of the Roman Empire*, Ch. XXVI, n. 136.

Not only in blood, but also in character, Rome changed. The decline of the farmer class meant a decline in the heroism of old Rome, as Horace realized.[1] The effect of urbanization itself was a moral degeneration which Romans deplored.[2] "Every age has a Clodius, but not every age has a Cato," observed Seneca.[3] Cato (Uticensis) had his obvious faults; but he had such honesty, doggedness, shrewdness, and love of country that he served as the typical old-fashioned Roman of his day, as the elder Cato was of his day. There were others like him, perhaps, in later ages; but certainly they were less common. Symptoms crowd the memory: the misuse of wealth; the contempt for industry, as fit only for slaves; the treatment of provincials not as new allies, in the old spirit, but as subjects to be exploited, in the manner of Carthage and the Hellenistic kings, whose rôles and methods Rome had assumed. The provinces had once seemed to the Romans a godsend, manifestly destined to be plundered and to save them from having to serve in the army; yet the political and moral results of provincial administration proved the provinces to have been as much a curse as a blessing. Not without reason has it been declared that Rome began to fall from the moment when she annexed her first province. Greek and oriental culture captured Rome, for better and for worse, certainly at the cost of a loss of discipline and moral fibre. Even Greek philosophy, so stimulating in the days of Cicero, and Greek and oriental mystical religions were not an unmixed blessing; and the old Roman religion, with its emphasis on the family cult, was

---

[1] Horace, *Odes* III, 6.

[2] Note the use of the word *corruptio*. Livy's *Praefatio* is devoted to this theme. Cf. also G. Ferrero, *Characters and Events in Roman History*. "'Corruption' in Ancient Rome, and its Counterpart in Modern History," and *passim*.

[3] Seneca, *Moral Epistles*, 97, 10.

almost dead except in the country districts. Polybius and Cicero agree that Greeks are not to be trusted even under oath, whereas Romans are instinctively honest; but the evidence of wholesale dishonesty among Romans in Cicero's day is convincing.[1] Public amusements, almost always crude and commercialized, absorbed more and more of the leisure of the idle classes. The pacific ideals of the Christians have been alleged, though without sufficient evidence, to have been an important reason in a later period for the decline in efficiency of the Roman army.[2] Their preoccupation with another world may well have caused the affairs of this life to seem to them so mean and transitory as to deserve little effort; yet the Christians seem to have fought as well as the pagans.

Most of the symptoms that we have discussed may be detected in the last years of the Republic, and Gibbon erred in not finding the seeds of decay earlier than the Age of the Antonines. But there was still sufficient vigor left at the end of the Republic for a real revival in the early Empire; and this might have become permanent if other forces had not impeded, and if the Roman political system had not come to the end of its resources.

It is easy to say, with Benjamin Franklin, and it is partly true, that "in the hands of good men the worst form of government will succeed, and the best will fail in the hands of the bad." But it is only partly true. The Roman principate, with its concentration of power in the hands of one man, came into being, was tolerated by the Senate, and was even welcomed by the people, because it was better than the

---

[1] Polybius, VI, 56; Cicero, *Pro Flacco*, 9, 10; but see also *ad Att*. IV, 18, for an example of wholesale dishonesty.

[2] E. Gibbon, *op. cit.*, Ch. XV, and in "General Observations on the Fall of the Roman Empire in the West," following Ch. XXXVIII.

anarchy that it replaced; and this anarchy, in turn, had been the joint result of the failure of the Senate to deal with economic abuses at home and abroad, which supplied the tinder, and the rise of irresponsible or short-sighted generals, who were the spark. The principate was efficient, in the main; but by no means can it be considered an ideal form of government. At its best a benevolent despotism, at its worst a military tyranny, it never pretended to express the will of a citizen body. The Assembly, of course, was now meaningless; it could not formulate public opinion on any subject. The Senate was at first given a semblance of power, which it used to a considerable extent; nevertheless its composition, controlled by the emperor, kept it from being a truly representative body. No reformer could be anything more than a temporary leader of the opposition, or a leader in a revolution against the government. "Rome never developed a political organ capable at once of continuous action and peaceful reform." [1] Even for the perpetuation of the principate, there was no accepted principle, whether of heredity, or of adoption, or of election by the Senate; intrigues, assassinations, and civil wars of succession were the consequence; a considerable majority of Roman emperors met violent deaths, often after very short reigns.[2] "The crown of the Caesars," writes De Quincey, "was a crown of thorns; and it must be admitted that never in this world have rank and power been purchased at so awful a cost in tranquillity and peace of mind." [3] For the Roman people

---

[1] W. E. Heitland, *The Roman Fate: An Essay in Interpretation* (Cambridge, 1922), p. 27.

[2] Through M. Aurelius, the reigns averaged 13 years and 3 months; from then till Carinus, only 3 years and 6 months; from Diocletion till 476 A.D., 5 years and 5 months; the percentage of violent deaths during these periods was 52, 73, and 51 respectively.

[3] De Quincey, *The Caesars* (Boston, 1851), p. 261.

the cost was even greater: in the thousands of deaths in war, in the draining of treasuries and the diverting of capital, in the suppression of personal liberty under emperors whose very insecurity made them tyrannical.

The spectacle of anarchy and of bad emperors is sad enough; but it is less tragic than the spectacle of well-meaning emperors striving impotently amid forces that they could not comprehend. The economic resources of the empire were by no means depleted beyond recovery in the second and third centuries A.D.; but they were misused under stress of military and political necessity. Here again we find a vicious circle. The mounting expenses of defense and government raised the question whether even the rapidly urbanized empire could be managed efficiently enough, and whether it could be civilized fast enough, to support a single sovereign state; yet only the continued sovereignty of this state stood between safety and anarchy. Safety depended on organized man power and organized taxation; these in turn were made to depend on urbanization of the provinces, which was artificially stimulated at the expense of the peasants. As Rome had once contrived to live on Italy, and later on the provinces, so during the first and second centuries A.D. the provincial towns and their wealthy citizens, egged on by Rome, had repeated the process, to the great disadvantage of the provincial peasants; these municipalities, despite superficial evidences of prosperity and "Romanization," were not so much healthily functioning centres of districts as mere tax-collecting centres.[1]

The anarchy of the third century A.D. intensified the opposition between the municipal bourgeoisie and the peasants. The army was now drawn almost wholly from pro-

[1] Cf. W. E. Heitland, *Iterum, or a Further Discussion of the Roman Fate* (Cambridge, 1925).

vincial peasant conscripts (so far as it was not an imperial bodyguard of barbarian mercenaries); and these peasants, resenting bitterly their exclusion from the opportunities and privileges still open to the municipal bourgeoisie, were ready to resort to civil war, especially when they could find emperors of their own class, or at least sympathetic with their class, to lead them. The emperors could do nothing without the army, and, being themselves foreigners in many cases, did not hesitate to buy present security at the expense of crushing the municipal bourgeoisie. Nor did the ensuing despotism greatly improve matters. What had been a noble philosophy in the teaching and the example of Marcus Aurelius, the transcendent claim of the state over the claims of individuals, became a grim fact in the practice of Diocletian and his successors. Confronted by the bankruptcy of the state after generations of anarchy, Diocletian determined at whatever cost to reëstablish the solvency of the state and its military efficiency. This he did, as we have seen, by imposing on the already struggling municipal bourgeoisie the task of finding the sinews of war. Thus was removed from small men of business the incentive to become magistrates or *decuriones*, since they would be charged with the grievous burden either of gathering the taxes (or produce) or else of footing the bill themselves; and most of the bourgeoisie was gradually crushed out of existence. Meanwhile the most hopeless class of all, the serfs, who were now not permitted to leave the estates to which they were "adscribed," had nothing to gain by industry or thrift, and the productivity of the soil further diminished. Society was stratified in castes, and there was little possibility, and hardly any motive, for one to change one's status, for each caste had its grave disabilities; cynical apathy or resignation seemed to be the only recourse. The emperor and his bureaucracy of military officers and civil administrators now formed the only really privileged caste. The state had become an end in itself, a lifeless machine rather than a self-directing organism with a power of self-expression; neither the state nor any emperor had power to stop the ever-accelerating tendency toward centralization and autocracy. Only here and there, in emperor or in subject, could the qualities of the free citizen show themselves; nor is it strange that the ablest men of the day turned from politics to the hopes of another world offered by religion, to literature, or to lives of pleasure.

"The interests of the people were sacrificed to what seemed to be the interests of the state. . . .[1] The emperors of the fourth century, and above all Diocletian, grew up in the atmosphere of violence and compulsion. They never saw anything else, they never came across any other method. Their education was moderate, and their training exclusively military. They took their duties seriously, and they were animated by the sincerest love of their country. Their aim was to save the Roman Empire, and they achieved it. To this end they used, with the best of intentions, the means which were familiar to them, violence and compulsion. They never asked whether it was worth while to save the Roman Empire in order to make it a vast prison for scores of millions of men."[2] Should we consider these words, which are true, to be an indictment or an apology? It is easy for us to be wise, so long after the event; but it is not so certain that any of us, given the opportunities of the several Roman emperors, would have done much better. The great mischief had been done by their predecessors who had built an empire

[1] M. Rostovtzeff, *Social and Economic History of the Roman Empire*, p. 461.
[2] *Ibid.*, pp. 477 f. Cf. the same author's *History of the Ancient World*, Vol. II, Chs. XXIV, XXV.

without adapting to it a just and elastic social and political system. But if even the settlement of Augustus left seeds of discord, if Vespasian and Trajan and the Antonines built on unstable foundations, it is not surprising that mere soldiers like Septimius Severus and Diocletian, with their very diferent antecedents, should have met still graver economic and military situations with mere palliatives that served only to prolong the life of the state. What is surprising is not that the fabric of the Empire finally succumbed to the mistakes of emperors and the successive blows of the barbarian invaders, but rather that it lasted as long as it did. And can we feel sure, after all, that it would have meant greater happiness for the wretched inhabitants of the empire if the barbarian invaders had been allowed to flood the empire a century or two earlier than they did? Let us agree with Mr. Rostovtzeff that the most prominent feature in the development of the ancient world during the imperial age, alike in the political, social, and economic and in the intellectual field, is "a gradual absorption of the higher classes by the lower, accompanied by a gradual levelling down of standards." [1] It is nevertheless true that what was left of Graeco-Roman civilization, when Rome suffered its political overthrow, was precisely what served to civilize the upper classes, and to a large extent also the masses, of the peoples of northern Europe in all subsequent ages. One must therefore at least consider how far it is likely that this civilization, with its social traditions, its arts and letters, its legal principles, and its organization of Christianity, were ready to endure and to influence the millions of barbarians, if one is to entertain the hypothesis of an earlier surrender to the barbarians. The question is highly speculative, and involves

[1] M. Rostovtzeff, *Social and Economic History of the Roman Empire,* p. 480.

one's whole conception of the meaning of civilization and of the extent to which it can be spread.[1] Here we can only note that the decay of Rome ended one chapter, as it began another, in the history of civilization. It is a notable chapter, impressive in every phase:

> First Freedom, and then Glory — when that fails,
> Wealth, vice, corruption, — barbarism at last.
> And History, with all her volumes vast,
> Hath but *one* page.[2]

3. CUSTOM AND REASON

If we endeavor, reviewing the thousand years and more during which the Romans built their civilization, to appraise their genius for social organization and citizenship, we are confronted by a curious circumstance. We find that very seldom did they deliberately initiate any far-reaching policy with a conscious appreciation of motives and objectives; almost always theory followed, rather than anticipated, practice. By instinct conservative upholders of custom and tradition, the *mores maiorum*, they changed only when they were compelled by contingencies to change. There is no expression in Latin that just corresponds to our English word "reform"; for *res novae*, the nearest equivalent, smacks of revolution.[3] Of course the Roman constitution, like the British constitution, was never a complete paper constitution drawn up at a given moment under the inspiration of a particular philosophy or of a definite movement, but was rather the resultant of a series of precedents, revolutions,

---

[1] See further Chapter VIII.

[2] Byron, "Childe Harold's Pilgrimage," Canto IV, cviii.

[3] If the Romans had been wiser, they might have been advised by Aristotle and avoided revolution by building up a large, contented middle class, and by creating a system of public education. Cf. W. W. Fowler, *The City-State of the Greeks and Romans*, pp. 259–273.

compromises, and adaptations. Meanings were extended to suit altered conditions, legal fictions were created, and naturally many inconsistencies remained. On the other hand, the Romans did gradually develop in this process a rational conception of the relationships of men to each other and of Rome's relation to the world that is one of their most lasting achievements. It would be too much to say that reason ever replaced custom as their guide; but reason flashed through many a practice and served to illuminate the path of men of later ages.

If the government of the Roman Republic was moderately good, it was more because of the comparative honesty of its officials than because of the adequacy of its machinery.[1] The Senate was for a long time conspicuously honest. We have already noted that the body that showed the most propensity to declare aggressive wars in a jingoistic manner was not the Senate but the Assembly,[2] a fact worth remembering when we consider proposals for the prevention of war by transferring the power to declare war from legislative bodies to popular referendum. Yet the Senate was not particularly well organized for its work: meeting without docket or minutes, without regulation for a quorum, without committees and without any system of determining the precedence of motions, it was only during the early Republic that it could be efficient, as an informal advisory body for the magistrates. When its personnel deteriorated, late in the Republic, and when it undertook the management of the provinces, its value waned. And although the Romans were not ignorant of the principle of representative government, they never introduced it in any important way at the heart of the state. Where, then, could intelligent, effective, and

---

[1] Cf. Polybius, VI, 56; XVIII, 35; XXXII, 8.
[2] Pp. 48, 52–54.

responsible leadership be found? Seldom among the magistrates, for in their fear of monarchy, the Romans had clipped the wings of their magistrates by limiting their tenure, by employing the collegiate principle with the veto of a magistrate's colleague or of a tribune, and by elaborate restrictions as to the magistrate's age and the sequence of his offices. Dictators were only for exceptional military emergencies.

The failure of would-be reformers like the Gracchi to recast the political system to meet the social and economic needs of the people was perhaps inevitable, but was certainly ominous; and the political domination of military leaders and their agents during the last century of the Republic was an indication of the bankruptcy of the whole system. This was confirmed by the emergence of the efficient principate with its bureaucracy, in which democracy was sacrificed to peace and prosperity or to ambition. Here at last was leadership, benevolent or despotic as the case might be, which perforce built up administrative machinery to carry out its purposes. Democracy tends to intrust power and responsibility to a comparatively small class, whether openly, as in England, or less obviously, as in America; conversely, autocratic power tends to seek willing agents and to build up a governing class.[1] Thus in practice democracy and autocracy tend to approximate each other. Now although we may have sound reasons for putting faith in the ultimate possibilities of democracy, we must penetrate to the reality behind the outward political form, and discover the *ethos*, or spirit, of a given system. For example, the British system is more democratic than the American in its more rapid response to public opinion, through general elections on definite issues, and through the presence of cabinet ministers in

[1] See Viscount Bryce, quoted on p. 199, n. 1, and W. B. Munro, *The Invisible Government* (New York, 1928).

Parliament; it is less democratic, in that its social classes are relatively stratified, whereas in the United States individuals find their way much more readily from class to class. The Roman system was seldom really responsive to public opinion, which, to be sure, could hardly be formulated at all; and despite its early concessions to democracy, which virtually ended in B.C. 287,[1] it remained an oligarchy, changing chiefly in the composition of its governing class, as the old patrician nobility was flooded, and eventually replaced, first by wealthy plebeians, later by the municipal bourgeoisie, and under the empire by the provincial bourgeoisie and by a new military aristocracy. If we ask where in the Roman system is to be found a rational principle, it must be answered that it is not in the constitution as a whole, but in three or four phases of it, as they came to be understood by the Romans themselves.

It is well known that not only Cicero but many later writers, and in particular Montesquieu and Blackstone, admired in the Roman constitution the separation from each other of the legislative, the executive, and the judicial branches, and the "checks and balances" provided by the collegiate principle and the tribunician veto. Indeed, it was partly from their writings that the authors of the Constitution of the United States derived these principles, and enforced them far more consistently than did the Romans. For the Roman magistrates sat in the Senate; moreover the Senate itself sometimes sat as a judicial court, and during the Empire it at least nominally chose emperors and magistrates. Nevertheless, the separation of functions prevailed in the main, and served during the Republic to protect the liberties of the people. Even to the end of the Republic popular leaders could appeal, as by a "referendum," to the

[1] Cf. p. 198.

sovereign Assembly; and there are a few cases in which the Romans impeached or "recalled" a magistrate who appeared to have betrayed his trust. It might be helpful if members of the Cabinet in the United States were sometimes present in Congress to be questioned, in order to make the executive constantly responsive to public opinion: but the existence of congressional committees does something to connect the two branches. In the end, moreover, policies are planned in the United States by "the administration," that is, by the executive branch, rather than by Congress; and the executive is frequently the more genuinely popular branch, in touch with public opinion.

Far more important than their constitution, as it was far more characteristic and influential, was the great body of Roman law slowly built up throughout the empire, chiefly by men whose names are forgotten. The very vocabulary of Roman law supplied similes and metaphors for all manner of literature, both Latin and modern. And although the law itself is vast in extent and technical in its terminology, even the layman finds it interesting to trace the growth of the law from the acorn to the oak, and to observe how the Roman mind manifested itself in legal forms.

The acorn is to be found in the early period, when the family was supreme and custom was the norm of action. What should be done? Why, obviously what had been done in the past. And who knew the customs of the elders and ancestors, the *mores maiorum*? Naturally the *patres*, the heads of the patrician families, whose traditional lore was invoked as a court of appeal. Probably little was written down, except such decisions as were gathered by the *pontifices*. This early law had a semi-religious character, though it presently distinguished between duties owed to the gods (*fas*) and the human rights that rested on the sanction of custom (*ius*, or *boni mores*). Custom is a powerful controller of action; even in our day fashion, "what is done," "the spirit of the times," serve as the flywheel of social behavior. And religious sanctions had much force in an age when the head of the family alone could consult the will of the gods, and could, as it were, excommunicate a recalcitrant member. Even in much later times legal business could be done only on *dies fasti*.

Such a simple body of custom might suffice for a primitive tribal society. But there must have been cases of conflict between the authorities of two families. Arbitration, at first voluntary, and later made compulsory by the growing state, marked the transition to the time when the state assumed full jurisdiction over law. And the new non-patrician families could not have been satisfied to be denied access to a body of secret, unwritten law that could be invoked against them. The codification of the existing law, in the twelve Tables (451 B.C.), was a great landmark in the growth of liberty. Along with *fas* and *ius* and *boni mores* there now grew up new sanctions, the pronouncements of definite groups of human beings under proper safeguards. These were the votes of the duly convoked assemblies (*leges*) and, after the Hortensian Law of 287 B.C., those of the plebeian *concilium* (*plebiscita*), and of course the votes of the Senate (*senatus consulta*). Many of these were of the nature of fundamental law, a constitution or charter of liberty, even if they were technically only votes, like Acts of Congress, which might be superseded. For ordinary affairs, there were the decisions or edicts of the praetors, the magistrates who, though not given exclusively legal functions, were primarily law officers. It was their decisions that came to comprise the most substantial part of the law toward the end of the Republic. Naturally a praetor, though in theory quite free to use his discretion, would follow in the main the precedents established by his predecessors, so that his *edicta* were apt to include a "part taken over" (*pars tralaticia*), as well as what he added or modified. This is what we call "judge-made law," and it lent itself to whatever rational powers of interpretation and whatever progressive spirit or deference to public opinion the several praetors might possess.

The process of interpretation was tremendously assisted by the enlightened attitude of a class of legal experts, not mere practicing lawyers, whose rôle it was to give advice somewhat as patrons had advised their clients. These *prudentes*, or *juris consulti*, were ordinarily of noble birth (Cicero, a *novus homo*, never became one), and of course received no pay, in accordance with the Lex Cincia; [1] they were unofficial statesmen. But Augustus gave to certain jurisconsults the right of pronouncing on matters in his behalf,[2] a right which Hadrian confirmed. Their *responsa* were ordinarily based on rational principles derived from precedents and on philosophic grounds; but Seneca says that their personal prestige carried sufficient weight even when they assigned no reason for their decisions.[3] The emperors also gave *responsa* or *rescripta*, answers to questions referred to them, which were of course incorporated in the law. At least a few of the great jurists of the Empire deserve to be remembered. Four of them held the important office of *praefectus urbi*, which in their day gave them powers legal, administrative, and military, second only to the emperor. Such was Julian, who served under Hadrian and Antoninus Pius; such was his successor Papinian, the faithful assistant

---

[1] Cf. p. 207. For a hint of their rôle see Horace, *Odes* III, 5, 53 f.

[2] "Ius respondendi ex auctoritate eius."

[3] "Juris consultorum valent responsa etiamsi ratio non redditur." (Seneca, *Epist.*, 94, 27.)

of Marcus Aurelius and Septimius Severus, and the greatest
of all Roman jurists; such, also, were his two pupils and successors, the great Ulpian, and Paul, both prolific writers.
Excerpts from all these writers are preserved in the later
Digest. Nor should we overlook Pomponius, whose *Handbook* cited in the *Digest* throws light on legal history; nor
Gaius, a professor of law living probably under the Antonines, whose *Institutes*, a textbook, after being ignored for
three hundred years, was largely incorporated in Justinian's
Institutes. The work itself was then lost, till Niebuhr found
a manuscript of it in 1816, making it possible to get new light
on Roman law during the early Empire.

So far we have mentioned only the law pertaining to *cives*,
Roman citizens, known as the *ius civile*. This is the law that
was administered by the *praetor urbanus*. As Rome, however, absorbed other Italian communities with laws of their
own, and came to include many foreigners (*peregrini*) in the
city itself, a *praetor peregrinus* was created (242 B.C.) to administer cases arising among foreigners or between them and
citizens; his principles were based more on common sense
than on ancient Roman precedents, and influenced even the
ius civile. Furthermore, when the Romans assumed provincial responsibilities it was out of the question to impose
the rigid Roman system on all the manifold races and communities within the empire, many of whom already had
ancient legal traditions or systems of their own. The Roman administrators tried to build as far as they could on the
existing traditions of the several provinces. But they and
the jurisconsults soon came to recognize that there were certain common principles among different peoples. Whether it
was the principles common to them, or whether it was the
principles which they all shared with the Roman *ius civile*,

that the jurists named the "law of the nations" (*ius gentium*) is disputed even to-day.[1] However that may be, it is clear that the *ius gentium* was recognized as something arising from the common experience of many peoples, and that it served to knit together the Roman empire in an international or universal system. The jurisconsults, many of whom were Stoics, went still further, and identified the *ius gentium* with the Stoic conception of the "law of nature," *ius naturale*, principles binding on all men equally as sharers in the divine reason.[2] Thus merely legal technicalities and precedents were gradually swept aside, and all law tended, at its best, to approximate universal justice or reason, and was interpreted in the light of common sense and fair play (*aequitas*). The very maxims of the *Digest* show this scrupulous devotion to custom penetrated by the newer devotion to equity. Of the old tradition are these: "By no means are those things to be changed that have always had a certain interpretation;" and "The best interpreter of laws is custom." But in the new liberal spirit we find: "To know laws is to grasp not merely their words, but their force and

---

[1] Sir Henry Maine, *Ancient Law*, Ch. III; F. de Zulueta, in *The Legacy of Rome*, pp. 199–204; W. C. Morey, *Outlines of Roman Law*, pp. 63–71, 107–115. The *ius gentium* of course must be distinguished absolutely from what we call "international law," usages followed by nations in their dealings with each other; yet the possibility of an "international law" rests on the same hypothesis of a common participation of all men and peoples in the universal reason that was held by the Roman jurists. (Cf. Maine, *op. cit.*, Ch. IV.) Not without justice has it been said that classical Roman law is "a product of jurisprudence rather than of legislation." (De Zulueta, *op. cit.*, p. 188.) The jurisconsults drew largely on the Hellenistic law of the Greek states, which in turn was derived to a considerable extent from Plato. Cf. J. Burnet, *Platonism* (Sather Lectures), pp. 86–94.

[1] "The law which natural reason has constituted for all men obtains equally among all nations, and is called *ius gentium*." Gaius, *Inst.* I, 1. Here again it may be necessary to warn the reader against confusing this principle with the romantic or sentimental conception of "natural law" (i.e. instinct).

power;" and "Laws should be interpreted in the more generous spirit, that their will may be preserved.[1]

It was during the later Empire that the great codifications of Roman law were made; first, in 438 A.D. by command of Theodosius, and again the more important Codex of the eastern emperor Justinian, in 533–534, when the Western Empire had already fallen away from the East. The Corpus of the Roman Law, as it came to be known in the Renaissance, now comprised four parts: the Institutes, a brief manual and text-book of the whole law; the Digest (or Pandects), excerpts from Ulpian and many other legal authorities; the Code, a miscellaneous collection of decrees, laws, and imperial rescripts; and the Novels (Novellae), supplementary laws, added later in Justinian's reign. In the Western Empire, Roman law had meanwhile been mixed with Frankish law, and the mixture was carried throughout western Europe. In the eleventh century the Code of Justinian was rediscovered to the West, and henceforth exerted, through the study of jurists, an enormous influence on western legal systems, serving as a common language even amid local differences. Thus Roman law serves to-day as the foundation of the law not only in the Latin countries but in Holland, French Canada, the southwestern states of the United States, and even in Turkey. Apart from direct survivals and direct borrowings (as in the French Code Napoléon and in Turkey), principles derived directly from Roman law have penetrated even the quite different system of

---

[1] "Minime sunt mutanda ea quae interpretationem certam semper habuerunt" (Paul, *Dig.* 1.3.23). "Optima est legum interpres consuetudo" (Paul, *Dig.* 1.3.37). "Scire leges non hoc est verba earum tenere, sed vim ac potestatem. . . . Benignius leges interpretandae sunt quo voluntas earum servetur" (Celsus, *Dig.* 1.3.17, 18). All four passages are quoted by Zulueta, *op. cit.*, p. 206. See further Gaius, *Dig.* 50.17.56: "Semper in dubiis benigniora praeferenda sunt."

the Common Law of England and the United States; [1] and
the ideas and phraseology of international law are under a
great debt to Roman law. It is held by the most eminent
lawyers that even for the practice of the Common Law the
best foundation is the study of Roman law. "It is in their
command of leading principles, and the certainty with which
they apply those principles to concrete cases, that the Roman jurists excel. A lawyer, it goes without saying, always
seeks the principle underlying the decision of any case which
he may consult, or upon which he may rely in argument. He
wants the *ratio decidendi*, and having found it he asks himself what is the reason for the rule. When he has obtained a
clear perception of the principle, he is the more able to determine whether the case he relies upon, the facts which may at
first sight appear to be almost on all fours with those of his
own case, really support that case, or whether the two cases
are distinguishable." [2]

The Corpus of the Roman Law fills several stout volumes.
Nevertheless, it may be worth while here to indicate, however briefly, the scope of the private law, and the general
conditions under which the criminal law was administered.
It was important in the first place to define the status of an
individual, distinguishing freeman from slave, Roman from
alien, the head of a family, who was *sui iuris*, from his dependents. The full-fledged *civis* enjoyed a complex of
rights (his *caput*), — ownership of property, doing business,
inheritance, will-making, marriage, suffrage, office-holding,
— but might be mulcted of any or all of these; others enjoyed only partial rights, and might change these on marriage or adoption or emancipation, or on the death of the

---

[1] See further F. de Zulueta, *op. cit.*, pp. 173–181.

[2] Lord Chief Justice Hewart, addressing the Canadian Bar association in
Toronto, August, 1928, as reported in the London *Times*.

pater familias. The use of property was likewise defined not only as to absolute ownership but also as to prescriptive rights (like "squatters'" rights) and as to licensed use. Such distinctions appear widely even in literature, as in the famous saying of Lucretius: "Life is given to none outright, but to all as tenants." [1] So, too, of inheritance. The old custom of automatic inheritance on the part of direct heirs was gradually modified so as to permit legacies to more distant kinsmen or to friends; but at least till imperial times it was made difficult to will much property outside of the family. Later such restrictions were largely removed; legacy-hunters then courted the wealthy, and tyrannical emperors made life dangerous for prosperous persons who did not remember them handsomely in their wills. Lawyers, forbidden to receive pay, could not be forbidden to receive legacies; and a will was a convenient place in which to place the names of friends or of great personages whom one would like to have the world regard as one's friends, *honoris causa*, without any legacy necessarily being forthcoming. The Roman law of contracts, with their various kinds, oral or written, with or without pledges, is closely related to modern law. The Romans valued the written contract as much as we do, the oral promise more than we do, — in fact, preferring it to any other kind.

We cannot here discuss the complicated methods of procedure of the Roman courts except to observe that a distinction was often made between the part of a trial in which the praetor determined what legal principle was involved and the part in which subordinate judges (*iudices*), acting under instructions (*formula*) from him, tried out the facts in the case. Though there were many other forms of trial or arbitration in different courts, this "formulary" procedure, used

[1] Lucretius, III, 971: "Vitaque mancipio nulli datur, omnibus usu."

till the time of Diocletian, was perhaps the most significant, in distinguishing between fact and law, — the same general distinction, it may be noted, that modern law preserves when it intrusts to the common sense and judgment of an untrained jury the finding of the facts, reserving points of law to the trained judge. There is also some reason for believing that the jury system of England and America is ultimately not of Germanic but of Roman origin.[1] Under the later Empire the formulary system disappeared, and all cases were decided outright by the numerous judges who represented the emperor. There was also, even in earlier times, provision for *interdicta*, commands or prohibitions on the part of judges, corresponding somewhat to our "injunctions" and our police regulations.

Criminal law naturally was removed very early from the control of the *pater familias* and put under the jurisdiction of magistrates, qualified by the right of appeal to the assemblies. From 149 B.C. it began to be intrusted to special courts (*quaestiones*) with large juries drawn from the upper classes;[2] finally, in the third century A.D., it was absorbed by the emperor and his staff of judges, the right of "appeal to Caesar" already having been substituted for the earlier appeal to the Assembly.[3] But Rome suffered from the fact that she never provided in her system for a public prosecuting attorney, and relied on voluntary prosecutions on the part of ambitious young lawyers with reputations to make. For this reason culprits might escape, if they could find accomplices to prosecute them; and innocent men were often the victims of blackmailers or informers (*delatores*). Wit-

[1] Cf. F. F. Abbott, *Roman Politics*, pp. 97–99.
[2] Till 123 from the Senate; 123–81 from the *equites*, thanks to G. Gracchus; restored by Sulla to the Senate, 81–70; thenceforth from panels including both classes.
[3] Cf. *Acts*, xxv, 11.

nesses were summoned by allowing their ears, the seat of hearing, to be touched.[1] Some persons, whose moral character was under a cloud, were debarred from giving testimony; and during the Republic slaves, whose loyalty to their masters was assumed, were examined only under torture; freemen were not so tortured. Penalties might concern either the legal status (*caput*) of the convicted man or his property (being fines, or *multae*), but seldom both. Imprisonment was for those awaiting trial, and was not ordinarily a form of punishment. The death penalty was seldom inflicted during the late Republic, and if imposed could usually be avoided by the legal fiction of voluntary exile, since the sentence merely forbade the use of water and fire in Rome (or Italy), and permitted one to withdraw, often to some delightful retreat. Under the Empire the increasing rigor of the government showed itself in the increasing use of the death penalty and its extension to some minor crimes. Voluntary exile was no longer a permitted substitute, though distinguished persons convicted of political offences were often permitted to anticipate execution by suicide. Old penalties were revived, or were extended from slaves to freemen: flogging and beheading by the rods and axes, crucifixion (till Constantine, moved by religious considerations, abolished it), and death in the arena by combat or by the jaws of hungry wild beasts. Penal servitude was introduced, as well as exile, whether in its old form or in the form of deportation to an island with loss of status, or as *relegatio*, compulsory residence at a definite, remote place, without loss of status. Free witnesses, as well as slaves, might now be examined under torture. On the other hand, the same crime was punished more severely in the case of the lower

---

[1] Cf. Horace, *Sat.* I, 9, 77 ff.; this was for Horace preferable to the continued company of the bore.

classes (the *humiliores*, or *tenuiores*) than in the case of the upper classes (the *honestiores*). Perhaps the chief alleviating fact in this trend of the criminal law is that the state tended to take over from masters their jurisdiction over their slaves, and to protect them from abuses.

From this brief glance at the administration of justice during the Empire one may receive a melancholy impression, if one fails to recall the humane and liberal spirit that the jurists were coming to manifest. The chief source of cruelty and injustice, it cannot be doubted, was the general political trend toward autocracy caused in the main by military and economic pressure; and this, as we have seen, was apparently inevitable. It is worth asking, however, what the Romans thought of their whole political and legal creation. Was it beneficent? Had it a definite goal?

We begin, as usual, with a fact, — the fact that Rome acquired, without any particular plan, an empire.[1] Cicero was not far from the truth when he said that Rome gained the mastery of the world by coming to the aid of her allies. If she did incidentally confer on her subjects great blessings and build up a universal empire in which a common language,[2] a common legal system, and a common religion prevailed, it was only very slowly that she realized what she was about. First it was military conquest that she understood,

---

[1] On this whole subject, see E. Barker's admirable essay, "The Conception of Empire," in *The Legacy of Rome.*

[2] For the value of Latin as a bond of empire, see J. W. Duff, *Literary History of Rome*, pp. 13–18; F. F. Abbott, *The Common People of Ancient Rome*, Chs. I, II; Lord Cromer, *Ancient and Modern Imperialism*, quoted by F. F. Abbott, *Roman Politics*, pp. 126 f.; and Viscount Bryce, *The Ancient Roman Empire and the British Empire in India* (Oxford, 1914), pp. 65–68. Cromer and Bryce both emphasize the advantage which a common language gave the Roman empire, the absence of which in some of the British dominions is a grave difficulty. Rome was also lucky in having generally homogeneous peoples to govern (practically no "color question," for example). Cf. R. G. Collingwood, *Roman Britain*, pp. 14 and 15.

then the moral qualities on which it depended; only later was there any appreciation of the growing unity within the Pax Romana and of the Roman destiny or mission. So, for example, Polybius gave to his history an artistic unity by emphasizing its central theme, Rome's winning of world-empire within two generations. So Livy in his Preface announces a similar theme, but with a moral coloring: "Let each reader, I beg, direct his attention to the life and character, the men and the arts manifested at home and in the field of war, by which our empire was won and increased." And Livy goes on to drive home the moral that history's chief purpose is to hold up examples and warnings.[1] Here and there he hints that the growth of Rome was under divine guidance; but its purpose is not even hinted at. Tacitus is a bit of a fatalist, as well as a moralist; and for him the best days of Rome were those of republican "liberty." It is not surprising that he is pessimistic and satirical about the Empire, reconciling himself to it with difficulty; he and his class have suffered from it. The monuments and inscriptions of the Empire, especially those coming from the provinces, do tell an eloquent story of empire-building, but necessarily without giving much insight into its significance. With the Augustan poets it is somewhat different; and of them something will be said later.[2] But from the bare fact of empire grew at least the legal conceptions of empire that were bound up in the very words *imperium, provincia, potestas*, and the like, all of which denoted or involved the right of the magistrate to issue commands, and were now used in a special sense of Rome's relation to her new subjects. Whether the right implied obligations to the subjects was a

---

[1] Livy, *Praef.*, 9, 10. See further below, pp. 415 f.
[2] Pp. 347, 349–356, 476 f., 484 f. See also W. Y. Sellar, *The Roman Poets of the Augustan Age: Virgil*, Ch. X.

question which did not immediately arise, — hardly, indeed, till the legal concept was interpreted in the light of philosophy.[1] But all Romans must have felt the moral difference between the empire-builders of the Punic Wars and their luxurious heirs who profited by the empire. They must sometime face the question as to why the world was becoming one, and also as to what body or person should be sovereign. Could any individual, indeed, claim sovereignty?

Few Romans would have been inclined to ask these questions if the empire had not existed as a fact, and if contingencies had not turned the republic into what rapidly became a monarchy. Given these facts to explain or justify, the Romans found sufficient precedents and arguments to build a strong theory of empire which has lasted, in various forms, till the present day. In the East, where they had absorbed Alexander's empire and the remains of other oriental empires partly built into his empire, they found an ancient tradition of autocracy, tribute-bearing subjects, and the worship of a god-king, in which municipalities and nations were fused. Each of these precedents was followed: emperor-worship provided a universal religion,[2] commerce brought about economic unity, ambition and contingencies united to precipitate the change from the constitutional principate into a tax-gathering absolutism. The Stoic philosophy that developed the conception of the *ius naturale* also held up an ideal of cosmopolitanism; the counterpart of the rational universe was a world-state, in which all men were equal as citizens of the world, and nations and petty states pooled their differences. Here again facts seemed to support theory; the population of the empire was becoming fused; the franchise was extended and Roman law was

---

[1] Cf. B. W. Henderson, in *Companion to Latin Studies*, p. 394.
[2] See further, pp. 347 f.

standardized with a consequent levelling of privileges; emperors were drawn from remote provinces; and even diverse religious cults approximated a single type.

Even if the theory of the empire were accepted as satisfactory, one might still raise the question whether it carried with it the justification of an absolute monarchy. Once more the theorists sought to proceed from a basis of fact. This time the fact was that sovereignty, which during the Republic had undeniably rested with the people when duly assembled, had passed to the emperor, subject only to the merely formal consent of the Senate or of the Praetorian Guard.[1] The jurists sought both to recognize the fact and to give the emperor an appearance of constitutionality. By one account he is the "living law on earth"; [2] but Ulpian, in laying down the principle that "The will of the *princeps* has the force of law," gives the reason, "because the people confers upon him and into his hands all its own sovereignty and power." [3] From this ambiguity of theory may be traced some of the conflict of opinion that raged in the Middle Ages as to the claims of pope, of emperor, and of people. Meanwhile, however, had occurred the division of the empire, which in a sense had combined church and state, or rather had used religion (first emperor-worship and later Christianity) in the interests of the state. And here we may note a curious paradox. "The East, which gave religion and the Church to the West, fell under the control of the State. The

---

[1] Even during the Republic, Cicero had tried to find room in his ideal state for a *rector* or *moderator* or *princeps rei publicae*, perhaps on the analogy of the Platonic philosopher-king, and possibly with Pompey in mind. (*De Rep.* V, VI.)

[2] From such views were derived in part later arguments for the "divine right of kings."

[3] Such sayings, which could be paralleled in Cicero and in Greek philosophy, suggest to us, if they did not influence, the theory of Hobbes, of sovereignty delegated by society to a king, and that of Rousseau, of the individual's surrender to society by a "social contract."

West, which gave politics and the State to the East, came under the sovereignty of the Church. We may almost say that there was an interchange of gifts and of rôles. The western state moved into the East, to Constantinople, and subjugating the Church produced Byzantinism. The Church which arose in the East moved into the West, to Rome, and enthroning the Papacy produced Latin Christianity." [1]

Where, then, was sovereignty to be found? Wherever the idea of empire persisted and could make itself recognized. In the East there were still emperors, who assumed control of the Church. In the West, there were no more emperors, and the popes assumed control of temporal affairs, armed not only with the terrible weapon of excommunication but with great estates and considerable experience in administration. Quite apart from the original claim of Christianity to become a universal religion, which now took the form of the claim of the popes to sovereignty as the earthly representatives of God, the popes naturally assumed by default the claims to sovereignty of the emperors whose places in Rome they had taken. The Eastern Church, despite its differences, was recognized by the popes till the eleventh century; the eastern emperors only till 800 A.D., when the coronation of Charlemagne in Rome at the hands of a pope marked the creation of the new "Holy Roman Empire." This creation did not actually change the theory of empire; for it had long been held that the pope was the earthly head of the Church, which was the visible counterpart of the City of God, while the emperor exercised a parallel sovereignty over temporal matters, till 800 A.D., at Constantinople, and thereafter in the West (and the eastern emperor was thereafter necessarily ignored). The Germanic emperors of the "Holy Roman Em-

[1] E. Barker, *op. cit.*, p. 78.

pire " were able to assert their claims to parallel sovereignty
only till Pope Gregory VII, whose humbling of the emperor
Henry IV in 1077 A.D. symbolized the new claims of the
Papacy to absolute supremacy over all society, both spiritual
and temporal. The struggle between popes and emperors
continued for several centuries. Dante put the case in favor
of parallel sovereignty: "Man had need of two guides for his
life; whereof one is the Supreme Pontiff, to lead mankind to
eternal life, according to the things revealed to us; and the
other is the Emperor, to guide mankind to happiness in the
world, in accordance with the teaching of philosophy." [1]
Nevertheless, the supremacy of the popes endured till the
rising political and national feeling of northern Europe and
the religious movement of the Reformation broke down in
practice the imperial claims of the Papacy. The "Holy
Roman Empire" continued, at least in name, till 1806, when
its last representative abdicated his claims to empire, thus
ending what was at the time "the oldest political institution
in the World." [2]

The survival in modern times, at least in theory, of the
claims of the Papacy to universal sovereignty may be regarded as a heritage from the Roman Empire. It is clear
that centralization is a condition of efficiency in many matters; and the centrifugal tendencies of Protestantism, often
due to small, even accidental, historic differences as to matters of doctrine or of ritual, have reached absurd extremes.
The continuous tradition of Catholicism has also gathered a
precious harvest of experience, artistic and political no less
than religious, which could ill be spared. Nevertheless, what
the Protestant will find it hard to give up is his conviction
that religion is the last sphere in which authority has any

[1] *De Mon.* II, 16.
[2] Viscount Bryce, *The Holy Roman Empire*, p. 1.

right to penetrate. For him, as a believer in democracy, any authority is merely delegated; and the less authority the better. This will for him outweigh any papal claims based on supernatural grounds, either logical or quasi-historical. And even if he were disposed to grant spiritual authority to a supreme earthly Vicar of Christ, for reasons of efficiency, he may still question the right of any spiritual authority to temporal authority, either in the form of universal sovereignty (as claimed by the popes of the Middle Ages), or of the Papal States (terminated, except for the Vatican itself, in 1870, when united Italy was created), or in the limited form of a small Vatican City (the form in which the "Roman Question" was settled by agreement in 1929).

The idea of empire, strong from the time of Alexander the Great till a few centuries ago, is unpopular to-day. The sentiment of the world is against any nation that undertakes to build a new empire by military conquest. But there are empires in existence, surviving from the past, including diverse nationalities and civilizations; and nations sometimes find themselves creating what amounts to empire, either by deliberate economic penetration and development, or accidentally, as in the case of the United States in Cuba and the Philippines. These empires must determine what their moral and political obligations are toward their subject peoples. The United States has liberated Cuba, but has not yet found a final solution for the Philippine problem.[1] Great

---

[1] Other questions involved in the imperial position of the United States naturally occur. As to population, the present restriction of immigration assumes, probably rightly, that a saturation point of aliens has been reached (though with only negative tests for selecting the aliens to be admitted). But what is to be the status of the immigrants? Are they to be fused in a "melting pot," or to keep their national character, manners, etc.? Is the foreign-language press a menace? Should American citizenship be a requirement or a privilege? If a privilege, what tests can be applied? Again, what is to be our attitude toward our Latin neighbors in Central and South America? Can we

Britain has a special set of problems in Ireland, India, and Egypt, complicated by historical, racial, religious, and military considerations; she is ready to intrust local self-government to her dominions so far as is consonant with her own safety; but no dogma whether of imperialism or of the sacredness of national independence will avail to establish *a priori* a final settlement either for England's good or for that of her dependencies.[1]

The modern world of intense economic competition and highly developed means of communication has shrunk so violently that conflicts become more and more inevitable, unless means of adjustment can be found. The oldest system meant constant wars and the emergence and decay of successive empires built on force, mitigated by ties of race, language, religion, or institutions. The more recent system meant an attempt of governments, guided by what appeared to be enlightened self-interest, to act through more or less honest diplomacy in preservation of the status quo, and to use war only as a more or less unpleasant last resort for cases of "vital interests" or "national honor." The results, seen in the Great War, are not reassuring. Some way must be found of forwarding the common interests of humanity, which are by no means fully represented by the competition of nationalities, even in times of peace; above all, the resort

convince them of our unselfish policies in view of our vested interests in their countries? Some rational system, beyond ordinary diplomacy plus the "big stick," is needed for the settlement of differences. And finally, how far shall the federal government encroach on state and local government? Which interests gain by being dealt with from Washington, and which suffer?

[1] See the illuminating discussion by Viscount Bryce in *The Ancient Roman Empire and the British Empire in India*, and his *The Diffusion of Roman and English Law throughout the World* (Oxford, 1914), both revised and reprinted from his *Studies in History and Jurisprudence*. Two interesting points are that the Romans Romanized their empire far more than the British have Anglicized theirs, and that Roman and English law now practically control the world.

to war must be forever removed. The vision of another world-empire in any literal sense is not within the range of practical consideration at present. And it may be a very long time before most of us could contemplate without misgivings a vast imperialism in which the local differences, the quaint provincialisms, the rights of minorities, the habits of centuries, might be overruled by a bureaucracy, wherever situated, or by a majority vote of peoples across the globe. Something less ambitious than such imperialism must suffice, at least for centuries. The Hague Tribunal, the World Court, regional understandings, the Monroe Doctrine, disarmament compacts, the Kellogg Treaty, the codification of international law, — all these are highly useful instruments for settling special disputes and for creating an international habit of peace. But none of them supply a continuously functioning organism of flesh and blood, bringing together men of good will from different nations in such friendly association that they can promote their common peaceful interests and exert their wills to prevent war. That is the special rôle of the League of Nations. Not an empire in the old sense, in that the sovereignty of even its smallest constituent nations is safeguarded, it nevertheless speaks for the conscience of the world. Using the representative principle far more than did ancient Rome, it is in a sense a "Parliament of the World," and helps to bring about, but only by the force of reason and public opinion, that habit of justice which Rome at her best built up within her Pax Romana.

If the habit of peace and coöperation and understanding is to grow still further, it will not be primarily because of any material or economic causes, but because of the wills of men who have had a common experience. There are fortunately many elements that may assist to build up this sense of partnership: religion (especially, but not exclusively,

Christianity), international educational movements and exchanges, the travel of educated persons, the diffusion of the arts and of scientific information. But it will not do to be too sanguine, and to overlook the fact that international relations and social well-being depend above all on enlightened leadership, without which the discoveries of science, the far-flung voice of the radio and the tale of the moving film, even the religious ideas of the man in the street, are helpless if not worse than useless. On the fund of ideas of the leaders depends the hope of the rest of mankind. And it is not a little thing that the majority of the leaders who are now guiding the destinies of nations and of international relations are still moving in the two traditions that have tried, amid many failures, most consistently to build up institutions based both on ancient custom and on reason, with a view to real justice: the Roman, or Latin, tradition, and the English tradition. The future of the world depends to no little extent on its continued utilization of these two great sources of stability and progress.

CHAPTER VI

FLAMMANTIA MOENIA MUNDI

Felix qui potuit rerum cognoscere causas,
Atque metus omnis et inexorabile fatum
Subiecit pedibus strepitumque Acherontis avari.
Fortunatus et ille deos qui novit agrestis
Panaque Silvanumque senem Nymphasque sorores.

Virgil, Georg. II, 490–494.

1. SUPERSTITION AND RELIGION

IN HIS earliest conflicts with the terrors of the forest and
the plain, the Roman felt his insufficiency; beast and
fellow man, fever and famine, were ever to be feared, and
he felt a shudder, a sense of awe, or *religio*, in the presence
of the unknown, the barrier and limit of his own powers.
This insufficiency he expressed in various ways. He sought
to surmount it by ritual acts of magic that might control
hostile powers; he endeavored to penetrate the obscurity of
the future by rites of divination or by the lore of astrology.
Even in the more enlightened ages of Roman civilization,
when he had learned much from his neighbors and from
Greece and the Orient, the Roman's *religio*, controlled and
ordered by the institutions of the state, preserved a fundamental attitude which we can describe only as superstitious.
Indeed, even though his attitude came at times to include
also what we must recognize as truly and profoundly religious, it would be rash to use without qualification the
English word "religion" as the equivalent of what the Roman meant by *religio*. In the sceptical age of the late Republic, to be sure, Stoics or Platonists like Cicero tried to

define the firm structure of the universe in terms either of
matter or of divine reason, and to lay down principles of
human conduct in harmony with nature. The solitary rebel
Lucretius, despising traditional "religion," sought to rise
with Epicurus even beyond the "flaming ramparts of the
world" and by the "living force of his soul" to gain a
victory over ignorance and a tranquillity that knows not
the idle fears of "religion."[1] By most Romans, however, the
"ramparts" were to be scaled, if at all, not so much by the
unaided reason as by ever-changing manifestations of faith
and will and love. It would be a mistake to interpret the
Roman's religious experience wholly in terms of its origins
and its materials or methods, rather than in terms of its maturity and its goal; for any religion is essentially not so much
an institution or body of beliefs as an attitude, a way of
meeting a perceived need or insufficiency which is perennial.[2] The forms may change; the need remains.

The need is perhaps most frankly recognized in those
primitive phases of superstition which were always near the
surface, and which emerged in times of national fear. Earthquakes and places struck by lightning were viewed with misgivings, and must be treated with special rites. Acts of
"sympathetic" or "imitative" magic were performed in the
hope of influencing persons or things to a similar behavior;
so Virgil, following Theocritus, depicts a girl binding an
image of her lover Daphnis with three threads in order to

[1] Lucretius, I, 62–79.
[2] Cf. the definition of religion by I. W. Howerth: "Religion is the effective desire to be in right relations with the Power manifesting itself in the
universe," (quoted by W. W. Fowler, *The Religious Experience of the Roman
People*, p. 8. Cf. also *ibid.*, pp. 459–462, tracing the Latin history of the
word *religio* from "the feeling which suggests worship" to "the forms under
which we perform that worship," or both together, or again to separate
religious systems contrasted with each other, and especially to Christianity
as the school of character).

bind Daphnis himself to her; [1] and Dido pretends to use black art in order to destroy Aeneas.[2] Certain people, unfortunate or envious, have been supposed not only by the ancient Romans but by many modern Italians and other peoples of our day to be endowed with *fascinatio*, the "evil eye," and thus to be able to blast the lives of those whom they look upon, or to bewitch and spirit away their neighbors' crops; charms, such as the child's *bulla*,[3] or the stripe that fringed the garments of boys and of magistrates, must be worn, or gestures must be made, to avert the "evil eye." Even to-day the Italian peasant may extend the index finger and the smallest finger of one hand to avert this baleful influence; and under the carts that bump along the ways leading in and out of Rome dangle animals' horns that point as they turn, like extended fingers, at all persons by the way. Some people, it was supposed, could change themselves into wolves,[4] becoming "were-wolves," and devour human flesh. Even in Horace's day there were hags who, like his Canidia, traded in charms and love-philtres made of gruesome objects, — dead men's bones and young boys' fresh corpses.[5]

To be sure there were attempts to suppress magical arts. The Twelve Tables (450 B.C.) expressly forbade the spiriting away of crops; and laws were passed repeatedly against the use of magic and astrology. Nevertheless, whereas magic, the attempt to control unseen powers by mechanical means, lingered chiefly in private life, in the state religion the attempt was made to propitiate such powers by prayer and by other elaborate and legalized institutions. Many of these attempts were originally "sympathetic" magic of the crudest sort, intended by the performance of certain ritual acts

---

[1] *Buc.* VIII, 64–109. [2] *Aen.* IV, 474–521.
[3] Cf. p. 104. [4] Virgil, *Buc.* VIII, 98.
[5] *Sat.* I, 8; Epodes 5 and 17.

to bring about similar desired results; thus the wetting of "rain stones" was supposed to produce rain, the fertility of women was supposed to be assisted by their being whipped with thongs by priests known as Luperci ("goat-men"),[1] and the sacrifice of a red dog was performed to avert the red mildew from the crops, or perhaps also for other purposes as well. The meaning of many primitive rites and prescriptions was completely forgotten, though the customs or phrases derived from them persisted, to puzzle the Romans themselves and learned students like Plutarch.[2] In times of danger, such as Hannibal's invasion of Italy, the Social and the Civil Wars, and the death of Caesar, a wave of superstitious panic was apt to recur; signs and omens were reported, and recourse was had to ancient or to exotic practices. Reports of earthquakes and floods and the overthrow of statues, the veiling of the sun, temples struck by lightning, and wolves raiding the city were met by extraordinary sacrifices, on very rare occasions even by human sacrifices. Tacitus, telling of a panic in 69 A.D., caused by such reports,[3] observes: "Such stories are listened to now in times of national anxiety, though in less civilized days they commanded attention even under normal conditions." It is clear, moreover, that not only the ignorant but the most eminent Romans were the victims of superstition. Sulla used to carry with him a little image of Apollo, which he kissed frequently, and to which he prayed before his soldiers on the eve of battle.[4] Cicero found it worth while to devote a treatise to an attack on the pretences of the art of divination to foretell the future; yet the emperor Tiberius kept an astrologer in his

---

[1] Cf. p. 320.

[2] See his *Roman Questions*. On magic and primitive religion in general, see Sir J. G. Frazer, *The Golden Bough*; H. J. Rose, *Primitive Culture in Italy*.

[3] *Hist.* I, 86.

[4] Valerius Maximus, I, 2, 3 (epitomators).

retinue.[1] And the survival in Italy and in many other countries to-day of such superstitions as the "evil eye" gives us
glimpses of the average Roman's state of mind; nor is it very
long since the belief in witchcraft was almost universal in
English-speaking countries.[2] It ill becomes us, then, to look
down patronizingly on the superstition of the Roman;
scratch many a modern man, and we shall find under the
skin just such a frightened creature doing his best to cope
with unfriendly powers.

Even the officially regulated religious system of the Romans, however, differs fundamentally from what we associate with religion, and especially from Protestant Christianity. The great and essential point of resemblance is
obviously the common recognition of something divine
which should be approached in the attitude of worship. But
the Roman's divinities are many and are tolerant of each
other; and they require of him not so much beliefs in revealed truths as ritual acts, which in general have to do with
the physical well-being of the community, rather than of the
individual. Health, food, success in war, rather than virtue,
are the chief desiderata, for which rites are performed and
prayers are offered. A great deal of Roman religion is local
in origin and specialized in scope; a great deal is imported
from other Italic or from Etruscan towns, or from the Greek
cities; the result is a mass of accretions which almost pre-
vents us from regarding Roman religion as truly Roman,
save as it is carried on in a Roman spirit, or as religious, save
as this spirit suffers a metamorphosis. In externals, the ancient Roman's worship is strikingly different from Christian
analogues. He has no "church" building to house the wor-

---

[1] Tacitus, *Ann.* VI, 20–22; cf. Louis XI of France.
[2] Cf. G. L. Kittredge, *Witchcraft in Old and New England* (Cambridge,
Mass., 1929).

shipers; for the pagan temple is built primarily to house the image of a deity and the treasures. He recognizes no difference between "church members" and the unchurched; for all, as citizens, are included in the religious observances of the state, though they may also participate in newer and alien cults. The Roman has not a "service," except for the sacrifice, the procession, and similar symbolic or magical rites; he has no sacred book, except for the treasured collection of advice on ritual attributed to the Cumaean Sibyl; no imaginative mythology of his own; no profound theology; no sermon, till the Stoic supplies the gap.

But the most striking difference lies in the Roman's separation between religion and ethics. The Roman's gods are powers who can help him, but they are not necessarily patterns of conduct; and the Roman's prayers, Cicero observes, do not ask the gods to make him virtuous, but rather to give him health and wealth.[1] His ritual acts may be supposed to help him, but they do not, at least for a long time, require of him a purity that is more than ceremonial. Nevertheless, it is possible to trace in this formal, conservative, somewhat legalistic Roman religion the growth of a tradition and an attitude which was of great moral value; and then, as the old forms and symbols outgrew their usefulness, to see how the same sense of insufficiency and the craving for salvation both of the whole people and of individuals finds an answer in new forms of experience, intellectual and spiritual and political. The Roman at his best is less imaginative than the Greek; less spiritually ardent than the Hebrew prophet

---

[1] Cicero, cited without reference by Fowler, in Sandys, *Companion to Latin Studies*, p. 152. For illustrations of this statement, and also for examples of prayers for blessings of a more spiritual sort, see E. E. Burriss, "The Objects of a Roman's Prayers," *Classical Weekly*, XXIII (February 3, 1930), 14. And the old formula *macte virtute esto*, "be blessed because of thy virtue," suggests another attitude.

or the Christian martyr; less intent on reforming his fellow
men than the modern American. But he lives in constant
relationship with the unseen world, and his character is
deepened by it. It is the story of his long development which
we must now follow.

That the earliest Romans felt a special awe attaching to
trees, and still more to groves and wooded hills, is clear from
many bits of evidence. Like the Greek, in the presence of the
oak of Zeus at Dodona, so the Roman, piercing the gloom of
a copse or of a cave, was troubled by a sense of something
sacred which he could not name. Such places were invested
with dread, as holy ground (*loca religiosa*) by nature, not set
apart by any act of consecration (*loca sacra*). So Virgil represents Evander as showing Aeneas "a great grove" (*lucum
ingentem*) on what was destined to be the Palatine Hill, and
"the copse (*nemus*) of the sacred Argiletum. . . . Thence
he led him to the Tarpeian rock and the Capitol, now golden,
but once rough with silvan thickets. Already a dread awe of
the place (*religio dira loci*) struck fear into the timid rustics,
already they trembled at the wood and the crag. 'This
copse,' he said, 'this hill with its leafy summit a god in-
habits, but who it is we know not.'" [1] Evander quotes his
countrymen as believing that it is Jupiter; but in the earliest
period no name or personality was associated with these
sacred spots, though they were later connected with special
divinities, — the Aventine and Nemi with Diana, Caere
with Silvanus, the little *bosco sacro* just south of Rome with
the wise Egeria.[2]

---

[1] *Aen.* VIII, 342–354.

[2] Cf. Ovid, *Fasti* III, 295 f.

> "Lucus Aventino suberat niger ilicis umbra
> quo posses viso dicere 'numen inest.'"

Note that, as Ovid suggests, no special "god" can yet be associated with the
place, only a vague undifferentiated *numen* or spirit. Cf. further Seneca,

The vague awe that was localized in groves was felt also in the performance of the varied activities of the farm. If the care of herds was the earliest occupation of the nomadic settlers of Latium, and gave rise to the earliest festivals,[1] agriculture was the most characteristic activity of the Romans when they had settled in a fixed region; and of the two most important phases of early Roman religion one is the religion of farm life. With each act or department of agriculture was associated a power or spirit (*numen*), sometimes conceived in later times as a god or goddess in human form (like Ceres), which could help or hinder the farmer's efforts, and whose favor must therefore be won with "first fruits" or whose blighting influence must be averted by rites of lustration or symbolic riddance. Let Virgil set forth the spirit and the ritual of the Ambarvalia, the spring processional round the boundaries of the farm or the hamlet, intended to purify the growing crops.

> But chiefly pay
> Fit worship to the gods.   Make sacrifice
> Each year to sovereign Ceres, when the grass
> Is green and glad, the winter making end,
> And gentle Spring is in the air, when lambs
> Are fattening, when the wine grows smooth and mild
> And sweet is slumber in cool hillside shade.
> Let all the country youth of manly prime
> On Ceres call, bearing her tribute due
> Of honey mixed with milk and sweet, new wine.
> Three times around the freshly bladed corn
> The blessed victim guide, while all the choir
> In gladsome company an anthem sing,
> Bidding the goddess to their lowly doors.

Epist., 41, 3; Otto Kern, *Religion der Griechen*, pp. 21, 82 f.; Sir A. Geikie, *The Love of Nature among the Romans*, pp. 141–150. Nemi, lake and village in the Alban Hills, takes its title from its grove (*nemus*) of Diana.

[1] E.g. the *Parilia*; cf. p. 16. April 21, on which the Parilia fell, is now appropriately celebrated as the birthday of the City of Rome.

And let no reaper touch the ripened corn
With sickle keen until his brows he bind
With twine of oak-leaf, while he trips along
In artless dance with songs in Ceres' praise.[1]

Here Virgil preserves for us, together with the simplicity
and reverence, the hopefulness and gaiety of the farmer's
religion in general, the essential part of the Ambarvalia; the
procession, thrice performed, of the sacrificial victims round
the fields. We know that the victims were the three animals
most prized by the farmer, the pig, the sheep, and the bull
(*suovetaurilia*); they are represented in a bas-relief still
standing in the Forum Romarum (the Anaglypha Traiani).
After the third round, the victims were sacrificed, and a
prayer was made. In Virgil's account the prayer is to
Ceres, the goddess of grain; Cato gives the formula, in old-
fashioned language, as directed to Mars, who was originally
a rustic god: "Father Mars, I pray and beseech thee to be
willing and propitious to me, my household, and my slaves;
for the which object I have caused this threefold sacrifice to
be driven round my farm and land. I pray thee keep, avert,
and turn from us all disease, seen or unseen, all desolation,
ruin, damage, and unseasonable influence; I pray thee give
increase to the fruits, the corn, the vines, and the planta-
tions, and bring them to a prosperous issue. Keep also in
safety the shepherds and their flocks, and give good health
and vigor to me, my house, and household. To this end it is,
as I have said, — namely for the purification and making
due lustration of my farm, my land cultivated and unculti-
vated, — that I pray thee to bless this threefold sacrifice of
sucklings. O Father Mars, to this same end I pray thee bless
this threefold sacrifice of sucklings." [2] Could any prayer be

[1] *Georg.* I, 338–350, tr. T. C. Williams, Harvard University Press.
[2] Cato, *De Re Rust.*, 141, tr. W. Warde Fowler, in *The Roman Festivals of the Period of the Republic*, p. 126, which should be consulted also for interest-

more severely limited to petitions for material blessings for
the immediate family and belongings of the petitioner? It is
no wonder that the religion of the Romans has sometimes
been described as a "bread and butter religion." Nevertheless, even this prayer, in its attempt to win the good will of
the god ("be willing and propitious"), marks an advance
over the magic that seeks by crude, mechanical acts to control a god.

A special interest attaches to another of the agricultural
festivals, inasmuch as something of its spirit has been preserved in our Christmas observances. The Saturnalia, which
fell between the middle of December and the winter solstice,
marked the time when the autumn sowing was finished and
the farmers and their slaves could rest. Saturn himself, the
shadowy spirit who lived in the sowed fields, was sometimes
identified by the Romans with the Greek god Cronos, the
dethroned father of Zeus, and was supposed by popular and
poetic fancy to have presided, in the dawn of Italian civilization, over a golden age, the *Saturnia regna*.[1] This time of
plenty and good will was symbolized in the Saturnalia of historic times with sacrifice and feasting, kindly visits from
friends, games, and presents of waxen candles and little
images; slaves and masters waited on each other at the feast
on an equal footing.

Of the festivals of early Rome, all occurring on odd, or

ing illustrations of the survival of similar customs in modern times, such as
the "beating the bounds" of English parishes with peeled wands (which I recall having seen in Oxford). Similar are the "blessing the fields" and the
"blessing of the fishing fleet" in France, and Italian village processionals.
For lustral rites in ancient Italic communities, see the inscription from
Iguvium (Gubbio) in Umbria (the Tabulae Iguvinae, ed. Bücheler, in *Um-
brica*; brief comment by Fowler in the *Companion to Latin Studies*, pp. 163 f.).
For modern analogies and survivals, see H. M. Bower, *The Elevation and
Procession of the Ceri at Gubbio* (London, 1897); T. Ashby, *Some Italian
Scenes and Festivals* (New York, 1929), esp. pp. 94–97, 122–129, 147–159.

[1] Virgil, *Georg.* II, 538.

lucky, days of the month, no less than thirteen spring from
the activities of an agricultural society; two have their roots
in the earlier, pastoral life, two in war, and seven in the activities of the household. Naturally it was in the country
districts, among the *pagani*, that this rustic religion of early
Rome was most firmly rooted and lingered longest, even
during the Christian centuries, till at last *pagani* were indeed, by contrast, "pagans"; and it is this rustic religion,
with its simplicity of heart and its nearness to the elemental
processes of nature, that seems to have appealed most
strongly to Roman poets of a sophisticated age. Virgil
counts him happy who knows the gods of the countryside
(*deos . . . agrestis*),[1] and in a powerful passage calls upon the
native Italian divinities, the *Di indigetes*, to protect young
Octavian after the death of Caesar.[2] Horace calls upon
Faunus, the deity of woodland pastures, to befriend his
sunny farm, if properly appeased on his winter festal day,
while the laborers and the oxen make holiday;[3] yet *rustica*
Phidyle ("Dame Frugal") needs no lavish gift to propitiate
the powers that preside over her little farm, if she will but
offer dutifully the grain and salt that are expected.[4] And
Tibullus delights in painting the old rustic processional and
ritual of the Ambarvalia because it preserves the country
sentiment at its best.[5]

In Horace's ode addressed to rustic Phidyle the poet
names, among the powers to be placated, the Lares and the
Penates. The Lares, which appear originally to have been

[1] *Georg.* II, 493; see the lines quoted at the head of this chapter, translated
below, p. 352.
[2] *Georg.* I, 498–501.   Cf. p. 337, n. 3.
[3] *Odes* III, 18.
[4] *Odes* III, 23.
[5] II, 1.   Readers of Walter Pater's *Marius the Epicurean* will recall with
what a kindly understanding his earlier chapters interpret this religion of the
countryside (and of the home).

the spirits that protected the farmer's plot of land, and which were worshiped at little shrines where his land adjoined his neighbor's (the *compita*), were presently brought into the home along with the slaves of the *familia*; in the form of small images of dancing young men they were placed by the central hearth, and later at one side of the *atrium* on a special shrine or altar, the *Lararium*.[1] Here, as the *Lares Familiares*, they shared the worship of the household with the Penates, the spirits that preserved or increased the family larder (the *penus*), and that came to be identified by each family with some special divinities, such as Ceres or Juno, like patron saints; the Penates were attended especially by the children of the family, dressed in the fringed *toga praetexta*. The Lares and Penates thus came to symbolize all that was most sacred in the associations of the home, and received honor and offerings of salt cakes each morning and at dinner ("grace before meat"), and of course on all important occasions, and when members of the family entered or left the home for a journey. The *pater familias*, as the priest of the family, or in his absence the overseer of the farm or his wife (the *vilicus* or the *vilica*), presided over the worship of Janus, the spirit of the house-door, that breach in the walls through which danger might enter. In the care of the *mater familias* and her unmarried daughters was the worship of Vesta, the primitive Italic spirit of the

---

[1] Such a shrine, from the "House of the Vettii," at Pompeii, is represented in the illustration opposite. It suggests the appearance of a small temple, which frames a painting. The *Genius* of the family (see below, p. 313) stands with toga drawn over his head, as in a sacrifice; he holds in his left hand an incense box and in his right hand a *patera*, or saucer used for pouring a libation. On either side are the garlanded Lares, stepping lightly forward, with drinking cups extended. Below, a crested serpent, another symbol of the *genius*, approaches the offerings, among which an egg may be distinguished. Above, in the pediment, the decoration includes a large *patera*, a sacrificial knife, and the skull of a sacrificial victim.

FAMILY SHRINE, "HOUSE OF THE VETTII," POMPEII

fire on the hearth. Thus the house, its entrance and its fire, and its food, growing or stored away, were all under divine protection, and every member of the family had his part in securing this protection and a free and direct approach to divinity.

In the home were worshiped also other spirits of a less material significance. In his *genius* the Roman recognized an *alter ego*, not so separate as a "patron saint" or a "guardian angel," but almost equivalent to his "self"; it was the *numen* or spiritual counterpart of his personality and powers, particularly of his power to beget offspring and to enjoy life. Originally, it was supposed to have come into existence with his birth and to perish with his death, and was symbolized, even when the gods were conceived in human form, by the snake that might glide in and out of the house; later, the *genius* was supposed to survive the *pater familias*, or to be the expression of the continuing vital force of the family which was for the time expressed in him. A place or a city, or even a club, might have its *genius*, for example a *genius loci*; so Aeneas, sacrificing to his father's spirit, and seeing a snake appear from the altar, is uncertain whether it is his father's *genius* or the *genius loci*.[1] During the Empire, possibly under Stoic influence, the feminine counterpart of the *genius*, attached to a Roman matron, was her Juno.[2] The respect given to the spirits of departed members of the family was at least for a long time less often paid to the *genius* of an individual than addressed to *Di Manes* collectively, as "hallowed spirits," perhaps in the attempt to win their good will. But in countless Roman gravestones dating from the end of the Republic we find evidence, in the

---

[1] *Aen.* V, 95.
[2] Cf. Seneca, *Epist.*, 110, 1; and E. V. Arnold, *Roman Stoicism*, p. 232. As the matron's attendant in childbirth, Juno received the epithet Lucina.

introductory formula D(is) M(anibus) S(acrum), of the continuing affection of the living for their dead, now individualized; moreover, in the offerings paid at the household shrine, the living, their gods, and their dead are united as members of one family. Naturally, as we have observed in an earlier chapter, the great occasions were marked by special solemnity, — birth, marriage, and death, and their anniversaries, — but every aspect of life was invested with a homely dignity and sense of the continuity of life retrieved somehow from the dangers and chances of disease and famine and death. Ritual and rubric, the custom of the ancients, find due observance, and foster in turn a discipline and habit of mind that is singularly expressive of the Roman character.

Before we leave these earliest, and in some ways most characteristic, phases of Roman religion, it is important to notice that for a long time the Romans can hardly be said to have had gods, certainly not gods fully developed in human form, with images and temples, even if there were symbols of divinity, such as the shields of Mars. *Numina*,[1] spirits or wills, they had, — functional powers that corresponded to their daily activities on the farm, in the home, and at war; and these are minutely subdivided. There are spirits of the harvest (Consus and Ops), of the growth of the grain (Ceres), of the blight that destroys crops (Robigo); in the home, besides Janus and Vesta, there are *numina* that correspond to the child's drinking (Potina), to the bride's homecoming (Domiduca), and many others. Unlike the later abstractions of moral qualities, such as Concordia and Fides, these *numina* are inherent in the material objects and acts of the people, and can hardly be separated from them. It

---

[1] The word *numen* is derived from the verb *nuere*, "to nod assent," and signifies will power, whether good or evil; it is the special office of religion to make sure of its friendliness.

was the task of later priests and antiquarians to record in their ritual books (*indigitamenta*) the names and functions of these countless spirits. And it goes without saying that the Romans did not yet attempt to trace any family relationship between their *numina*; they were not even sure of the gender of Pales. Beneath the southwest corner of the Palatine there is still an archaic altar dedicated to a divinity *sei deo sei deivae*, "be it god or goddess." [1] Other divinities were perhaps paired, but not wedded; some believe that female *numina* in such cases were merely the counterparts of the male divinities, worshiped especially by the women of the household. There was not yet an Olympus or a Pantheon, nor were myths told of individual gods. Many of their *numina* and their cults were still restricted to special localities, — a spot struck by lightning, a single farm, a particular village.

So far we have been considering the Roman's religious attitude as that of a member of a family engaging in his activities on the farm and in his life in the home; the family, as we have seen, is the characteristic unit of Roman society. But groups of families formed tribes and villages, which in turn were united in the city of Rome. This larger body, too, required means of expressing its corporate religious attitude; a great part of the state religion of Rome is nothing more than the adaptation or expansion of the farmer's and householder's religion. Certain rites, to be sure, were still reserved for families; and others were introduced at a later time by the plebeians, who were not citizens in the fullest sense, or by alien immigrants, and continued as tolerated but unofficial cults. The official religion of Rome, on the other hand, represented the organized endeavor of the state to secure the help of potentially helpful *numina* in the struggle for bounti-

[1] *C. I. L.*, VI, 110 (= Dessau 4015).

ful harvests and for success in war, — what the Romans came to describe as *pax deorum*. To secure this help became a highly technical process, hedged about by ancient prescriptions the meaning of which had often been long forgotten; it was the province of the *ius divinum*, a mass of legal tradition no less portentous than the *ius civile* itself, and was controlled by experts, priests or priestly colleges, who were trained in the traditional lore. On what day should a particular festival be held? The priests made the announcement; and in a later period the Calendar, exhibited in the Forum, showed the dates of the chief festivals. Which of the countless *numina* should be invoked in an emergency? Again it was the priests whose guidance was sought, since they alone had access to the ritual books, or forms of invocation. Had divine sanction been secured for a given undertaking? Were the *numina* propitious? Only the priests charged with the rites of divination could say.

All but one of the copies of the Calendar now extant belong to the imperial period; but they preserve a record of the festivals of the early period soon after Rome had absorbed the settlements on the Quirinal Hill, the earliest festivals being indicated by the use of large letters. Festivals of some of the greater gods who were worshiped in Rome in the historic period are here conspicuous by their absence; the Calendar may be regarded as a record of the period of the early monarchy, or indeed of Numa, to whom Roman tradition ascribed the organization of the religious institutions of the state.[1] Besides indicating Kalends and Nones (the new moon and the first quarter), and the religious festivals of each month, the Calendar named those days on which it was

---

[1] Ovid's *Fasti* was intended, in its twelve books (one for each month), to trace the festivals throughout the year, with myths (largely from Greek sources) and speculations as to their origins. Only six books, those dealing with the months from January through June, now survive.

lawful (F = *fastus*) or unlawful (N = *nefastus*) to do secular business, or on which the *Comitia* might meet. Most of the festivals have to do with the *numina* associated with the farm; even Mars, for example, appears to be still chiefly a wild agricultural spirit of the outland fields and forests, where war is to be feared, though he is gradually acquiring a personality and becoming a god, rather than a mere *numen*, and is gradually associated with warfare rather than with farming.

The spirits that watched over the home, too, were similarly transformed into guardians of the City. Janus, the spirit of doors, of openings (and shuttings) and of beginnings, was given an arch, and later a temple, on the northern edge of the Forum, as well as the month opening after the winter solstice, and finally a two-headed figure representing his double-facing aspect. Vesta, the spirit of the fire on the hearth, was now given in the Forum a round House which perpetuated the primitive Italic wigwam type of house; on the City hearth burned Vesta's fire throughout the year, rekindled only on the first of March, the beginning of the old Roman year; in the City *Penus*, the counterpart of the domestic larder, were kept various sacred emblems and utensils, including the Penates of the State. In Vesta's House, too, wills were deposited. As the unmarried daughters of the family cared for the hearth and the larder, so the six Vestal Virgins, originally the daughters of the king (the "father" of the state), during the Republic were carefully chosen from old Roman families, and were regarded in the eyes of the law as the daughters of the Pontifex Maximus. They devoted the best part of their lives to their holy office, tending the City hearth, preparing by primitive methods the sacrificial salt cake (*mola salsa*) needed for certain rituals, and carrying water from a sacred spring. Their secluded home, the Atrium Vestae, adjoined the House of Vesta; and if their life was hedged by archaic taboos, nevertheless theirs was an honored position and maintained among the Romans for more than a thousand years a conception of domestic simplicity, of peace, and of purity.

With "the religion of Numa" the Romans associated the elaborately organized and subdivided functions of the priests and priestly colleges. During the monarchy the king acted as chief priest, asking advice of the board of *pontifices*. During the Republic, this board was the supreme authority in religious matters; its members held office for life, though they might also hold civil magistracies; its chairman, the *Pontifex Maximus*, was the heir of the kings so far as religion is concerned, and used as his office the Regia, the "King's House," in the Forum (a neutral site between the rival settlements on the hills). The *pontifices* decided questions involving places, dates, procedures, burials, wills, and adoptions, and kept archives; they were present at confarreate marriages; the *Pontifex Maximus*, as we have seen, was legally *in loco parentis* to the Vestal Virgins. Many of the emperors held the office of *Pontifex Maximus*, and the title is still borne by the popes.

If the legal aspects of religion were controlled by the *pontifices*, its ritual aspect was intrusted to the *Rex Sacrorum*, who like the Athenian *Archon Basileus* continued the religious duties of the kings, especially in the actual performance of certain sacrifices. He was appointed by the *Pontifex Maximus*, and served for life, being debarred from civil office because of his handling of sacred objects. Similar, or even greater, taboos attached to the *flamines*, "blowers" or "kindlers," members of priesthoods of great antiquity connected with the cults of Jupiter, Mars, Quirinus, and other divinities. The *Flamen Dialis* (of Jupiter), for example, must not appear out of doors without the pointed cap (*apex*), must not touch a dog or a goat, eat beans, use an iron knife, wear knots or rings, or leave Rome for more than two nights.

The other priestly colleges were charged with responsibility over special interests. The *augures*, for example, were expert in the interpretation of the omens, generally from the flight or the feeding of birds, which were reported to them, and on which the success of a proposed course of action was supposed to depend. For this purpose they might mark out with a crooked stick, as an augur had marked for Numa,[1] the quarters of the sky or the plot of ground, known as the *templum*, in which the omens were to be sought. Since the Roman augur faced south, whereas the Greek diviner faced north, and both Greek and Roman sought omens in the east, there is a discrepancy between Greek and Roman terms; Romans found lucky omens on the left, Greeks on the right.[2] Temples could be consecrated only by the augur's art, and the Senate could meet only in a *templum* marked out by him. Despite the tendency of the Romans to suppress irresponsible rites of divination, the augurs were in high repute till late in the Republic, though they were often manipulated for political ends, and were superseded, at least in emergencies, by decree of the Senate, by the perversely ingenious art of Etruscan soothsayers (*haruspices*). This art was based chiefly on the inspection of the organs of sacrificial victims, but included also the study of lightning and of other prodigies that might be observed, and laid down methods of expiation for such phenomena.

To the *fetiales* belonged the ritual of declaring war and making treaties. One member of the board, the *verbenarius*,

[1] Livy, I, 18.
[2] But the Romans were not consistent. See Cicero, *De Divinatione* I, 12; II, 82; and the passages assembled by A. S. Pease in his commentary *ad loc.* (Urbana, 1920–23).

carried a bunch of grass, symbol of inviolability, with which he consecrated his colleague, the *pater patratus populi Romani*, the "father made for the purpose of the embassy." The latter, if a dispute arose with another state, advanced to the border, called Jupiter to witness the claims of Rome, and repeated this formula thrice in the alien territory. If within thirty days Rome's claims had not been met, he hurled across the frontier a spear of ancient form, the tip of which had been dipped in blood.[1] When Octavian declared war on Cleopatra, the old rite was revived, a spear being hurled into a plot of ground feigned to be hers.[2] In concluding treaties the *pater patratus* also acted, striking the sacrificed victim with a flint, and praying Jupiter to strike the Roman people even so, if they should not observe their oath. Another survival of primitive customs was the rapid war-dance, from temple to temple, of the Salii, the "leaping priests," each spring and autumn (the beginning and the end of the fighting season); their shields, the *ancilia*, of the primitive figure-eight type common in Mediterranean lands, included a shield thought to have fallen from heaven into the house of Numa.

Other priestly colleges sought to win prosperity for fields and flocks; the Arval Brothers conducted processions and sacrifices, especially in the Ambarvalia and later in worship of the Bona Dea, a goddess of fertility.[3] Perhaps it was both protection from wolves and purification and fertility for flocks and human beings that the Luperci sought by their curious rites at the Lupercal, the cave beneath the Palatine where the wolf suckled Romulus and Remus. Young men

---

[1] Livy, I, 24.
[2] Dio Cassius, I, 4, 5.
[3] The Song of the Arval Brothers invokes, with triple repetition, the aid of the Lares and of Mars against any blight that may befall the harvest. (*Oxford Book of Latin Verse*, No. 2.)

had their foreheads smeared with the blood of sacrificed goats, and wiped with wool dipped in milk, and were required to laugh; then, wearing the skin of the goats, and carrying strips of the skin, they ran round the base of the Palatine striking all whom they met with the thongs. The agricultural origin, the magical character, the accretion and the conservative repetition of forms whose precise meaning was forgotten, and the social organization of "the religion of Numa" could hardly be better illustrated. Fortunately for Rome, as the legal monopoly of the *pontifices* was abolished and law was secularized, so the other priestly colleges, and in particular the futile but dangerous college of augurs, remained as merely advisory bodies, and never secured a political control of the republic. So far was Rome from being ruled by a hierarchy that religion was finally degraded into becoming the tool of politicians.[1]

The primitive religion of the Romans was further organized during the Etruscan occupation of Rome. To the native *numina* or gods, the *di indigetes*, worshiped chiefly inside the *pomoerium*, were added new or foreign gods, the *di novensides*, who found a foothold outside the *pomoerium*, and were worshiped with rites conducted by non-Roman priests. These accretions to the old religion reflect the political solidarity and the territorial expansion of the growing state; they are gods of the Rome that now dominates the Latin League, gods of the conquered towns of Latium and Etruria, gods of the new plebeian citizens who cannot share in the old patrician rites and cults. No longer standing merely for agricultural increase or domestic security, they preside over the fortunes of a political and military state; they no longer dwell in groves or are worshiped at humble shrines, but are given by the Etruscans temples, built somewhat in the Greek

[1] Cf. pp. 334–336 and 339–348.

manner, and often providing shelter for a triad of divinities in three *cellae* under one roof; and they are embodied in statues of human form.

It was during the Etruscan period that Jupiter, a sky-god associated with agriculture and worshiped on the Alban Mount by the members of the Latin League, was given a temple on the Capitoline Hill,[1] and received, as a political and military divinity with vague ethical potentialities, the significant title of "Best and Greatest" (*Optimus Maximus*). To this temple, where Jupiter's statue stood, its face smeared with red war-paint, marched the Roman generals and their men, in celebrating the Etruscan ceremony of the "triumph," the general's face also being smeared with war-paint.[2] Juno, too, possibly also originally a divinity of the bright sky,[3] was housed on another summit of the Capitoline. Jupiter, Juno, and Minerva (a goddess of handicrafts coming from the semi-Latin town of Falerii, in southern Etruria, and probably already worshiped on the Aventine by the plebeian artisans), were known as the Capitoline Triad, and inhabited the Temple of Jupiter Optimus Maximus. They gained in prestige at the expense of Mars and the other Roman divinities; they were presently identified with the Greek gods Zeus, Hera, and Athena, whose functions and myths they accordingly appropriated. Their cults were monopolized by the patricians; when Rome dominated the Latin League the plebeians established in their settlement on the Aventine the cult of Diana, who had been worshiped

---

[1] Probably not completed till the early years of the Republic. Its foundations have very recently been exposed to view.

[2] Roman generals during the Republic who had not been granted a triumph at Rome sometimes celebrated a sort of unofficial triumph on the Alban Mount, which they ascended by a triumphal way whose lava paving stones may still be seen. Cf. Livy, XLII, 21, 7.

[3] Cf. J. Whatmough, C. Q., XVI (1922) 183–185; and E. L. Shields, "Juno", *Smith College Classical Studies*, (1926).

by the Latin cities in her grove on the shore of Lake Nemi, in the Alban Hills.

To the last Tarquin Roman tradition ascribed the purchase from the Cumaean Sibyl of the books which their special committee consulted from time to time, by command of the Senate, when the state needed advice in an emergency. There are grounds for believing, however, that the Sibylline Books did not reach Rome till early in the Republic, and that they were bought under the influence of Apollo, the god of prophecy, whose cult probably preceded them.[1] These treasured books, written in Greek hexameter verse, were destroyed by fire in 83 B.C., and a new collection was made from oriental sources. The books seem to have contained not prophecies in the usual sense but advice as to procedure, usually the rite necessary for the placation of offended divinities. In most cases the divinities indicated were those of Greek origin; during a failure of crops, Demeter, Dionysus, and Persephone, deities associated with growing things, were brought to Rome and Latinized as Ceres, Liber, and Proserpina, a new "Triad"; from Cumae, where they had been worshiped by Greek settlers, they moved to Rome along with the Cumaean grain, and were housed on the Aventine. Greek traders brought their patron gods with them, — Hermes, Hercules, Castor and Pollux, and Poseidon; these, too, found their way to Rome, chiefly under the influence of the Sibylline Books, sometimes by way of Latin cities and in Latinized form, as the protectors of the plebeian craftsmen and merchants of Rome.[2]

[1] Cf. Fowler, *Religious Experience of the Roman People*, p. 268, n. 29. The cult of Apollo carried on in the Campus Martius was at least earlier than his earliest temple, built on this site in 431 B.C. See further J. B. Carter, "The Coming of the Sibyl," in *The Religion of Numa*.

[2] For an example, see J. G. Winter, *The Myth of Hercules at Rome* (New York, 1910).

The form of ritual enjoined by the Sibylline Books was also not Roman. In the place of rites performed by experts with veiled heads, in the presence of the passive people who kept holy silence, were enjoined celebrations of a more spectacular sort into which the people could join in some measure. Such was the *supplicatio*, a festival once of appeal to offended divinities, and later of thanksgiving, performed by processions of men, women, and children wearing garlands and carrying laurel boughs to the shrines of various deities. Such, too, was the *lectisternium*, at which images of pairs of divinities were exhibited on couches, with offerings of food laid on tables before them. Such, again, were the various *ludi*, games celebrated by the people in accordance with a special vow, or as a regular festival, athletic or dramatic in character. These rites occurred whenever the Romans were hard pressed in war and their old religion seemed inadequate to save them, and especially during the terrible days when Hannibal was in Italy. After the battle of Lake Trasumenus, not only *ludi* and a *lectisternium* were invoked but an old Italic rite, the "Sacred Spring" (*Ver Sacrum*), by which all animal and human increase of the year was dedicated to the gods.[1] After Cannae the Romans, dismayed by a portent, resorted to human sacrifice, a practice "by no means Roman," as Livy remarks, doubtless correctly;[2] and, to relieve the strain of the war, they instituted new games in in honor of Apollo. Finally, when they had all but despaired of driving Hannibal from Italy, the Senate authorized, in 204, the introduction from Asia Minor to Rome of the black lump of meteoric stone which represented the oriental goddess Cybele, the Great Mother of the Gods.

[1] Livy, XXII, 10.
[2] Livy, XXII, 57. Yet a few other cases of human sacrifice were known to the Romans; cf. C. Saunders, "Human Sacrifice," in *Vergil's Primitive Italy* (Oxford, 1930), pp. 97–120.

Before we consider the results of this invasion by a new type of religion, let us pause to take account of the achievement of the three centuries between the Tarquins and Hannibal. The Etruscans found at Rome a religion, derived from scattered agricultural communities, but already crystallized in the fabric of the newly unified state; this they exploited as the cohesive force of an expanding state. New citizens often meant new gods and new cults, beside the old ones; but the young Republic perpetuated in its religious institutions the traditional usages, even if it was only a dwindling minority of the people who actively participated in them or, indeed, understood their meaning. It would be idle to suppose that the magic of the ritual accomplished what it professed to do, and as idle to see in the state religion any lofty ethical guidance or any clearly conceived theology. But it did stimulate a corporate solidarity of feeling and purpose, a hallowed patriotism, a discipline of the individual in the service of the state, a grave yet hopeful sense of unseen realities, that was of incalculable value to the Roman character; it was the cradle of Roman *pietas*. The individual felt himself to be weaker than the group, to owe obedience to the group, to be helped by the group; he felt himself to be impotent in the presence of powers unseen, yet not unfriendly or at least not implacable; he would do in his place and in his generation what he as a Roman was bound to do. He might die in battle; sooner or later he would surely die and join his fathers. But the Temple of Jupiter Optimus Maximus would continue to stand, the pontiffs and the silent Vestals would forever move in solemn processional to the Capitoline; [1] if he himself deserved well of his generation his *imago* would be treasured by his descendants and would appear at their triumphs and funerals. Thus *gloria*, the in-

[1] Horace, *Odes* III, 30, 8 f.

dividual's sense of personal pride, might serve the common cause. Judged by any pragmatic test, the religion of the middle Republic had at least a "survival value"; and it would be easy to underestimate the value of the routine performance of ritual for the inculcation of discipline and the habit of order and respect for authority, even of fear. The Greek's religion, we have been told, "made him at home in the world"; [1] at times the Greek was almost too much at ease among his gods. The Roman, at least during this period, knew his place and kept it, so far as the gods were concerned; his "fear of spiritual powers" (*deisidaimonia*), accounted among other peoples a source of weakness, was regarded by Polybius as having held together the Roman people.[2]

The gods of the Romans, to be sure, though powerful, were not in origin or in essence conceived as patterns of moral conduct for humanity; and the more they approximated human forms and appropriated Greek myths, the less they tended to deserve reverence. They lagged behind the standards of decency of enlightened mortals, who in the end had recourse for ethical guidance to philosophy rather than to religion. On the other hand, there was a tendency for abstract words and ideas to become deified. Some of these began as epithets of divinities whose functions were subdivided. Thus from Jupiter Fidius, the god invoked when oaths were made, was detached the independent divinity Fides, the protector of good faith, by Roman legal instinct given concrete form and personality. Concordia perpetuated the harmony between patricians and plebeians that was at least sought in the political arrangements of the

---

[1] G. L. Dickinson, *The Greek View of Life*, p. 9.
[2] VI, 56; cf. Cicero, *De Natura Deorum* I, 2, 3, claiming for the Romans preëminence in this one trait.

year 367 B.C., and had a temple in the Forum. So in due season devotion was given to Pudor, to Victoria, Salus, Libertas, Spes, Pietas, and many other virtues, *numina*, as it were, expressing moral aspiration.[1]

That the average Roman could find during times of stress any adequate emotional outlet in the religion of Numa it is not easy to believe; for he must stand, a silent spectator, while the experts conducted the traditional rites. But in the Greek rites, the *supplicationes* and *lectisternia* and *ludi* introduced under the influence of the Sibylline Books, he could participate more actively and emotionally, as the astute religious officials must have realized. In the inclusiveness of this religion, which was open to the whole people, in its many-sided appeal to all sorts of people, in its succession of festivals, in the pageantry of its ritual, with sacrifices, processions, and tableaux at countless temples and shrines, in the architecture and sculpture and mythology freely adapted from Greek sources as a vehicle for Roman attitudes, the religion of the middle Republic might be described, in a phrase which some modern men have used of themselves, as "Catholic but not Christian." Yet it cannot be doubted that the rites which it introduced under the influence of the Sibylline Books did more to arouse than to allay superstition; moreover it was hardly yet a personal religion, and gave little comfort to the individual in distress, unless perchance in the ritual of the home. Its guidance in questions of personal conduct was neither adequate nor rational. Ethical guidance was to come chiefly from the subtle theory of the Greek philosophers, tempered by Roman common sense; the craving for personal religion was to come chiefly from the newly imported mystery religions of Greece and the Orient.

[1] See further H. Axtell, *Deification of Abstract Ideas at Rome* (Chicago, 1907).

For the Greek world, too, had passed through a similar appeal from the religion of the state to something more personal. We are so familiar with the religion of the Greek city-states and their worship of the Olympian deities, Zeus and Apollo and Athene and the rest, that we often forget that there was in Greek lands an earlier form of religion, which had been driven into obscurity by the coming of Homer's "Achaeans." This was the cult of spirits of the dead and of the underworld, who had power to help or to thwart mortals, and who therefore received their homage and their libations. And in the seventh and sixth centuries B.C., when men realized that the Olympian religion had little hope to offer the humble and the unhappy, a remarkable revival and expansion of the older religion took place. Rites of expiation and the worship of dead heroes were revived; and the newly arrived god Dionysus upheld new hope. Bringer of the vine and protector of all living things, he was the god of a blessed release, through intoxication, from the troubles of life; he expressed the return to nature, the death and rebirth of vegetation. He was even supposed himself to have suffered death and resurrection, and his worshipers sought by union with him to win a release from mortality. So, too, in the worship at Eleusis of Demeter and her daughter Persephone, who died and rose every year, the death and the revival both of the grain and of mankind were symbolized; and the brotherhoods that claimed Orpheus as their founder and the communities that were supposed to have been founded by Pythagoras hoped through purifications and an ascetic life to set the soul free from the body. The cult at Eleusis and the cults of the Orphics were commonly known as "mysteries," and tried by rites of preliminary initiation and by subsequent ceremonies such as a "sacred feast" or a "sacred marriage," carried on in secret, to bring their adherents into an ecstatic or a solemn state of mind in which they could commune directly with the god. The exact nature of the ritual remains obscure, and was doubtless often enough trivial; but the tendency, among at least the better adherents of the mysteries, was to forget the crude origins of their cult, and to emphasize the imaginative myths that pointed to a purification not physical but moral, leading to a future life such as the Olympian religion had never offered. The happiness of the initiates who have won Elysium is described in a fragment of Pindar: "For them the sun shineth in his strength, in the world below, while here 'tis night; and, in meadows red with roses, the space before their city is shaded by the incense-tree, and is laden with golden fruits. Some of them delight themselves with horses and with wrestling; others with draughts and with lyres; while beside them bloometh the fair flower of perfect bliss. And o'er that lovely land fragrance is ever shed, while they mingle all manner of incense with the far-shining fire on the altars of the gods." [1] We can hardly overestimate the value that such poetic imagery, in ritual and in myth, had and indeed still has for the creation of a personal attitude. Man acts not because of the reason alone, but quite as much through habit and emotion and the force of images and personalities which turn logical assent into action. Mystery religions and passion plays speak directly to the heart.

It was in 204, during the terrible days when Hannibal was at large in Italy, as we have seen,[2] that the cult of the Magna Mater was brought to Rome; the next year, Hannibal left Italy. "Post hoc, propter hoc," the Romans argued; it must be because of the good offices of the new divinity that the state was saved. A dozen years later there was built on the

---

[1] Fragment 129, tr. Sandys.
[2] Cf. p. 324.

Palatine the temple of the Magna Mater, the foundations of which, overgrown by a grove of ilex, may still be seen. Other oriental cults were soon brought to Rome by foreigners or by returning legionaries, and were at least tolerated. And Rome continued to borrow Greek deities, identifying them with old Roman divinities, often on slight grounds; the richer art and mythology of the Greeks was thus added to Rome's store, but the cults of the Roman gods suffered accordingly. If we wonder at this hospitable attitude on the part of the Romans, we must remember that their traditional attitude toward their gods had been a legalistic one; they contracted to do certain things for the gods, expecting to receive in return certain blessings. Now in the Hannibalic War the old Roman gods had not seemed to fulfill their part of the bargain; and the Romans, like patients who had lost faith in their family physician, called in foreign specialists. But when peace and prosperity returned, these alien cults remained, not lifted, to be sure, to the level of the old religion, but as barely tolerated, non-conformist tabernacles. They might be useful to the state in emergencies; they might serve the needs of foreigners and of many high-strung individuals. Normal public opinion, as such, was apt to look askance at them. Indeed, when the rites of Bacchus (Dionysus), which had lately been brought from Greece through Etruria to Rome, had given rise to grave scandals, and were curbed by the Senate in 186, and all but suppressed, the cult was described not merely as a "foreign superstition" but as a *coniuratio*, a conspiracy against the *ius divinum* of the state.[1] We must not fail to note, however, that the Senate nevertheless did tolerate the Bacchanalian rites, even if in a severely limited and licensed form; so much, they felt, must be conceded to the craving of an appreciable proportion of the

[1] Livy, XXXIX, 18.

people for religious experience more personal and ecstatic than that of the state. In fact, the Greek mystery religions and the other oriental cults that found their way to Rome increased during the late Republic and the early Empire till, although not officially recognized by the state, they became of enormous importance: even at the beginning of the Christian era they flourished in Rome and in many parts of Italy; [1] in the second century A.D. the strongest rival of Christianity was not the old Roman religion but Mithraism.

Each of the mystery religions shared with the rest certain common traits, and each had its peculiarities of myth and ritual and doctrine, and its especial appeal to some race or social class or sex or temperament. Thus Cybele, the Great Mother, though officially introduced into Rome in an emotional crisis and officially welcomed by the noblest Romans, was viewed askance during the Republic, and only foreigners held her priesthoods. Yet her loud and orgiastic ritual, and her myth (setting forth the love of a nature-goddess for the young mortal Attis and his act of self-devotion to her), exercised a strange fascination on the feelings both of common folk and of Romans of a finer mould. [2] They expressed somehow the romantic "call of the wild" that is instinctive in human nature, even if they could not moralize or rationalize it. During the Empire the noblest Romans as well as depraved charlatans participated in the cult. The ritual now included the *taurobolium*, the rite of baptism in the blood of a bull, by which were symbolized rebirth and purification from sin and the hope of salvation, often "for twenty years" and occasionally even "for eternity," as some inscriptions attest (*in aeternum renatus*). In the end, Cybele became,

---

[1] Cf. M. Rostovtzeff, *Mystic Italy.*
[2] Catullus, 63, the "*Attis,*" an amazing poem, which inevitably invites comparison with the *Bacchae* of Euripides.

more than the other oriental mother-goddesses, the type of the gentle universal mother, and appealed to women more than did the rugged religion of Mithras.

The cult of Isis, brought from Egypt by way of Delos and Campania, also appealed especially to women. Its myth told of the death and dismemberment of Osiris and the discovery of the fragments by Isis; but the Egyptian Osiris was all but forgotten in Italy, and was replaced by Serapis, almost a sun-god or a lord of all life, while Isis herself became a gentle queen of the lands of the living and of the dead. After the partial suppression of the Bacchanalian worship, some of the religious feeling that it had satisfied was perhaps transferred to Isis. During the late Republic there were repeated attempts to suppress the cult, an old-fashioned consul in 50 B.C. even taking an axe in hand to lead in the destruction of the Temple of Isis; but the sect continued to be popular in Rome and in the country towns, and was triumphant soon after the establishment of the Empire. It was all things to all men, inculcating asceticism for those who were capable of leading a holy life, and indulgent to those of frailer virtue; to the masses it offered processions of tonsured, white-robed priests, and hymns and liturgies; it even sought at times to fall in step with the monotheistic leanings of men like Plutarch.[1]

The cult of Mithras, an ancient Persian religion carried west by Roman armies, particularly by Pompey's soldiers, in its emphasis on the idea of a struggle between light and darkness was essentially a soldier's religion. Mithras was represented as having slain a bull, for the good of men, and his act was perpetuated in the rite of the *taurobolium*, which was

---

[1] Cf. Apuleius, *Metamorphoses* XI, the *locus classicus* for the mystical aspects of the cult of Isis, and for her rites of initiation; Apuleius is writing in the second century A.D.

borrowed from the worship of the Magna Mater. But the chief influence of Mithraism in the west was to be felt during the Empire.[1]

Each of the mystery religions was concerned only with its own initiates, to whom it held out hopes of a personal salvation; the rites were observed in secrecy, and were not to be divulged to the uninitiated; they were conducted in secluded chapels or apartments, such as the subterranean "Basilica" of the Porta Maggiore, in Rome, the decorations of which beautifully symbolize the craving of the Neo-Pythagorean worshipers for immortality, or such, again, as the secluded "House of the Mysteries," outside Pompeii, whose frescos depict various scenes in the initiation of the god Dionysus and his worshipers.[2] For obvious reasons our knowledge and understanding of all these matters is tantalizingly imperfect. But from the paintings and reliefs and from the accounts of initiations we gather at least one fact of great importance. The people who resorted to the mystery religions were not living in any real world which science or common sense could recognize; they were seeking an escape from their immediate experience into a world of hopes and visions. They despaired of human society and sought, as individuals, a personal fulfilment of their cravings and in the end a personal survival, sometimes a celestial immortality, such as the vague old Roman ideas of an after-life had never promised them.[3]

---

[1] See further, pp. 356–358.

[2] See G. Bendinelli, "Il Monumento Sotteraneo di Porta Maggiore in Roma," *Mon. Ant.*, XXXI (1927), 602–847, also figures and 43 plates; J. Carcopino, *La Basilique Pythagoricienne de la Porte Majeure* (Paris, 1927); A. Maiuri, *La Villa dei Misteri* (Rome, 1931), a sumptuous work, with many plates (also 17 in color in a separate portfolio); V. Macchiero, *The Villa of the Mysteries in Pompeii* (Naples, n. d.); M. Rostovtzeff, *Mystic Italy*, pp. 40–98, 130–142.

[3] See further Fowler, *Religious Experience of the Roman People*, Ch. XVII,

Other Romans, equally disillusioned by the future of the old Roman religion during the Punic Wars, sought during the last century of the Republic to find a substitute for religious sanctions in a more exclusively human and secular point of view. For the educated few, Greek philosophy seemed to offer a substitute. Epicureanism pointed to an escape from the distressing demands of life in pleasure more or less refined, or in the scientific outlook and the high resignation of a Lucretius; Stoicism, with a more Roman insistence on character, gave a new sense of direction to any man who would school his will to serve under the banner of reason, and became, in fact, a philosophical interpretation of *pietas*. The success of the sage, the *vir sapiens*, in retrieving for himself from the wreckage of the common disaster a happy life of reason, will concern us later;[1] we have already noticed how the Stoic jurisconsults used their philosophy to bring a theory of law and the state into accord with the principle of the cosmic reason. But it goes without saying that most ancient Romans, like most men to-day, were not philosophical, and were less scientific in their outlook than were the ancient Greeks; Epicureanism and Stoicism alike failed to reach them effectively. The average man toward the end of the Republic either observed the state religion mechanically or found emotional support in the mysteries; even Cicero, unnerved by the death of his daughter, built for her a shrine (a *fanum*, not a *sepulcrum*) in the Greek or oriental manner.[2]

How far it was worth while for the state to perpetuate the

"Mysticism and Ideas of a Future Life"; F. Cumont, *After Life in Roman Paganism* (New Haven, 1922); C. H. Moore, *Pagan Ideas of Immortality during the Early Empire* (Cambridge, Mass., 1918); Mrs. Arthur Strong, *Apotheosis and After Life* (London, 1915).

[1] Pp. 373–398.

[2] *Ad Att.* XII, 12, 1; 36, 1. "I am anxious to avoid any likeness to a tomb . . . in order to attain as nearly as possible to apotheosis."

institutions of the state religion, in the efficacy of which educated men could no longer believe and the significance of which common men could no longer understand, we may find it hard to say; Roman statesmen and thinkers doubted not that it was worth while, for it provided a bond of solidarity among the ignorant. They themselves kept their attitude toward this religion quite distinct from their own philosophical attitude. A famous jurist, Mucius Scaevola, who was also *Pontifex Maximus* during Cicero's youth, held that there were three kinds of religion: one of the poets, whose imaginative stories were worthless,[1] one of the philosophers, which might be true but which was injurious to the state, and one of the state, which must be accepted because of its social utility.[2] So Cicero's own contemporary, the antiquarian Varro, likewise recognizing three "theologies," argued that though the state religion was not necessarily true it could be purified of false mythology, and was a good sedative for the common people.[3] Cicero himself, though certainly disbelieving in most of the old gods, regarded the old religion as a useful symbol of the conservative, respectful attitude on which political security and the *status quo* rested; hence it was the duty of the state to administer the *ius divinum* as scrupulously as any other part of the *ius civile*. It was a legal matter, pure and simple. Cicero's own views, of course, were to be reached by philosophic speculation, in the spirit of Plato's attempt in the *Laws* to formulate a tenable theology.[4]

[1] Though the major myths of the earlier Greeks were often beautiful and capable of spiritual interpretation, many of them, because of their anthropomorphic character, seemed to an enlightened age neither plausible nor edifying; when used in burlesque by Greek and Latin comic poets they appeared positively scandalous.

[2] "Expedire igitur existimat falli in religione civitates." St. Augustine, *De Civitate Dei* IV, 27.   [3] *Ibid.* VI, 5–7.

[4] What is now called "natural theology." Cf. A. E. Taylor, *Platonism and Its Influence*, pp. 97–99.

Even the priesthoods and the practices of this utilitarian religion had suffered neglect or perversion. Cicero, though proud to be an augur, because the office carried political prestige, was ignorant of the augural lore. The office of *Flamen Dialis* was avoided because of its taboos, and was vacant from 89 to 11 B.C. There is a record of one young ne'er-do-well whose family had him appointed to the office of *Rex Sacrorum*, in 209 B.C., in order that the taboos attaching to it might keep him straight. A similar cynical attitude was to be seen in the case of the other priesthoods, which were elective, and were now thoroughly political, especially from the time of Sulla, who for all his superstitions was also sceptical, and perceived that since the state religion was being maintained for political reasons, it might as well be used to promote the political ends that he favored. He increased the membership of the priestly boards, so as to have more handles by which to control legislation. Cicero's son and other boys from time to time were given a major priesthood, like mediaeval "boy bishops." The Calendar was exploited to prolong a military command, and the consul Bibulus obstructed legislation by announcing every day, in ancient formula, that he was "observing the heavens." But the obstruction was ignored by his colleague, Caesar, who was at the same time *Pontifex Maximus* (as indeed he continued to be all the time that he was in Gaul).

During the terrible years of the Civil Wars, when brothers fought against brothers and whole families were wiped out in battles and proscriptions, and the ancient devotion to farm and home was trampled upon, the feeling grew among Romans that such evils must be signs of the anger of gods who were offended by the wickedness, the greed and cruelty, of men. The Golden Age, the *Saturnia regna*, was gone; if it lingered amid the rural piety of the farmers, it had surely vanished in the city, where family life and its loyalties had vanished both in tenement and in palace. Only by contrition and the emergence of some new manifestation of divinity could a better age dawn among men. Catullus wrote wistfully of the earlier age, when righteous men beheld the gods who were now lost to the view of a sinful race;[1] but his was only a passing fancy. Horace, in a hopeless mood, proposed that the better Romans abandon Rome, and sail away to some pastoral retreat in the Western Isles, such as the Greek romancers had depicted;[2] his, too, was but the gesture of helplessness. After the murder of Julius Caesar, Virgil gave powerful expression to the terrorized feelings of the people: the very sun veiled his head, while dire omens, phantoms and voices and all manner of prodigies, were reported, and battlefields were again stained with Roman blood. Finally the poet prays fervently to the oldest gods of Rome to spare that divine young man who may bring succor to an age in which right and wrong are inverted.[3]

So Virgil writes before Actium; yet he has already written, immediately after a temporary reconciliation between Octavian and Antony (the Treaty of Brundisium, 40 B.C.), of a Golden Age that is being ushered in by the birth of a child during the few months of Pollio's consulship (the end of the year 40). The age is described with pastoral imagery and prophetic fervor that recall Messianic prophecy; and the poem concludes with words of unique tenderness addressed to the child.[4] It is a moving expression of the aspirations of

[1] Catullus, 64, 384–408.
[2] Horace, Epode 16.
[3]   Di patrii, Indigetes, et Romule Vestaque mater,
    quae Tuscum Tiberim et Romana Palatia servas
    hunc saltem everso iuvenem succurrere saeclo
    ne prohibete." *Georg.* I, 498–501.
[4] *Buc.* IV. For the whole idea, see Mayor, Fowler, and Conway's *Virgil's Messianic Eclogue*, in particular the essay of Conway contained therein,

war-weary and conscience-stricken pagans. The child, it may be, died in infancy; and the Treaty of Brundisium was surely a false dawn; but Virgil's hopes were not long deferred. For in Octavian, the young man for whom he prayed in the *Georgics*, the pagan world indeed found a new and growing spirit of beneficence which it could worship as divine, and who brought back the Golden Age;[1] moreover, during the halcyon days of his reign Bethlehem saw the birth of another child[2] whose reign, longer deferred, is still striving to bring about the regeneration of man. One need not, like the early Christian readers of Virgil, attribute to the poet (or indeed to the writers of the Old Testament) a conscious prophecy or literal prediction of Christ in order to recognize in Virgil the best pagan embodiment of the universal craving for peace and regeneration and for a single figure in whom might be expressed the hopes of diverse religions.[3]

Octavian, soon to be known as Augustus, did not altogether disappoint the hopes of his age, even if he had to be educated in office. As his political position masked a monarchical power under republican forms, appearing in the East to be truly monarchical and in Rome to be a restoration of the Republic,[4] so the religious movement of his age has a dual aspect. Though not personally a religious man, he was doubtless sincere in holding that peace and prosperity and a decent spirit among men depended on a revival of the old Roman virtues of discipline and *pietas*. Further-

---

"The Messianic Idea in Virgil" (esp. pp. 33–48). J. Carcopino, in *Virgile et le Mystère de la IVᵉ Eglogue* (Paris, 1930), makes a strong case for identifying the child with Saloninus, a son of Pollio who died in infancy.

[1] *Aen.* VI, 791–794.

[2] Cf. Milton, "On the Morning of Christ's Nativity."

[3] Among the philosophers of this age is to be found the belief that different religions are but different expressions or epiphanies of the one God, — a tendency known as syncretism.

[4] Cf. pp. 232–234.

more he knew that few men are capable of being philosophical and that all men are more easily reached through the emotions than through the reason. Hence he was at pains to represent his religious reforms as being a revival of the old state religion, enhanced by new dignity and splendor. In his autobiography he tells us [1] that he restored eighty-two temples which had fallen into neglect; and he also revived several priesthoods and cults, notably the Arval Brotherhood with the cult of the Bona Dea, and the *Flamen Dialis*. After the death of Lepidus in 13 B.C., Augustus assumed the office of *Pontifex Maximus* and held it for the rest of his life; it came to be held regularly by subsequent emperors. In 17 B.C. the celebration of the *Ludi Saeculares* and the singing of the *Carmen Saeculare* on the Palatine and the Capitoline marked in solemn yet hopeful manner the firm establishment of the new age, gratitude to Apollo and Diana, as well as to Jupiter and the other divinities, and the return of the long-neglected virtues.[2] Even if the revival of the old Roman religion savors of antiquarianism, it was inspired by moral motives, and symbolized, like the waving of a flag, a loyalty to the living past.

More difficult to understand, and more important, is the ascendancy of the emperor's prestige, culminating in emperor-worship.[3] Here the motive is more clearly political. Earlier Roman religion, we have seen, was largely the creation of the state; since Augustus might truthfully have said, "L'état, c'est moi," the *ius divinum* also naturally came under his control. This result came about partly through the attach-

---

[1] *Monumentum Ancyranum* IV, 17.

[2] Cf. p. 245.

[3] The best general account of this subject is now that of Miss L. R. Taylor, *The Divinity of the Roman Emperor* (Monographs of the American Philological Association, No. 1, 1931); see also references below to several of her previous papers.

ment of certain phases of the old Roman religion to the personal fortunes of the Julian line, and partly through the influence of Hellenistic ideas. After the death of Julius Caesar, Octavian, as his heir, vowed to build a temple to Mars Ultor ("the Avenger"): this was dedicated in the new Forum of Augustus in 2 B.C., and drew to itself important observances.[1] It was to this temple that boys proceeded after they had donned the *toga virilis* in the Temple of Jupiter Capitolinus; the standards recovered from the Parthians were kept there; and in its wall henceforth, instead of in the Temple of Jupiter Optimus Maximus, was driven a nail at the end of each *lustrum*. Moreover, since Augustus professed to feel a special debt to Apollo, particularly for the victory of Actium, he built for the god a new temple on the Palatine, adjoining his own house, and transferred to it the Sibylline Books. But he did not undertake to elevate the worship of Apollo at the expense of the Capitoline Triad; and in fact the old gods in general amounted during the Augustan age to little more than shadowy symbols of forces or activities.[2] Since Augustus did not wish to dwell in the house next to the Regia in the Forum (especially in view of its ancient and dangerous associations with the kingship), and yet must, as *Pontifex Maximus*, dwell in a public building, he gave the Regia to the Vestal Virgins, and declared a portion of his own new palace to be public property; by declaring his hearth to be a public shrine of Vesta he identified his family worship with the fortunes of the state.

The actual deification and worship of Julius Caesar, of Augustus, and of later emperors must, nevertheless, be regarded as an innovation quite alien to the spirit of the earlier

[1] See the illustration opposite.
[2] Cf. Fowler, *Roman Ideas of Deity*, Lecture VI, "The Degradation of the Idea of Deity in the Augustan Age."

TEMPLE OF MARS ULTOR, IN THE FORUM OF AUGUSTUS

(Photo by Alinari)

Roman religion. For gods and men had been considered distinct, even if a man's *genius* had something of the supernatural. But during the closing years of the Republic Italy had been flooded by throngs of people of foreign races, particularly from Greece and the Orient, where god-kings and heroes of divine ancestry were familiar conceptions, and where the mystery cults brought divinity much nearer to humanity. Moreover educated Romans, and especially Stoics, were coming to think of heroic and beneficent action as an expression of divinity or the divine reason. Amid the decay of the older cults it was natural to transfer divinity from the gods who had failed to human beings who had succeeded in helping man, "a very present help in time of trouble." [1]

In the East such ideas had long been prevalent. The Persian king seemed to the Greeks to be thought of as a god on earth. Alexander found the assumption of divine honors in the cities of Greece to be a strong cohesive force, a political unity disguised under religious forms, in which his absolutism received a specious legalism, for a god may do anything! In Egypt he was the heir of the Pharaohs.[2] The Greek Euhemerus (third century B.C.), who was familiar with Hellenized Egypt as well as with Greece, declared that gods are but deified men; his views, it may be noted, were translated into Latin by Ennius, and perhaps assisted in the

---

[1] Cf. Lucretius V, 8–12: "deus ille fuit, deus, inclute Memmi, | qui princeps vitae rationem invenit eam quae | nunc appellatur Sapientia," etc. (of Epicurus); Virgil, Buc. I, cf. "deus nobis haec otia fecit. | Namque erit ille mihi semper deus," etc., and 42: "praesentis . . . divos" (of Octavian). Virgil's language expresses in the most natural manner the spontaneous feelings of his contemporaries. See further Fowler, *Roman Ideas of Deity*, Lecture IV, "The Idea of the Man-God."

[2] Cf. W. W. Tarn, in *C. A. H.*, VI, 424: "In Egypt Alexander was an autocrat and a god. In Iran he was an autocrat, but not a god. In the Greek cities he was a god, but not an autocrat. . . .'"

growing disbelief in the Roman gods. Plutarch, several centuries later, and with many more examples both Greek and Roman in mind, poured contempt on the assumption of divine honors by rulers; virtue was the only link between king and god.[1] But in Greece, at any rate, the line between gods and great men had all but vanished; and when the Romans acquired piecemeal the fragments of Alexander's Hellenized empire, the veneration which earlier Greeks had given to dead heroes and kings and benefactors, like Lysander and Alexander and Demetrius, was now transferred spontaneously to Roman generals or to the personified City of Rome. Thus the general Flamininus, the victor of Cynoscephalae, as "Savior" and "Deliverer" was associated with Zeus, and public buildings were dedicated to him. Pompey, who had saved the East from the pirates and from Mithradates, was also hailed as a "Savior" and a god. Roman governors in Greece and the East, even if of indifferent or of bad character, were given divine honors, temples, and festivals;[2] since individual Roman governors were superseded, shrines were built also to "Rome the Benefactress," or to "The Good Faith of the Roman People," as well as to Jupiter Capitolinus. Roma, then, was a political personage, worshiped by provincials among their gods, but by them only.

From Greece and the East such conceptions were carried to Rome by humble immigrants and by returning governors during the closing years of the Republic.[3] The common

---

[1] Cf. K. Scott, "Plutarch and the Ruler Cult," *T. A. P. A.*, Vol. LX (1929). A. D. Nock finds ruler-worship in Greek lands wholly distinct from native customs. Cf. Σύνναος Θεός, *H. S. C. P.*, XLI (1930), 1–62.

[2] Cicero declined such an honor, though he could have had it, thinking it set a bad precedent. *Ad Quint. Frat.* I, 1, 26.

[3] See in general W. S. Ferguson, "Legalized Absolutism en route from Greece to Rome," *American Historical Review*, XVIII (October, 1912), 29–47.

people were ready to turn instinctively to a human benefactor as to a manifest god; the governing class was willing to manipulate and to control for political purposes an idea that clothed rulers in a much-needed dignity. Julius Caesar appears not to have been deeply interested in the idea, nor indeed to have lifted a finger to claim divinity for himself,[1] though he became familiar with the practice of deification during his brief stay in the East while dealing with Pompey and his party. At Pharsalus he gave as his watchword "Venus Victrix," which suggested that the Julian *gens*, like at least one other Roman family of the day, professed to look upon Venus as his ancestress; and in 46 B.C. he actually built in his Forum the Temple of Venus Genetrix. After the victory over Pompey he was given divine honors by the Greeks. But Caesar was not a familiar figure in Rome itself during these years, and doubtless had nothing to do with the placing of his statue in the Temple of Quirinus (Romulus) or the carrying of it in processional along with statues of the gods, — neither of which acts as a matter of fact quite amounted to deification, though the former suggested that he was a second founder of Rome. He was apparently not interested in the attempt of Antony and others, during the last months of his life, to secure for him divine honors and a cult; yet he apparently acquiesced, and wore the *corona radiata*, which was the emblem of a sun-god, and accepted other regal and divine honors.[2] After his death and the read-

---

[1] Cf. Fowler, *Roman Ideas of Deity*, Lecture V, "The Deification of Caesar"; Miss Taylor finds more reason to attribute to Caesar himself the motive power behind his regal and divine honors (*The Divinity of the Roman Emperor*, Ch. III, "Caesar's Attempt to Found a Divine Monarchy").

[2] See F. Folliot, "De Principiis cultus imperatorum Romanorum," etc., *H. S. C. P.*, XXXVIII (1927), 143–147, who holds that "Fowler in his *Roman Ideas of Deity* seems to have underestimated the degree to which Caesar flouted Roman religious practice"; Miss Taylor independently reaches similar conclusions.

ing of his will, however, the people realized that he had indeed been a "Benefactor" and "Savior," and spontaneously proclaimed him a god; the comet of the following summer, the eclipse of the sun of the following autumn, and the other prodigies that were reported assisted in promoting the deification.[1] On January 1, 42 B.C., Octavian persuaded the Senate to vote that Julius Caesar was divine and that he should have a cult and a temple in the Forum Romanum on the spot where his body had been burned; the temple, a sort of memorial shrine, was dedicated in 29 B.C.,[2] and the altar and part of its foundations may still be seen. Thus the veneration of "the deified Julius," *divus* rather than *deus*,[3] it must be noted, was sanctioned by the state and duly regulated; not yet, in all probability, had a living Roman been actually worshiped in Rome.[4] But Caesar had all but set up an oriental monarchy in Rome, which inevitably gathered about itself "the divinity that doth hedge a king." Roman sentiment had been offended, at least during his lifetime, and political reactionaries had struck him down. Antony, not profiting by the lesson, played with monarchy and divine honors in Egypt, as the "New Dionysus," and met his miserable end. It was Octavian whose political sagacity in determining his constitutional position was equalled only by the skill with which he recognized the religious sentiment of both halves of the Empire.

---

[1] Cf. Virgil, *Buc.* IX, 47; V, 56–80.

[2] "To the *genius* of the Divus Julius, *pater patriae*, whom the Senate and people of Rome have received into the ranks of gods."

[3] *Divus* and *deus* were at this time practically synonymous; but *divus* was presently differentiated, as meaning "one made into a god."

[4] But cf. L. R. Taylor, "Divus Julius," *Proceedings of the American Philological Association*, Vol. LVIII (1927), dating the title before the death of Caesar; the deification in this case becomes the putting into effect of the decree passed early in 44 but held till now in abeyance. See further Taylor, *Divinity of the Roman Emperor*, Ch. IV, "Divus Julius Enshrined in State Cult."

The people of the Greek and the Hellenized cities of the eastern half of the Empire had long worshiped the Fortune (*Tyche*) of their own personified cities, or of Rome, the new mistress of the Mediterranean; it was their way of expressing faith, political and religious, in the vitality and the promise of the greatest power that controlled their lives. During the reign of Augustus they spontaneously added to such cults that of Augustus himself, with altars and priestly boards or sodalities, of which the leading provincials were members; for did not he now embody that power and hope? Thus altars were dedicated to "Roma et Augustus," or to Augustus as a "savior . . . through whom come good tidings," and to "God, the son of God, Augustus the Benefactor." Even in the western provinces of the Empire we find a cult of *Roma et Augustus*, which in a sense took the place of the earlier allegiance to the *Senatus Populusque Romanus* as the politico-religious expression of the "dyarchy" and the worship of deified emperors whether living or dead.[1] The official title Augustus (in Greek, Sebastos) signifying one consecrated and endowed with *auctoritas*,[2] suggested to orientals a vague deification such as was congenial to their traditions, and was yet not offensive to Romans. In Egypt, of course, Augustus was a god-king, the heir of the Pharaohs and the Ptolemies.

In Rome and in Italy, however, Augustus was careful not to permit anything that savored of actual worship of himself on the part of Roman citizens. The office of *Pontifex Maximus*, which he assumed after the death of Lepidus in 13 B.C.,

---

[1] This cult was deliberately introduced into Gaul. Cf. also G. C. Fiske, "Notes on the Worship of the Roman Emperors in Spain," *H. S. C. P.*, XI (1900), 101–140.

[2] Perhaps the title also designated its bearer as the new Romulus, the second founder of Rome. Cf. K. Scott, "The Identification of Augustus with Romulus Quirinus," *T. A. P. A.*, Vol. LVI (1925).

was in fact incompatible with divinity. His *genius*, to be sure, was included among the *Lares Compitales* worshiped in the *vici* of Rome, and priestly boards of *Augustales*, usually though not always consisting of freedmen, not of citizens, were to be found in Italian towns, as well as temples dedicated to the emperor's *genius*; [1] the *genius* had always been considered not quite identical with the self. Doubtless Augustus found it useful to exploit the original association of the *genius* with a family's vital force in connecting the divine ancestors of his line (Venus Genetrix and Mars Ultor) with the perpetuation of his house; it is interesting to note that it was in the same year (2 B.C.) in which the Temple of Mars Ultor was dedicated, and associated with the *iuvenes* of Rome, that Augustus was hailed as *pater patriae*.[2] In the inscription on the *Ara Narbonensis*, dedicated to the *Numen Augusti*, the *numen* is invoked as an independent deity; but there were innumerable other deities, abstractions like Victoria and Concordia, or even older deities of the state religion like Jupiter and Hercules, which were now venerated with the epithet Augustus (or Augusti), that is, as guardian spirits or functions attached to the person of the emperor, or as expressions of his personality equivalent to his *genius*.[3] And since at Rome there was no special temple of Augustus, and his cult encroached on that of the older temples, there was some justification for the complaint of certain Romans, immediately after his death, that "no honor was left for the gods when Augustus chose to be himself worshiped with temples and statues, like those of the deities, and with fla-

---

[1] H. F. Pelham, "The Domestic Policy of Augustus," in *Essays on Roman History*, esp. pp. 105–113; and L. R. Taylor, "The Worship of Augustus in Italy during His Lifetime," *T. A. P. A.*, Vol. LI (1920).

[2] Cf. L. R. Taylor, "The Worship of Augustus . . . ," p. 127.

[3] Cf. Folliot, *op. cit.*; W. M. Green, "Notes on the Augustan Deities," *C. J.*, Vol. XXIII (November, 1927); A. D. Nock, "Studies in the Graeco-Roman Beliefs of the Empire," *Journal of Hellenic Studies*, XLV (1925), 92.

mens and priests." [1] Augustus had indeed utilized the old gods, as well as the popular conception of the *genius* or *numen*, to suggest that he was the visible embodiment of Providence.

Doubtless it was difficult for Augustus even in Italy to prevent himself from receiving during his life the deification which he was obviously destined, as benefactor and as son of the Divus Julius, to receive at his death; men tended spontaneously to give it by anticipation, and Augustus had to resist the adulatory decrees of the Senate. The poets perhaps assisted in the process. But we must observe that in Virgil, at least, Augustus is regarded as a divine incarnation or epiphany only when acting as a benefactor of mankind.[2] Thus he has "the germ of a deity in him, which may be developed at his death." [3] Virgil, just before Actium, suggests that the gods already are impatient for Octavian's return to heaven; [4] Horace prays, a couple of years later, that this return may be delayed.[5] Soon Augustus will drink nectar among the gods; [6] when the Britons and the Persians are subdued he will be held a *praesens divus*, a manifest god.[7]

In these ways the faith of Romans and Italians was allowed to express its loyalty to the divine element in the living emperor. After his death, his *acta* might receive a special ratification by his deification, as in the provinces he had already been worshiped; soldiers took their oath of allegiance to his *genius*, and, later, to the *Divi Caesares*. Tiberius, the

---

[1] Tacitus, *Ann.* I, 10.

[2] Cf. R. S. Conway, "An Unnoticed Aspect of Vergil's Personality," in *Harvard Lectures on the Vergilian Age*, pp. 68–71.

[3] Fowler, *Roman Ideas of Deity*, p. 126.

[4] "Iam pridem nobis caeli te regia, Caesar, | Invidet." *Georg.* I, 503 f.

[5] "Serus in caelum redeas, diuque | Laetus intersis populo Quirini." *Odes* I, 2, 45 f.

[6] *Odes* III, 3, 12, reading (as the context demands), with the best Mss., *bibet*; some editors read *bibit*.   [7] *Odes* III, 5, 2–4.

conscientious successor of Augustus, to be sure, accepted divine honors for Divus Augustus as a matter of course; he went through the form of refusing such honors for himself, except in the East, but in the end accepted about all the honors that Augustus had accepted during his lifetime. Actual deification he never received, since his reign was unpopular in Rome, and his successor Caligula did not press the matter.[1] Claudius was deified after his death (rather to the amusement of Rome),[2] and Vespasian and many later emperors. The cult of the emperors, living or dead, a fusion of patriotic and religious feeling, served, like a union of church and state, as a bond of union among diverse peoples, and became presently, as the Christians were to discover to their sorrow, the most convenient test of loyalty. The motive was still political, but it meant the extension of *pietas*, once a peculiarly Roman quality, to all the diverse peoples of the Empire. As a matter of fact, it is almost impossible to make a large number of people think alike or feel alike; but it is not difficult to get them to dress alike or act alike. The odd yet significant fact is that from similar acts come similar feelings and thoughts and an *esprit de corps*. "You don't cry because you are hurt," William James once said: "you are hurt because you cry." So it was with the subjects of the god-emperor, whose common acts of worship bred a common loyalty, a *pietas* not to be distinguished from patriotism. Under the form of religion, as Tacitus observed, had been established in the Empire a stronghold of everlasting domination.[3]

[1] Cf. L. R. Taylor, "Tiberius' Refusal of Divine Honors," *T. A. P. A.*, Vol. LX (1929); K. Scott, "Tiberius' Refusal of the Title 'Augustus,'" *C. P.*, Vol. XXVII (January, 1932).

[2] Cf. the *Apotheosis Divi Claudi*, attributed to Seneca, referred to also as the *Apocolocyntosis* ("Pumpkinification").

[3] *Ann.* XIV, 31.

However political in motive and in results may have been the religious revival and the imperial cult introduced by Augustus, there was one of his subjects in whom something nobler was stirring, and who brooded now doubtfully, now hopefully, on gods and men and fate. Virgil is at once the priest of the older Roman religion and the prophet of the new age of humanitarianism and of Rome's mission to the world; he is conscious, also, of problems beyond human power to solve. No reader can fail to note how observant he is of the canons and the rubrics: how his heart delights in picturing a sacrifice performed *ritu*, or *more maiorum*; how the funeral of Misenus prefigures the ritual of funerals in Virgil's own day; how the cheerful account of the funeral games for Anchises serves to suggest the Roman memorial festival of the *Parentalia*. But this is not mere antiquarianism; the Homeric gods are morally ennobled, and amid the details of ritual over which Virgil affectionately lingers he seeks to penetrate to the *pietas* of which they are symbols.

So far Virgil is the priest. But elsewhere he shows himself the prophet or the hierophant,—in the "Messianic Eclogue," in the gradual revelation of the goal of Aeneas given in the third book of the *Aeneid*, in the visions and divine prophecies of Roman greatness, above all in the sixth book of the *Aeneid*. Here Aeneas, fresh from his lapse at Carthage and from the penance done in the funeral games, undergoes what amounts to initiation into a mystery cult. Virgil builds on the all but universal belief in immortality or craving for a blessed hereafter expressed by poets from Homer down. He fuses the popular mythology that Lucretius rejected with the doctrines of purification taught by the Orphics and by Plato, and represents the act of *pietas* of Aeneas, his visit to his father, as culminating in a vision of last things, an eschatological myth, in which Roman ideas of conduct, a pagan decalogue, are sanctioned by noble examples and dreadful warnings, and the future course of Roman history and the Julian line is unfolded in the light of the Platonic theory of the rebirth in divers forms of purified spirits that partake of the universal spirit. Like the Platonic myths, Virgil's apocalypse is a spiritual affirmation.

Aeneas has struggled, sinned, and done penance; the command laid upon him to rescue the Trojan Penates and to found a new city has gradually become more and more precise, and has been connected with the destiny of Rome, the Fatum Romanum; but this destiny has brought unhappiness to Aeneas and death to warm-hearted Dido, and will bring death to noble Turnus. Nevertheless, in the first book of the *Aeneid* Virgil has suggested in the conversation between Jupiter and Venus that there is some connection between *Fatum*, fate, and "what is said" (*fatum*) by Jupiter;[1] if at times it seems to be inexorable predestination, it is at other times the beneficent freedom of his will. Although the Roman Empire is a hard, ineluctable fact, the result of chance and the will to survive, Virgil contrives in the sixth book to view it as foreordained in the nature of things to prevail and to prevail for the good of the world. Thus the conflict of the individual with apparently capricious gods or with an apparently ruthless Fate, — a conflict which in the tale of Dido sorely tries the reader's faith, — finds some sort of reconciliation; freedom of the will finds repose in *pietas*, nor is Dido's poet unable to "justify the ways of God to men."

.This vision, the aspiration of Virgil and of all good Romans, is given a dramatic setting of the most profound mystery, hardly to be surpassed in impressiveness by Dante. Virgil leads us to the portal of the Lower World, in a region

---

[1] *Aen.* I, 223–296, esp. 239, 241, 257–262.

already full of prophetic associations: Avernus, the Sibyl,
and Apollo. He leads our minds to Crete, the earliest home
of European civilization, and thus to the myriads of forefathers already entombed. How naturally the death of
Misenus and his funeral cause us to follow him to the Lower
World, even as the impending death of Socrates sets the
minds of the philosopher and his companions on the destiny
of the soul! The Golden Bough, too, found in the course of a
quest enjoined by *pietas*, has its own mystic significance as
an emblem of life-in-death. And as we move obscurely with
Aeneas amid the dire divinities of Limbo, amid spirits un-
buried or buried, first those who died but lately and presently those who died earlier, as we hear of the dooms inflicted in Tartarus and behold the abodes of the Blessed, and
come at last into the presence of Anchises, there is no point
at which we are impelled to say, "Thus far I believe, but now
I doubt." So perfectly has Virgil made palpable the obscure,
even while hinting again and again at its unsubstantial nature. What wonder, then, that the words of Anchises have
the weight of true prophecy, as he expounds the Platonic and
Orphic doctrines of the *anima mundi*, of purification and
reincarnation? What wonder that the heroes of Roman
legend and history seem to carry the banners of crusaders
charged with a holy mission? At the last, just as the picture
of Marcellus, dead ere his prime, has brought us to the threshold between world and world, Anchises leads Aeneas forth
through the gate of *false* dreams, wondering whether it was
only a vision. The ships stand on the shore, anchored by the
prow; there at least is reality once more. Yet the vision of
Aeneas is a secret vision, for which nothing in the earlier
books prepares us, and to which nothing in the later books
makes reference; Aeneas keeps the secret revelation in his
heart as faithfully as did the initiates into the mysteries. He

introduces no new rites, sets forth no new doctrines, departs from none of his accustomed activities. Only in the strengthening of his purpose, which no longer vacillates, and in the purifying and enlarging of his sympathies, are we henceforth conscious of the experience through which he has passed, an experience fairly to be described as religious "conversion."

Besides setting forth his interpretation of the old Roman religion, then, Virgil has been moving toward a more profound reading of life. Even in the *Bucolics* we find him yearning for peace and turning to successive champions who may save Rome, and finally to Octavian. In the *Georgics*, the piping shepherd of the *Bucolics* has almost disappeared, supplanted by the hard-working farmer. Yet Virgil is writing no less of and for him who is endowed with what Wordsworth called "a wise passivity," for one who delights to brood upon things and their inwardness. But who is this person, poet or philosopher? As frequently, Virgil seems to halt between two opinions, between the Lucretian or Epicurean scientist and the more instinctive lover of nature who trusts to the promptings of his poet's heart. He pays his homage to Lucretius, and in the same breath flings him a challenge. Before all else he would fain know the causes of natural phenomena; but if such knowledge be denied him, may he, lost to fame, find his delight in the countryside, the streams that water the valleys, the woods. "Happy the man who has availed to learn the causes of things, and has trampled under foot all fear and inexorable fate; . . . blessed, too, he who has known the gods of the country, and Pan, and old Silvanus, and the sister nymphs!" [1]

In the *Aeneid* we are still more fully aware of the author's deliberate purpose to reveal the conflict of forces that must

[1] *Georg.* II, 490–494, quoted at the head of this chapter.

be reconciled, and of his brooding on human problems that can at best be thrown into relief without ever being fully solved.[1] Dealing both with the remote legendary past (the founding of Rome) and with recent events and their possible consequences (Rome's recent struggles with her Italic *socii*, the civil wars, and the founding of the Empire), he shows past and present, Italy and Rome, converging in a great process of reconciliation. *Pietas*, the devotion of Aeneas, is brought into conflict with the human affections of Dido and with the patriotism and the *violentia* of the Italian Turnus and his allies, in two episodes of truly tragic character. The *pius* Aeneas himself does not ride triumphantly over all obstacles, but for years is rewarded with hardships and anguish of heart. For Virgil's golden age [2] is no longer an accomplished fact, past, present, or imminent, but the world in process of being remade by the forces of humanity and tolerance. As for his qualms and misgivings, the failures and broken lives that he records, that is a part of Virgil's glory; he has seen at what cost all progress is made. At the heart of things remains the mystery, unsolved by man, of undeserved suffering, of single wills thwarted for some good end which is not their end, — the problem of evil.

Yet despite his sense of the pathos, the futility, the evil, that is in life, Virgil reveals himself best when he betrays his own affections and loyalties to friends and causes and the characters whom he has created. These, he seems to imply, are the abiding things, whatever may be their fortune in this transitory world; to love them is to spend one's days well. The beauty of nature and the joy of country life kindle his delight; the sufferings of dumb animals and above all the deaths of young warriors arouse his pity. Thus we come to

[1] Cf. R. S. Conway, "The Philosophy of Vergil," in *Harvard Lectures on the Vergilian Age*, pp. 94–112.   [2] Cf. pp. 336–338.

realize the meaning of *lacrimae rerum*, the tear of sympathy for suffering, the heart that is touched by our mortal lot, which is Virgil's peculiar gift. We feel it in the lines in which the poet, after telling of the deaths of Nisus and Euryalus, those brothers-in-arms whose very devotion to each other was the ultimate cause of their deaths, drops his epic reserve and in person addresses the dead warriors in almost lyric strain. And in what manner? Not to commiserate with them on their sad doom, but to congratulate them. "O happy pair, if aught my song avail, no day shall ever blot out your names from the memory of time, while Aeneas' line shall dwell upon the Capitol's immovable Rock, and the Roman father holds sovereign power." [1] When all is done, Virgil would have us admire and emulate true heroism and *pietas*, wherever they be found, and bow our heads in resignation before those dispensations whose motives and issues lie within the shadow, keeping for all suffering in high and in lowly creatures alike our deep and instant sympathy.

The *Aeneid* itself is in every true sense a poem inspired by a religious idea, — man gradually realizing the guidance and support of divine powers and struggling to do his duty.[2] Virgil's influence on the better minds of his own age and of succeeding ages was considerable; it helped to refine the conception of human character, and especially of the ideal ruler, and was not without practical effect in moulding the statesmanship of Augustus and of later emperors.[3] The political

---

[1] *Aen.* IX, 446–449. See also X, 507, and 791–793, the poet's lyric outcries on the death of Lausus.

[2] Cf. further G. Boissier, *La Religion Romaine*, Vol. I, Bk. I, Chs. V and VI; and H. Nettleship, *Suggestions Introductory to a Study of the Aeneid* (Oxford, 1875), reprinted in *Lectures and Essays* (Oxford, 1885).

[3] Cf. R. S. Conway, "Politics and Government", *Proceedings of the (English) Classical Association*, Vol. XXV (1928); D. L. Drew, *The Allegory of the Aeneid* (Oxford, 1927); R. M. Henry, "Virgil and Roman Civilization," *Proceedings of the (English) Classical Association*, Vol. XXVII (1930).

ideal of the Republic, personal liberty for self-governing citizens, was as dead as the Republic itself; benevolence on the part of the ruler and loyalty on the part of the governed form the ideals of the new age. Marcus Aurelius, the weary *defensor pacis*, is a true incarnation of the *pietas* of Aeneas; and even in the panegyrics lavished on unworthy emperors one feels chiefly the pathetic or even ironic contrast between the actuality and the ideal that Virgil has created. The tradition of pagan civilization, infused by Virgil with a new spirit of humanity and a sense of new frontiers of religious experience, is accepted even by the Christians as part of their heritage, especially after the triumph of Christianity, and the Church fathers often recognize in Virgil a spiritual ally. The Christians are loyal to the Roman state, and pray for the emperor; the one test of loyalty to which they will not submit is the actual worship of the emperor, which unfortunately is precisely the crucial test imposed by the state.

Nevertheless,Virgil hardly represents the average religious feeling of his own or of the next age; even in those poems of Horace, his successor as "poet laureate," which most directly deal with the ideals and needs of the new age [1] we are aware, amid striking phrases that haunt the memory and amid unimpeachable moral commonplaces, of a more perfunctory attitude. In Virgil and in Horace alike the gods of the state religion are chiefly literary artifices; but whereas Virgil's human beings are pilgrims and crusaders battling for eternal realities, Horace's men are moving in a matter-of-fact world, a world singularly like our own, to be sure, but one whose horizon discloses no "flaming ramparts," no mysterious portals opening into the unknown. And if even Horace is so much the product of his own realistic age, we may be sure that ordinary men were not deeply affected by

[1] E.g. *Odes* III, 1–6.

the religious reforms of Augustus, by the visions of Virgil, or even by emperor-worship save as a political symbol draped in religious forms. If Virgil's Messianic hopes were only partly realized in Augustus, his spiritual message was imperfectly understood, and was kept alive chiefly as a dream in the minds of men of good will.

The following centuries accordingly are characterized principally by two developments. On one hand there is the dignified continuation of the formal ritual of the state religion, subordinated more and more to the worship of the living and the deified Caesars. On the other hand there is the rapid increase of the proselyting mystical religions from the East, and an anti-scientific, obscurantist spirit, the very negation both of the rational, philosophic outlook of Greece and of the practical legalistic attitude of Rome. Chaldaean astrologers, once debarred from Rome, now move freely among rich and poor. Not only in the numerous precincts of the healer Asclepius, with their mixture of common-sense living and calculated hallucination, are visions and dreams interpreted with superstititious and painstaking care. Miracles are expected, and miracles are therefore reported, whether by the credulous or by the impostor. Gods and *daemones*, good or evil, are always ready to appear to men; Delphi and the other older oracles are neglected amid the new methods of approach to divinity that are crying for attention. Especially the oriental mystery religions continue to break down the old Greek and Roman barrier between god and man. Mithras, Isis, the Great Mother, and the Neo-Pythagorean cult claim new devotees and turn men's thoughts and hopes to another world and to personal salvation.

Since Pompey's soldiers brought westward the cult of Mithras, its invigorating influence had spread along the military roads throughout Italy and the western provinces even as far as Britain. Mithras had borrowed freely: from Phrygia, the characteristic cap of its people; from the Great Mother, the baptismal rite of the *taurobolium*. The latter perhaps suggested that the ancient myth of the slaying of the bull by Mithras be represented in bas-reliefs of a conventionalized form in the Greek manner; these were placed in the scores of small subterranean chapels as the sacred symbol of the cult, much as the image of the Crucified has been used in Christian churches.[1] This symbol, with the other vague, almost heraldic, figures and emblems, and the sacramental character of the ritual, suggestive of the Christian Mass, naturally appealed to minds that craved support in an obscure world; nor was the appeal less strong because the myth and the symbols were themselves obscure. At least Mithras was a hero, a mediator saving man from evil, and aiding Ahura-Mazda in his eternal struggle with Ahriman. His worshipers were by him nerved for the struggle against the powers of darkness, and proceeded step by step, through an almost Orphic or even Platonic discipline and through successive grades of initiation, toward immortality and a return through the spheres of the planets to the divinity whence they originally came. Thus Mithraism preserved for better and for worse something of the purity of the earlier Persian sun-worship. The sun had already served even Plato as the visible symbol of the Idea of the Good, the unifying principle of all existence; and absolutist Roman emperors were soon to claim reverence as unique expressions of the Invincible Sun (*Deus Sol Invictus*). With the tendency of the age set toward syncretism, Mithras led the way;

---

[1] Cf. F. Cumont, *Textes et Monuments Figurés Relatifs aux Mystères de Mithra*, 2 vols. (Brussels, 1899, 1896). See also S. Dill, *Roman Society from Nero to Marcus Aurelius*, bk. IV, Ch. VI; and W. R. Halliday, *The Pagan Background of Christianity* (Liverpool, 1925), Lecture IX.

his sacramental religion had a far greater appeal than any philosophy; his cult was cosmopolitan, and though unfriendly to inferior cults and never officially accepted by the Roman state, it was at least more tolerant than Christianity; he presented a stirring ethical appeal, at least to men. To women the appeal was less strong; and Mithraism had furthermore the essential weakness common to all religions that are at heart nature-cults. Moreover, it was prone to link itself with all manner of astrology and demonology. At its best a pure and noble religion, Mithraism was nevertheless capable of becoming a crude superstition. As the strongest rival of Christianity during the third century, and as offering in its myth and in its ritual certain analogies which Christians could not but regard as travesties of their own sacraments, it was subject to their violent attacks.

In the provinces, the mystery cults reached their zenith in the second century A.D.; in Rome they lingered for a century or two longer, checked or assisted by the hostile or the friendly attitudes of some of the emperors. From the time of Septimius Severus (193-211), whose wife was a Syrian, it was still more conspicuously the oriental cults that displaced Roman or even Greek religious ideas in Rome and in the provinces.[1] Caracalla admitted all the foreign deities to the state cult; so Rome became the home of Baal and Astarte. Caracalla himself and his crazy successor Elegabalus were both worshiped as (Deus) Sol Invictus; Aurelian assumed royal and divine emblems, — on his coins he is described as "Deus et Dominus Noster." Throughout these centuries the old Roman gods were given foreign epithets, — for example, Jupiter Optimus Maximus being identified with Baal and worshiped with the epithet *Dolichenus*, derived

[1] Cf. C. H. Moore, "Oriental Cults in Britain," *H. S. C. P.*, XI (1900), 47-60.

from a petty town in eastern Asia Minor. This is typical of the syncretism of the age, which tended to view all religions as but aspects of a single religion.

Among the oriental cults that were scattered westward and that found their way to Rome during the late Republic was that of the Jews. Originally a united people with a theocratic form of government, they had enjoyed in their homeland the tolerant attitude of the conquering Romans, who seldom interfered with the religions of their subject peoples unless they appeared to be inconsistent with morals or with political security. For reasons of expediency, Julius Caesar, Augustus, and Tiberius granted to the Jews various special privileges and exemptions, in the East to the nation, in the West to individual Jews as tolerated aliens or even citizens. After the destruction of Jerusalem (70 A.D.), the Jews ceased to exist as a state; yet their religion continued to enjoy the protection of the Roman state, and was specially licensed. Nevertheless, the fierce monotheism of the Jews, the toleration of their uncompromising refusal to join in the politico-religious cult of emperor-worship, and their general exclusiveness, all conspired to make the Jews very unpopular among the Romans. Nor was it to be expected that the toleration which they enjoyed would be extended to another cult, equally monotheistic, and more given to proselyting, if this cult seemed to threaten the peace and security of the Roman state.

Such a cult, of course, Christianity appeared to be. With the real spirit of Christianity and with its theology, this is not the place to deal; the attitude of Roman society and of the Roman state toward it is our immediate concern.[1] To the Romans, to the Jews, and to themselves, the Christians

---

[1] See in general E. G. Hardy, *Christianity and the Roman Government, A Study in Imperial Administration*, 1894 (reprinted, New York, 1925).

at first seemed to be merely a sect or offshoot of Judaism; and they were persecuted, if at all, by the Jews or by injured pagan trade interests.[1] The Roman government tended to regard differences between Jews and Christians as mere internal differences between fanatical Jewish sectarians, and intervened only to protect the Christians. It was not till the Jews accused the Christians of disloyalty to the Roman state that the government regarded the Christians as persons to be dealt with severely. The difference between Christians and Jews was emphasized not only by their acceptance, as an honorable designation, of the name "Christian," first given them at Antioch as a jeering epithet, but also by the spread of the new religion among Gentiles, especially through the efforts of St. Paul, and the consequent claim of Christianity to be a universal religion.

By the end of the first century A.D. the Christians were very numerous in the provinces and even in Rome, and were regarded with universal antipathy by Jews and pagans alike. No Roman would have hated them for purely religious reasons alone, for the Romans never objected to a new god as such. The real reason for the unpopularity of the Christians was the whole social and political trend of their faith, which was incompatible with the ideas of the Romans and in particular with the new imperial cult. Because their minds were filled with the hope of a speedy second coming of Christ, and their interests were "other-worldly," they appeared not to be good citizens of a state that required much in terms of this world. Because their somewhat individualistic religion tended to break up families, to promote celibacy, to divert family property to a common Christian fund, to oppose the ordinary social and religious activities of amphitheatre and temple and service in the army, and also be-

---

[1] E.g. the Ephesian silversmiths (*Acts*, xix, 23–41).

cause their necessarily secret meetings and their sacred meals were misinterpreted as shielding gross immoralities (*flagitia*), the Christians were credited with harboring a hatred toward civilized society.[1] As early as the reign of Nero the Christians in Rome, chiefly converts from paganism rather than from Judaism, had been understood to be a separate sect; and when Nero was suspected of having set the great fire, he sought to divert the suspicion to this hated sect. The examination of the Christians resulted in their being convicted, as Tacitus says, "not so much on the charge of incendiarism as on that of hatred toward civilized society." [2] They were, nevertheless, made the scapegoats of Nero, and suffered cruel martyrdoms, even arousing a certain pity from the populace.

However accidental this persecution in Rome may have been, it was bound before long to result in repercussions in the provinces; the Christians had been put to death not for any overt crime or treasonable act, but because they were Christians, that is, members of a hated sect, suspected of disaffection. It did not follow that the Christians were likely to suffer a general persecution. Even as members of groups which Roman governors would be apt to regard as unlicensed *collegia*, and therefore frowned upon or forbidden by the state from the days of Julius Caesar,[3] they would not necessarily be attacked, for the government tended to treat such matters as fit for the mere police regulation of the

---

[1] See the pagan view of the Christians vigorously set forth toward the end of the second century by the Christian Minucius Felix in his *Octavius*, 8–13.

[2] *Ann.* XV, 44. Tacitus also speaks of Christianity as a "dangerous superstition"; Suetonius refers to it as "a new and maleficent superstition" (*Nero*, 16).

[3] Cf. p. 241. *Collegia* had been alternately repressed and tolerated, according to political exigencies; Trajan refused even to allow a fire brigade to be formed in Bithynia, lest it breed political disturbances. (Pliny, *Epist.* X, 34.)

urban prefect or of provincial governors, and to be as lax as conditions warranted. So in an earlier age the Senate had dealt with another alien cult, the *Bacchanalia*, at once firmly and leniently.[1] Nevertheless, to be a Christian, to confess the name of Christ, quite apart from the *flagitia* supposed to pertain to it, was at least in theory to be a criminal, to be guilty of *odium humani generis* or of *maiestas* (treason). A Christian was always liable to prosecution if the state saw fit to revive the state religion, or if there was a political disturbance in a given area, or if he happened to be accused by interested persons. And it should be remembered that the Roman legal system still lacked a public prosecutor, so that private denunciations and blackmailing were commonly carried on. Furthermore, the worship of Rome and Augustus, or of the reigning emperor, already a more or less spontaneous phenomenon in the East, was introduced probably under Domitian, not, to be sure, as a universal obligation but as a test to be used in identifying Christians who were under accusation. On their compliance or refusal might turn their dismissal or conviction.

The state, then, was not carrying on a systematic policy in dealing with the Christians, but was applying police court methods to sporadic cases as they arose, in a thoroughly opportunist manner. It inclined on the whole to be lenient toward the Christians, unless provoked by difficult situations; in such cases there were precedents for putting to death Christians as Christians, and there was a convenient test for identifying a Christian. It was because Bithynia was a province in which there were many Christians and also many political disturbances, and in which vested interests (the purveyors of fodder and sacrificial victims for the pagan temples) were injured, that its governor, the younger Pliny,

---

[1] Cf. p. 330.

found a difficult situation. He wished to be lenient, and the information that he gathered from the confessing Christians and the renegade Christians who were brought before him disclosed nothing in the way of crimes, but only a "base and fanatical superstition" or a "madness"; [1] their meetings and their common meals seemed innocent enough, and when Pliny in his attempt to suppress *collegia* bade them give up their common meals they complied at least to the extent of omitting the daily "love feast" (though they may without his knowledge have kept, as did Christians elsewhere, the weekly Eucharist). Nevertheless, the spread of Christianity and anonymous accusations perplexed Pliny so much that he wrote to his "master," the efficient emperor Trajan, for instructions, hinting that leniency might accomplish more than severity. Need the *nomen ipsum*, the mere fact that one was a Christian, if not connected with crimes, be punished? Might a former Christian receive pardon if he recanted? Might not a general policy of clemency, replacing the opportunism of previous administrations, turn the tide once more toward paganism? Meanwhile he had been doing his best to extort from the accused a recantation and a formal act of reverence to the emperor's image which might save them from punishment; failing such amends, he had not hesitated to execute them for their very "stubbornness." They had indeed checkmated Pliny's well-meaning attempts to find a loophole by which to save them. The meaning of Christianity, and the reason why real Christians refused the loophole, Pliny simply could not understand; and there is irony of the most tragic sort in the spectacle of this kindliest of pagans striving, at cross-purposes with his Christian subjects, to save them from their "madness."

[1] Pliny, *Epist.* X, 96, which is the source of most of the paragraph above, and a *locus classicus* for the subject; for Trajan's reply, and the following paragraph, see X, 97.

Trajan's rescript, also kindly in intent, reaffirmed the opportunist attitude. The Christians were not a great enough menace to the state to be hunted out; nevertheless, Christians, if duly brought to trial and unwilling to meet the usual test of loyalty to the state, must be punished accordingly. Pardon might be given those who would recant and meet the test. Anonymous accusations deserved no consideration here or elsewhere; they set a bad example and were not in keeping with the "spirit of the age." So easily did Trajan remand to the police courts the difficult problem that Pliny referred to him. It was natural for Christian apologists like Tertullian, a hundred years later, to wax indignant at this inconsistency.[1] Why should only those Christians be punished who happened to be brought to trial? If to be a Christian was a crime, all should be hunted out; if it was not, none should be punished. But as Pliny and Trajan failed to understand the religious position of the Christians, so the Christians failed to realize why the Roman government followed a deliberately opportunist policy in dealing with them, not prosecuting them except where their "stubbornness" (always a potential source of disloyalty to the state) seemed actually dangerous. This policy, or lack of policy, was probably operative in other provinces and in reigns subsequent to Trajan's; Christianity only gradually became organized enough to seem worth suppressing deliberately. Not till Septimius Severus forbade the Christians to make converts (202 A.D.) did the state take the initiative. Decius (250) launched an attack on the Christian leaders, and offered certificates to Christians who would give formal assent to the state religion, exempting them from further trouble. Finally Diocletian (284–305), irritated by the refusal of Christians to serve in the army, set in motion a series of ter-

[1] *Apologeticus*, 2.

rible persecutions, which ended with the edict of Galerius (311), proclaiming a policy of clemency.

"Semen est sanguis Christianorum," wrote Tertullian,[1] with as much truth as rhetoric, for the Christians had indeed multiplied under opposition and persecution and martyrdom; they now comprised perhaps a half of the population of the empire. Constantine found it politic, just after his defeat of the pagan Maxentius (312), to assume that the God of the Christians had been on his side; he recognized Christianity as a tolerated religion, and later made it the official religion of the Empire, though without suppressing the pagan cults. That Constantine's conversion to Christianity was sincere need not be doubted, if one may speak without qualification of the conversion to any religion of a man whose interests and motives were primarily political rather than religious. Even his calling of the Council of Nicaea was animated chiefly by the desire of reaching some definition of the new state religion. Not only were the Christians no longer subject to persecution but Christianity had now supplanted the old religion in the new union of church and state. It was now the pagans who were on the defensive, and whose futile attempts to revive the religion of their fathers have for us the romantic interest of a lost cause. Julian ("the Apostate"), the young emperor who, reared a Christian but loving his Homer and his Neo-Platonic philosophy, felt moved to purge and exalt the pagan religion and to prohibit Christian teachers of rhetoric from meddling with pagan literature, was a sensitive and a lonely soul; but his mystical philosophy had little appeal for the average man, and the chief result of his edict (soon repealed) was to make later Christians realize that though they could dispense with the pagan religion they could not dispense with

---

[1] *Apologeticus*, 50.

pagan culture. His tolerance of Christian worship stands in contrast with the disestablishment of the pagan cults by the emperor Gratian, who unlike several of his Christian predecessors had already declined the office of Pontifex Maximus. In this matter the power behind the throne was doubtless St. Ambrose, who in all the struggles of this period was building the secure foundation of the claims of the Church to temporal power. The pagan literary circle of the aristocratic Quintus Aurelius Symmachus represented a cultivated, rather than an effective opposition. Christian emperors now fulminated against pagan cults, Theodosius even forbidding the worship of Lares and Penates and Genius; temples were converted into churches, bishops and popes were the real statesmen of the age.

Yet there were trying days for the faithful. The capture of Rome by the Visigoths (410) and by the Vandals (455) seemed to argue that, judged as a political instrument, Christianity could not save Rome as had the old state religion; the *Civitas Dei* of St. Augustine provided a consolation in the conception of a kingdom not of this world, and foreshadowed the later separation of church and state, even though his imagination was also kindled by the thought of the earthly Rome and its Christian emperors as a noble, even a holy institution. Theodoric's Ostrogothic Kingdom proved at times less civilized than his pretensions, and Belisarius, fighting in the name of the Eastern emperor Justinian, hardly succeeded in restoring the prestige of Rome in Italy. The times were waxing evil, and good men sought at least to save their own souls, and if possible the souls of others, by withdrawing to hermitages and monasteries. St. Jerome had already founded a monastery in Bethlehem; early in the sixth century St. Benedict wrought a vital work in establishing at Monte Cassino, on the lofty site of an ancient temple of Apollo, a monastery organized and stabilizcd by his "Rule," and animated by the ideal not only of a disciplined life of prayer and meditation but of useful tasks. The monastic orders of the Middle Ages all derive in some degree from the example set by St. Benedict, and from his contemporary Cassiodorus, at whose monastery in southern Italy literature both Christian and pagan was studied and copied. But it was not from monasteries that Rome could hope to find strength to cope with the confusion that arose with the Lombard invasion and attack on Rome, or with the despair that pestilence brought. It was rather the strength of will of St. Gregory, who, already trained in civil posts and in diplomacy and given to service as monk and abbot, moved his people to penitence; then made pope against his will, he carried on his varied labors, sending the monk Augustine as missionary of Romanism to the Angles, dispensing charity to the poor, reforming the liturgy, and by diplomacy and courage dealing with negligent emperor and brutal Lombard. Gregory the Great not only saved the dignity of Rome in his day but laid the foundations of the Holy Roman Empire of two hundred years later.

Christianity had triumphed over paganism. One can hardly refrain from asking why it had spread so rapidly, met with such obstacles, and at last won its victory; and it is hardly less interesting to ask whether it won its victory without itself suffering change. At first it had shared with the other oriental cults the advantages of rapid means of communication and stable forms of government which enabled it to travel quickly and to exist with some security. Like them it found men's minds longing for personal salvation, for an escape from a sinful, struggling world into a blessed immortality, seeing with the eye of faith rather than of unaided reason; like them it had a sacred story, sacred symbols, and rites or sacraments uniting worshipers with divinity. But unlike them it made exclusive claims which aroused the animosity of ordinary men and the united opposition of all the other mystery religions as well as the suspicions of the state; how easy might have been a partial victory for Christianity if the Christians had been willing to have their cult hero become, like that of many other oriental gods, a mere *numen Augusti*.[1] Since the easy way was disdained, Christianity must triumph, if at all, by the intrinsic superiority of its religious teaching and example. Here was its unique advantage. The state religion of Rome had been confined too much to the preservation of the state by covenants with the gods and the scrupulous performance of ritual; it had condoned cruelty and slavery; its conception of deity had seldom risen to the idea of the fatherhood of God; it had not thought of all men as brothers. The Greek philosophies which some Romans had embraced, even the refined Neo-Platonism of the third century A.D., had been too vague, and had lacked organization; even if they upheld an ethical ideal singularly like that of Christianity, it was a rational rule for the few, which hardly touched the lives of the many, and theory and practice were too often divorced. The cult of Mithras did touch the lives of the many, but its central figure lacks the appeal of an actual and historic person, an ever-living Savior whose message is to the weak and suffering as well as to the strong, and in whom is perfectly incarnate the goodness of God. Above all, Christianity called upon men not only, if need be, to die for their religion, but to live it, and to find as the universal solvent of life's problems the person of Christ,— not an easy task, and a task which required more of ordinary men than they could always achieve; but it was the secret of the triumph of Christianity.

[1] Cf. pp. 345–348.

Every victory affects the victor, sometimes as much as the vanquished. Rome had conquered Greece, but had herself been conquered by Greek culture. So Christianity, moving westward, gathered strength; but the more inclusive it became, the more it was gradually transformed. Appealing first to simple fishermen, it soon learned to speak to educated Greeks in their own tongue and in terms of their own philosophies. It addressed itself both to superstitious orientals, who looked above all for miracles, and to legally-minded Romans. It developed creeds and "apologies"; it elaborated an organization with "elders" (presbyters, or priests) and "overseers" (bishops), and in Rome a more developed system of priesthoods and of canon law, with the Bishop of Rome as Pontifex Maximus. More and more it adapted to its own purposes the ancient traditions and institutions of Roman paganism. It discovered in the Latin language such words as "sacrament," "saint," "piety," and "religion." In part this was a *damnosa hereditas*; more often it was a salvaging and revivifying of treasures that the world could not afford to lose.

The ritual of the early Christian Church was in part an inheritance from Judaism, transformed by specifically Christian ideas and symbols; naturally some of its rites approximated, consciously or unconsciously, the rites common to many of the oriental and Greek mystery religions, — purifications, sacred meals, and symbols of the passion and resurrection of a lord.[1] When it reached Italy, and especially after it triumphed, there passed into it something of the old pagan Roman religiousness, the sense of spiritual presences

---

[1] Cf. E. Hatch, *The Influence of Greek Ideas and Usages upon the Christian Church*, 8th ed. (1901); W. R. Halliday, *The Pagan Background of Christianity*, Lecture X, "The Similarity of Christian and Pagan Ritual"; Gordon J. Laing, *Survivals of Roman Religion* (1931); E. J. Strittmatter, "Classical Elements in the Roman Liturgy," *C. J.*, XVIII (January, 1923), 195–207.

in all the little things of life as well as in the great occasions, and the scrupulous performance of rites by priests set apart for their sacred office. Colors, numbers, emblems, vestments, relics, sacred spots, all formed powerful aids to the imagination, special channels through which divine grace was sought. Something of the private religion of the Roman family invested the Christian rites of baptism, confirmation, and marriage. Many of the old pagan festivals found their way, in new forms, into the "Christian Year," — the Saturnalia and the birthday or resurrection of the Sol Invictus, appropriately celebrated at the winter solstice as Christmas (previously celebrated at various times of the year); the Robigalia and the Ambarvalia as the Major and the Minor Litany; the Lupercalia as the Purification of Mary. The evil spirits of paganism, though relegated to Hell, still might tempt the faithful; but the devotion once given to good spirits and protectors, to Hercules and Castor and Pollux and others, was now transferred to saints, often at the same shrines. The Genius became a guardian angel. The craving for help once sought from the Great Mother and other goddesses now invoked the intercession of Mary the Mother. Hymns, long used both by Jews and by Greeks, were now written with a new beauty by men like Prudentius, who knew the lyric art of Horace, or who experimented with the new accentual and rhyming verse. The whole liturgy was reorganized by Gregory the Great, who enriched the music of the Church and standardized it. Early Christian painters transferred to the conception of the Good Shepherd the pagan types of Mercury and Orpheus, and used pagan emblems for Christian ideas without hesitation; Christian sculptors continued pagan traditions; Christian architects adapted to their needs the subterranean mystery chapels and the basilica form of law court.

The thinkers of the Church profited no less from their pagan forerunners. In the eastern part of the empire it was natural to use Platonic and Aristotelian philosophic conceptions, — substance and attribute, God and the World, the *Logos*, — in the formulation of theology and creeds; Christ was the Word, the incarnation of the divine *Logos*. In the West, if Tertullian would fain ignore pagan culture, a different spirit animated his successors; Virgil and Horace and even Terence were as familiar to Christian schoolboys as to pagans. But it was especially Cicero's ethical treatises, and only to a less extent the writings of Plato and Aristotle, that controlled the thought of Ambrose and Jerome, of Augustine and Boethius, each in his way a humanist, imbued with devotion both to the tradition of Roman culture and to Christian ideals. Each borrowed what he chose, using the materials now critically, now in the spirit of the casuist, for the building of a new edifice, the foundations of the mediaeval Church and of mediaeval thought.[1]

The Church was, for better and for worse, in the world; was it to be also of the world? At first it was a select company of devoted souls seeking to redeem an evil world; now that it was becoming all-inclusive and yet could not immediately reform the world, it must adopt some attitude toward the world. Several distinct attitudes indeed are to be noted. When Christianity was first freed from persecution and became powerful, and during a few later periods, it turned against its enemies and even against its own heretics the terrible instrument of persecution; furthermore, in different ages some Christians became thoroughly worldly, as critics so different as Jerome and Augustine and Savonarola and Martin Luther bitterly complained. Fortunately, intolerance and worldliness were on the whole the exceptions. An-

---

[1] Cf. E. K. Rand, *Founders of the Middle Ages* (Cambridge, Mass., 1928).

other attitude was expressed, especially in periods of political and economic disturbance, by those who withdrew from the world into monasteries,—churches, as it were, within the Church. In their works of mercy and in their scholarly labors they made the world their debtor by keeping alight the flame of religion and of culture in evil times, even if they also deprived their contemporaries of more active and secular labors. On the other hand, it was still other leaders, bishops and popes, who received from the dying Roman Empire the theory of empire and who amid the barbarian invasions built up strongholds of civilization. If the Empire, by preserving its fabric during the third and fourth centuries, staved off the barbarians and enabled Christianity to secure its foothold in Italy, it was now in turn the Church that preserved Roman civilization.

So Christianity gradually took possession of the mansion that had been prepared for it by Roman paganism and learned new ways. The Church of the Middle Ages and of modern times is not identical with the religion of the New Testament, nor could it well remain the same if it was to be a living thing in a changing world. It has shown at times the human failings of its human members. Sometimes it was only by a certain intolerance, a claim that it held a monopoly of the truth, that it could preserve itself; sometimes a group within the larger group has been equally intolerant. Too often, in the struggle for existence and power, it has mistaken the means for the end, unduly exalting mere conformity with its ecclesiastical authority or its temporal power; too often it has upheld its special channels of grace as of magical potency; too often it has upheld the letter at the expense of the spirit of religion. These failings, be it noted, are legacies not so much from essential Christianity as from the exclusiveness of Judaism, and still more from Roman paganism, — from the austere discipline of the Roman state, the superstitious attitude of Roman ritual, the legalism of the Roman tradition. Antidotes have been needed from time to time in the free play of a critical spirit, in attempts to seek anew the sources of Christianity and of all religion. The Roman tradition, pagan and Christian alike, is conservative; therein lies both its glory and its peculiar danger. For religion at its best is not passive conformity with an institution but an active and living experience, a spiritual adventure; it takes risks, or it withers and dies in its shell.

2. Vir Sapiens

That the Romans, a practical people, should have allowed in their religious life so large a measure of superstitition might appear curious if it were not also apparent that superstition and a flair for getting things done are by no means incompatible. The successful "practical" man needs only energy, discipline, a knack of using other people and their ideas, and a certain resourcefulness in making adjustments with his immediate human and material environment, — Roman (and American) qualities, which are enhanced rather than diminished by a naïf attitude toward the unknown. The real antithesis is not between superstition and practical "success" but between superstition and wisdom, or between an intuitive kind of goodness and an ethical system based on reason. The Romans were engineers, but not men of pure science; they were sometimes humanitarians, but generally for patriotic rather than for peculiarly religious motives. In fact their religion was useful chiefly as a social cohesive force, first for the young, struggling city-state, and later in a different manner for the varied peoples of the empire. If their conception of the structure of the universe was to be at all consistent and scientific, if their conception of duty was to be rational, philosophy must try to do what the old Roman religion failed to do; the *vir sapiens* must come to the rescue.

How little the old Roman religion could do in the period of the Punic Wars and afterwards either to enlighten or to edify the Romans, we have already observed. Indeed, we find certain Romans of the last two centuries of the Republic treating with open contempt the rites of the augur and the priest. Furthermore, since the state religion was the support of the state, it was itself supported by the state; but if a state consisting only of wise men could exist, remarked Polybius, such an institution would be unnecessary.[1] Scepticism of this sort perhaps did not do so much to undermine religious faith as did that of Ennius, who a few years later voiced not only the Epicurean doctrine that though the gods exist they do not care how the human race fares, but also the notion of Euhemerus that gods are only deified heroes; or of Plautus, who did not hesitate to represent Jupiter as a Don Juan. Moreover, patriotism declined as selfish individualism gained headway. By these negative, destructive attacks on the moral values of Roman religion the way was being prepared for whatever positive enlightenment Greek philosophy could offer.

The Romans were suspicious of philosophy and resisted its intrusion. In 181 B.C. writings purporting to be Numa's discussions of Pythagorean philsophy were unearthed on the Janiculum, and were burned in the Comitium by the Senate's order as forgeries subversive of religion. The far more subversive ideas of Ennius somehow escaped a similar fate; but in 173 B.C. two Epicureans, and in 161 philosophers in general, were expelled from Rome. In 155, however, there came to Rome on a political mission three philosophers from

[1] VI, 56.

Athens, Carneades of the (sceptical and eclectic) New Academy, Diogenes the Stoic, and Critolaus, a Peripatetic; they not only conducted their diplomatic business but discoursed to large audiences on philosophic themes. Carneades in particular made a good impression; but Cato advised that men who could apparently argue either side of a question equally well were dangerous, and should be sent away. In the circle of the younger Scipio Africanus, soon after the middle of the century, the Greek Stoic Panaetius was made welcome, and henceforth philosophers lived on intimate terms with the Roman aristocracy. Not infrequently a Roman set before himself as his ideal the *vir sapiens*, the sage and the rational man of affairs.

The desire to know, and the desire and will to act rationally, these were the two motives or ideals of philosophy in Rome; the one took the form of scientific speculation (hardly of experimental science), the other of the rational handling of ethics and law (hardly of metaphysics, except incidentally). Everywhere the Roman acknowledged his debt to the Greek, by translation, paraphrase, adaptation, or illustration; nevertheless, he made his philosophy his own in several significant ways, and wrought it into his law and later into Christian theology.

The early interest in Epicureanism at Rome rapidly waned; Ennius was almost alone among his contemporaries in embracing it. During the first century B.C. there was a revival of Epicureanism; Philodemus and others taught its doctrines in Rome and Naples; Julius Caesar and T. Pomponius Atticus, the friend of Cicero, had Epicurean leanings; even Virgil, in his youth, and the eclectic Horace, in his laxer moods, were attracted by different aspects of Epicureanism, Virgil by its philosophy of nature, Horace by its genial view of the principles of daily living. But the great Roman champion of the school was, of course, Lucretius, a poet second only to Virgil, a spirit deeply religious, and for that very reason committed to the task of exposing the religion of his day. Since the influence of his tremendous poem, the *De Rerum Natura*, after moulding to a considerable degree the thought and the verse of Virgil's earlier works, then faded away, we must try to understand the motives of his undertaking and the reason for his failure to affect his fellow Romans more profoundly.

Foremost in the mind of Lucretius is a contrast. On the one hand he sees men fettered by superstition, cowed by their fear of Tartarus, cringing before capricious gods, perpetrating cruelties and follies in the name of "religion"; on the other hand he looks back to Epicurus, the philosopher of the Garden, who, borrowing from Democritus, had explained the universe in terms of indestructible material atoms in constant motion, now forming temporary unions and now suffering dissolution. No gods are needed here, unless Nature herself, ruling by immutable law, be thought divine. Nothing is born of nothing; even what we call "soul" is only a temporary union of moving atoms, albeit of extraordinarily fine atoms, which therefore like all other unions is presently dissolved; there is no immortality, therefore death is but an endless sleep, and need not be feared. This doctrine, the other side of the contrast, is what seems to Lucretius a veritable gospel of salvation; to it his imagination kindles, for here is release from fear and all disturbing emotions in the rapt contemplation of Nature's infinite wonders and her majestic processes. Indeed, Lucretius appears almost to forget that no gods are needed; at the beginning of his poem he apostrophizes Venus, goddess of the fructifying forces of nature, as if she were a real being.[1] Or is she a mere

[1] Cf. p. 470.

convention, a concession to traditional religion and poetic tradition? Epicurus, to be sure, agnostic though he was, had seen no reason to quarrel with popular beliefs in the existence of gods, but had relegated them to a supercelestial region where, devoid of any responsibility, and indifferent to mankind, they lived a carefree, philosophic life. The gods of Lucretius, superfluous for his mechanistic system, require no worship and exact no special moral code; at most they serve as a poetic symbol of vital and destructive forces, opposite aspects of the identical process of growth and decay which Epicurus had described (comparable to the "Love" and "Strife" of Empedocles) or as additional, idealized objects of contemplation for mankind.[1] The real veneration of Lucretius, however, is reserved for that "god" or savior, Epicurus himself,[2] who "passed far beyond the flaming ramparts of the world and traversed in mind and spirit the immeasurable universe; whence he returns a conqueror to tell us what can, what cannot come into being; in short, on what principle each thing has its powers defined, its deep-set boundary mark. Therefore religion is put under foot and trampled upon in turn; us his victory brings level with heaven."[3] Of Epicurus, then, Lucretius is the fervent prophet, who finds in his master's teaching not merely pleasure but "medicine" and a way of life.

One who turns the pages of Lucretius to-day is moved first of all by a feeling of respect for his honesty and courage. Then one is apt to be struck by the eager curiosity of his observation and by the orderly exposition of the thought; now it marches with a military vigor and plainness of style, now it pauses for copious imaginative illustration, and at in-

---

[1] Cf. G. F. Else, "Lucretius and the Aesthetic Attitude," *H. S. C. P.*, XLI (1930), 149–182.
[2] V, 8.   [3] I, 72–79.

tervals breaks out in expressions of mystical wonder, or hails
with gratitude his deliverer from darkness, Epicurus. Book
One presents the doctrine of matter; the second book dis-
cusses motion; the third, the soul and its mortal nature; the
fourth deals with the theory of sense-perception and of
thought as derived from it; the fifth book is a cosmogony
and a history of civilization; the last book explains various
extraordinary natural phenomena on a purely physical basis.
The poet, like a hound on the scent,[1] presses on, now proud
to traverse the pathless haunts of the Muses,[2] now content
to follow the footsteps of his master,[3] and thus feels "a kind
of godlike delight mixed with shuddering awe" at the spectacle of nature thus revealed.[4] If his doctrine be a bitter
draught for others, at least it is to be drunk from the hon-
eyed goblet of his verse; [5] but he whose citadel has been
fortified by learning should feel a sense of relief in contem-
plating the plight of others from which he has escaped, as
from shipwreck or battle; scorn and pity are mingled in the
poet's satiric picture of benighted and erring mankind: "O
miseras hominum mentes, o pectora caeca!" [6]

To the thought of Epicurus his Roman disciple has not
added much save fertile illustration and a tone of perfervid
enthusiasm. But the vision of a unified cosmos penetrated
by inflexible law, in which inevitable cause leads to inevitable effect, might be expected to appeal to thoughtful Romans in whom the unity of their highly ramified legal
system seemed a necessary fact. Not that Lucretius dis-
penses with the freedom of the will; in fact he argues, like
Epicurus, that the atoms, besides streaming downwards in
parallel lines have a swerve or "declination" by reason of

---

[1] I, 404.   [2] I, 926.   [3] III, 5.
[4] III, 28.   [5] I, 936–950.
[6] II, 14 (cf. the whole passage, II, 1–61).

which they come into contact; they are in fact alive, like the
"substance" of the earliest Greek physicists. And if the
soul is material, its self-motion, of which we are conscious,
must be derived from a matter that has a life or will, since
"nothing comes from nothing." Man, then, is not a helpless
automaton. But it is when Lucretius attempts to show what
use is to be made of the freedom of the will that he begins to
forfeit the interest of his Roman readers. His gods need
nothing of man in the way of worship or prayer or even of
conduct; for a consistent materialism requires no ethical
system at all, since a mechanical "nature" knows no "better"
or "worse," and has no favorites, though man has his special
interests and standards, and must feel sad when cherished
persons or things are swept away. Man's conduct, then,
must be regulated on a purely human basis, and on a rather
individualistic basis at that. Although Epicurus, following
in his fastidious way the Cyrenaic doctrine of pleasure as the
end of life, has professed to make much of the refined pleasures of society, of friendship, of the tranquillity of an ascetic
life of contemplation, he is really timid and afraid to give his
heart away; detached observation is his best resource. Lucretius, too, determined to find in death no painful surrender of all that is precious, tends to think only as the solitary philosopher who is not deeply in love with life, and
whose interest in nature's vital processes is only that of the
spectator. Young Virgil may be entranced for a time by the
ideal; but it is all rather austere for the average Roman.
And though Lucretius is himself far from ignoble in his
standards of conduct, and hardly refers to the word pleasure, there are other Epicureans of a humbler sort for whom
their master's "science" has little meaning but who gladly
accept "pleasure" as their sole guide. A deceptive guide, it
proves, without the authority of the stern "Duty" whom

the Romans know so well; Cicero, in fact, asks: "If they are right who deny that the gods have any interest in human affairs, where is there room for *pietas*, for *sanctitas*, for *religio*?" [1] Indeed, the essential social virtues cannot be deduced exclusively from the pleasure of the individual.

If Lucretius is painting an ideal of a scientific, intellectual life that is above the reach of average Romans (and more's the pity); if the humbler, pleasure-loving Epicureans are apt to sink below the customary practice of average Romans, they agree in doing violence to the character of all Romans, which is active rather than theoretical. The Epicurean gods have abdicated; they neither love men nor use their power to save a chance-made world. So men, immersed in thought or in pleasure, are not nerved by Epicureanism for the struggle of life; they are not taught how to use their conscience or their precious freedom of the will. If this world is mostly evil and is hastening to its decay, as Lucretius implies, he has no counsel but acquiescence and the contemplation of the awesome majesties of nature, for he knows of no activity that can make this life better. But to ignore all appeal to the active will is to perpetrate a slander on human nature, which gives much when much is asked of it. Again, though death may be a blessed release, he has no hope of a better life hereafter; in death, he urges, one cannot indeed enjoy the sweetness of life and of loved ones, but neither will one be conscious of any loss. This consolation, if valid, sets a mean valuation on life, by preferring annihilation to it. But the real reason why men fear death is not that they suppose death to be intrinsically evil, but that they love and cling instinctively to life. Though the art of living is full of compromise and surrender, Lucretius surrenders altogether too much. To be *securus*, free from anxiety, to give no "hos-

[1] *De Natura Deorum*, I, 2.

tages to fortune," is after all a purely negative ideal. In his eagerness to get rid of capricious gods he has got rid also of responsible gods; now in his desire to rob death of its terrors, he both slanders life and rules out immortality of a different kind, perhaps even of a better kind, thus setting himself against the rising tide of Roman feeling.

Lucretius is nobler than his philosophy, and the modern world can sympathize with him better than could his fellow-Romans. We admire, more than they, his individualism and his defiance of popular beliefs; the spectacle of Lucretius *contra mundum* is inspiriting. Better than they we can feel respect for his scientific spirit, for his picture of a universe in which law is paramount, in which all forces are interdependent, in which time-space is infinite, in which growth and cause and effect are to be tracked relentlessly, without appeal to the supernatural or to metaphysical abstractions and final causes. The atomic theory, revived in the seventeenth century, is the basis of modern chemistry; if the qualitatively different units, combining according to specific affinities (the "*concilia*" of Lucretius), are being broken down in our time into smaller units, the principle is not different; and if the method of Lucretius is that of observation and speculation rather than of experiment, the very entities now supposed to underly the atom are mental constructions assumed to support observed phenomena. Lucretius anticipates many other modern principles: the indestructibility of matter, the conservation of energy, the nebular hypothesis, spontaneous generation, and (in part) the evolutionary hypothesis,[1] are to be recognized in his system.

On the other hand, the modern world will not feel bound

---

[1] Curiously enough, the evolutionary hypothesis of Lucretius supposes the fixity of biological species, so jealous is he of allowing nature any spontaneity that might upset his conclusions.

to accept all of the conclusions of Lucretius. Some of his lapses in matters of fact may be readily disregarded as unimportant or as unavoidable. More significant is the unwarranted dogmatism with which Lucretius proclaims that the universe is without conscious direction. He overworks the atomic system, as some exponents of evolution or of theology have overworked their favorite theories, seeking to explain what lies beyond their provinces. Science can describe phenomena, and to some extent it can trace causes and effects; but it has no answer to the ultimate question, the primary "Why" of all existence, still less as to the "Whither." These are questions of values, and hinge on conceptions of mind, of goodness, and of the will, and must be dealt with by another method. Even if mind and matter are to be reduced, as Lucretius would argue, to a single substance, it does not follow that this substance is what is commonly described as "matter" or that its organization is mortal; even the "matter" of Lucretius is alive, as we have seen, and the "matter" of modern science is rapidly becoming a complex of relationships in a vast rational system.[1] In a field so highly speculative, he must be a bold dogmatist who is willing to assert that purpose can be proved not to animate the universe, or to hold that human wills and goodness are conditioned only by forces that can be measured in the laboratory. Finally, the modern man may join the ancient Roman in feeling that the contemplative quietism of Lucretius is not the only inference to be drawn from his

---

[1] Cf. Sir James Jeans, in *The Mysterious Universe* (New York, 1931): "The universe begins to look more like a great thought than like a great machine. Mind no longer appears as an accidental intruder into the realm of matter. . . . The old dualism of mind and matter, which was mainly responsible for the supposed hostility [of the universe to life], seems likely to disappear . . . through substantial matter resolving itself into a creation and manifestation of mind."

premises. If the poet can so nobly tread under foot the fear of death, could he not also find active ways of meeting the demands of life, and extend his moral sympathies to other people, to the remote past and the distant future? Need the *sapientia* of Epicureanism descend to the level of its humbler and more gross representatives in order to find a zestful philosophy of daily living? Need contempt for ignorance and superstition breed despair and intolerance? An answer to these questions we shall perhaps find in the poems of Horace;[1] meanwhile we must return to consider how a rival school of philosophy ran its course among the Romans, and what it could offer them in the way of an explanation of the universe and of man's place in it.

Stoicism originated in the borderland between Greece and the Orient, and was ultimately derived both from Greek and from Oriental ideas. On the mind of its founder, Zeno of Citium (350–260 B.C.), the religion of ancient Persia, as interpreted by Zoroaster, made a deep impression: a single deity, identified with fire, warring with evil, and attended by, or manifesting himself through, ministering "angels" bearing such names as "the Best Reason" and "Immortality." We have seen that from this religion issued also Mithraism, which thus displays both in its origins and in its features its kinship with Stoicism.[2] But Stoicism explains away evil, or interprets it as a partial phase of the whole scheme of things. Like the Chaldaean astrologers, the Stoics believe in fate, written in the heavens; but they combine with this belief a faith in the wise guidance of the universe by the Deity, and in the freedom of the human will. It is barely possible historically that Buddhist influence also reached the Greek world in time to contribute to Stoicism

[1] Cf. pp. 439–451, 483–489.
[2] Cf. pp. 356–358.

the ideal of the voluntary subordination of the individual's will to the Supreme Being, and the sufficiency of virtue, devoid of external goods, for happiness; at least it presents analogies with Cynicism and Stoicism. From Heracleitus, Stoicism drew the monistic materialistic conceptions of the cosmos, consisting of ever-living fire, and of the universal *Logos*, the Word or Reason, which animates both the natural world and mankind. Here, then, are a number of fundamental ideas, often contrasted, which Stoicism was to attempt to relate to each other and to life, often without complete consistency or success: God and the created world, *Logos* and matter, soul and body, fate and free will, nature and human nature, death and immortality. Some of these are still the battleground of theology and metaphysics. But at any rate Zeno, after his years of schooling in the doctrines of the Cynics, of the Megarian dialecticians, and of Plato's followers in the Academy, taught in the Painted Porch at Athens what may be called the normal or essential doctrine of Stoicism, which his successors merely revised or illustrated or diluted. Normally Stoicism is monistic and materialistic; God and the *Logos* are identical, and are moreover identical with the Fire of which all things consist, though Stoics sometimes strayed into the dualistic separation of mind and matter which Platonism and the later Academy seemed to support. To rival schools of philosophy, Stoicism presents both resemblances and contrasts. With Cynicism it shares a moral earnestness; but it derives virtue from the universal reason rather than from the intuition of the individual. With Epicureanism it shares a materialistic physics and a conception of Nature as a closed system; but it differs from the Epicurean attempt to derive thought only from sense perception, and to derive virtue from pleasure. With the New Academy it shares an interest in the reason or mind, and (presently) in literary, grammatical, and logical studies; but for a considerable time it is more confident than the sceptical Academy of the possibility of attaining to certainty.

The followers of Zeno mould Stoicism in their several ways. Cleanthes makes the philosophy into a religion, in his noble Hymn to Zeus addressing the Creator as Law and Reason, and Father as well as Fate. The Hymn begins thus:

> Supreme of Gods, by title manifold
> Invoked, O thou who over all dost hold
>   Eternal dominance, Nature's author, Zeus,
> Guiding a universe by Law controlled;
>
> Hail! for 'tis meet that men should call on thee
> Whose seed we are; and ours the destiny
>   Alone of all that lives and moves on earth,
> A mirror of thy deity to be.[1]

The prolific Chrysippus standardized the tenets of Stoicism; nevertheless, in his time began the gradual compromise of the School with the sceptical views of the Academy. Thus in defining the supreme good as "a life according to Nature," he adds, "that is, both general Nature and our individual human nature, for our individual natures are parts of the Nature of the all." And Diogenes the Stoic tolerantly defined the good as "reasonableness in the choice of natural ends," giving free play to the individual. Casuistry thus became part of the Stoic's activity. Meanwhile, doubts were entertained as to whether the universe, being derived from fire, must periodically be consumed in a conflagration, as Heracleitus held.

---

[1] Tr. W. H. Porter (with an emendation by E. V. Arnold, in the latter's *Roman Stoicism*, p. 85). The sixth line contains a reminiscence of a phrase from the Stoic poet Aratus, which St. Paul quoted in Athens. See also the translation by James Adam, in *The Vitality of Platonism* (Cambridge, 1911), pp. 105 ff.

It was a modified form of Stoicism, therefore, that reached Rome in the person of Panaetius (*circ.* 189–109). More literary, interested in a wider range of philosophical subjects, and more eclectic in his doctrines than the grim Stoics of an earlier age, he also discarded such physical theories as the periodic conflagration, and such extreme ethical paradoxes as the Stoics had elaborated from the tenets of the Cynics. Indeed, without disparagement of his character it may be said that he stooped to conquer; he presented Stoicism as a gentleman's philosophy, not as the system of a fanatic, and science as a recreation rather than as a vocation. Virtue is knowledge; virtue is the sole good; the wise man never errs: these Cynic and Stoic paradoxes he accepts as the implications of a rational universe. But they are for him counsels of perfection: virtue may be enhanced by external goods, which are not to be despised on their own account; not every man can become the perfect *vir sapiens*, but all can make progress in wisdom and virtue by practising duties, "what come in one's way to do." [1] The virtues are not absolute, but as Aristotle has argued, means between extremes; for Panaetius the most important of the virtues appears to be temperance, or decorum. This is a suave, not a militant, form of Stoicism. In Posidonius,[2] on the other hand, Stoicism appears once more as a religion. He returns to the Heracleitean notion of the conflagration, but he asserts none the less the divine origin and the immortality of every soul, thus seeking to graft on the monism of Stoicism a Neo-Pythagorean dualism of soul and body which he doubtless derived from his studies in Plato; he revives also a belief in astrology and divination. This is a mystical, not a purely rational, form of Stoicism. Nevertheless, it was in such a

---

[1] τὰ καθήκοντα, translated by Cicero as *officia*.
[2] Of Apamea in Syria, and of Rhodes, born *circ.* 150.

direction that Roman thought and experience were moving in the last years of the Republic, when Nigidius Figulus, a Roman senator, was propagating Neo-Pythagoreanism and the mystery religions were attracting converts.

Cicero's ambition was to be the Roman Plato, as he was in fact the Roman Demosthenes. Yet his most useful achievement in philosophy was not the building of a new philosophic system, for he had little original thought, but the popularizing of Greek thought in readable forms, and above all in the creation of a Latin vocabulary for the discussion of abstract ideas. Not only have many of the ideas that he first expressed in Latin become the commonplaces of modern discussions of conduct, but we owe to him the very words and phrases on which many of our discussions turn. The sceptical views of the New Academy were congenial to him; but he did not hesitate to write expositions and criticisms of Stoical and Epicurean thought as well, or tacitly to use Stoic materials. He borrowed both from the ingratiating, utilitarian ethics of Panaetius and from the theological treatises of Posidonius, whom he had heard in his youth in Rhodes. Panaetius is paraphrased in the *De Officiis* (on the practical applications of ethics), Posidonius in the second book of the *De Natura Deorum* (on physics and theology); Stoic ethics fills the third book of the *De Finibus*; several other works mingle the logical, political, and moral philosophies of Platonism and Stoicism. In his later years, however, disappointed in his political ambitions, he showed a more mystical turn of mind. Indeed, as early as 54, he had placed at the end of his *Republic* an impressive vision, in partial imitation of the Myth of Er at the end of Plato's *Republic*. In this *Somnium* the Scipio Africanus who destroyed Carthage receives in a dream a revelation from the earlier Scipio Africanus, now enjoying a celestial immortality. From his vantage point in the Milky Way the elder Africanus discloses to his namesake the splendors of the universe, the nine spheres, the planets, the stars, and the music of the spheres, and unfolds Platonic arguments for a blessed immortality to be won by virtue. It is a noble passage which inevitably reminds the reader of the mystic revelation of the lower world made to Aeneas by his father. In his last years, crushed by domestic troubles, and especially by the death of his beloved daughter Tullia (in 45), Cicero wrote his major philosophical works, turning here and there to the consolations of Platonism. We have noted [1] how Tullia's *fanum* was designed to suggest apotheosis; the first book of Cicero's *Tusculan Disputations*, based largely on Posidonius and on the *Phaedo* of Plato, is devoted to demonstrating the immortality of the soul.

The Augustan age, if we may believe Horace, was full of Stoics, familiar with the paradoxes, old and new, and ready to lecture on them, or on the allegorical reconciliation of physics and mythology, or on grammar. During the early Empire, Stoicism had a political color; just as the praetors and jurisconsults of the Republic had interpreted the *ius gentium* as an expression of Nature or of the universal reason of the Stoics,[2] so Stoicism now became the philosophy of the opposition to upstart imperialism, the ideal republic being opposed to a *de facto* government. Or Stoicism could be used to justify withdrawal from an evil world and the private cultivation of the life of reason, or even to condone the evasion by suicide of incurable disease or of a hopeless political situation. Both of these uses of the system were employed in turn by Seneca, the ascetic millionaire who, after serving as tutor and as minister of Nero, withdrew from active life to

---

[1] P. 334.
[2] Cf. pp. 284 f.

study, and who finally committed suicide when suspected of
conspiring against the emperor. Seneca, like Cicero, had no
great originality; but he had considerable gifts as a philosophic essayist. With him, Stoicism was a religion; the divinity is no longer a fiery substance but a benevolent, personal god, like the creator in Plato's *Timaeus*. Indeed, the
ethical bearing of Seneca's thought is in substantial agreement with much of Plato; and though its rhetorical and
sometimes inconsistent expression does not always bear the
stamp of sincerity, it is not to be doubted that Seneca was
sincere in his attempt to use philosophy in the most practical
way for the "cure of souls" and the reform of a decadent
society. Among the aristocrats he played the rôle of "philosophic director"; [1] he showed them how by self-examina-
tion, renunciation, and skill in the art of living they might
approximate the Stoic ideal of the *vir sapiens*. Not that the
ideal can ever be fully realized; human beings are human,
and compromises with the environment must be made; reason must include casuistry. Yet life is also a struggle, and
progress in virtue is possible, till one becomes free from the
seductions of the world, living a life of inner serenity; thus
one becomes a citizen of two worlds, the city of one's birth,
for which one must not lose sympathy, and the divine city
of one's longings.

The message of Seneca was for the aristocrats of his own
circle; but the masses were also reached by philosophers with
a missionary zeal. There were teachers of tremendous moral
earnestness, like Musonius, itinerant preachers like Dio of
Prusa, the "golden mouthed," pagan friars who denounced
vice and luxury, evangelists who sought "conversions," and
lecturers who sought fine rhetorical effects, as well as many

---

[1] The phrase is borrowed from the title of an excellent chapter in S. Dill,
Roman Society from Nero to Marcus Aurelius.

impostors or *faux dévots*. Though there was nothing new in
the philosophic teaching of the slave Epictetus (*circ.* 50–
130 A.D.), his moral earnestness and his concrete applications
of Stoic and Cynic commonplaces to life have a lasting human interest. A similar interest attaches to the attitude of
the emperor Marcus Aurelius (121–180 A.D.), an amateur in
philosophy, and no consistent exponent of the details of
Stoicism, whose paradoxes and whose claims to certain
knowledge he discards. Of what, then, can he feel sure in
this perplexing world of struggles, on which death is closing
in? The empire and his personal duty to it and to the old religion he takes for granted. That there is a cosmos, that
"blind atoms" do not control all, is for him self-evident;
therefore he does well to believe in the rule of reason, to put
his trust in the gods. For the rest, the world is not a kindly
place; strength of character to resist evil, resignation of the
will to the universal reason, tranquil submission to death as
a natural event, *aequanimitas*, these are the counsels that
will win what contentment there is in life; but Marcus
Aurelius is confident of no personal immortality to be enjoyed when his time comes to be reabsorbed in the greater
whole. A melancholy philosophy, full of a pathetic dignity,
this is the last significant utterance of Stoicism, before the
waves of mysticism sweep over Rome. The next age will see
Stoicism lost in Neo-Platonism and Neo-Pythagoreanism,
and daemonology and magic will replace the Stoic rational-
ism or even its allegorical interpretation of mythology, until
Christianity in turn absorbs much of the Stoic and Platonic
method of dealing with theology and ethics.

No general account of the Stoic philosophy will quite fit
every one of those who at different times called themselves
Stoics; how varied they were may be judged even from the
preceding brief sketch of the Stoic movement, in which we

have not found space to deal with the Stoic studies of the theory of knowledge, of logic, and of grammar. The main trend of Stoicism, however, we may now sum up and examine, for it is close to the heart of the achievement of Rome. It begins with the physical universe, and asserts a stubborn monism. Its "body," the substratum of what we call both "mind" and "body," is not quite the same thing as the "matter" or the "atoms" of Epicureanism; it not only has life (like the Epicurean atoms) but it contains the seeds of life. Whereas Epicureanism underlies modern physics and chemistry, Stoicism may be said more nearly to harmonize with at least some phases of modern biology and the evolutionary hypothesis; whereas Epicureanism begins with atoms, and goes as far as it can by combining them, Stoicism begins with the whole, and subdivides and differentiates it as far as it can. This whole is guided by a simple first cause, the divine reason or *Logos*; nevertheless, intermediate, coöperating causes, subject to the first cause, are not ruled out, and the freedom of the will, itself a cause, is thus at least possible. The physical universe excites the mystical wonder and reverence of the Stoic; it is finite, symmetrical, rational, and divine, and (he believes instinctively) the earth is its centre; the fiery stars, too, are divine.

The universe *is*; may one say further that it is *good*? From its rational structure, and the design implied in it, the Stoic infers a Creator, — not merely an external Fate, but the immanent Reason (*Logos*) that creates the conditions within which other rational beings may also work out their destinies. Thus determinism for physics and freedom of the will for ethics are combined. And it is natural for the Stoic, as it is not for the Epicurean, to regard the Creator as a Providence, a living, active, benevolent, rational, immortal

hostile to what we suppose to be the moral interests of man, the temporary inhabitant of this inconsiderable speck of gradually cooling star dust. Moral values on this hypothesis are purely human, perhaps utilitarian; man must do the best that he can for himself in this unfriendly universe, but in the end he is doomed to failure. Shall we then suppose that God is quite separate from the physical universe and is merely a projection of our human moral ideals, our coadjutor in the struggle against Nature? It is comforting to think of God as on our side; but it would be hard to demonstrate that He actually does approve of all our conflicting ideals, or even of many particular ideals. Perhaps those who cling to a humanized God do so because they began with a Creator-God whom science has shown to be morally backward; they have therefore dethroned Him from His cosmic tyranny and transferred their devotion to a shadow of themselves. This is surely democratic; but the nemesis of democracy is the fall from popular favor of idols who have had their day. Man may find this shadowy God to be a superfluous luxury and decide to shift for himself.

Is it possible, then, to conceive of God as both the Creator of the natural universe and the Sustainer of a moral order within the physical order? Are mind and matter ultimately one, or at least so mysteriously interrelated that we can exile neither God nor men from either category? Such a solution, on the whole, has been attempted by most Stoics and, in various ways, by most Christians. Evil remains; but physical evil and moral evil present different faces. The good man who violates the laws of the physical order will suffer physical evil, — for example, disease. Morality, however, and happiness and unhappiness turn rather on the state of the will, which should be in harmony with the Divine Reason, or with God, a moral Being with moral purposes, who answers men's prayers for spiritual blessings, if not for material benefits. "Undeserved suffering," such as disease or the loss of a loved one, must be accepted as a physical evil produced by physical causes (bacteria, or the collision of vehicles). Yet it may serve the sufferer as a school of character in fortitude or sympathy, and thus create moral good; this rests with his will. Death, ordinarily a physical evil and usually the curtailment of moral activities, can be regarded as a moral gain only by one who regards this life as evil, or on the other hand by one who regards moral values as eternal and personal, and immortality therefore as at least a reasonable hope. These moral gains and losses can be measured less by logic than by the practical test of actual living. Biography is the complement of metaphysics and theology; thought proves its claims only as it is lived.

How well suited the Stoic philosophy was to interpret and to build up the Roman character we can now understand. From the days of the younger Scipio and his circle, it served to foster among Romans the ideal of *humanitas*, the life of reason and peace, inspired by patriotism and devoted to true culture. For the satirists it helped to paint the background of normal human nature against which they could hold up to ridicule the abnormalities of their ages; Lucilius and Persius and Juvenal weave patterns of character largely on the Stoic loom, and if the warp of Horace's web is Epicurean, the woof is Stoic. Not only did the Roman lawyers who developed varied customs into an equitable system for a cosmopolitan society think in terms of natural law, but thousands of obscure civil servants throughout the empire endeavored to give it effect. Men of affairs during the Republic as varied as the ingenious Mucius Scaevola and the unyielding Cato (the younger) and the high-minded Cicero derived their ideals of citizenship perhaps chiefly from Stoicism. During the Empire it was Stoicism that inspired certain opponents of the Caesars to become martyrs, and Marcus Aurelius himself to practise virtue "even in a palace." Finally, if the Aeneas of Virgil is only partially a Stoic *vir sapiens*, and if Virgil's own philosophy, so far as it is set forth in the sixth book of the *Aeneid*, is partly Stoic and rather more Platonic and mystical, Lucan's *Pharsalia* is thoroughly Stoic in its inspiration, and Cato is perhaps its hero.

Epicureanism, by asking little of life and by making little use of the will, robbed man of much of his dignity. Stoicism demanded more of life, required more of man, and achieved a healthy "tone" and an active mastery over circumstances. Doubtless men adopt special philosophical views partly because of temperamental propensities, and it was to be expected that active, intelligent Romans would adopt Stoicism more readily than Epicureanism, because it better supported and interpreted their personal and national activities. But what of ordinary men, ancient Romans or men of our time, to whom the voice of reason speaks only faintly, or to whom the abstract image of the *vir sapiens* appears even repellent? It must be admitted that to such men Stoicism makes little appeal and speaks with little authority. Moreover, we have seen that in Stoicism itself there is a strain of quietism; the will does not merely assert itself, but moulds itself to the divine will. And from this self-surrender to a spirit of resignation, even of pessimism, is no long step; we have seen it manifested in the case of Marcus Aurelius, who resolutely kept his colors flying in an evil world, and who in a cosmopolitan age was driven into the citadel of himself, finding an inner peace in his approving conscience. Yet even the *vir sapiens* knows that there are times when his philosophy is put sorely to the test, and his virtue, ordinarily self-sufficient, does not seem enough; what hope or consolation is left? Should the good soldier, fighting in a hopeless cause, desert the ranks by suicide?

From the slings and arrows of fortune there seem to be at least four well-marked avenues of escape. There is the humbler sort of Epicureanism in which the individual makes what he can of the moment, and enlarges his personality with social pleasures; "eat, drink, and be merry, for to-morrow we die," — and thus the inevitable shadow closes in on the brief moment. Or, again, there is the higher Epicureanism, a spirit of pure detachment and contemplation of Nature's processes; the individual minimizes his personality and his claims on life, and is the less a loser when death ends all. Once more, there is the Stoic's active sympathy and coöperation with Nature or the Divine Reason; he himself matters little, but the task is good and the chance to take part in it is the best that life holds; all the more tragic, then, is the frustration of goodness and the annihilation of the good man, if this life be all. Can he hope that the ideal, that his own self, will not be snuffed out in the passing of time? The mystery religions, Platonism, Cicero, perhaps Seneca, the semi-Platonic, semi-Christian Boethius, and Christianity itself unite in answering this question in the affirmative; what is good, and the personality of the individual, are not hostages to time, but defy death.

These other ways of dealing with life's ultimate problem gained headway, as we have seen, not only over the old Roman paganism but even over the phase of Stoicism that denied personal immortality. Perhaps it was chiefly for this reason that they outstripped it; they agreed with the Stoic will to live, but they carried it beyond the grave, and they had other appeals beside the unaided reason to support their faith, — ritual, poetic myth, and in the case of Christianity the example of a personal Founder who had "overcome the world," and who was still a living force. Thus the Christian could say with his Master, "I have meat to eat that ye know not of." [1] This reserve force, "grace" reaching down from heaven to lift up virtue, is what makes the difference between the resignation of the intellectual Stoic and the good cheer of the average Christian; it is fundamentally the distinction, as St. Paul sees it, between the "darkness" and "light." [2] Furthermore, whereas the Stoic gives his intellectual assent to the proposition that all men are brothers, the Christian, so far as he is a Christian, acts on the belief. Nevertheless, some of the best in Stoicism and in Platonism was absorbed in Christianity, and helped not a little to form the thought of St. Paul himself; [3] this was possible only because it had already explored with considerable success the conditions under which human character grows and finds itself.

In this chapter we have been threading some of the Alpine trails by which religious and philosophic Roman explorers sought to reach a promised land; now we may descend to the plains and follow some of the highways and byways, to learn what Roman chroniclers and poets can tell of life.

---

[1] *John*, iv, 32.

[2] Cf. II *Corinthians*, iv, 6.

[3] Cf. E. V. Arnold, *Roman Stoicism*, Ch. XVII, "The Stoic Strain in Christianity."

CHAPTER VII

THE MAGIC OF WORDS

Carmina vel caelo possunt deducere Lunam
Carminibus Circe socios mutavit Ulixi.
Virgil, Bucolics 9, 69–70.

1. THE ROMAN CHARACTER

Moribus antiquis res stat Romanan virisque.
Ennius, Annals 500 (Vahlen).

I F IT is the power of speech that constitutes man's greatest
advantage over the other animals, perhaps the greatest
difference between civilized and primitive peoples, or between extraordinary and ordinary men, is the degree to
which they can compel words to do their will. Speech is indeed magical in its power of transmitting thought and feeling;
even the words of prose are winged, and songs (*carmina*) are
charms. Not the slightest achievement of Rome is her trans-
mutation of will and action into words, and of words into
feeling and action. Though Roman literature is not the
most original of literatures, it has a unique interest as the
adequate expression of a powerful national spirit; increasing
familiarity with it results in an ever-growing admiration for
its strength, its resourcefulness, and frequently for the
charm with which many of its authors, employing either
prose or verse, have gained our ears.

In these few pages it would be idle to attempt even a
cursory survey of the whole vast field of Roman literature,
extending in the classical period alone over some six cen-

turies, and embracing every literary form. What is more to our purpose is to observe how the literature unfolded itself in successive periods, and how successfully it expressed the national character and aspirations, following its greater movements now in retrospect, now in partisan strife, and occasionally leading the way. Usually an aristocratic literature, as we shall see, and seldom giving voice to the common man, it nevertheless makes vocal the experience of a widening circle of citizens, Roman, Italian, and provincial. Now and then a clearer voice speaks of a rare personal experience, with which kindred spirits may feel sympathy; more often the appeal is to a universal human understanding not limited to any age or nationality.

The earliest native Latin literature is popular in form and origin, — songs of the priestly colleges, rude hymns and charms against illness, impromptu farces borrowed or imitated from the towns of Campania. Verse, as usual, precedes prose; and the songs are all anonymous. With the Punic Wars begins the deliberate borrowing and adaptation of Greek epic and drama. The Greek freedman Livius Andronicus in 240 B.C. translated the *Odyssey* into the accentual "Saturnian" verse that was indigenous in Italy. Naevius followed the annalistic method in his *Bellum Punicum*, and wrote drama also. Ennius (239–169 B.C.), deservedly called the "father" of Latin poetry, also put into verse in his *Annales* the real and the imagined history of Rome, and composed as well both tragedies and comedies adapted from the Greek, and *saturae*.[1] We know that tragedies and comedies on Italian themes (*togatae*) were written at this time, but none have survived; and of the earlier comedies adapted from the Greek (*palliatae*) only fragments remain. Plautus, however, a contemporary of Hannibal, has left us twenty of

[1] Cf. pp. 431 f.

his racy comedies; and the freedman Terence, the intimate
of the younger Scipio Africanus and his cultivated circle,
wrote comedy as remarkable for its fathoming of human
nature as for its humor. In the satiric medleys of his associate Lucilius is revealed the eye of a keen observer and a
vigorous personality. Prose meanwhile lagged behind, and
confined itself to law and chronicle and didactic treatise,
hardly blossoming into literary form, in oratory, earlier than
the generation just before Cicero's. With Cicero himself,
Latin prose, considered as style, reached its apogee, — tense,
copious, magnificently cadenced, responsive to every demand.
And in his matter Cicero well illustrates the many-sided
interest of the Roman humanist, pouring forth speech, philosophic essay, letter, and even verse with equal readiness.
Beside his works, how comparatively slight appear even the
shrewdly composed political pamphlets of Julius Caesar (his
narrative of campaigns), even granted that we know that he
composed also treatises on grammatical and literary subjects,
and was sufficiently busy in other ways! Their contemporaries in prose, the encyclopaedist Marcus Terentius Varro
and the historians Sallust and Nepos, are distinctly lesser
men, but illustrate excellently both the didactic bent of Roman literature and its fruitful preoccupation with national
events and with human nature. Poetry meanwhile achieved
a quality that must have mystified many Romans in the
strangely contrasted didactic epic of Lucretius and the sometimes intensely personal, sometimes perversely learned
poems of Catullus.

The Augustan Age succeeded the Republic, and was an
age of poetry; Virgil and Horace had made considerable
reputations before there was an Augustus, but their major
work was done in the new age, heralding it, guiding it, adorn-
ing it. Tibullus and Propertius, elegists wistful and passion-

ate, and Ovid, elegist and much more, the wizard of words who could control everything except the stern necessities of the times, — these names, a few among many, must suffice to suggest what a galaxy of poets gathered in the literary circles of the emperor and of his friends Maecenas and Messalla. One name will suffice for the prose of the age, that of Livy, who amid the glories of the new era preferred to "avert [his] gaze from the troubles which [his] age had seen so long," and to dwell in imagination among the faded memories of the past, commemorating the heroism, the simplicity, the independence of Republican Romans from the legendary days of the Kings down to his own time.

It is interesting to note how few among the leading writers of the later Republic and of the Empire were strictly Roman in origin; perhaps Lucretius and Caesar alone. Ennius was a Calabrian, Plautus an Umbrian; Terence came from Africa, Lucilius from the borderland of Latium and Campania; Cicero was born in Arpinum, in the territory of the once hostile Volscians; Catullus was a native of Verona, in Transpadane Gaul. Of the Augustan poets, Virgil also came from across the Po, from the neighborhood of Mantua; Horace was a south-Italian from Venusia, far down the Appian Way; Tibullus derived from the edge of the Sabine Hills, and Propertius from Assisi in Umbria, while Ovid's birthplace was chilly Sulmo, in the Apennines considerably to the east of Rome. Livy came to Rome from the north-Italian town of Padua, the local speech of which (*Patavinitas*, or "*patois*") he was accused by Asinius Pollio of having retained.[1] Nor would it be difficult to extend indefinitely the list of "Roman" writers of this period who had come to Rome from other parts of Italy.

---

[1] Quintilian, I, 5, 56. On the nature of this "Patavinity," see J. Whatmough in *H. S. C. P.*, Vol. XLIV (1933).

In the next age, the hundred years that followed the death of Augustus, an age which not unjustly has been termed "Silver" by contrast with the "Golden" century that embraced the best writers of the Republic and the Augustan writers, the eminent men of letters were as apt to be provincials as Italians. Tacitus, to be sure, came probably from Interamna, a little northeast of Rome, the two Plinys from Como in northern Italy, and Suetonius presumably from Italy; but the two Senecas, Martial, Quintilian, and Lucan were all Spaniards, like Prudentius of the fourth century. Moreover, the second century brought to Rome from Africa the rhetorician Fronto and the novelist Apuleius; and, not to prolong the list, the fourth century gave us the poet Claudian, of Alexandria, and Ausonius, of Gaul, the last of the Roman and the first of the French poets.

The Silver Age was primarily an age of prose and criticism. History, biography, didactic treatise, philosophic essay, and epistle flourished during periods when the turn of politics made political oratory superfluous if not unsafe, and expressed the Roman tendency to deal with solid masses of fact. After all, there was need enough to organize and popularize the vast amount of tradition and theory that Rome had accumulated; and the critical spirit of the historian and the satirist, in prose or in verse, needed to catch up with the tremendous activity of previous centuries. That was the task of Tacitus, a caged lion, whose smouldering genius dealt relentlessly with the transition from the moderate rule of Augustus to the tyranny of later emperors and the turbulence of civil war; of the doctrinaire young Persius, who contrasted Roman society with Stoic ideals; of the bitter Juvenal, whose satires are masterpieces of foreshortening. Their pictures of Roman society are supplemented by the extravagant, semi-realistic romance of Petronius; by the biographical sketches of the gossip Suetonius; by the self-conscious letters of the amiable though pedantic Pliny the younger; by the brilliant epigrams of the shameless *flaneur* Martial, to whom all life was but copy for a shiftless poet-in-need-of-a-dinner. The other poets of the age may be dismissed briefly as capable, though seldom inspired, imitators of previous epics, who found their themes either in Greek mythology or in Roman history: Lucan, who sought to revive a dead issue in glorifying the republican resistance to Caesar, in his "Pharsalia"; Statius, the author of frequently graceful occasional verse (the *Silvae*) and of an epic on the threadbare theme of the Seven against Thebes (the *Thebais*); and the lesser writers of traditional epic, Valerius Flaccus and Silius Italicus.

Even less can we linger with the writers of the centuries that followed the Silver Age, though they learned to command new prose rhythms and new richnesses of style, and though the later poets, such as Ausonius and the unknown writer of the lovely *Pervigilium Veneris*, lead us to the threshold of mediaeval and modern verse. But the romantic tale of Apuleius, the haunting refrain of the *Pervigilium*, and the rhyming, accentual Christian hymns, delightful in themselves, no longer express the essential Roman character. We must return, therefore, to consider with some care the place that literature held in Roman life and the peculiar qualities of the Roman character that it expressed.

Like Roman sculpture and architecture, Roman literature tended to serve a practical social purpose in the recording of great deeds and personalities. No less than *imagines* of ancestors and funeral inscriptions, triumphal arches and bas-reliefs, Roman literature was commemorative. And as the Romans and their descendants of modern Italy have always been gifted in making spectacular use of occasions and buildings, naturally resorting to insignia and display and festive demonstrations, so Roman literature naturally turned to the rhetorical; oratory, *eloquentia*, is perhaps the characteristic Roman literary form, to which history and even poetry approximate. In reading it one is conscious of being a member of an audience on whom the writer has designs, rather than of overhearing his secret thoughts. There is something similar in the Roman's view of conduct. "The Greek," it has been said, "was concerned with what he himself felt about his actions; the Roman was concerned with what they would look like to other people, and the credit or discredit that would be reflected back on himself."

The Roman was willing to subordinate, if need be, the pleasant to the useful, though he often learned with Horace to combine the two.[1] For the Roman was fond of orderly thought not on its own account but as a means to some practical end; therefore treatises and didactic works, even if in verse, appealed to him and needed little apology. When to this intellectual or at least practical bent is added a strong social or moral sense, flavored with the tart Roman scorn for idiosyncrasy, we have satire, another characteristic Roman vehicle for guiding action according to recognized standards. Few Roman writers, historical, philosophical, or even epic, are without at least some satiric leanings. Thus Latin literature is apt to express not so often merely individual taste as the institutional, traditional ideals of society; and the poets at an early time were organized as members of a *collegium*.[2] In form and content, much of the literature is traditional or imitative, as was natural in view of the conservative character of the Romans and of the preëminent quality of the Greek literature that they came to know. Some of these questions of literary form and individual temperament may

[1] Cf. p. 454. [2] Cf. p. 427.

well wait, however, till we have considered further the essential quality of the Roman character.

That the Romans were a strong people, a conquering people, is their first and most obvious quality. If they did not deliberately set out to conquer the world, they at least had unlimited powers of endurance and discipline to deal with the immediate situation. As Napoleon said of the English, "They do not know when they are beaten." [1] This determination to finish the matter in hand, to sacrifice oneself and even one's dearest for the common end, is stamped indelibly on Livy's pages, which go far to explain the greatness of Rome as the natural outcome of the Roman character. One recalls the two bearers of the name Decius Mus, father and son, who "devoted" themselves to death that Rome might live; one thinks of the first Brutus, who condemned to death his own sons for treason,[2] and of T. Manlius Torquatus, who gave his gallant son over to the executioner not for treachery but for excess of patriotism in slaying a Latin chief in single combat when such combats had been forbidden;[3] no wonder that the Romans of the day shuddered, or that Virgil called Torquatus "*saevus.*" This tradition of patriotism bore more pleasant fruit in the natural expectation of ordinary citizens that they would make whatever sacrifice might be demanded of them; thus the elderly centurion Spurius Ligustinus, after reciting in a simple but impressive manner his long and distinguished record of military service, makes it clear that he does not intend to claim exemption from further service if it be demanded of him.[4] The Roman idea of patriotism is well summed up in the words of Cicero, at the conclusion of a

---

[1] Cf. *Aen.* XI, 306–307, of Aeneas and his men: "quos nulla fatigant | proelia, nec victi possunt absistere ferro."

[2] Livy, II, 5.   [3] Livy, VIII, 7.

[4] Livy, XLII, 34.

passage in which he has discussed family and friendship as bonds of union. "But survey the whole range of philosophic thought," he says, "and you will find no tie which appeals so strongly to the conscience and to the heart as that which binds each one of us to the State. Parents, children, relations, friends, — all are beloved; but all loves of all men are embraced by our common fatherland. What good man and true hesitates to die for it, if his death will profit?" [1]

The word patriotism has been somewhat sullied by abuse; it may well be urged that exclusive nationalism appears less admirable to-day than formerly, less beautiful to aliens than to hard-pressed Romans. What if we had an account, let us say, of Caesar's campaigns written from the point of view of a patriotic Gaul? And indeed the historian Pompeius Trogus, who had Gallic blood, has put into the mouth of Mithradates a jibe at the Romans because of their veneration for "their founders, nurtured at the breast of a she-wolf; so has that whole people the spirit of wolves, insatiate of blood and rule, greedy and hungry for wealth." [2] Generosity and consideration for others are perhaps late arrivals among the virtues of the Romans. But in the matter of patriotism let us give them their due. Solidarity and loyalty are real virtues, in which the Romans surpassed the more fickle Greeks. Rome had a Coriolanus, but not quite an Alcibiades. Nor was it only the great men who were steady; the common folk were hardly inferior, if only they were treated fairly. Like their god Mars, they were farmers first, and warriors only by necessity; politicians they never were by choice.

In their daily affairs the Romans were a curious mixture of the shrewdly practical and the superstitious, as we have

---

[1] Cicero, De Off. I, 17. See further G. Showerman, "The Citizen-Soldier of Rome," in Eternal Rome.

[2] Pompeius Trogus, XXXVIII, 6.

already noted in their religion. The practical quality has its unattractive side. The elder Cato's canny system for the treatment of slaves and animals wins no friends to-day. Nor had he any room in his life for sentiment; he never embraced his wife, he said, unless it thundered loudly.[1] The ruggedness of the self-made Marius has perhaps a moral basis, narrow though it be; he has never studied Greek literature, for it has been of no use to its teachers in promoting virtue.[2] Ovid's father was impatient of his son's verse-writing, but for another reason: Homer himself left no property.[3] Even Cicero and Horace, knowing their public, emphasize the practical value of having virtue immortalized by verse. Some people will go so far as to say that the Romans were an essentially unattractive people. They will contrast the stodgy figures and the coarse features of many Roman portrait statues with the grace and refinement of most Greek sculpture. The comparison, to be sure, is partly between two artistic ideals, and not merely between the physical or moral qualities of two peoples. But one may find symptoms of a certain Roman ruthlessness in the preference of most Romans for gladiatorial combats and other sensational entertainments to drama and intellectual pursuits, with the callous cruelty that this preference implies. This is a more serious indictment; even though gladiatorial games may have come to Rome from Etruria, by way of Samnium, as funeral rites, they found a firm lodging in Roman life, and help to account for the Latin fondness for bullfights in modern times.

---

[1] Plutarch, *Cato*, 17.
[2] Sallust, *Jug.* LXXXV, 32. The whole speech is worth reading as a sample of the Roman character at its simplest; translated in J. W. Duff, *Literary History of Rome*, p. 419. Something perhaps may be explained in Cato's case by the fact that he had red hair. See further Plutarch, *Cato*, 4–9; and Livy, XXXIX, 40.   [3] Ovid, *Tristia* IV, 10, 21–22.

More attractive is the Roman fondness for other public entertainments and holidays, such as the Saturnalia, frequently religious in origin and name, but celebrated both in ancient and in modern times in a cheerful and social spirit; it is the natural counterpart or reaction to a life of toil, and governments both ancient and modern have therefore sought to foster it. To offset the cruelty of the amphitheatre, we may recall the fondness of the Romans for dogs and birds and other household pets. Then, too, the home life of the Romans and their love of home [1] was far superior to that of the Greeks, if we except the pictures given in Homer and a few other cases. The treatment of children and the position of women was much nearer to the modern ideal. It is hard to think of Greek women of the classical period who deserve to be set beside Cornelia or Arria, or to remember any Greek father whose interest in his son's education is as admirable as that of old Cato, as it is recorded by Plutarch.[2] Serious the average Roman was, even if fond of sociability and festivity; and Romans in public life seem often weighed down by responsibility. One cannot imagine a Roman soldier indulging in superfluous gestures, riding into battle like the Norman Taillefer at Hastings, tossing his sword and catching it, and singing as he went; or like Achilles singing in his tent, or shouting at the trench. Off duty, however, the Roman of the later Republic learned how to doff formality. Cicero, we learn from his letters, used to kill time by visiting the shore and counting waves, if bad weather prevented him from catching lizards.[3]

For the Romans, despite their doggedness, were learners in matters both serious and trivial. They were trained in a school of experience in war and practical undertakings and

[1] Cf. pp. 144–147.   [2] Plutarch, *Cato Maior*, 20.
[3] Cicero, *Epist. Att.* II, 6.

increasing political responsibilities. Their characters, thus forged by hardship, were in some ways tempered, in some ways softened, by contact with the culture of other peoples. Etruscan grimness and Etruscan dexterity in shaping metal and stone entered Rome at an early time; somewhat later the Romans who penetrated Campania found a Greek and an Oscan art of a luxuriance and an aristocratic quality that beggared their own rude attempts, and that set an example of lightness of touch in painting and in dramatic mimicry. Still later it was the steady flow of Greek influence that moulded and refined the thought and the manners of the Roman aristocracy, and that surrounded the populace with buildings and sculpture of a new dignity and charm, and gave them at least an opportunity of sharing with the Greeks the imaginary world of the tragic and the comic stage. Until the days of Pompey, to be sure, there was a conservative opposition to the building of a permanent theatre in Rome, lest Rome become a Greek city; an opposition unnecessarily prolonged, we may now feel, for tragedy was never really popular at Rome, as in Athens, and even the Latinized comedy of the Greeks lost favor as the cruder appeal of the amphitheatre gained ascendancy.

For such Romans as the members of the Scipionic circle, in the age of the Punic Wars, and for most writers till the end of the Republic, as for Roman-statesmen and jurists generally, the Greek influence, and especially the influence of Stoicism, could not but be beneficial. For another sort of Roman there was an element of danger in Greek literature. The cynical travesties on mythology and the contempt for conventional morality implicit in many of the plays of Plautus fitted the war-weary mood of the Romans just after the Hannibalic War; but the results were lasting. Moreover, the cynical attitude toward politics exhibited by many Roman aristocrats during the last fifty years of the Republic was assisted by the diffusion of Epicurean doctrine; the state now mattered less than the individual. It was chiefly the Hellenistic Age, rather than the great age of Greek activity and thought, that was at work in the mind of Rome, till the closing years of the Republic and the Augustan Age; only then, in the thought of Cicero and Virgil and Horace and some of their contemporaries, did the last protest of the Republic and the rising spirit of the new age find congenial nourishment in the best age of Greek literature.

Another test of the ability of Rome to profit, rather than to lose, by contact with other peoples came when her conquests abroad brought wealth and freedom from taxation. She literally plundered the opulent East, and lived on the spoil; from this time the words "luxury" and "extortion" were added to her vocabulary. It was Scipio Nasica who declared solemnly, after the fall of Carthage and Corinth, "Now is our position really dangerous, since we have left for ourselves none to make us either afraid or ashamed." [1] What indeed was to become of a nation whose chief rivals were crushed? Would the self-discipline and simplicity of life bred by danger continue to live after the danger was removed? The next century gave the answer; the wealth that reached Rome brought splendor, but it also brought a softening of character; and it was as unevenly distributed as in the old empires of the East. Rome never succeeded in Romanizing the eastern half of her empire as thoroughly as the western half, and adopted for herself more and more the oriental system of capitalism and autocracy, with the sharp contrast of rich and poor, of ruler and subject. Culture itself was more and more in danger of becoming a veneer, a cosmo-

---

[1] Plutarch, *De Capienda ex Inimicis Utilitate*, 88; cf. Plutarch, *Cato Maior*, 26–27.

politan commodity to be imported and diffused, rather than a natural expression of the native life. The economic historian of Italy will point out that during the last hundred years of the Republic the culture of the vine, which was not indigenous and which implies a capitalistic system, more and more tended to supplant cereal crops. Horace, for all his praise of the blessings of the vine, constantly harps on the encroachments of rich landlords' estates, both vineyards and parks, on the dwindling acres of the poor and even on the sea; [1] and Livy is as insistent that the simplicity of an earlier day has been spoiled by the *luxuria*, the *corruptio*, made possible by wealth. One may admit that standards of living and the term "luxury" are relative, and that much of what conservative Romans of Livy's day would call "luxurious" appear to our age only decent comfort, not to be resisted because of an undiscriminating wistfulness for "the good old days"; one may agree, on the other hand, that progress is in the end to be measured more by moral and intellectual standards than by material things. The fact remains that the contact of Rome with the East bred wealth and the self-seeking ambition of individualists at the expense of the traditional Roman character, and that from the opposition between the new spirit and the old tradition grew many of the dramatic conflicts of the last days of the dying Republic and the first century of the Empire.[2]

Apart from the inevitable moulding of the Roman character by foreign influences, the Romans themselves made a

---

[1] *Odes* II, 15 and 18.

[2] G. Ferrero, in his *Greatness and Decline of Rome*, and in his *Characters and Events of Roman History*, doubtless exploits too far the antithesis of oriental and occidental ideals; yet there remains much that is sound in his explanation of the conflict between Octavian and Antony and Cleopatra, between Tiberius and Julia, and between Agrippina and Nero. See also the same author's "Puritanism," *Atlantic Monthly* (July, 1910).

conscious effort to modify or to guide their national traditions. We have seen that by the invention of legends and genealogies they contrived to give continuity to their past, and to connect it with Trojan legend. Farther than that, they undertook to emphasize and perpetuate the old-fashioned type of character that they admired. The functions of the censors, though at first concerned with the economic classification of the citizens, came to take into account also their moral qualifications at least by the negative expedient of degrading unworthy citizens, so that the word "censure" conveys to us chiefly the idea of moral disapproval. But there is abundant evidence in Roman literature of a positive interest, if not in the theory of character, at any rate in the procession of heroes that marched through the national history. The Romans liked to describe characters, and not always soldiers at that. Here is part of the picture given by the poet Ennius, generally supposed to be a portrait of himself, but modestly used of another: "... a learned, trustworthy, pleasant man, content with his own, serene, tactful, speaking men fair in season, courteous, sparing of words; the keeper of much antique buried lore; one whom lapse of time made master of customs old and new, of laws of many ancient gods and men; a man whose wisdom told him when to speak and when to hold his peace." [1] There may be here a bit of self-idealization. There is no doubt that Cicero idealizes the uncouth reactionary, the elder Cato, in the dialogue named for him (*Cato Maior*, or *De Senectute*), in painting him as a delightfully garrulous old gentleman who has learned Greek to good advantage. For Cicero is himself helping to create the ideal of the gentleman;

---

[1] Ennius, *Annales*, 234 ff. (Vahlen), quoted by A. Gellius, XII, 4; *Oxford Book of Latin Verse*, No. 17; translated in J. W. Duff, *Literary History of Rome*, p. 140.

and nothing in Cicero's thought is more typical of the soundness of his humanism than his insistence that the orator must not be merely a clever manipulator of words, but must be a well-rounded man of stable character.[1] Even if Cicero's political views may have been short-sighted, his emphasis on character as the foundation of the state is sound, and is in the Roman as well as in the Platonic tradition.[2]

As a people, the Romans were given to hero worship; and their national history provided them with many types for emulation. Thus the Decii were a byword for fortitude, Cato Uticensis for constancy and *duritia*.[3] Though public education under state control was curiously lacking during the Republic and the early Empire, it is evident that the young were imbued by their masters with admiration for these exemplars of the Roman tradition, and precept was fortified by concrete model. Seneca expresses the principle when he writes to his friend Lucilius, "Hear and take to heart this useful and wholesome motto: 'Cherish some man of high character, and keep him ever before your eyes, living as if he were watching you, and ordering all your actions as if he beheld them,'" — and he gives as examples the severe Cato and the gentler Laelius.[4] If we remember this tradition, we find in the central part of the great speech of Anchises to Aeneas in the Lower World much more than a prophecy of Roman greatness; it does indeed pass in review a pageant of Roman heroes, but they serve to inculcate the ideal of patriotism in war and in peace, and the episode ends

---

[1] See Cicero, *De Oratore, passim,* and the younger Cato's definition of the orator: "Vir bonus dicendi peritus," cited by Quintilian, XII, 1, 1.

[2] Cicero, *Dc Rep.* V, 1–2.

[3] See H. W. Litchfield, "National *Exempla Virtutis* in Roman Literature," *H. S. C. P.,* XXV (1914).

[4] Seneca, *Epist.* XI, 8–10, tr. R. M. Gummere; cf. XXV, 5–6.

with the famous characterization of the Roman's mission,
the firm establishment of law and the "habit of peace." [1]
Horace, too, as the Ship of State passed from the dangers of
civil war into the haven of the Pax Augusta, sought in the
clarion note of his six patriotic odes, the opening odes of the
third book, to recall the rising generation to a new sense of
the national tradition, and to warn them against an undue
sense of security. If they were content to allow the disgrace
of the defeat of Crassus by the Parthians to go unavenged,
let them remember the example of Regulus, who, according
to the legend, returned calmly to be tortured by the Carthaginians rather than counsel the Romans to accept disgraceful terms.[2]

On a less lofty plane, too, Roman literature sought to
guide the development of the national character. Roman
comedy was intended first of all, of course, to amuse an
audience. Yet it learned, as we shall see, to hit off the foibles
of people, real or typical, and to supply a standard of conduct which, if not noble, would at least escape ridicule.
Needless to say, it is not a picture of actual Roman society.
Satire much more obviously contrasted life as it was with life
as it might be. And the greater historians are at pains to
point out the difference between the great days of old (which
they saw through rose-colored spectacles) and the more de-
generate days nearer to their own times. Livy's *Preface*, indeed, is largely devoted to this contrast.

Here are the questions to which I would have every reader give
his close attention — what life and morals were like; through
what men and by what policies, in peace and war, empire was
established and enlarged; then let him note how, with the gradual

---

[1] *Aen.* VI, 851–854.
[2] *Odes* III, 5. See further p. 485; and R. S. Conway, "Horace as Poet
Laureate," in *New Studies of a Great Inheritance.*

relaxation of discipline, morals first gave way, as it were, then sank lower and lower, and finally began the downward plunge which brought us to the present time, when we can endure neither our vices nor their cure. What chiefly makes the study of history wholesome and profitable is this, that you behold the lessons of every kind of experience set forth as on a conspicuous monument; from these you may choose for yourself and for your state what to imitate, from these mark for avoidance what is shameful in the conception and shameful in the result.[1]

If Livy is thus animated by a moral interpretation of history, Tacitus is even more vehement in his denunciation of the growing tendency toward absolutism in government. Even the reign of Augustus seems to him to mark a decline, and he closes his brief summary of it with the exclamation, "How few were left who had seen the Republic! Thus the state had been revolutionized, and there was nothing left of the old sound morality. Stript of equality, all looked up to the commands of a sovereign."[2] Bitterly resenting the tyranny of Nero and Domitian, which have stifled the best Romans for more than a generation, he holds that "the chief office of history is to make sure that virtue shall not be ignored, and that the fear of posterity and disgrace shall attend evil words and deeds."[3] He employs the weapons of the satirist, as well as of the historian, to analyze the motives of the men and women who have played their parts in this vast tragedy. We have learned how to discount part of his biassed narrative, and to supplement it by the evidence of inscriptions and other archaeological material, especially from the provinces; but it remains a masterpiece of literature, not to be classified in any single category, whether of

[1] Livy, *Praef.*, 9–10, tr. B. O. Foster.
[2] *Ann.* I, 3–4.
[3] "Praecipuum munus annalium reor, ne virtutes sileantur, utque pravis dictis factisque ex posteritate et infamia metus sit." (*Annals* III, 65, 1. Cf. *Agricola*, 1.)

history, of satire, or of drama. Like the satires of Persius
and of Juvenal, it must be read not as a sober scientific account of deplorable social and political conditions, but
rather as an indication of a powerful and stubborn movement that measured Roman achievement against a visionary standard.

Thus Roman literature emphasized the character on
which the Roman greatness rested, and invested it now and
then with a visionary gleam; from the welter of primitive
warfare and party politics emerged the typical Roman
gentleman, in whom the features of real Romans were fused
under the influence of a philosophical ideal. Into the Aeneas
of Virgil has entered not only the saga hero, and something
of Augustus himself, but the education of a Stoic *vir sapiens*.
At times he seems to carry too great a burden to convince us
of his actuality; such *pietas*, we exclaim, is not of this world.
And indeed Aeneas is sprung of divine ancestry, and is kept
by the poet in the mythical past. The Cato of Lucan's poem
is supposed to be an historical character, but is even more
overlaid with philosophic conceptions; he is a type, always
"in his humour," like one of Aristotle's or Ben Jonson's
ethical marionettes, to the detriment alike of artistic considerations and of verisimilitude.[1]

In fact it is perhaps just here that one may put one's
finger on a weakness in the Roman tradition: national greatness was bought at the expense of submerging salient personalities. The Roman gentleman at his best had perhaps
birth and breeding, certainly a sufficient intellectual training
and experience to grapple with affairs, and a dogged devotion to duty. What he often lacked was originality. If he
did act independently, like Julius Caesar, he was subject to
suspicion, and might have to pay the penalty. In Greece the

[1] Cf. E. E. Sikes, *Roman Poetry*, pp. 185-209.

tendency was otherwise. "In the history of Rome the man is often sunk in the Roman; his features are in low relief; we are led to forget the individual in the type. In Greece great personalities with an ineffaceable stamp of their own are far more numerous — men not only great in the things which they accomplished, but interesting in themselves, in endowments of mind and force of character, in the union of many outwardly discordant gifts — idiosyncrasies, it may be, but the idiosyncrasies of genius." [1] The Greek valued leisure and personal freedom perhaps more than did the Roman; the state with him was precious, but was nevertheless a means to an end, which was the life of the freeman. The Roman claimed that the ideal of the individual could be realized through the state, and did in fact find more place for the family and for country life than did the Greek in Greek states whether actual or ideal. Attempts to enforce uniformity in Greece were apt to result in civil war and failure. It was partly for this reason that Plato would fain curb the self-seeking man bred by a democratic society, and mould the citizens of his ideal state to the norms required by the needs of an aristocratic polity; this, he held, was for the common good.

Roman education, even if largely not state-controlled, also tended to produce a standardized type of aristocratic Roman; in this respect it may be compared with the English "public school" system. The type is on the whole a fine one, reliable, patriotic, a little narrow and class-conscious, a little lacking in imagination, but sportsmanly to the last degree. It is a type needed especially under the conditions of war and of pioneer work among backward peoples. It may prove now and then to flower in scientific achievement; less often in artistic expression, or even in the sympathetic or

---

[1] S. H. Butcher, *Harvard Lectures on Greek Subjects*, p. 156.

imaginative treatment of new political problems.[1] It is interesting to note that Quintilian, however, in the first book of his treatise on the training of the orator suggests that the object of education is not to introduce external matter into the pupil, but to foster his mental growth and ambition, and should therefore be adapted to the individual. He nevertheless believes that pupils gain more by being members of a class than by learning only from a tutor. Education in Quintilian's day, as in Cicero's, is still ostensibly devoted to the utilitarian end of producing orators; but in both cases the ideal is really higher and aims at nothing less than the formation of minds imbued not merely with the national *mores* and with technical skill in oratory but also with a broader humanism.

Such a humanism was doubtless beyond the reach of most Romans; and, though we are slow to admit the fact, it is not possible to instill it by means however mechanically perfect in persons of mediocre intelligence. Hard is the path of wisdom, as of virtue. Universal education is a noble ideal; but education must be a diversified and a selective process, and in the end there must be something of the aristocratic, in the true sense of the word, in its goal. Roman education and Roman literature remained for the most part aristocratic, though in the more usual sense.

The decline of acted drama at Rome and the increase of interest in the exhibitions of the amphitheatre is the most obvious symptom of the paradoxical fact that Roman literature, though intensely national, is not often the expression of the common people's life. It was written largely by and for aristocrats. If we wish light on the life of the common people, we must go to the scraps of folk poetry that have survived, to inscriptions and to scribbled *graffiti*, for example

[1] Cf. W. E. Heitland, *The Roman Republic*, I, 184 f.

at Pompeii; we must read between the lines of comedy, always remembering that its social background is chiefly Greek; and we must glean cautiously from history and from satire. In general, however, life is depicted chiefly from the aristocratic point of view. Plautus appealed to the bourgeoisie, and was played often before the populace whose votes candidates for political office wished to gain. But Terence, though formerly a slave, was absorbed in the circle of Scipio, who was even supposed to have collaborated with him in producing his refined comedies; and Terence complains in a prologue that the people would rather see rope-dancers or gladiators than his plays. In fact, his plays were over the heads of most of them, and we cannot but draw a contrast between the Roman public and the intelligent audience of the Athenian democracy which appreciated Sophocles and relished Aristophanes. Tragedy was even less within the comprehension of the Roman populace, and remained the perquisite of the educated aristocracy; it was chiefly a rehandling of Greek myths, and though it survived till the end of the Republic it finally left the stage for the library of the studious. Although Roman themes found their way into satire, they seldom appeared on the stage. No complete example of the *togata* comedy has survived, and but a single example of the *praetexta* tragedy, — the *Octavia* attributed to Seneca. Even history and the epic are tinged with the aristocratic coloring. Ennius glorifies the nobles as the bulwark of Romans against Carthaginians, and gives no hint of the "unknown soldier"; Livy, drawing partly on ancient chroniclers, possibly on ancient bards, who sang the prowess of certain great Roman families, likewise foreshortened the picture. On the other hand we must not overlook Naevius, who jeered at the noble Metelli, and Cato, who in his *Origines* deliberately omitted the names of the generals in the Hannibalic War, though he named the gallant elephant Surus.[1]

The literature of the late Republic, oratory and history excepted, was not directed toward the common man. Lucretius, of course, and Catullus, save in a few of his lyrics, and much of Cicero, could be fully appreciated only by those who knew Greek. Still more in the Augustan Age literature was formed by the tastes and interests of cultivated literary circles, the associates of Maecenas and Messalla and the emperor himself. Virgil's themes were of concern to all Romans, — country life, and the national destiny, and the heart of man, — and like the greatest literature in all tongues his poems had a certain appeal to the unlettered and the learned alike; but he was seeking in particular the ear of those cultivated Romans who could understand the inner burden of his verse. The *Georgics* was not merely a handbook of husbandry, nor the *Aeneid* merely a tale. Satire, too, diverged more and more from its dramatic beginnings, and became a vehicle for philosophic doctrine. Even the *Satyricon* of Petronius, the single semi-realistic romance of the early Empire that has survived, though it deals with *nouveaux riches* freedmen and with low life, deals with them from the point of view of a sophisticated aristocrat. Finally, the Latin that we read is mostly a literary Latin somewhat removed from the daily speech of even the educated, and of course still more remote from the speech of the lower classes and of rustics.

If Roman literature appears not often to be the expression of the life of the ordinary people, it would not be fair to conclude that it was a sealed book to them. On the contrary, there is good evidence that during the Empire there was considerable familiarity with the more important writers of

[1] Pliny, *Nat. Hist.* VIII, 5.

Rome and even of Greece. Schools and public libraries
diffused this knowledge, and Pompeian wall paintings attest
a wide acquaintance with mythology. Virgil was so well
known that his verses were scribbled on Pompeian walls by
schoolboys and gladiators, illustrated by paintings on walls,
and even parodied by members of the guild of fullers.[1] Thus
did Roman literature at least make its way into the lives of
the people.

2. SATIRE: INDIGNATION AND QUIET SMILE

> Facit indignatio versum.
>> Juvenal, I, 79.

>> Ridentem dicere verum
> Quid vetat?
>> Horace, *Sat.* I, 1, 24–25.

> Laetus in praesens animus quod ultra est
> Oderit curare et amara lento
> Temperet risu: nihil est ab omni
> Parte beatum.
>> Horace, *Odes* II, 16, 25–28.

Matter first, and the manner of expression afterwards;
this certainly would be the order in which a Roman would
have considered any question of literary composition. The
Roman character, then, which is the heart of Roman literature, has been our first concern; and a recent volume presenting in English translation a number of extracts from the
literature is not without good reason entitled "*The Mind of
Rome*,"[2] for there is in at least the greater part of the literature an intellectual, or at least practical, quality, which ap-

---

[1] "Fullones ululamque" [the fullers and their sacred screech-owl] "cano,
non Arma virumque"; M. della Corte, *The New Excavations* (Pompeii, 1925),
pp. 30–33. See further F. F. Abbott, "Literature and the Common People
of Rome," in *Society and Politics in Ancient Rome* (New York, 1911).

[2] Edited by C. Bailey, Oxford, 1926.

peals more obviously to the reason than to the aesthetic sense. In fact the older Romans were apt to brush aside too easily all questions of literary form. "Rem tene, verba sequentur," old Cato remarked: "Get a firm grip on your subject matter, and the words will come of their own accord." Wholesome doctrine though this may be for some young writers who are too exclusively preoccupied with the graces of style, it is not a complete philosophy for the writer. The words will come, indeed; but what words? Will they adequately express the matter? Will they convey anything of the writer's personal quality? Will they have the potency of magic?

The writers of Rome had certain assets that made for a literature of force. The Latin vocabulary abounds in words that present definite concrete images; even the more abstract thought of law and of philosophy never travels very far from these tangible foundations, with results beneficial in lucidity.[1] All poetry, of course, deals largely in metaphor; Latin poetic diction tends in particular to employ images drawn from farming and war and business and law, the characteristic Roman occupations.

The Latin genius, moreover, is strong, if not in metaphysics, at least in the phrasing of terse and memorable remarks about human nature. The vigorous saws of the older generation (*sententiae*, or *veterum praecepta*) became proverbial, and were inevitably quoted not only in popular speech but by later writers. Their sententious gravity, their compact and often lapidary brevity, sometimes barbed with epigrammatic sting, proved again and again that Latin is the predestined tongue for motto and familiar wisdom. A glance

---

[1] Cf. O. Weise, *The Latin Language and Character* (English translation, London, 1909); M. B. Ogle, *English and Latin* (New York, 1926), Ch. I, "English and Latin Modes of Expression."

through the pages of such an author as Montaigne is perhaps the best proof of this assertion; not merely epigrams in the strict sense but countless passages from every sort of Latin writer meet us on nearly every page, passages that seemed to invite Montaigne to gem the many-colored beauty of his discourse with their sparkle, passages that seemed to have been written in order to be quoted. No doubt the Roman often carried his gift too far. The rhetorical training of Roman lads who were intended for public life put too great an emphasis on making effective appeals to a court or a deliberative body, and truth was sometimes sacrificed to effectiveness. The declamations of the schools, both the *suasoriae* (speeches discussing a proposed course of action) and the *controversiae* (arguing both sides of a proposition), invaded general literature, giving an artificial, rhetorical flavor to drama and epic. Even the best Latin poetry is often dangerously near to what the Romans called *eloquentia*.[1] The influence of the author's reading, the *recitatio*, which Asinius Pollio instituted in the time of Augustus, also tended to concentrate the writer's attention on the production of well-distributed pointed sentences that would evoke applause.[2] An epigrammatist like Martial was forever preoccupied with the problem of cracking his whip smartly, whether or not he happened to write truly. Yet another author of the Silver Age is able to reveal truth in lightning flashes of innuendo and epigram. The Romans, Tacitus makes a British chieftain say, pose as civilizers: "They make a solitude, and call it peace."[3] Nor will sober thought disagree with his own

---

[1] Cf. A. S. Wilkins, *Roman Education*, Ch. V (on the influence of rhetorical training); W. C. Summers, *The Silver Age of Latin Literature*, Ch. I, "The Declamations and the Pointed Style"; G. Boissier, *Tacitus and Other Roman Studies*, pp. 163–194, "The Schools of Declamation at Rome."

[2] Cf. J. E. B. Mayor's note on Juvenal, III, 9.

[3] Tacitus, *Agricola*, 30.

judgment: "It is human nature to hate those whom you have injured."[1] Once more, in describing a funeral, what an oblique thrust he delivers by his quiet concluding remark: "The images of twenty of the most illustrious families, the Manlii, the Quinctii, and other names of equal splendor, were carried before [the bier of Junia]. Those of Brutus and Cassius were not displayed; but for that very reason they shone with preëminent lustre."[2] Avowed satire could not more powerfully perform its peculiar task than does this professed historian.

Forcible, memorable expression, then, was native in Rome. But what of literary form? It is no secret that the Romans, who borrowed from the Greeks most of their philosophy, much of their religious forms, more of their legal science than we formerly realized, and of sculpture and architecture a large part, not only borrowed Greek literary forms and materials but gloried in the fact. The Roman, even more than the Greek, regarded himself as but a member of a long succession of proprietors whose gains might come from any source but were thenceforth entailed on the estate; or, if the figure be preferred, he was a craftsman working in an ancient tradition, for whom appropriation was the economy suggested by common sense. And if he acknowledged a special debt to the Greeks in matters literary and artistic, it was perhaps partly because his supremacy in such tangible matters as war and government made it easier to condescend to borrow the non-essentials. Let others, then, excel in calling to life the bronze and the marble, in pleading cases, and in tracing the paths of the stars; he will rule peoples, will crown peace with law, will spare the conquered and crush the proud.[3] Greek literature, in its various forms, he will

---

[1] *Ibid.*, 42.   [2] Tacitus, *Annals* III, 76.
[3] Virgil, *Aen.* VI, 847–853.

appropriate and colonize, as it were, on Roman soil. So Horace boasts not of the originality of his thought but of his pioneer work in bringing Greek lyric measures, and especially that of Alcaeus, to Italy:

> princeps Aeolium carmen ad Italos
> deduxisse modos.[1]

And Virgil in the *Georgics* tells of his ambition, if his life be spared, to be the first to lead home with him the Muses from their Aonian hill:

> primus ego in patriam mecum, modo vita supersit,
> Aonio rediens deducam vertice Musas.[2]

We note in both passages the verb *deducere*, the word regularly used of colonization.

Roman poets, it appears, far from apologizing for their borrowings from Greece (and from earlier Roman poets), insist on them; and the borrowing extends not only to literary forms but to phrases, lines, and whole ideas. The comic poets paraphrase Greek originals, or "contaminate" their plots by fusing them; the epic and lyric poets practice, like their Greek forerunners, a sort of liturgical repetition of words, phrases, and ideas. They are not conscious of plagiarism, nor should we accuse them of it; we should rather see in their practice "a kind of apostolic succession of imagery and phrase." [3] To quote, to adapt, to echo a brother-poet's line is more than "the sincerest form of flattery"; it is an indication of the fact that poets are "bound each to

[1] Horace, *Odes* III, 30, 13 f.; cf. *Epist.* I, 19, 32.
[2] Virgil, *Georg.* III, 10 f. See further the well documented essay of W. Kroll, "Römer und Griechen," in his *Studien zum Verständnis der Römischen Literatur* (Stuttgart, 1924).
[3] E. K. Rand, "Catullus and the Augustans," *H. S. C. P.*, XVII (1906), 22.

each by natural piety," that they are members of a guild. The poets were actually incorporated as a *collegium poetarum* in early times, with a meeting-place in the Temple of Minerva on the Aventine.[1] This tradition was perhaps a more cohesive force than the later institution of literary circles, like those of Scipio and of Maecenas; but able poets, like Lucilius and Horace, held aloof from the guild. Still less productive of real poetry were the contests, the Agones Capitolini, instituted by Domitian; prize contests stimulate the use of the reason more than of the imagination.

We are now in a position to understand why the younger Pliny could admire the poems of his friend Spurinna as "*lyrica doctissima,*" that is, poems written in a conscious tradition. It is a poor economy, the ancients felt, for the poet to try to begin at the beginning with his personal experience, singing as the bird sings; he had better build on the experience of the race, adding what he can of his own; a poet is both born and made, the product both of nature and of art.[2] Both Greeks and Romans were familiar with the notion that poets write by the promptings of a Muse, through irresponsible "inspiration," or in a state of "ecstasy" or divine "madness"; they also recognize the notion that poetry is a manifestation of learning, the result of art.[3] Yet the Romans incline on the whole to the latter view: Horace disclaims any pretention to Pindar's swan flight, and is only a toilsome bee

---

[1] E. G. Sihler, "The Collegium Poetarum at Rome," *A. J. P.*, XXVI (1905), 1–21.

[2] Horace is quite definite on this point; see *Ars Poetica*, 408–411, and below, pp. 453 f.; also Quintilian, X, 2, on the advantages and the dangers of imitation. Cf. the theory masterfully exploited by J. L. Lowes in *Convention and Revolt in Poetry* (Boston, 1919). Art, and civilization itself, mediates between crystallization of the old and experiment with the new. See below, pp. 533 f.

[3] See W. C. Greene, "Plato's View of Poetry," *H. S. C. P.*, XXIX (1918); E. E. Sikes, *Roman Poetry*, pp. 55–105; W. Kroll, *op. cit.*, pp. 24–43.

filling cells with honey of the thyme.[1] If this seems at first sight to be an odd theory to apply to the lyric, of all poetic forms, one may observe that even the proverbial bird's song has in it not a little of convention. For the dramatic or the epic poet a better case may be made. There is a best way of doing everything: "C'est imiter quelqu'un que de planter des choux."[2] To lean heavily on one's predecessors is, within reason, merely a wise economy. And the epic poet is at pains to emphasize the fact that he is only telling the tale as it was told to him: *fama est, fertur,* are among Virgil's favorite *formulae.*

Originality among the Romans will seldom consist in absolutely new beginnings; it will mean oftener the use of old material in a new manner or for a new purpose. The same statement might be made, of course, with regard to almost any other race or any great artist, — even with regard to the Greeks or to Shakspere; true originality is the quality not of mere novelties and idiosyncrasies, but of the perfect work that comes at the end of a series of experiments, and that differentiates it from them. Thus Virgil is not merely what is left after we have subtracted all his borrowings from Homer and the rest of his "sources"; Virgil is the magician who has transmuted all his borrowings into something new.[3] And in the case of the Roman the point goes a little deeper than with the Greek, and involves the whole theory of a master's relation to his predecessors. For the Roman, even more than the Greek, regards the individual's work as but a moment in a greater tradition; the crest, it may be, of a wave, yet nevertheless the crest of a wave in a tide that has set in a definite direction. This it is that makes a master's work, if in a sense imitative, something more than mere imitation; it

---

[1] Horace, *Odes* IV, 2.   [2] Alfred de Musset.
[3] E. K. Rand, *The Magical Art of Virgil* (Cambridge, Mass., 1931).

is at its best the high-water mark of a long process, a "first-class" work, a "classic." Let us translate from an essay by Sainte-Beuve some memorable sentences that bear on the point.

A classic, according to the ordinary definition, is an ancient author, already enshrined in admiration, one whose word is law to others of his ilk. The word "classic," taken in this sense, begins to appear among the Romans. They called properly *classic* not all the citizens of different classes, but only those of the first, who possessed at least an income of a certain fixed figure. All those who possessed an inferior income were designated by the denomination *infra classem*, — below "the" class. In the figurative sense, the word *classicus* is used in Aulus Gellius [N. A. XIX, 8, 15], applied to writers: a writer of value and mark, *classicus assiduusque scriptor*, a writer who counts, who has a position in the world, and who is not confounded in the crowd of the proletariat. Such an expression presupposes an age sufficiently advanced for it to have already passed through a recension and grouping in literature. . . . The idea of the word "classic" implies something that has issue and consistency, that makes mass and tradition, that is sufficient in itself, that transmits itself to future generations, and lasts.[1]

It is therefore the quality of a work, as Sainte-Beuve argues, that constitutes its claim to be regarded as a "classic," rather than mere chronological priority, and a modern "classic" is no anomaly. The Greek and Latin classics did, however, have the advantage of priority, and except in uncritical ages have served to form standards of taste. One of the major tasks of criticism must always be to determine how far such standards should be considered permanent and how far they are merely historic landmarks in a continuing process which will go on forever. The Roman, at any rate,

---

[1] Sainte-Beuve, "Qu'est-ce qu'un Classique?" in *Causeries du Lundi*, Vol. III. See further G. C. Fiske, *Lucilius and Horace*, esp. Ch. I, "The Classical Theory of Imitation."

tended to be conservative in his attitude toward recognized masterpieces, to "imitate" them, to adapt them; and it may be that we can perceive to-day more of independence in his attitude, more intrusion of personality and new ideals, than he would have dared to claim for his work. Let us observe the working of these forces as they manifested themselves in two great fields of Roman literature: first in the field of comedy and satire, and then in the more ideal world created by the lyric and the epic poet.

Comedy and satire we must consider together; they appear to have had a common origin, and although their fortunes varied they kept a somewhat similar relationship to the more sedate forms of art. Satire, indeed, Quintilian claims in an oft-quoted sentence as the special province of Rome: "Satura quidem tota nostra est";[1] and though Greece might present the rival claims of Archilochus and Semonides of Amorgos and Hipponax, of the sillographers and the Cynic and Stoic satirists, to say nothing of the satiric bent of Aristophanes and of the New Comedy of manners, it is nevertheless true that Rome did perfect the "satire" as a literary form, and that satire in a more general sense pervades other Roman types. We shall not go far wrong if we see in the background of Roman comedy and satire alike the *versus fescennini*, the improvised scurrilous verses with which the common people in early times sought on joyous occasions, such as harvests, weddings, and triumphs, to avert malicious powers (for example, the "evil eye") from the happy cynosure of all eyes. This friendly abuse has its parallel, perhaps, in the γεφυρισμός ("bridge banter") that greeted the mystics as they marched along the Sacred Way from Athens to Eleusis. But it invited repartee, doubtless also in crude form, as in some of the pastoral verse that

[1] Quintilian, X, 1, 93.

we know.[1] Something more truly dramatic was the medley
known as the *satura*,[2] which though accompanied by music
and dancing at least as early as 389 B.C.[3] appears to have
had hardly any plot. It might serve to give clever actors a
chance for impromptu fooling and "wise-cracks," but gave
little scope for an author to develop plot and characterization. Nevertheless, when it was driven from the stage by
more artistic plays of the Campanian and the Greek type, the
satura, still a medley, had a distinguished career as a literary
form. It might include a hodgepodge of topics; it might
combine verse and prose (the "Menippean *satura*" of Varro
and later imitators); it often reverted to the dialogue form;
and it gradually developed from personal abuse to social
criticism and even philosophic doctrine. There are analogies, of form or of spirit, with the modern essay, pamphlet,
novel, drama with a thesis, popular science article, literary
criticism, editorial article, and sermon.[4]

Meanwhile, comedy with a plot had taken its place on the
stage. In the Campanian towns, and especially at Atella, a
kind of popular farce had long exploited comic situations and
burlesqued myths, and had invented stock characters not
unlike those of their descendants Punch and Judy; at Rome
these farces were acted by young men of good family who did
not suffer the social obloquy of ordinary slave-actors. But it

[1] Cf. Virgil, *Buc.* III, *passim*; and esp. l. 59: "alternis dicetis; amant
alterna Camenæ." Horace, *Epist.* II, 1, 146: *versibus alternis*, of a vintage
festival. It is worth noting that Thalia was the muse both of the pastoral and
of comedy.

[2] The word *satura* as used for a *lanx* ("platter") signifies a dish full of
various kinds of food; used for a *lex*, it means a law that included odds and
ends of legislation; in the literary sense the term also seems to have referred to
the miscellaneous content and form of sundry works (e.g. of Ennius, Lucilius, and Varro), only in Horace's age acquiring the specific connotation of
'satire," and being used still later to indicate a single poem of this type.

[3] Livy, VII, 2.

[4] Cf. A. Y. Campbell, *Horace*, esp. pp. 180–191, comparing also Browning.

was the Greek freedman Livius Andronicus, the translator of
the *Odyssey* into Saturnian verse, who at the close of the first
Punic War first had the courage to displace the dramatic
satura by introducing a plot; [1] in other words he produced
Latin versions of a Greek comedy and a Greek tragedy.
Aristophanic comedy, to be sure, the comedy of political
satire and biting personal ridicule, had long since died in
Greece; it was the Middle and the New Comedy of stock
characters and generalized social satire that Livius and
Naevius and Ennius, that Plautus and Terence presented to
Roman audiences. Even democratic Athens, hard-pressed
during the latter part of the Peloponnesian War, had tried,
though with imperfect success, to curb outspoken attacks on
statesmen; and the Roman tradition, with its discipline and
its respect for the great families, was even less tolerant of
comic tirades against its aristocratic leaders, as Naevius
learned to his sorrow when he pilloried a Scipio or sneered at
the Metelli. Strictly Italian dramatic elements and themes
were thus largely relegated from Rome to country districts;
"Roman" comedy is chiefly an adaptation of late Greek
comedy. [2]

In the age of Plautus, at the end of the third century B.C.,
comedies were still given on only a few days each year, before
noisy audiences which stood or which sat on improvised

---

[1] Livy, VII, 2, 8: "Livius . . . ab saturis ausus est primus argumento
fabulam serere."

[2] The foregoing account of the origin of satire and comedy is in outline the
orthodox one. (See further H. Nettleship, "The Original Form of the Roman
Satura," in *Lectures and Essays, Second Series.*) It may be added that the
trustworthiness of the tradition has been impugned in recent years by F. Leo
and G. L. Hendrickson; early dramatic *satura* is by them supposed to be an
attempt to imagine a Roman parallel for the Greek Old Comedy. This view
cannot be considered to have won general acceptance. See (*pro*) Hendrickson, *A. J. P.*, XV (1894), XIX (1898); *C. P.*, VI (1911); also (*contra*)
C. Knapp, *A. J. P.*, XXXIII (1912); R. H. Webb, *C. P.*, VII (1912);
A. L. Wheeler, *C. P.*, VII (1912); B. L. Ullman, *C. P.*, VIII (1913), IX (1914).

seats; not an easy audience to entertain. And Plautus, himself a poor Umbrian, who had possibly been an actor in Atellan farces, undertook to learn Greek and to convey to this
Roman audience the humor of a subtle foreign drama, keeping its conventions of plot, character, and costume. It is
surprising that he succeeded so well as he did. For although
Plautus comes, for us, for all practical purposes, almost at
the beginning of Latin comedy, he represents, with Terence,
the end of the highly-developed Greek comedy of Menander
and his colleagues, — a drama that has travelled so long a
road that its plots have become hackneyed and tiresome, its
characters stereotyped, while its Hellenistic social setting
and ideals are rather disagreeable. Amorous intrigues, virtue hoodwinked, confusions of twins, the timely discovery of
a long-lost child; passionate youth, mercenary courtesan,
stern father, shrewish wife, shameless slave-dealer, glutton-
ous parasite, braggart soldier, impudent slave: these are the
rubber stamps with which, even before Menander, countless plots have been fabricated, plots that could entertain
only the very unsophisticated. But something else has intervened to save Greek comedy: the crossing of comedy with
Euripidean romantic tragedy, and infusion of a mild and
tolerant philosophy of life, expressed, at least by Menander,
in a polished, sententious style. The interest, in other words,
has come to be far less in the plot than in the poet's knowledge of human nature, in his power of breathing new life
into a stock character, in his gift of phrasing. Comedy is
once more, in the works of Menander, for the sophisticated.

This Hellenic world is what Plautus dishes up for his audience, keeping the essentials of its social setting and its
plots, and introducing only incidental allusions and asides
that suggest a Roman setting. It is beside the point to object that Plautus by no means presents the Roman point of

view, — for example, the Roman conception of social relationships, of family life, of slave and master. He does not pretend to do so; in fact, he allows himself the loophole, if his situations seem too daring for Roman taste, that after all this is not Rome but Greece! For the whole aim of Plautus is to get a laugh in the easiest way; and his great merit is his sense of the theatre, his knowledge of what will please a difficult audience. He has not the refinement of expression of Menander; he lacks insight into subtleties of character. But he is comic; writing for an audience that we might characterize to-day as "low-brow," he writes "low-brow" comedy. Rapidity, versatility, broad horseplay, comic exaggeration, are in his arsenal. Social satire is hardly there, unless we find it in the willingness of the playwright, a man of the people, to depict slaves more admirable than their masters. There is a fair range of subjects: burlesque on a Greek myth (*Amphitruo*), something like character study of a miser (*Aulularia*), a really touching picture of a slave's devotion to his master (*Captivi*), a romantic tale of shipwreck (*Rudens*), a comedy of errors which Shakspere hardly surpassed in his more elaborate imitation (*Menaechmi*), a travesty of an empty-headed braggart soldier's taking down (*Miles Gloriosus*), the ruse of a "haunted house" to veil a revel (*Mostellaria*): these are the kernels of a few of the twenty plays that survive. Plautus served his generation by providing a safety-valve for over-wrought feelings in the years during and after Hannibal's stay in Italy. He helped men to laugh, when laughter was sadly needed; he relieved the sobriety of Roman letters by a lighter touch; he taught Romans, perhaps, to conceive as a possibility something different from conventional Roman customs and standards of conduct by making vivid a fantastic world of make-believe. In its unreality, in its specious realism, in its appeal to the common

denominator of average humanity, in its attempt to provide
an escape from the workaday world, the drama of Plautus
comes nearest to the modern moving-picture.

In order to be fully appreciated, Plautus must be seen on
the stage. Terence can be adequately appreciated when
read. For Terence, slave from Africa though he had been,
undertook the more difficult task of reproducing Menander's spirit; his prologues make abundantly clear the difficulty that his restless audience and rival attractions caused
him. Discarding all pretense of a Roman coloring, he invited his audience to imagine themselves in Athens, and built
his plots from one, or more often from two, Greek plays. Professing to paint the same Hellenistic society as Plautus, he
contrived to soften some of its harsher aspects, to refine feeling and character, to express in polished verse a proverbial
wisdom. In Terence comedy once more becomes intellectual; and though truly comic situation is by no means absent, rollicking fun is comparatively rare. One is moved to
smile, rather than to laugh. One pictures the author brooding over the perfect phrasing of a *sententia*: "fortune favors
the brave," "old age is itself a disease," "lovers' quarrels renew their love." Low-keyed these sayings are, in the diction
of prose; they are the pronouncements of the student of human nature who records a diagnosis. Yet it cannot be said
that the plots always turn on a convincing analysis of character. What, for example, are we to say of the change of
heart manifested in the *Adelphoe* by old Demea, who without apparent reason passes at a leap from utter crustiness to
absolute indulgence? Or has Demea (and Terence) had
his tongue in his cheek all the while? In the *Phormio*, the interest is chiefly in the plot, which is manipulated consistently
enough by the scheming parasite, who feathers his own nest
while helping a pair of cousins to advance their love-affairs,

all to the discomfiture of the contemptible father of one of them. The interest of the *Andria*, again, turns on a sentimental situation; yet the dénouement (the revelation of the Andrian woman's identity) is mechanical. The realism of Terence, in other words, does not go far enough; he neither depicts the real world of Greece or Rome, nor does he consistently create an imaginary world of people whose motives are completely intelligible. His merits are of detail, rather than of general conception; single scenes and detached utterances fill us with admiration, as they did the more intellectual members of his audience and his educated readers in ancient times. The populace meanwhile turned to the more realistic *fabula togata*, with scenes in Latin towns, to the Atellan farce, to revivals of Plautus, and to the vulgar mimes and pantomimes that finally drove comedy from the stage.

Far more important and more characteristic of Rome than the acted comedy is the satire that was intended only to be read. Here the name of Lucilius deserves more attention than one would suspect from a casual inspection of the fragments that survive, hardly 1400 lines, mostly in bits of only a line or two. For Lucilius resumes in himself the long tradition of Greek satiric writing, as it was known to the cultivated Scipionic circle, and the farce of the native Italic *satura*; and in Lucilius we find the germ of all that flowered in the mature satiric art of Horace, of Persius, and of Juvenal.[1] From his Hellenistic predecessors he derived especially the interest in expressing practical wisdom in narrative form (the *Chreia* of the Cynics and Stoics), or in the form of dialogue and declamation, partly autobiographic, partly de-

---

[1] Indispensable for the study of this difficult subject are the text of Lucilius, with commentary, of F. Marx (Leipsic, 1904–05), and G. C. Fiske, *Lucilius and Horace* (Madison, Wis., 1920).

scriptive (the *Diatribé*, as developed by the eclectic Cynic Bion of Borysthenes), infused with borrowings from other literary forms, — fable and mime, symposium and epistle. The Scipionic circle was committed to the doctrine of the "plain style" refined by Panaetius. It meets us in the "*purus sermo*" which Caesar attributed to Terence, an easy, conversational, ironic style approximating the "Socratic discourses" of Plato in the informal, good-natured give and take of well-bred talk. Lucilius, however, permitted himself also to disturb this controlled, ironic style with a vigorous invective which his contemporaries must have thought more in keeping with the "grand style." For Lucilius appears to have been in earnest; and a man who is in earnest is apt at times to chafe at well-meant forms and rules. Horace might indeed learn how to "tell the truth with a smile"; but Lucilius, and in a later age Persius and Juvenal, wrote (or at least professed to write) because indignation cried for expression.

Between these extremes, outraged expostulation and amused comment, Roman satire makes its way; both qualities are rife in Lucilius. In a society in which organized religion gives little ethical guidance, and philosophy is over the heads of the many, but in which the force of tradition and public opinion is strong, satire serves as the most available vehicle of popular philosophy, doubly effective because of its comic armor.[1] But it is of the greatest importance to observe whether satire will merely record the trend of public opinion or will assert an independent attitude, whether it will follow or whether it can lead. Small towns are apt to be conventional, critical of innovators, easily roused to anger against

---

[1] Cf. H. J. Rose, *Primitive Culture in Italy*, pp. 215–218 (on public opinion); C. W. Mendell, "Satire as Popular Philosophy," *C. P.*, XV (1920), 138–157.

individualists; yet their social conscience is not necessarily enlightened. Rome in the day of Lucilius still kept the traits of the small town; but the Scipionic circle was more cosmopolitan in the range of its interests, more tolerant in its attitude. Here is the inner contradiction in the work of Lucilius; he knows how to laugh, to laugh cruelly, but he has imperfectly learned the far greater power and value of a smile.

Lucilius writes, he tells us expressly, not for the very learned, nor again for the ignorant; he aims between them, and names the reader whom he does not wish and the reader whom he wishes,[1] reminding one, though remotely, of Addison, who hopes that *The Spectator* may reach coffee-houses and tea-tables.[2] Born on the Campanian border, and in spite of his close connection with the Scipionic circle not a participant in Roman politics, Lucilius remains a somewhat detached observer of Roman life. A partisan of the Scipios, he takes a fling at their political opponents, not unlike Aristophanes in his personal attacks; but he also launches his attacks against universal types: at the iniquities of the Forum;[3] at the miser, who "keeps his purse with him, dines with it, sleeps with it, takes his bath with it." [4] He indulges in autobiography, recounting with rollicking humor, for example, the toilsome stages and the grotesque adventures of a journey by land to Puteoli, and thence by sea along the coast to Sicily.[5] Harsh, even coarse at times, in his language as in his spirit, he can also turn out well-phrased commonplaces whether original or traditional: "to find a knot in a bullrush"; [6] "we cannot all of us do all things"; [7] "one of the

---

[1] Lucilius, Frags. 593–596 (Marx).

[2] *The Spectator*, Nos. 4 (March 5, 1711; Steele) and 10 (March 12, 1711; Addison).

[3] Lucilius, 1228–1234.   [4] *Ibid.*, 244.   [5] *Ibid.*, 98–147.

[6] *Ibid.*, 36; cf. Terence, *Andria*, 941.

[7] Lucilius, 218; cf. Virgil, *Buc.* VIII, 63.

many." [1] If he takes small pains to charm his readers, he nevertheless has an ideal of refined social pleasures; he enjoys, he says, "food well cooked, and its seasoning, good talk, and that right gladly." [2] In the longest fragment that survives, a passage of thirteen lines, he carelessly strings together definitions of virtue in such a way as to give color to Horace's remark that Lucilius would dictate two hundred lines in an hour while standing on one foot; [3] yet the closing couplet is effective: virtue, he says, "consists in putting first one's country's good, then one's parents', and third and last one's own." [4]

No less pungent in his satire, no less keen in his observation of human nature, but learning to smile as well as to gibe, is Horace, the admirer and emulator of Lucilius. Emulator he is, and not mere imitator; for though he borrows themes and lines and the general conception of satire from Lucilius, Horace seeks to surpass his master. Like him, Horace calls his satires *sermones*, "conversations," and cultivates a studied informality; he likewise exploits or criticizes Stoic paradoxes, does battle for the respectable virtues, paints genre pictures, and recounts his own experiences. Painstaking investigation has shown how freely he quarried from the works of Lucilius, and his admiration for the older poet's wit is frankly and generously expressed. But he is also frank in denouncing his turbid diffuseness and his occasional coarseness. For the century and a half that separates the circle of Maecenas from the Scipionic circle has brought a refinement in taste and in literary style that requires of poets a greater *urbanitas*; political satire and personal attacks are now taboo. Only a few of the earliest of Horace's poems are marred by coarseness; his political manifestoes

---

[1] Lucilius, 448.   [2] Lucilius, 1122.
[3] Horace, *Sat.* I, 4, 9.   [4] Lucilius, 1326–1338.

are programmes, rather than attacks; his personalities are comparatively harmless. Since the bond of union of a literary circle is now only that of a common interest in literature, Horace is free to devote all his energy to "filing" his work to the last degree of polish, and to expressing a personal philosophy that becomes more mellow as the years go by.

Of the first book of the *Satires*, published in 35 B.C., perhaps half may be said to be studies in the traditional manner. The fifth satire recounts a journey to Brundisium, partly in company with Maecenas and Virgil and others, with realistic details reminiscent of the similar sketch of Lucilius. The ninth, telling with irresistible humor of Horace's desperate attempts to shake off the bore who attached himself to the poet as he strolled along the Sacred Way, combines character study, Lucilian touches, and a tribute to the unspoiled social atmosphere of the circle of Maecenas. The sixth satire also does homage to Maecenas who, though high-born, values character more than high birth, and has befriended Horace, the son of a freedman; Horace, in turn, owes his character to his father's devoted care and education of him, which he would not exchange for illustrious ancestry and the cares that it would bring, preferring to live simply and comfortably, noting the activities of Rome, dining frugally, sleeping soundly (and late), suffering no social stigma if he travels on a bob-tailed mule. Satire here mingles the personal and the universal; it obliquely rebukes *ambitio*, while making out a case, based on genuine experience, for practical democracy.

The remaining satires of the first book are more concerned with the literary problem of the nature and end of the satire itself. Horace gives no ground for complaint to individuals unless they have a guilty conscience; no, his satire is merely the putting on paper of the sort of observation, the teaching by examples, that his father gave him. This habit of observation, of self-communing and self-criticism, has kept Horace free from the greater vices, though perhaps not from foibles, including this minor foible of writing!

The first satire, which serves as a dedication of the whole book, well illustrates the method, interlarded though it is with Cynic and Stoic commonplaces and with Lucilian reminiscences. Why is it, Horace professes to ask Maecenas, that no one is content with one's lot, but that no one, if given the chance, would exchange one's lot for another's? Enough to make Jupiter furious! Really, to be serious, — yet why not tell the truth with a smile? — yet, to be serious for the moment, the cause of discontentment is the mad race for wealth, not mere foresight, like that of the prudent ant who enjoys what she saves, but endless hoarding. However, there is a natural limit to what one can enjoy; for one who lives "within the limits of nature" a hundred acres are as good as a thousand. "Ah, but," they say, "there is no such thing as enough; you are rated by what you have." No; beyond a certain point wealth brings misery. Tantalus is a universal type: change the name, and the tale applies to you. You sleep with money-bags piled high,[1] getting no real use or pleasure from them. Yet money is good only for what it will buy; beyond one's needs it brings only worries; poverty is better, for the miser has no friends. Nor need one be a spendthrift. There is a measure in all things; there are fixed bounds, within which the right is to be sought.[2] Discontent comes from greed; we match ourselves with others, rather than with our own needs, and thus fail in the end to

---

[1] Cf. Lucilius, Frag. 244, quoted on p. 438.
[2]   "Est modus in rebus, sunt certi denique fines
        Quos ultra citraque nequit consistere rectum."
                                                Sat. I, 1, 106 f.

take our leave of life like a guest who has had his fill.[1] Ah, but Horace fears that he will seem to be stealing from the Stoics, and suddenly ends his satire.

Chiefly during the decade before the battle of Actium, Horace tried his hand at another form of satiric writing, and published in 30 B.C., under the name of *Epodes*, "refrains," a group of seventeen poems. The majority are iambic, and therefore invite comparison with the poems of the Greek satirist Archilochus; all but one of them, moreover, are written in couplets, in which the second line forms a sort of refrain to the first. Several of them deal with the fortunes of the Roman state; desperation at the renewal of civil war in the year 40 (the 16th), joy at the victory of Actium (the 9th). Others are realistic sketches, or experiments in more lyric vein; one (the second) is a delicious picture of country life with a sudden ironic conclusion that just saves it from sentimentality. Finer lyric poems, however, Horace was to achieve in more characteristic lyric measures, in the *Odes*; and his satiric vein was still to find its best expression in the second book of the *Satires* and in his *Epistles*.

The second book of the *Satires*, indeed, was ready for publication in the same year as the *Epodes*. Now the accepted friend of Maecenas, and from about the year 33 the grateful possessor of the Sabine Farm that Maecenas has given him, Horace shows a new ease and confidence. He has lived with the great, but does not presume on his relations with them; he knows the handbooks of the Stoics and of the Epicureans alike, but he is not slavishly tied to any creed, as he can boast ten years later.[2] This eclectic, or rather independent, attitude is greatly assisted by his reversion in most of the poems of the second book to the dialogue form of earlier sat-

---

[1] "Uti conviva satur," *ibid.*, 119; cf. Lucretius, III, 938 f.
[2] "Nullius addictus iurare in verba magistri." *Epist.* I, 1, 14.

ire, manipulated with delicate irony; for it enables him to put in the mouth of a second speaker, sufficiently remote in epoch or in social station, what he wishes to say or to hold up to ridicule, without seeming to preach unduly. He can thus express, or disclaim, Stoic or Epicurean doctrine at will; he can include himself in a universal ridicule, which disarms any charge of censoriousness. Indeed, one must read Horace warily, with the whole burden of his teaching in mind, in order to know when he is laying bare his heart and when he is writing with his tongue in his cheek. Frequently he seems to have learned the Socratic or Platonic irony that represents Socrates as being told by another what Plato himself holds; [1] in other instances the principles laid down by Horace's interlocutor are so extravagant as to refute themselves. And Horace can always claim the indulgence that is freely accorded the dramatic artist.

How well Horace manipulates this game of make-believe! Does he wish to lecture on frugality, the advantages of "living on a little"? He introduces us to the rustic Ofellus, a homespun philosopher,[2] whose life proves better than the commonplaces of the philosophic schools that exercise and hunger are the best sauces; that the pleasures of the table are not in the food but in the diner; that fashion, not taste, is the only impediment to the enjoyment of common fare. Though Ofellus has suffered reverses, he is no more frugal now, through necessity, than he was formerly by choice; fortune cannot take from him what he realizes was only a loan from nature.

Two of the satires are devoted to the exploitation of Stoic paradoxes, not without parody, though Horace is becoming more and more a convert to Stoicism; here, too, he gives the

---

[1] Cf. W. C. Greene, "The Spirit of Comedy in Plato," *H. S. C. P.*, XXXI (1920), esp. pp. 69-71.   [2] "Abnormis sapiens." *Sat.* II, 2, 3.

floor to others. Thus in the seventh satire Horace permits his slave Davus to exercise the privilege of the Saturnalia to harangue his master. Appropriately enough the theme is slavery; and Davus, remembering what he learned from the doorkeeper of the Stoic Crispinus, holds forth on the folly and fickleness of mankind. All men are fools, all are slaves to their desires; all save the wise man who alone is free because he is self-controlled and self-contained,[1] and therefore proof against the assaults of fortune. Even Horace himself is fickle in his vacillation between the charms of country and of city, between simple fare and the banquets of Maecenas; he cannot bear solitude, and is dogged by care. Davus has dared too much; his master exhibits a towering rage, and threatens to send him off to the hard labor of the Sabine Farm. Who can be deceived, however, by the rage, or fail to see in the wise Davus the wisdom of his master that freely mingles Stoic commonplaces and native wit, with a carica-ture of his own failings (not by any means to be taken liter-ally) to appease the feelings of susceptible readers?

The mention of the Sabine Farm reminds us that we have not yet referred to the most delightful poem in the second book. The sixth satire breathes a new atmosphere; in the detachment of the Sabine Farm, his "citadel" aloof from the city, he voices his fervent appreciation of country life. If he was inclined in the second Epode to poke fun at the money-lender Alfius, who praised country life but balked at taking the final step of turning countryman, Horace himself is country-bred and feels nothing but relief on leaving Rome for the Farm. But there is something here beyond the under-standing of the mere countryman; it is the country enhanced by contrast with the city, a sophisticated love of country life, a mature and mellow variety of Epicureanism. The

---

[1] "In se ipso totus." *Sat.* II, 7, 86.

very form of the poem, a triptych, carries out the contrast, [1] — the morning tranquillity of the Farm, contrasted with a busy, fretful day in Rome amid men jealous of his friendship with Maecenas, a day that causes him to long for the peacefulness of the Farm.

O country, when shall I behold thee? When may I drink sweet oblivion of life's anxieties, now from the books of old sages, now from sleep and idle hours? O when shall the bean . . . and the garden mess, well larded, be set before me? O nights and banquets fit for the gods, when my friends and I feast before my own fire-side and feed my saucy home-born slaves on what is left! Each guest, according to his pleasure, drains cups large or small, not bound by foolish rules, whether he be man enough to carry strong bumpers or whether he more gladly grow mellow with milder potations. So talk springs up, not about others' villas and town houses, nor whether Lepos dances ill or no; but we discuss rather what concerns us more nearly and what 'tis base not to know: to wit, whether it is through wealth or through virtue that men are blest, whether expediency or uprightness leads us to friendship, what is the nature of the good, and what is the highest good.[2]

The contrast between city and country life is further enforced by his neighbor's telling a tale, — the poem is not otherwise given dialogue form, — the Fable of the Town Mouse and the Country Mouse. We are here given a glimpse of something beyond the world of satire, — the poet's private world that is always in the making. This world, and the magic casements through which Horace lets us view it in his *Odes*, lyric poems written for the most part during the next few years, will concern us later.[3] After the

---

[1] A similar architecture of contrasts may be traced in the arrangement of the poems within the second book: Stoic and Epicurean themes in juxtaposition, ironically treated (2 and 3, 7 and 8); two mock-didactic poems in succession (4 and 5).

[2] *Sat.* II, 6, 60–76; the first part has been quoted on p. 153.

[3] Pp. 483–496.

publication of the first three books of the *Odes* in 23 B.C., however, Horace turned again to his pedestrian Muse; the result we have in the two books of the *Epistles*, published respectively in 20 and (probably) in 13 B.C.

The *Epistles* are with few exceptions as much *sermones* as the *Satires*. They are, to be sure, addressed to individuals, but so are many of the *Satires* (and a few of the *Satires* of Lucilius); so are many of the *Odes*, so indeed are some even of the songs of the more truly lyrical Catullus. Like some of the self-conscious letters of the younger Pliny, like the "Letters to the Editor" to be found in modern newspapers, they are intended from the first more for the public than for the person ostensibly addressed. Why, then, the fiction of the epistolary form? Chiefly because of the apparent informality of tone that becomes it. The *Epistles* do, to be sure, generally fit the persons addressed, and convey news of special interest to them; but they differ from the *Satires* in the perfection of their form and in the amount of self-revelation that Horace permits himself; Lucilius is almost left behind.[1] Secure in the esteem of his friends, in the enjoyment of a literary reputation recognized by all whose criticism he values, and well established as a country squire on the Sabine Farm, he writes confidently, tolerantly, urbanely. His gratitude to Maecenas knows no limit; yet he reserves his independence, and would rather surrender the Farm than feel that he must dance attendance on his patron.[2] But Maecenas understands; and Horace is free to enjoy those nights and days on the Farm that he once craved. In his beloved valley, encircled by shadowing mountains, amid oak and ilex and fruit-bearing bushes, he can escape the

[1] See further E. P. Morris, "The Form of the Epistle in Horace," *Yale Classical Studies*, II (1931), 79–114.
[2] *Epist.* I, 7.

summer heat and quench his thirst from icy streams; [1] his
neighbors are amused by his clumsy attempts at digging and
moving rocks with his own hands. [2] Best of all, the Farm
"restores Horace to himself," [3] and teaches him its philosophy.

Long ago Horace has learned what he could from the
Stoics and the Epicureans; now he is living a philosophy
which owes much to them, but which is drawn quite as much
from his experience and observation of life. Deliberately
declining to write further lyrics, at least for the present, he
now addresses himself to the task of setting forth the secret
of happiness. And what is the key to this all-important inquiry? "To flee vice is the beginning of virtue, and to have
got rid of folly is the beginning of wisdom." [4] An obvious
point? Perhaps; but the world has not learned it; even boys
at play, singing the old adage "You'll be King if you do
right," are expressing a deeper wisdom than that of the business world, where the cry is: "O citizens, citizens, money is

---

[1] *Epist.* I, 16, 1–16; 18, 104–112.

[2] *Ibid.*, I, 14, 39.

[3] *Ibid.*, I, 14, 1. In the valley of the Digentia, near the village of Licenza,
may be seen the remains, recently excavated, of a villa which may reasonably
be supposed to be that of Horace. See G. Lugli, "La Villa Sabina di Orazio,"
Mon. Ant., 1926; architectural restoration of the villa by T. Price, in *Mem.
Am. Acad. Rome*, Vol. X (1932); E. K. Rand, *A Walk to Horace's Farm*
(Boston, 1930). The hills, if perhaps more bare than in Horace's day,
present the same gracious outlines, and the same inviting shade on a
summer afternoon. The frontispiece of the present volume shows the view
from the Farm looking northward. The cool stream that tumbles down the
hillside a few hundred feet to the west, if not Bandusia, is at any rate re-
freshing. In winter the sun warms the sides of the narrow valley. About
the farm are silvery olive trees, and vines "wedded" to the trees that support
them, as in Horace's day; each July the grain is threshed by the hand-flail on
a threshing floor a few feet from the poet's bedroom (if Lugli's identification
of a certain room with a handsome mosaic floor be correct); there are roses
and sweet lavender and hives of bees. The natives of the valley have a
Horatian courtesy and independence. One must be a very imperfect Horatian if one does not return from a visit to the Farm a better Horatian.

[4] *Ibid.*, I, 1. 41.

the first thing to be sought, virtue after coin." [1] The folly
of rich and of poor alike, dissatisfied as they all are, Horace
would fain avoid like any other inconsistency or indecorum;
only the *sapiens* is to be envied, and he is rich, free, honored,
beautiful, a king of kings, above all sound, — except when
he has a cold in the head! [2]

"*Nil admirari*, that is perhaps the one and only thing
that can make and keep one happy." [3] Not indifference, not
quite the imperturbability sought by Stoic and Epicurean
alike, but the maintenance of a mean between extremes,
lest even Virtue herself be sought extravagantly.[4] As usual
it is in his concrete illustrations that Horace gives the clue;
what folly to sacrifice real values to apparent ones, — piling
up wealth, for example, beyond what one can use, like Lucullus with his five thousand cloaks. Use, then, is the standard,
and the practical test is the true test of a philosophy. "He
is not poor who has enough of things to use; if stomach,
lungs, and feet are all in health, regal wealth can give nothing more; if you turn vegetarian, you are still further removed from the reach of Fortune." [5] One must keep oneself
independent of circumstances, esteeming character above
reputation. Why wander abroad in quest of happiness?
Better take gratefully what God gives; don't wait; stay
where you are; happiness is within: "they change their
climate, not their mind, who hurry across seas; it is a busy
idleness that is our undoing. . . . What you seek is here,
even in [a mean little village like] Ulubrae, if there fail you
not an even temper." [6]

This central thesis Horace qualifies and amplifies. To one
friend, Lollius, he sees fit to address an exhortation: "Well

---

[1] *Ibid.*, I, 1, 52, 59.   [2] *Ibid.*, I, 1, 106–108.
[3] *Ibid.*, I, 6, 1–2.
[4] "Ultra quam satis est." *Ibid.*, l. 16.
[5] *Epist.* I, 12, 4–11.   [6] *Ibid.*, I, 11, 27–30.

begun is half done; dare to be wise; begin! . . . Rule your
spirit!" [1] Another, the poet Tibullus, fortunate in wealth
and beauty and the art of enjoyment, but diffident, he bids
regard each day that dawns as if his last; and he invites his
young friend to visit him and find him, "fat and sleek, a pig
from Epicurus' herd." [2] To Maecenas, in claiming a dignified independence even from his patron, he protests against
any man being compelled to live on another's terms, however kindly the intent of the patron; he tells no less than
four stories to enforce the point, which is driven home in a
closing line: "'tis right that each man measure himself by his
own standard." [3] That this individualistic creed is only half
of Horace's philosophy, however, we may judge both from
his own life, which recognized a mature discipline, and from
other utterances. Not the pretensions of the individual,
after all, but Nature is the standard. To his friend the wag
Aristius Fuscus, "the lover of the city," writes "the lover of
the country," Horace; kindred spirits they are in all but this
difference. It is in the country that Horace lives and feels
himself a king; [4] it is there that one may "live naturally." [5]
Try though one may, there is no escaping Nature in the
country; "drive her out with a pitchfork, yet she will ever
in unexpected fashion return victorious." [6] Learn, then, to
discriminate, to set one's ambitions at a reasonable level, to
cultivate simplicity, to live content with little, and so to remain free.

[1] *Ibid.*, I, 2, 40, 62.   [2] *Ibid.*, I, 4, 15 f.
[3] *Epist.* I, 7, 98. Cf. I, 14, 44, another closing line ostensibly addressed to
his bailiff: "I think each had better ply contentedly the trade that he knows."
We have seen (p. 385) that the Stoic Chrysippus modified the prescription
that one should live according to Nature by taking into account not only
universal Nature but our individual natures.
[4] "Vivo et regno," *Epist.* I, 10, 8.
[5] *Ibid.*, I, 10, 12.
[6] *Ibid.*, I, 10, 24 f.

After all, one needs philosophy in order to live tranquilly, to estimate the claims of property, of nature, and of discipline in winning virtue and freedom from worry, — in a word, in order to live on good terms with oneself. What is it that brings tranquillity? Is it honor and wealth, or the quiet by-paths of life? Horace finds the answer to his question in his own experience. "As for me, as oft as I am refreshed by the cool stream of the Digentia, that Mandela drinks, that region wrinkled by the cold, what do you think are my feelings, what do you suppose, my friend, is my prayer? May I have what I now have, or even less, and may I live my own life (*mihi vivam*) for the time that is left, if the gods wish me to live longer. May there be the blessings of books, and enough food stored away for the year, and may I not be tossed about between hope and anxiety. 'Tis enough to pray to Jove for the things that he bestows and takes away; may he give life, and may he give sustenance; an even temper I will provide myself." [1] In the last poem of the book, an *envoi* to his manuscript, eager to find the stalls of the booksellers, he paints his portrait for friendly readers: a freedman's son, who has found his place among the leaders of the state, short, grey before his time, fond of the sun, quick to anger, but easily appeased.[2]

The Philosophy of the Sabine Farm, as it is often called, met at least one practical test: it made Horace happy. It has also endeared itself to many generations of men who may have been impatient of external authority, or sceptical of revealed religion, or impervious to technical philosophy. Sane, charming, not too exacting, it provides even to-day a guide to happiness, at least for some people of education and breeding. It imposes a discipline, but from motives of en-

[1] *Epist.* I, 18, 104–112.
[2] *Epist.* I, 20, 20–25.

lightened self-interest; self-realization comes only through self-denial. It encourages tolerance toward others, not because it regards all sorts and conditions of men with indifference, but because it realizes that one can affect what one does not approve less easily by showing anger than by the contagious influence of a gentle smile.[1] The Philosophy of the Farm is very wise; no man who masters it will ever make a fool of himself. What one misses in it is a sense that there are times when one must run the risk of being thought a fool in order to do something that needs doing. Ardor, recklessness, the spirit of the crusader, self-denial for the good of others, are seldom to be found in Horace, even in the *Odes*. He lives on none of life's frontiers, once he has thrown away his shield.[2] Perhaps it is for this reason that Horace is an author less appreciated by the young than by those whose early enthusiasms have cooled a little in the world of hard realities. What Horace loses in this respect he gains in the range of his sympathies and the common sense of his attitude. If he does not enter into our experience in moments of eager self-abandonment or of crushing sorrow, he represents the common denominator of our universal experience; and there are few ordinary occasions on which a well-turned phrase of Horace does not seem to the point.[3]

The second book of the *Epistles* consists of three long poems, epistles only in name, devoted wholly to the criticism of poetry and its place in life. The value of Horace's adventures in literary criticism consists less in the correctness of his knowledge of literary history than in the good sense with which he handles stock themes, with a real sense

[1] See the admirable characterization of Horace by Persius, *Sat.* I, 116 f.:
"Omne vafer vitium ridenti Flacco amico
Tangit et admissus circum praecordia ludit."
[2] Cf. *Odes* II, 7, 9–16.
[3] See also pp. 495 f.

of the potentialities and the social responsibilities of poetry, and the happy phrases and figures that he hits on to express his commonplaces. He never conceives of poetry apart from life; and his remarks always provide good reading.

Why consider only dead poets to be good poets, he asks in the epistle to Augustus that he prefixes to the other two? If it is only age that confers merit, how many years must a poet have been dead to be approved? A hundred? What of the poet who lacks a month or a year of this century? From this *reductio ad absurdum* Horace passes on to sketch the growth of literature in Rome, with special attention to drama and the present craze for writing, and deals finally with the beneficent influence of the emperor on letters. Patronage, we may remark in passing, was an almost necessary adjunct to the profession of literature, except for men of independent means who wrote only by way of avocation, until the invention of copyright about a century and a half ago. The institution has its grave dangers, in producing servility and insincerity; occasionally, as in the case of Horace, a Maecenas has known how to confer patronage without imposing conditions explicit or implicit.

In the third epistle, "To the Pisos," ordinarily known as "The Art of Poetry," and quite possibly written even before the first book of the *Epistles*, Horace chats informally on a series of loosely yet artfully connected topics, laying down principles for the guidance of the rising generation of writers and in particular for Cnaeus Piso. Many of these principles are the commonplaces of his Greek and Roman predecessors, more neatly expressed; some are observations on contemporary tendencies. Not all have a universal bearing; yet it is surprising how often Horace, taken with a reasonable allowance for changed circumstances, might seem to be commenting on our own literature. A sense of harmony and propriety is his first *desideratum*, a sense best cultivated through study of previous literature as well as of life itself; inspiration *and* training are alike indispensable.[1] Many a phrase and precept expressed in the development of this general thesis is unforgettable: "the purple patch";[2] "clever joiner's work";[3] "use, the law and norm of speech";[4] "sesquipedalian words";[5] "internal consistency" (in characterization);[6] the artistic advantage for a narrative or dramatic poet of plunging "in medias res";[7] "the labor of the file";[8] one is surprised "when Homer nods."[9] Never has there been a more memorable expression of the non-fulfillment of grandiose literary expectations: "Parturient montes, nascetur ridiculus mus."[10] One should not attempt to write "if Minerva be unwilling" (i.e. if the gods have not vouchsafed the proper gifts).[11] It is difficult *propria communia dicere*, "to appropriate what is common experience."[12] Hence the advantage of rehandling traditional themes, and, for this and for other reasons (particularly for versification), of studying Greek models daily and nightly.[13] Not that Horace would have Roman drama merely ape the Greek; he goes out of his way to commend the exploitation of Roman material.[14] Nor should the writer forget that wisdom, *sapere*, "is the beginning and fount of good writing";[15] a philosophy, for example one of Socratic

---

[1] *Epist.* II, 3, 408–411.

[2] "Purpureus . . . pannus." *Ibid.*, II, 3, 15 f.

[3] "Callida . . . iunctura." *Ibid.*, l. 47.

[4] "Usus | quem penes arbitrium est et ius et norma loquendi." *Ibid.*, II, 3, 71 f.   [5] *Ibid.*, II, 3, 97.

[6] *Ibid.*, II, 3, 119.   [7] *Ibid.*, II, 3, 148.

[8] *Ibid.*, II, 3, 290.   [9] *Ibid.*, II, 3, 359.

[10] *Ibid.*, II, 3, 139.   [11] *Ibid.*, II, 3, 317.

[12] The reference is to what has not yet been dealt with by others, as the context shows. *Ibid.*, l. 128.

[13] *Ibid.*, II, 3, 268 f.   [14] *Ibid.*, II, 3, 285–288.

[15] "Scribendi recte." *Ibid.*, l. 309.

origin, must animate one's treatment of the matter in hand.[1]
Thus instructed and guided in technique and in methods of
interpretation of material, the writer should look to life itself
for his pattern, observing character and reflecting it in vivid
speech.[2] The aim of poetry is to combine pleasure and
profit.[3] Structural qualities are more important than surface finish; yet without distinction all else is in vain; though
the world needs poetry, it has no need of mediocre poetry.[4]
Don't write *invita Minerva*; and don't be in a hurry to pub-
lish a poem, — wait for nine years.[5]

Even these few citations from the *Ars Poetica* may serve
to show Horace in the rôle of a conservative Roman, following the didactic tradition and conscious of the social importance of poetry; it is for this reason that he seeks to evoke
a worthy national drama, and binds the poet of the future,
inspired though he must be to deserve the name of poet, to
the painstaking working out of his share in something
greater than himself. Poetry is an honorable craft, not the

---

[1] A. Y. Campbell (*Horace*, pp. 250 f.) regards this advice as an example
of the "philosophic Fallacy, the intellectualistic conception of Morals," seeking to construct drama from sophistry plus realism; for examples, see Euripides, Seneca (*par excellence*), and Shaw. On the whole, yes; at any rate, we have
here the old quarrel between philosophy and poetry. (See W. C. Greene,
"Plato's View of Poetry," *H. S. C. P.*, XXIX [1918].) No one will doubt
that poetic expression suffers when it is "sicklied o'er with the pale cast of
thought." But are poets to trust wholly to their feelings? Have Aeschylus
and Sophocles and Shakspere satisfied our moral sense in the same degree
that they have aroused our feelings? Horace has not said the last word; but
he has thrown the problem into relief; in the *Odes* and in the first book of the
Epistles he proves in practice that thought and concrete imagery may help
each other.

[2] Epist. II, 3, 317 f.:
"Respicere exemplar vitae morumque iubebo
Doctum imitatorem et vivas hinc ducere voces."

[3] *Ibid.*, II, 3, 343 f.:
"Omne tulit punctum qui miscuit utile dulci
Lectorem delectando pariterque monendo."

[4] *Ibid.*, II, 3, 372 f.

[5] "Nonum . . . prematur in annum." *Ibid.*, l. 388.

impromptu expression of unschooled genius; that way lies
madness.[1] Such, at least, is the classical creed of Horace, a
perpetual challenge to the romantics of all ages. If it does
not account for all poetry (and who can really account for
poetry at all?), if it all but ignores the emotional and moral
depths of tragedy, if it failed to produce Roman drama, it
serves as a useful interrogation point in the consideration of
poetry. And it is not a little significant to follow the career
of Horace in his "Conversations"; after early experiments
in imitation of Lucilius, and satirical comments on life and
manners, he passes on to self-expression and a practical philosophy of mild individualism and of good sense, only to
return to the setting forth of a literary canon of propriety
and good sense. Consistent, however, Horace is, for his
ultimate appeal in literary standards, as in the conduct of
life, is to Nature, the great exemplar; literary traditions are
but economies within her all-embracing realm, and the world
of the poet is but a province subject to her laws.[2]

In his literary epistles Horace may seem to have strayed
far from the original conception of *satura*; yet he still plays
the rôle of the sophisticated *censor morum*, albeit in a special
field. Later writers, in very different veins, continue the
tradition. Phaedrus, with his versified beast-fables and racy
anecdotes, moralizes social situations; Petronius, in his
prose-and-verse picaresque romance, combines with his

---

[1] *Epist.* II, 3, 472.

[2] R. K. Hack, in "The Doctrine of Literary Forms" (*H. S. C. P.*, XXVII,
1916, 1–65), argues that the practice of Horace is at variance with his theory,
and that he is really an individualist. It is indeed true that literature, as he
criticizes it, is too departmentalized, and that he deals more with its forms
than with its spirit. G. C. Fiske, however, meets at least part of Hack's
argument, explaining "Horace's free and independent acceptance of the laws
of the genre of satire" and of the other forms in the *Odes* and *Epodes* as the
"expression of *common human* experience" (*Lucilius and Horace*, pp. 470–
471). As to the practice of Horace, see pp. 521–536 and 576–594; and
A. Y. Campbell, *Horace*, esp. pp. 192–232.

fantastic tale of adventure a realistic satire on upstart freed-man life. Also in Menippean (prose-and-verse) form is the audacious skit on the Apotheosis (or "Pumpkinification") of the deified Claudius that has come down under the name of Seneca, an unkind, doubtless unfair, but none the less brilliantly comic affair. The *gauche*, stupid, freeman-managed Claudius is seeking admission to Olympus; the gods meet in council to debate his claims. One of them speaks in his favor:

"I move then that from to-day the blessed Claudius be a god, with all the rights conferred on any previous creation, a minute to this effect being added to Ovid's *Metamorphoses*." Opinion was greatly divided, but it began to look as if Claudius would win. For one thing, Hercules saw that it was his own iron that was in the fire, and trotted to and fro, saying, "Now you mustn't stick at it; it means a great deal to me, and some time when you want something done I'll pay you back; one hand washes the other." Then the blessed Augustus rose, when his turn came to speak, and made a fine speech. "I call you to witness, gentlemen, that from the moment I became a god I have never spoken a word. I always mind my own business. But I can no longer hide my feelings or contain my anger, which my sense of decency makes all the greater. Was it for this that I made peace on land and sea? Did I end the civil wars and give Rome a constitution and fine buildings only in order that, — really, gentlemen, I don't know what to say: words are inadequate to express my disgust. I must fall back on eloquent Messala's *mot*, 'I blush to be an emperor.'" [1]

After the publication of such a satire, what wonder that some years later the blunt emperor Vespasian, who had throughout his reign refused divine honors, felt moved on his death-bed to remark drily, "Alas, I think I am becoming a god!" [2]

---

[1] *Apocolocyntosis*, 9, 10.   [2] Suetonius, *Vespasian*, 23.

Diatribe in the strict sense characterizes the slender volume of young Persius, who died in 62 A.D., at the age of twenty-eight. Of noble Etruscan lineage, able, trained in Stoic doctrine, surrounded by distinguished friends and doting "sisters and aunts and cousins," Persius addresses himself conscientiously to the task of castigating vice, of which he knows little, with an Etruscan flair for minutiae, in Latin of brilliant and willful obscurity. It is a literary exercise pure and simple; the unexceptionable moral purpose may attract those whom the sensational style does not repel; the more than Meredithian or Browningesque verbal contortions require elaborate commentary. The thread of thought is always there, however: Persius castigates now the shameless seekers for literary popularity, the product of a corrupt age; now the mercenary wickedness or the folly of most prayers; or again those sluggards who ignore or forget the claims of (Stoic) philosophy, or who aim at popularity rather than at self-knowledge; once more he contrasts the freedom won by philosophy with the slavery of the vulgar, or discourses on the advantages of moderation in the use of wealth. Snobbish, bookish, involved, Persius can nevertheless see what is under his nose and can reproduce it vividly in detached scenes, if not in larger imaginative pictures. Once in a while, too, he can strike out a memorable line: "Live with yourself, and you will learn how scanty is your moral furniture." It is not the fault of Persius if this line is, as Gildersleeve calls it, "one of the most threadbare quotations from Latin poetry." [1]

A tone of moral earnestness is the last thing to be expected of Martial; yet he, too, belongs in a sense in the tradition of

---

[1] "Tecum habita: noris quam sit tibi curta supellex." Persius, *Sat.*, IV, 52. See B. L. Gildersleeve, *ad loc.*; the same editor elsewhere calls Persius "a sensational preacher" (pp. xxvi, xxxiv).

Roman satire. Not to debate unprofitable questions of literary boundaries, it is at least obvious that an inscription, an "epigram" in the strict sense, and other brief elegiac poems, as written by the Greeks, tended to be "pointed," whether pathetic or witty; the funerary inscriptions of Simonides, and many of the poems of the Greek Anthology and of Callimachus have one or the other quality. Catullus, though first of all a lyric poet, gives vent to pungent and satiric effects not merely through the use of the traditionally satirical "limping iambic" metre and the hendecasyllabic that is associated chiefly with the lyric, but often too in elegiac couplets. Sometimes the effect is merely that of playful *vers de société*; sometimes the spirit is one of blasting satire directed against false friends or even against Lesbia.[1] In many ways, and incidentally in his use of the three metres just mentioned, Martial is the direct heir of the satirical bent in Catullus. In an age when the "pointed style" is the greatest asset in a writer, Martial makes his precarious living by the barbs of his wit, flattering and dancing attendance on the mighty. Naturally, in the exploitation of his art, Martial most often chooses as his subject the frailer aspects of society: the fools, the wantons, the parasites, the fortune-hunters. Yet there is no rancor in his attacks, and the objects of his satire are usually given fictitious names; the wit is of a purely intellectual sort, almost devoid of feeling, so that it is hard to feel resentment against even his most heartless jibes. His frequent coarseness, too, so far as it is not merely the licensed, conventional coarseness of Roman satire, is evidence not of any special depravity but rather of his inability to resist the temptation to make a telling epigram, whatever the cost in outspokenness. Like Catullus and like

[1] For the former type, see Catullus, *Carmina*, 9, 12, 13, 14, 22, 26, 53, 84, 86; for the latter, 23, 58, 70, 72, 73, 75, 85, 92.

Herrick, he distinguishes between his verse and his life.[1]
Zest for life and its many facets in the capital, Martial had;
humanity, he says truly, is the predominant flavor of his
page.[2] Probably it is from Martial and his friend the
younger Pliny and (with reservations) from Juvenal that we
gain our truest picture of the daily round of Roman life in
their ages. The variety of his vignettes is surprising. Why
does Gemellus so ardently court ugly Maronilla? She
coughs.[3] It is Martial's own book that Fidentinus recites;
but so badly does he recite it that he makes it his own![4]
Diaulus, once a doctor, is now an undertaker; no change at
all![5] Martial's clothes, he tells well-dressed Zoilus, are
threadbare; yes, but they are his own.[6] Philo swears he
never dines at home; quite true, when not invited out, he
starves at home.[7] Martial is hard up, Regulus; he must sell
off some of your gifts; will you buy?[8] So slow a barber is
Eutrapelus that while he goes over the cheeks of Lupercus,
his client's beard grows again.[9] Chloe, the wretch, set up
over the graves of her seven husbands the words, "Chloe's
work"; what could be franker?[10] Of such a sort are a few
among Martial's briefer epigrams that lose least by losing
the neatness of his versification. Perhaps Tom Brown's well-
known version of another, somewhat unfairly applied to the
excellent Bishop Fell of Oxford, is as good as its original:

> I do not love thee, Doctor Fell,
> The reason why I cannot tell:
> But this I know and know full well,
> I do not love thee, Doctor Fell.[11]

[1] Catullus, 16; Martial, I, 4, 8; Herrick, end of *Hesperides*: "Jocund his
Muse was, but his life was chast."
[2] "Hominem pagina nostra sapit." Martial, X, 4, 10.
[3] (And doubtless will soon die, — and leave him her fortune.)   Martial,
I, 10.   [4] I, 38.   [5] I, 47.   [6] II, 58.
[7] V, 47.   [8] VII, 16.   [9] VII, 83.   [10] IX, 15.
[11] I, 22; obviously indebted to the couplet of Catullus (85), "Odi et amo"
(cf. p. 479).

Nevertheless, Martial can use his wit with less devastating effect. Bachelor though he remains, he shows a tenderness for childhood. To a schoolmaster he addresses a poem bidding him spare his childish throng during the dog-days, and lay aside his rod: "in summer if lads keep well, they are learning enough." [1] To his own parents in the Lower World he commends the little slave-girl Erotion, dead when not quite six years old, lest she shudder at the dark shades and great Cerberus; may she play in their presence, and lisp his name; and may the earth, he prays, lie lightly on her tender bones, as her step on earth was ever light. [2] Martial strikes the epic note in a quatrain on the death of Arria: "Believe me," says the heroic wife, drawing the blade from her bosom and extending it to her husband, "the wound that I have made hurts me not; it is the wound that thou art about to make that hurts me." [3] A genial, indolent philosophy of life pervades Martial's enumeration of "the things that make life blessed:"

> An income left, not earned by toil;
> Some acres of a kindly soil;
> The pot unfailing on the fire;
> No lawsuits; seldom town attire;
> Health; strength with grace; a peaceful mind;
> Shrewdness with honesty combined;
> Plain living; equal friends and free;
> Evenings of temperate gaiety;
> A wife discreet, yet blithe and bright;
> Sound slumber, that lends wings to night.
> With all thy heart embrace thy lot,
> Wish not for death and fear it not. [4]

Something of this quiet life Martial enjoyed after his hand-to-mouth years in Rome, when he returned to his native

[1] Martial, X, 62. [2] V, 34.
[3] I, 13; cf. p. 94.
[4] X, 47, tr. Goldwin Smith.

town in Spain, Pliny paying the travelling expenses. While his friends must still walk the steep streets of Rome, and dressed in the "sweaty" toga go court the mighty, he can lazily turn rustic again in Bilbilis; can sleep late mornings, making up for the lost sleep of thirty years in Rome; no need for the toga, but whatever garment hangs on yon broken chair will serve; there's a fine heap of oak wood on the hearth, and a pot on the fire; the bailiff serves out rations to the close-cropped slave-boys. "Sic me vivere, sic iuvat perire."[1] Wit, good nature, and something more, an absolute freedom from cant (the *candor* that his friend Pliny perhaps admired the more because he himself lacked it), these qualities make Martial a very agreeable companion for an idle hour.[2]

Martial's formula for avoiding heartaches (along with joy, to be sure) is never to give one's heart away.[3] That is the secret of Martial's comic art, too; he views life as an intellectual, keenly aware of its incongruities, but not really caring greatly. Whether Juvenal was primarily a moralist or chiefly a rhetorician might well be debated. He says bluntly that it is indignation at the vice of the age that calls forth his verses.[4] Yet he seems to have lived through Domitian's reign of terror without publishing a satire, and it is under the good emperors Trajan and Hadrian that he undertakes to lash the town; it rather looks as if his pent-up rage is being spent in flogging a dead dog. Not that Rome or the Romans have suddenly improved so far that satire is now pointless; vice unfortunately is perennial, and instances that are no longer of timely interest may serve to point the moral of a

[1] XII, 18.
[2] See further K. F. Smith, *Martial the Epigrammatist*, and the essay on Martial by G. Boissier in *Tacitus and Other Roman Studies*.
[3] Martial, XII, 34, 8–11.
[4] Juvenal, I, 79.

poet whose theme is universal, and whose wrath therefore borrows from epic something of the grand style. Perhaps Juvenal is a moralist, after all; at any rate, his satire attempts to hold the mirror up to life, now tacitly and now explicitly contrasting it with an ideal standard, depraved Rome with the unspoiled country,[1] Catiline and his ilk with Cicero and Marius.[2] Yet this satirist, for all his sustained invective, betrays no sense of humor; for him folly is vice, and vice evokes ranting anger, not laughter. He has more of Swift than of Johnson in his nature, even if it is Johnson who has best reproduced in English some of the effect of his satires, — of the third in "London," of the tenth in "The Vanity of Human Wishes."

The two satires of Juvenal just mentioned happen to illustrate the two main types of his work. In the first nine satires he recalls more the miscellaneous character of the earlier *satura*, with its loose framework and its detached scenes. Dialogue he hardly essays, and though his personages are vigorously drawn we do not feel that we really know them or that they act of their own accord; puppets they remain. "Whatever mankind does, its prayers, fears, wraths, pleasures, joys, runnings to and fro, make up the hodgepodge of my book."[3] Such indeed is the impression that one gains from a reading of the third satire. Umbricius has determined to leave Rome and take up his abode at Cumae; Juvenal is sorry to lose him, but can only applaud his purpose. The Bay of Naples is so charming, Rome so distressing with its fires, falling houses, and poets reciting even in summer. Just outside the Porta Capena, near the grove of Egeria, now sadly vulgarized, Umbricius soliloquizes. Rome is no place for an honest man; only rascals can prosper

---

[1] *Ibid.*, III, 171–231. [2] *Ibid.*, VIII, 231–253.
[3] Juvenal, I, 85 f.

there; the city is full of hungry Greeklings and the dregs of the Orient, clever, conscienceless creatures; nothing is valued at Rome but wealth, and poverty is become ridiculous; it is only in country towns that one is safe from the dangers of the metropolis and can live a wholesome life. Such is the complaint that Juvenal puts in the mouth of Umbricius; the interest, however, is less in the thought, which is now a commonplace, than in the realistic details, the homely touches that give life to his descriptions of narrow, noisy streets, of humble, decaying quarters of the city, of dripping aqueduct, of the poor man in his garret, to the night scenes, presenting the hurly-burly of nocturnal traffic, and footpads' attacks, and the great man in scarlet cloak passing through the streets with his long retinue of torch-bearers. Is it only because they are not condemned to live there that modern tourists go far to see the quaintness of ancient but dirty little Italian towns, and enjoy the contrasts of grandeur and rusticity in many parts of Rome itself? Can it be that even Juvenal does not utterly despise Rome, and finds despite himself a certain pleasure in describing what he professes to scorn?

The last seven satires still deal with commonplaces, but like Horace's *Epistles* they are less dramatic, and more in the vein of moral essays with a literary background. Thus Juvenal attacks extravagance, legacy-hunting, and perjury. The tenth satire, already mentioned as Johnson's model, is a long and vehement attack on vain ambition. How few men know their own good, and how foolishly most men pray! The very granting of their prayers is often their undoing; wealth and power bring jealousy and ruin, as witness Sejanus, and Crassus, Pompey, and Caesar! Eloquence, too, is a deceptive boon; happier had Cicero been if his bragging verses about his consulate had been his worst folly, and De-

mosthenes if he had stuck to his father's anvil. As for the
spoils of war, many have ruined themselves and their countries in the pursuit of them. Hannibal, Alexander, Xerxes,
the world could not hold; but how pitiful they seem in defeat and in death! "Give me long life, Jupiter, give me
many years." Yes, and you will suffer the repulsive in-
firmities and the indignities of old age; you will outlive your
happiness, — like Nestor, and Priam, like Marius and Pompey. Even beauty is often a fatal gift. Are men, then, to
pray for nothing? Ah, no; but it is wisest to let the gods bestow what they think best. Still one may pray for a "mens
sana in corpore sano," for courage and freedom from passion;
in fact for the very things that one can bestow on oneself,
finding through virtue the path to a tranquil life.[1] Except
the dignified conclusion, there is not much in this satire, or
in any of the satires, that is not marked by overstatement of
a kind that sober second thought would modify or refute: it
is keyed too high, it is all shouting. But in its way it is effective, and Juvenal has the Roman gift for the telling, sometimes paradoxical phrase. "Integrity is praised, — and goes
shivering." [2] What folly "in the pursuit of mere living to
lose all that makes life worth living!" [3] "To your son you
owe the greatest respect."[4] The pauperized Roman people
now cares for nothing but "panem et circenses." [5]

Indignation or gentle smile, which is the more effective?
Both have had their vogue, not only in the later Roman
period, when the satiric tradition penetrated all manner of
writing from history to theology, but also in modern times.
It is well to know how to be angry on occasion, and the

---

[1] Cf. Horace, *Epist.* I, 18, 104–112, quoted on p. 450.
[2] "Probitas laudatur et alget." I, 74.
[3] " Propter vitam vivendi perdere causas." VIII, 84.
[4] "Maxima debetur puero reverentia." XIV, 47.
[5] X, 81.

world sometimes needs a draught of vinegar. But common
scolds achieve nothing. We read Lucilius with some little
interest; Persius with a bewildered, grudging attentiveness;
Martial with unfailing amusement, but not too much at a
sitting; Juvenal with admiration tempered by annoyance.
Horace we welcome as a familiar friend, the more so because
he smiles not only at us but with us, and includes himself
among the objects of his quizzical satire.

3. NATURE, HUMANITY, AND THE POET'S WORLD

> Fies nobilium tu quoque fontium
> me dicente cavis impositam ilicem
> saxis, unde loquaces
> lymphae desiliunt tuae.
>
> Horace, *Odes* III, 13, 13-16.

As the Romans went about their tasks on the farm, or
passed up and down their country roads, the beauty of Italy
was spread before their eyes.[1] Blue mountain range, snow-
crowned in winter, rich plain cropped by flock and herd and
threaded by gliding river, trim garden-plot, Mediterranean
of peacock blue and green; crisp day of the north wind, grey
sultry day of the African sirocco; green meadows freshened
by winter rains, sudden glory of the spring, parched brown
summer fields and hills; golden dawns, flushed sunsets, and
nights of stars: — what did the Romans make of it all?
First of all they valued the land itself as the source of the
farmer's livelihood. Shepherds and tillers of fields they were
in their earliest days: Cincinnatus, the hero of the plough,
remained their idol; if Rome absorbed thousands of countrymen, farming rather than industry continued to be the foundation of Rome's economy, and patricians by preference or

---

[1] Cf. pp. 3-10.

under compulsion kept their capital invested in land.[1] As a matter of fact they generally gave a good deal of personal attention to their estates, leaving detailed supervision to their bailiffs; the elder Cato and Varro both wrote treatises on farming for the guidance of landlords. The speakers in Varro's work are introduced as standing in a temple of Tellus (Mother Earth), examining a map of Italy on the wall. "You who have travelled over many lands," cries one, "have you ever seen any more richly cultivated land than Italy? . . . What spelt shall I compare to the Campanian? What wheat to the Apulian? Is not Italy planted with trees, so that the whole of it seems an orchard?"[2] The practical interest in Nature's bounty and patriotic pride in Italy come first. Nor is the long and splendid panegyric on the glories of Italy which forms the first climax of the second book of the *Georgics*[3] devoted so much to the beauties of the land (though the poet lingers over the lakes and streams and seas) as to its richness in grain and vine and olive, in white herd and flock, in metal, and in men, together with their crag-piled towns and harbor-walls. And although primitive Romans looked with awe on dark groves as the abode of *numina*,[4] it was not till they came into contact with Greek mythology that Roman poets easily thought of woods and springs as inhabited by gods and nymphs in human form.

After Rome became crowded and noisy, well-to-do Romans valued their country estates more and more as an escape from the "noise and wealth and smoke of Rome,"[5] and, in the last years of the Republic, from sordidness and

---

[1] Cf. pp. 207 f.
[2] Varro, *De Re Rust.* I, 2, 3–6.
[3] Virgil, *Georg.* II, 136–176.
[4] Cf. p. 307.
[5] "Fumum et opes strepitumque Romae." Horace, *Odes* III, 29, 12. Cf. W. W. Fowler, *Social Life at Rome in the Age of Cicero*, pp. 243–247.

civil war. Some, like Cicero and the younger Pliny, were fortunate enough to own several villas in the hills or by the sea. These are less productive estates, and their owners' delight in them is the symptom of a more sophisticated age; it is the pleasure of playing at being a country squire, the joy in cooling breezes, tranquil nights, and the spectacle of smiling nature. It is partly conditioned by the very contrast with city life, which true countrymen born and bred can hardly know, and it is not incompatible with a fondness for the sociabilities of city life, as Horace shows. In fact, the Roman's appreciation of nature is almost always an appreciation of an agreeable setting for human life, — an Italian garden, orderly, disciplined, bringing forth vegetables among its flowers and trees, with perhaps a view of a well-composed landscape from its *belvedere*; wild nature unreclaimed for human uses hardly interests them. Trees they love, in order to enjoy in their shade a *siesta* or a repast beside a brook; [1] flowers they welcome, especially when twined in chaplets or garlands for banquets and religious festivals; they not only plant them in their gardens but paint them on the walls of their houses. Peaceful rivers, smiling lakes, and resounding, tumbling waterfalls form a pleasant feature in a landscape; wooded mountains form a good background, but are in themselves rather dreadful, and tempt few Romans to climb them. The seashore attracts the Romans, when the sea is calm and the sun shines; it is good to look upon, and most of Cicero's villas are situated on the Latin and the Campanian coast. As for sailing the sea, that is quite another matter; the sea is treacherous, a barrier rather than a highway, [2] which few beside Catullus would tempt for pleasure. In a

---

[1] Lucretius, II, 29; Horace, *Odes* II, 3, 9 ff.

[2] Horace, *Odes* I, 3; the attitude is conventional, if exploited here with irony.

country in which volcanic activity, hot springs, gaseous vapors, and natural caves are abundant, — sure tokens of proximity to the Lower World, — the Romans naturally interest themselves in these dread phenomena, whether rationally or imaginatively. Yet even the Roman poets, true lovers of nature though many of them are, with many a fresh and individual way of dealing with its various aspects, resemble the Greek poets on the whole in an important particular. They seldom invoke the magic of words to describe nature without relating it to human interests; still more rarely do they merge themselves mystically in the vast processes of a personified Nature.

The mingling of nature with humanity meets us perhaps first in a fragment of one of the early Roman poets, Accius: ". . . perchance before Dawn, the harbinger of blazing rays, when from sleep they wake the horned oxen and drive them afield to cleave with the plough the red, dew-sprinkled soil, and to break into sods the yielding tilth." [1] But there is little here beyond a pleasing bit of country sentiment. Catullus, preoccupied chiefly with the human scene, is nevertheless not insensitive to the more tender or even to the grander aspects of external nature: the balmy spring breezes, felt in Bithynia, awaken his eagerness to wander; his yacht threads the island-jewelled Aegean; he rejoices, on his homecoming, in his own Sirmio, the gem of all islands and isthmuses, above the laughing waves of Lake Garda.[2] But of actual description there is hardly a word. When he does conjure up an image of nature, it is as a setting: we see Ariadne standing on the weed-strewn shore of Dia, oblivious of the waves at her feet, gazing at the flying ship of her false lover Theseus;[3] we see Attis, on the Phrygian strand, at

[1] From the *Oenomaus* of Accius (170–86 B.C.), lines 493–496 (Ribbeck).
[2] Catullus, *Carmina*, 46, 4, and 31.   [3] *Ibid.*, 64, 52–70.

dawn, looking ruefully across the vast seas toward his deserted home in Greece, and the power of the wilderness behind him is felt chiefly because of his forlorn state.[1] The delightful little picture of the calm morning sea, gradually ruffled by gentle breezes and moving more and more as the wind rises, is introduced as a comparison with the progressive leave-taking of the guests at a wedding.[2] Catullus loves flowers, but they appear in his poems chiefly in the form of similes: the bride Vinia, in one of the marriage songs, is "beautiful as the myrtle that the Hamadryads tend," or "the hyacinth in the pied garden of a rich lord"; she is "radiant as the white feverfew or the yellow poppy"; she is bound to her husband "like the clinging ivy that twines about its tree." [3] In the other marriage song the maidens liken the unwedded girl to the secluded flower in a walled garden, nurtured by breeze and sun and shower, and sought by many a lad and girl.[4] Catullus' own love for Lesbia, mortally wounded by her heartless infidelity, he likens to "the flower on the edge of a field that has been touched by a passing plough." [5]

Lucretius, whose theme is "Nature," has, to be sure, a watchful eye for the details of landscape and of natural processes, and surprises us at times by the accuracy of his observations. They all tend, however, to illustrate some tremendous generalization; for the unique gift of Lucretius is his conception of the unity amid the variety of Nature. He deals with the vast order of the cosmos, with the celestial regions of the world: "the sun and the moon rolling through the heavens, the moon, and day and night, and the stern con-

---

[1] *Ibid.*, 63, 39–49.
[2] *Ibid.*, 64, 276–277.
[3] Catullus, *Carmina*, 61, 21–25; 91–93; 192–195; 33–35.
[4] *Ibid.*, 62, 39–42.
[5] *Ibid.*, 11, 21–24. Cf. p. 480.

stellations of night, the night-wandering torches of heaven and flying flames, clouds and sun and rain and snow, winds, lightnings and hail, and the rapid roar and mighty murmur of their menacings."[1] These inspire in him "a kind of god-like delight and awe."[2] There are times when Nature has a kindly aspect, and her creative powers can be personified under the name of Venus. Thus his exordium hails her, invoking her aid in unfolding the secrets of Nature:

Mother of the race of Aeneas, delight of men and gods, fostering Venus, who beneath the gliding stars of heaven dost fill with life the ship-bearing sea and the lands that bring forth crops; since through thee every kind of living thing is conceived and comes to behold the light of the sun; from thee, goddess, the winds and the clouds of heaven flee, and from thy coming; for thee the daedal earth sends forth her sweet flowers, for thee the levels of the sea smile and the sky grown calm shines with light wide-poured. For as soon as the face of spring is revealed and the fruitful breath of the west wind, unloosed, gains strength, first the birds of the air, goddess, proclaim thee and thy coming, their hearts thrilled by thy power; then the cattle frisk wildly over the glad pastures and swim the rapid streams; so each, captivated by thy charm, follows thee eagerly wherever thou leadest. Yea, and amid seas and mountains and rushing rivers and the leafy homes of birds and green fields thou dost instil fond love into the breasts of all, so that all, after their kind, may be eager to continue their race.[3]

Yet Nature's designs are too far-flung to pay any special regard to humanity, to say nothing of the individual man; no poet is further than Lucretius from suggesting that Nature sympathizes with our joys and sorrows. That does not prevent him from devoting himself with eager curiosity to the magnificent spectacle of the heavens, the splendor

---

[1] Lucretius, *De Rerum Natura* V, 1188–1193.
[2] *Ibid.*, III, 28.
[3] Lucretius, I, 1–20; cf. p. 376.

of clouds and storms,[1] and the pageant of the seasons.[2] But man must sink his petty interests in the larger world if he is to keep on good terms with it and enjoy it.

With Virgil, humanity once more becomes a partner with nature. The *Bucolics* are not merely "Landscapes with Figures"; they are poems of country life and sentiment, interfused now and again with allegory, in which the landscape serves to provide charm and atmosphere. Borrowings of commonplaces from Theocritus, hints from the Mantuan landscape, and much of his own, Virgil essays to fuse. For indeed these are no merely Italian shepherds who pipe and sing, no mere shadows of Theocritean shepherds; these Arcadians inhabit no restricted province, least of all the bleak uplands of the real Arcadia. Tityrus piping under the spreading beech tree, distracted Corydon singing in the noon heat, wise, tipsy Silenus bound with garlands of flowers, the love-sick girl seeking by magic rites to recall her Daphnis, — these belong to no one time or place. The farm in the region "where the hills begin to drop away and with gentle slope to fall to the water's edge and the ancient beech trees with broken tops,"[3] may belong to the Mantuan district; but it would be futile to confine to a single setting such a universal scene as closes the first Bucolic: "and now in the distance smoke rises from the cottage roofs, and lengthening shadows fall from the high mountains."[4] Figures and landscape alike are, above all, the creations of the poet's fancy, a visionary world that is as old as time and as young as ourselves. "Nunc formosissimus annus," "now the year is in its most beauteous prime,"[5] and "Omnia vincit amor," "'Tis love that makes the world go round,"[6] are its maxims. "Here

---

[1] Lucretius, IV, 133–142; VI, 189–203; 256–261.
[2] *Ibid.*, V, 737–747. [3] Virgil, *Bucolics* IX, 7–9.
[4] *Ibid.*, I, 83–84. [5] *Ibid.*, III, 57.
[6] *Ibid.*, X, 69.

amid well-known streams and sacred springs wilt thou take
delight of the cool shade; here, as ever, the neighboring willow hedge, whose flowers the bees of Hybla feed upon, with
soft humming will oft invite thee to fall asleep; there, beneath yon crag shall the leaf-gatherer sing to the breeze;
nor meanwhile shall the hoarse wood-pigeons, thy pets,
cease to moan, nor the turtle dove on the tall elm." [1] Well
does Virgil paint the scene in the days of his youth, and well
does he send the song of the vine-dresser on into the future,
for it is a perennial song, such as one may hear to-day in
Italy or in America or wherever youth is happy and un-
trammelled. And well does Virgil describe, through the lips
of two of his shepherds, the effect of his own music. "Such
is thy song to us, divine poet, as sleep in the grass to the
weary, and as the quenching of one's thirst in summer heat
at a gushing stream of sweet water." So one shepherd; and
the other, anon: "Not so much delights me the whisper of
the rising south wind, nor the shores pounded by the surf,
nor the streams down-flowing amid rocky vales." [2]

Every sensitive reader of the *Georgics* realizes that although the professed purpose of the poem is didactic, the
work is much more than a handbook of farm-lore. On almost every page Virgil betrays his interest in all the natural
processes that bind man to the beloved land, and a passion
for the *divini gloria ruris*, for mother earth, for mother Italy.
It is not mere information about the economy of farming
and its value in healing the world of civil war that he aspires
to give, but a suggestion of the possible influence of an active
country life on a sensitive soul. An active life, for instead of
the *Omnia vincit amor* of the shepherd of the *Bucolics* we
read "Labor omnia vicit | improbus et duris urgens in rebus

---

[1] *Ibid.*, I, 54–59.
[2] *Ibid.*, V, 47–49, 82–84.

egestas"; [1] it is hard work that accomplishes everything, and necessity is the mother of invention. Nature, then, is not wholly kindly, nor on the other hand is she merely "red of tooth and claw"; she is bountiful, but not interested in those who will not help themselves. She must therefore be conquered by incessant toil. Yet labor has its indefeasible dignity; happiest of men, did they but know it, are the farmers. Far from the din of arms the earth gives them a livelihood; no luxury, to be sure, is theirs, but rather carefree repose, a life that knows no guile, leisure on broad acres, the delights of caves and lakes and cool vales; theirs are lowing oxen, pleasant naps under trees, good hunting, sturdy, frugal sons, true religion, and respect for age; when Justice fled from earth, her last footsteps were set among such as these. Their plough brings plenty the year through, — grain, olives, fruit, and wine. Their homes are pure; their sweet children hang about their kisses; on holidays they make sport and feast. Such was the life of the old Sabines, of Romulus, that made Rome the fairest of things; such was the golden age of Saturn.[2]

Moreover, the poet of the *Georgics*, who has paid homage to Lucretius only to challenge him,[3] "finds his delight in the countryside, the streams that water the valleys, the woods"; he loves to linger over the beauties of the natural world.[4] As a "landscape-lover" Virgil has not perhaps quite Homer's zest of the eye, his wonder at the commonplace, his gift for composing with his eye on the object with no *arrière pensée*. Yet Virgil excels in his appeal to the ear; in conveying to us the gush and the roar of waters, the rustle of trees, the buzzing of bees, the stillness of night. Let your sheep graze

[1] Virgil, *Georg.* I, 146 f.
[2] *Ibid.*, II, 458–474, 513–540.
[3] Cf. p. 352.
[4] "Singula dum capti circumvectamur amore." *Georg.* III, 285.

toward sunset, he bids, "when the cool evening star tempers
the air, and the moon, now dewy, refreshes the glades, and
the shore rings with the kingfisher's note, the thicket with
the finch." [1] He marks how a sea-wave begins to whiten off-
shore, and gather its curving mass, rolling landward upon
the rocks with a mighty roar and tumbling mountainously,
while the dark sand seethes in the undertow. [2] He describes
the signs that betoken an impending storm, and the hissing,
moaning tumult of the storm itself. [3] He watches with
amused sympathy the activities of bird and bee, of flock and
herd; his deeper sympathy goes out to the cattle who are
victims of the plague. He views particular scenes, moreover,
as does Wordsworth, as containing in little a whole world of
feeling and association; seen through his magic casement a
view has three or even four dimensions. A ploughing scene, a
tree with engrafted, alien fruit, the swarming of bees, is for
him something almost sacred, to be regarded with a sort of
mystical wonder. Not merely the external beauty and
symmetry of nature but her expression, — the phases of
weather and seasons and hourly changes, the beauties that
cannot be itemized, — have for him a haunting appeal. But
to describe nature on her own account, apart from human
associations, like a few late Roman poets and many Romantic poets, to regard her as a moral teacher, like writers as
different as the Stoics and Wordsworth, Virgil declines.
Like the ancients generally, he tends to keep nature subordinate to humanity; and if he wishes to regard nature as

---

[1] *Ibid.*, III, 336–338.

[2] *Ibid.*, III, 237–241; cf. *Aen.* XI, 624–628. In the last two lines of the lat-
ter passage, note how the repeated use of the letter *r* suggests the grinding of
pebbles, and the letter *l* suggests the liquid ebbing of the wave:
"Nunc rapidus retro atque aestu revoluta resorbens
Saxa fugit, litusque vado labente relinquit."
See further Sir A. Geikie, *The Love of Nature Among the Romans*, pp. 313–321.

[3] *Georg.* I, 316–334.

revealing a divine purpose, he personifies her powers. Mountains, for example, for all their grandeur, have no secrets to tell him of "something far more deeply interfused." [1] On the other hand, granted that humanity is "the proper study of mankind," as humanists from Socrates down have insisted,[2] Virgil goes further than most ancients in finding man at his best when living nearest to nature as a part of the greater whole. Even the individual's struggles and sorrows and perplexities, that seem riddles if isolated, gain dignity and beauty, if not illumination, when viewed against the greater mystery of all creation.[3] The struggles of the bees mirror the comic struggle, the battle of the bulls echoes even as high as Olympus, the storm that makes havoc of men's crops is but an incident in the inscrutable universal process that both creates and destroys. But why do the gods permit these things? Neither Virgil nor we can say.

To study nature dispassionately, then, is not enough; nor is it easy to love her in her angrier and more careless moods. Humanity comes first in our interests and affections. No wonder that the poets have ever sought to build a smaller world within the greater world, a *multum in parvo* that should compensate for their surrender of the greater world. Or else, bolder than the rest of men, they have sought to shatter "this sorry scheme of things . . . and then remould it nearer to the heart's desire." The simplest procedure is to forego the larger world and to let one's affections and dreams play about a single beloved spot, — one's birthplace or one's home. Cicero waxes almost lyrical when he writes of the gorges and the island of his native Arpinum; [4] Catullus

---

[1] Cf. E. E. Sikes, "Nature in Latin Poets," in *Roman Poetry*, pp. 106–152, esp. pp. 127–152.   [2] Plato, *Phaedrus*, 230b–c.

[3] Cf. R. S. Conway, "Man and Nature in the Augustan Poets," in *New Studies of a Great Inheritance*, esp. pp. 35–43.

[4] Cicero, *De Leg.* II, 1, 1–3.

at Sirmio, Horace at the Sabine Farm, Pliny at his Tuscan villa embowered in trees and shrubs, or at his Laurentine villa a stone's throw from the sea, live to themselves and their intimate friends.[1] The more reticent Virgil tells us less of his home, yet the north-Italian who lived much in central and southern Italy did not forget Mantua or the Italian Lakes.[2] But here we see how easily the poet passes from personal affection to patriotic pride in the natural resources and the historic traditions of his country. Not only the famous panegyric [3] but the whole of the *Georgics* may be read, if one pleases, as a long glorification of Italy, the favored land of plenty which Nature has permitted to exist between frozen north and parched south; but the climax of the panegyric comes when the Saturnian land is hailed not only as mother of crops but as mother of men. The *Aeneid* is of course still more obviously a patriotic poem, if it is also a poem of universal experience; yet it is interesting to note that despite its Italian character, particularly in the last eight books, Virgil is sparing in his pictures of Italian landscape. The reason is perhaps clear; the poet has already painted, in the *Georgics*, his canvas of Italy, and now he is more interested, even in the parts of the seventh book that call the muster-roll of the peoples of Italy, in suggesting the heroic origins and traditions of the men than in picturing their country.[4]

The world that Virgil is now creating is grandly conceived. It essays to trace an unbroken continuity between the age of the Trojan War and the age of Augustus, thus

---

[1] For passages bearing on these and other places with personal or historic associations, see F. E. Sabin, *Classical Associations of Places in Italy* (Madison, Wis., 1921).

[2] Cf. *Georg.* II, 159 f.; 198 f.; III, 10–15; *Aen.* X, 198–206.

[3] *Georg.* II, 136–176.

[4] See further J. W. Mackail, "Virgil's Italy," in *Classical Studies* (New York, 1926).

throwing the glamor of heroism and romance and antiquity over the present; the golden age of myth is in process of realization in the Roman destiny. How artfully Virgil makes fictitious genealogy, Roman legend and history, feigned prophecy, and evasive allegory contribute to his undertaking is common knowledge; and we have already considered some of the religious and philosophic phases of the poem.[1] What concerns us here is that Virgil is not writing history, not recording facts, but creating a new world from fragments of the dissolving world about him. Neither nature as it is nor humanity as it is suffices for this Prospero who by the sheer beauty and magic of words has called into being something new, something, moreover, that had its effect on the Rome of his day, that outlived the empire, and that in its own right lives on as a bond of union among men of different nations. The poet's world is a world that can be shared.

What is more, poets have a way of wishing to share even their most private world. Catullus had presumably the ability to become a successful soldier or lawyer or even statesman, if he played his cards correctly; he became instead the avowed lover of Clodia, wife of Metellus, — the "Lesbia" who first welcomed the young poet and then broke his heart. His best poems are called forth by the joys and the sorrows of this experience; some are addressed directly to her (or to her pet sparrow), others are self-communings, still others, though written to friends, revolve about his affection for Lesbia. None of his love-poems, unless perhaps the fifty-first,[2] are "Sonnets from the Portuguese"; for he was con-

---

[1] Pp. 349–356,
[2] Actually a free translation from Sappho, in the original metre, and possibly the first poem ever sent by Catullus to Clodia. The name "Lesbia" is the metrical equivalent of Clodia, and was suggested by the name of Sappho's island-home; the continued use of the name for Clodia would preserve associations with this passionate song of the outspoken poetess.

scious of no reason for veiling his experience under even so
flimsy a concealment. How many of the Lesbia poems, the
bitter as well as the tender, Catullus included in the little
book that he dedicated, "such as it is," to his friend the historian Nepos, hoping that it might last "more than one century," we shall never know; but we may feel fairly sure that
no excess of delicacy would have prevented him from publishing any poems about Lesbia that he had thus far written. When we read them, therefore, it is as though he had
left the door ajar and we were overhearing the spontaneous
outpourings of his heart. Never mind if there are eaves-
droppers; he would not sing differently in any case. And
what strikes the eavesdropper is the utter obliviousness of
Catullus to everything outside of the little world in which he
is completely absorbed, a world consisting of simply Lesbia
and himself; moral conventions, the claims of Metellus, the
Roman arena of war and politics and business touch him not
at all, external nature and friends and foes only in relation to
his ardors. The one exception is the death of the brother
"with whom is buried [his] joy"; to him Catullus recurs
again and again.[1]

His very blindness to all externals enables Catullus to
magnify his world till it fills the universe, and he encom-
passes every mood of longing, of exultation, of remorse and
despair in addressing himself to it. To Lesbia's sparrow,
wistful tenderness and envy of its privileges;[2] after its death,
a luxuriance of mourning on the dainty darling whose loss
has brought tears to the eyes of his "*puella*."[3] To Lesbia
herself, the exhortation to live and love, regardless of what
the censorious may say: "suns may set and rise again; for us,
when once the brief light of day has set, there is but one per-

---

[1] Catullus, *Carmina*, 65, 5–14, 68a, 19–26, 68b, 51–100, 101.
[2] *Ibid.*, 2.   [3] *Ibid.*, 3.

petual night to be slept through." What then? Kisses by
hundreds, by thousands, — but without counting them, lest
the envious know their number, and do harm.[1] How many,
then? Well, if Lesbia must know, as many as the sands of
the sea (and the poet keeps her waiting with a mischievously
pedantic bit of obscure geographical lore); or as many as the
stars that look down in the stilly night on the stolen sweets
of love.[2]

Doubts and disillusionment intervene. To Lesbia offering
"love," he sends grave acknowledgment and a prayer for
"friendship";[3] for he knows that "what a woman says to
her eager lover had best be writ on the wind or in running
water."[4] Yet another offer of reconciliation causes him to
exult from the bottom of his heart.[5] Gratitude to the friend,
Allius, at whose house Catullus first met his "light," Lesbia,
finds expression in the outer layers of a curiously involved
elegy;[6] at its core he addresses the lost brother at whose
tomb he was to write his hopeless "Hail and Farewell."[7]
Lesbia, he now realizes, is no more his alone; he seeks to
minimize her "rare lapses," to remember only the happiness
of the past.[8] Not "base" is her present infidelity, but "oh,
the pity of it!"[9] For the false friends who have abused his
confidence, he has nothing but bitter contempt; all the
world's ungrateful, even he who but lately claimed him as his
best friend, he cries in verses of deliberate harshness.[10] As for
Lesbia: "I hate and love; perchance you ask me why? I
know not; I only feel that it is so, and I am in torture."[11]

---

[1] Catullus, *Carmina*, 5.   [2] *Ibid.*, 7.
[3] *Ibid.*, 109.   [4] *Ibid.*, 70.
[5] *Ibid.*, 107.   [6] *Ibid.*, 68b.
[7] *Ibid.*, 101; see translation, p. 115.
[8] *Ibid.*, 68a, 95–108; cf. 8, 3–8.
[9] *Ibid.*, 68b, 27–30.
[10] *Ibid.*, 73. The last line is surely a *versus duriusculus*; cf. Pliny, *Epist.* I,
16, 5.   [11] Catullus, *Carmina*, 85.

Now that he knows her for what she is, esteem is out of the question; but he cannot help loving her, whatever she does.[1] He tortures himself with irresolution; seeking to forget Lesbia, he finds, just as his will is all but steeled against her, that his imagination is still playing with her image.

Poor Catullus, cease to play the fool, and count as lost what thou seest is lost. Upon a time brightly shone the suns on thee, when thou didst flit to and fro at the beck and call of the girl who was loved as none will ever be loved. Then many a prank was played, as was thy desire, and she was nothing loth; brightly indeed the suns shone on thee. Now she is loth; and do thou, too, desire no more, nor be weak-willed and pursue her who shuns thee, nor live wretchedly; but steel thy will, be obdurate. — Farewell, girl; now is Catullus obdurate, nor will he seek thee nor woo thee against thy will. Ah, but thou wilt grieve when thou art wooed no more. Out upon thee, what sort of life now lies before thee? Who will now visit thee? In whose eyes wilt thou seem fair? Whom wilt thou now love? Whose wilt thou be called? Whom wilt thou kiss, whose lips bite? O Catullus, be obdurate![2]

It is too late for Lesbia to send fair-spoken messengers to recall him; with elaborate irony, and significantly using for the second and last time the Sapphic strophe,[3] he thanks them for their devotion, and bids them take back a few words, not good ones, to his "girl"; let her live and fare well with her countless lovers, and give no further glance toward his love, slain as it is by her, like the flower by the passing plough. The world of Catullus has shrunk to the dimensions of his own breast, — or was it ever any larger? Be that as it may, the magnificent elegy in which he talks over with himself his plight, the "Litany of a Stricken Soul," as it has been called, is in the grand manner.

---

[1] *Ibid.*, 72 and 75. [2] *Ibid.*, 8.
[3] Cf. p. 477, n. 2.

If there be any happiness in store for one who reckons up his past kindnesses, remembering that he is true-hearted (*pius*) and has kept his faith, nor ever perjured himself in order to deceive, then many a joy awaits thee, Catullus, in the long vista of years, accruing from this thankless love of thine. For all the kindness of word or deed that men can say or do, all this has been said or done by thee; and all has gone for naught, intrusted to an ungrateful heart. Why then torture thyself further? Why not make firm thy will, and withdraw, and cease to be wretched, since the gods would not have thee so? — Ah, but it is hard all at once to lay aside a long-cherished affection. — Yes, it is hard; but this thou must do by one means or another; this is thy one safety, this the goal that must be won, this thou must do whether it be possible or no. — O ye gods, if yours it be to know pity, or if ever ye have brought aid to men on the very verge of death, look upon me in my misery, and if I have lived true-hearted (*si vitam puriter egi*) take from me this wrack and ruin. Ah, what a palsy has crept into the depths of my frame and driven all joy from my heart! No longer do I seek that she should return my affection, or, since that cannot be, that she should care to be chaste: I pray to be well myself and to put away this foul disease. O ye gods, grant me this in return for my devotion (*pietas*).[1]

"All the world loves a lover" and the pretty spectacle of a lover and his lass wholly absorbed in one another; Catullus himself has written their rapturous duet, with half-amused, half-pitying sympathy.[2] But "the course of true love never did run smooth"; surely Catullus would agree. It is too late to chide Catullus, even if we wished to do so, about the folly of that devotion which was for a time his whole world: any matter-of-fact, middle-aged person could have told him that he was headed for unhappiness. But what such a person could not have done is to write lyrics about his own unhappiness that would create happiness. Here again is the magic of words, the anodyne that eased for Catullus his suffering, and

[1] Catullus, *Carmina*, 76.
[2] *Ibid.*, 45.

that makes the pageant of his bleeding heart not painful but delightful to us. For, once more, poetry is not merely a record of experience, even if its roots are in experience; it reaches outside the limits of its creator's immediate environment toward a timeless region. Whatever else tragedy may be, it is pain made beautiful by being thus lifted into a new world, and universalized; the true lyric, too, even if it is, or gives the illusion of being, a personal cry, is the voice of the world. And a poem, or for that matter any significant work of art, is unique, something added to the wealth of the world; there is no transmuting or exchanging it for anything else.

Any poem is moulded more or less by definite though variable circumstances: its theme, the occasion that evoked it, the personality and intent of the poet, his audience, together with its special form and the devices of versification and of figurative language. Absolute poetry, divested of all these elements, cannot exist; the poetry that comes nearest to being "absolute" is that lyric poetry which, without losing its individual flavor, employs concrete images to express emotion of a universal sort while giving the ear as nearly as possible the sensuous pleasure of patterned music unspoiled by intellectual considerations.[1] Catullus at his rare best comes near the ideal; in emotional intensity he leaves nothing to be desired, though his sympathies have a narrow range; he is also adept in controlling the volume of his melody, and in manipulating alliteration and assonance and the echo of words and lines.[2] There is art here; but Catullus

[1] This statement is in all essentials in accord with the discussion of T. Watts-Dunton in his masterly article, "Poetry," in the *Encyclopaedia Britannica*, though he finds "absolute vision" more in drama than in the lyric. His definition runs: "Absolute poetry is the concrete and artistic expression of the human mind in emotional and rhythmical language."

[2] Note, for example, the long sweep of the opening sentences in *Carmina*, 76 and 8; the onomatopoeia of *tunditur unda* in 11, 4; the manipulation of the letters *m* and *f* in 100 (cf. E. E. Sikes, *Roman Poetry*, pp. 261–267); in 8 the

seems to be singing because his heart is full and sing he must. With Horace the case is different; he is master of a wider range of themes, of moods, and of metres than is Catullus, but his emotions are keyed far lower. Though he sings partly for the joy of singing, it is far more for the pleasure and profit of others; for he is conscious of a definite rôle which his gifts and the force of circumstances have called him to play.[1] There is genuine feeling in the *Odes*; but every one of them is a carefully constructed work of art, and the four books of the *Odes* comprise a triumphant elaboration of contrasting ideas, a poet's world built within a real world, inviting the wayfarer to step into its garden close for refuge, for pleasure, for inspiration to carry back into the work-a-day world.

There are many ways of reading the *Odes*. At times one may well let oneself be beguiled by their verbal melody, their genial revelations of the poet's personality, and their easy-going appreciation of the goodness and the brevity of life, without concerning oneself too much about technicalities of any sort. But Horace is not to be regarded merely as a graceful trifler. Even the casual reader cannot but be struck by the fact that the *Odes* reflect the age through which Horace lived, interpreting the great events and ideas in the light of universal experience. It is here that Horace, whose love-poems seem to be only pleasant *vers de société* compared with the intense outcries of Catullus, far outstrips the earlier poet. Like the poets who contribute to the London *Punch*, he plays delightfully with the oddities of human nature; but like them he can also rise nobly to a great occasion and touch our heartstrings. In his earlier years Horace has fought at

---

echo of *obdura* (lines 11, 12, 19) and of line 3 as line 8; in 3 the echo of "passer, deliciae meae puellae" from the preceding poem; in 11 the significant echo of the word *identidem* from 51; in 58, heartbroken echoes from 8 and 5.

[1] Horace, *Odes* IV, 3; III, 4, 1–36.

Philippi for Brutus, and ingloriously lost his shield (thus emulating more than one Greek lyric poet). [1] Presently, he sees in Octavian after all the hope of Rome; but he is anxious for the Ship of State, storm-tossed by the Civil Wars,[2] till the victory of Actium and the death of Cleopatra, noble only in her death, free Rome from the menace of the Orient.[3] Now it is the returning peace and prosperity of the Augustan Age that he celebrates; the Roman arms are carried to distant frontiers. Rome is rising in new splendor, but on that very account the young Romans are the more exhorted to renew the virtues of their fathers, — simplicity, manliness, steadfastness,[4] — for Horace is not impressed by mere material display. So the first three books of the *Odes*, written during something like a decade, were published in 23 B.C. A few years later, as Poet Laureate, he sings rather more perfunctorily the secure blessings of an established order, and praises the imperial dynasty.[5]

Of such weighty themes is Horace the oracular prophet, divinely endowed with the gift of song; but he is a prophet with a difference. Again and again he disclaims any gift for epic, and if he catches himself on the verge of preaching, he darts off obliquely, laughing over his shoulder.[6] He masks his message under traditional Greek forms: a prayer or a hymn to a divinity; an exhortation to a young aristocrat; a casual, friendly letter in lyric measure. His most serious counsels are delivered not in abstract terms but in pictures.

---

[1] Horace, *Odes* II, 7.
[2] *Ibid.*, I, 14; cf. II, 1; I, 2; Epodes 7 and 16.
[3] *Odes* I, 37.
[4] *Ibid.*, III, 1–6.
[5] *Ibid.*, IV, 4; 5; 14; 15; and the *Carmen Saeculare*. Cf. H. Nettleship, "Horace, Life and Poems," in *Essays in Latin Literature*, pp. 143–167; R. S. Conway, "Horace as Poet Laureate," in *New Studies of a Great Inheritance*, pp. 44–65.
[6] Horace, *Odes* I, 6; III, 3, 69–72; II, 1, 37–40.

The secret of Rome's greatness in earlier days was the manly son of a peasant soldier, "trained to till the soil with Sabine hoe and at the bidding of his stern mother to cut and carry in the fire-wood, as the sun shifted the shadows on the mountains and let the yoke drop from the weary oxen, bringing with its departing chariot the friendly time of day."[1] Better still, it was Regulus, who would not let his fellow-countrymen ransom the captured Romans from the Carthaginians; indeed would not let himself, as no better than a captive, kiss his wife and children, and returned from his grieving friends to his foes, though knowing all the while what tortures they had in store for him: "yet not otherwise did he push aside those who sought to hinder him and the people delaying his return than as if he were leaving the wearisome business of his clients when a lawsuit had been decided, and he were taking his way toward the fields of Venafrum or Lacedaemonian Tarentum."[2]

If Horace knows how to convey even serious thoughts with a light touch, he also takes delight in interspersing his book with poems whose chief aim is to give pleasure; and these are doubtless the odes that most instantly win their way to our hearts. The naturally Stoic Roman needs to be shown not only how to act honorably but also how to relax, how to enjoy the art of refined Epicurean living. For him, and for us in our less strenuous moods, Horace celebrates the joys of friendship and conviviality. A birthday, a festival, a friend's visit, a homecoming, or any other occasion, is sufficient excuse for broaching a jar of Massic wine, and prolonging the feast with carefree talk and wit, perchance with the company of Venus and the Graces, till Phoebus routs the stars.[3] Wine, however, must be used in moderation, not with

---

[1] *Ibid.*, III, 6, 37-44.   [2] Horace, *Odes* III, 5, 13-56.
[3] *Ibid.*, III, 21; cf. I, 20; I, 36; III, 8; II, 7; III, 29; IV, 11.

the wild excesses of the barbarians.[1] Bachelor that he is, Horace writes love-poems, or at least refers in the language of gallantry, to a bevy of ladies, — Chloe, Pyrrha, Lyde, Lydia, Phyllis, Lalage, Myrtale, Neaera, Chloris, Cinara, Glycera, Tyndaris, and the nameless "fair mother's fairer daughter." Perhaps there is safety in numbers, and Horace never really gives his heart away, unless possibly to "good Cinara," who died early; he is always thanking his stars that he has escaped the tyranny of some charmer, and dreading the onset of some new love-affair. Hapless the slender lad who now courts Pyrrha, the "auburn-tressed," plain in her neatness; Horace knows better how fickle she is, for he has been shipwrecked in that sea.[2] But whatever persons may be concealed under the pretty Greek names that adorn his verse, they certainly belong to a class of women, frequently foreign-born, in whose society Roman gentlemen often found pleasure but whom they did not dream of marrying. The Roman code, and even the moral reforms of Augustus, tolerated such casual affairs, provided that they did not usurp the place of the legal *matrimonium*. Horace contrasts the fickle lover with the thrice-happy ones whom "an unbreakable bond holds and a love that is torn by no quarrel before life's last day."[3]

For the rest, Horace commends the life devoted to the study and enjoyment of poetry and philosophy, especially if it be spent in some secluded nook in the country. Again and again the *Odes* reflect his own life at the Sabine Farm and his happy, tranquil enjoyment of nature, and impart to his friends the fruits of his impressions and ponderings. What does the poet ask of Apollo, newly enshrined on the Palatine? Not ample grazing-grounds and choice vineyards, not

---

[1] Horace, *Odes* I, 18; I, 27.
[2] *Ibid.*, I, 5; cf. IV, 1; III, 26.   [3] *Ibid.*, I, 13, 17–20.

gold and ivory, but rather simple fare, health, a contented mind, and an old age still not without song.[1] In ad-
versity and in prosperity alike, 'twere best to keep one's
equanimity; for death comes, indifferently, whether one has
lived sadly all one's days or whether one has kept holiday in
some secluded grassy nook, indulging oneself with the best
of Falernian wine. Indeed, why do yon towering pine and
yon white poplar join their hospitable shade, or why does
the fleeting stream fret its quivering way between winding
banks, unless to invite us, while still we may, to enjoy wine
and perfumes and the all-too-brief bloom of the lovely rose?
Better not heap up wealth for the morrow, to be enjoyed by
an heir; Charon's bark is no respecter of persons, and will
sooner or later take us to our eternal exile.[2] Seek not to
know the future; even while we speak, flies grudging time;
carpe diem![3] Let others build palaces resplendent with gold
and ivory and marble, crowding the sea, and driving their
wretched clients from their homes, in their forgetfulness of
the inevitable end of all; Horace is rich enough in his one
dear Sabine Farm, endowed as he is with good faith and a
kindly vein of talent which brings him the respect even of the
mighty.[4] Others are richer, more ambitious; but appetite
and sleep come not so readily to them as to poor rustics who
dwell amid shaded, wind-blown valleys. Why should Horace
wish to exchange his Sabine valley for wealth that would
only bring care?[5] Here he is content to dwell, strolling
about his woods, welcoming his friends, ennobling by his
song the Bandusian spring that provides cool draughts even
during the dog-days for tired oxen and wandering herd;

---

[1] Horace, *Odes* I, 31.
[2] *Ibid.*, II, 3; cf. II, 14.
[3] *Ibid.*, I, 11.
[4] *Ibid.*, II, 18.
[5] *Ibid.*, III, 1, 9–48.

from hollow rocks under an ilex tree leap its prattling waters.[1]

The seasons come and go. Winter casts a snowy garment even on Mount Soracte; trees are heavily laden, and streams stand still under the ice. Pile high the hearth with logs, and broach the Sabine wine, careless of the battling winds and the morrow's worries; now is the time for the young to enjoy the sweetness of love and the dance, the nocturnal *rendezvous*, the merry tell-tale laugh of the girl who hides in a corner and hardly resists when her token is taken from her wrist or finger.[2] Spring returns, with pleasant breezes; fled are the snows, the grasses come back to the meadows, their tresses to the woods; ships are launched again, the cattle leave their stalls, the ploughman his fireside; Venus with the nymphs and Graces leads her dances, Vulcan and the Cyclopes return to their anvils. Yes, the seasons follow in their annual round, and the swift moons repair the losses of the heavens; but as for us, when once we have descended where are the heroes of old, we are but dust and a shade. Pale Death knocks with impartial foot at the huts of the poor and at kings' palaces. Best not hope for immortality, or even for an earthly morrow, but be warned by the flight of time to enjoy the present; nothing can take from us what we have already enjoyed.[3] This note of melancholy, the presentiment of impending death, troubles Horace as often as he is reminded of the flight of time, even by the genial return of spring; it is indeed a weak point in the Epicurean's armor. Even on the death of a beloved friend, the best consolation that he can offer Virgil is the counsel of a Stoical endurance: "'tis hard, but patience helps us to bear what we may not

[1] Horace, *Odes* III, 13. See the Latin, quoted on p. 465.
[2] *Ibid.*, I, 9.
[3] Horace, *Odes* I, 4; IV, 7; cf. IV, 12.

change." [1] Something like immortality, however, may be conferred by song; it rescues mortality from oblivion. Many brave men lived before Agamemnon, but were overwhelmed by unending night, with none to mourn them, because no poet sang their deeds.[2] The poet, too, achieves immortality by reason of his song, and a great part of him escapes the funeral pyre.[3]

True it is that with Horace the art of living and the art of poetry are inseparable; the sage of the Sabine Farm lives now only because his life and thought were embodied once and for all in verse of consummate art. Like the best of Greek lyric poetry, his verse seeks to unite the expression of personal feeling with the treatment of large themes, whether in serious or in playful mood; it says much in a little space, cultivating the allusive, suggestive style, rather than the exhaustive. Though Horace is by no means so ornate and elaborate in his pattern and style as Pindar, he has a similar fondness for calculated effects produced by violent contrasts and abrupt transitions; he likewise disposes of his announced theme briefly or by *praeteritio*, and turns to some more or less loosely related theme, perhaps a myth.[4] It follows that one's enjoyment of an Horatian ode is as complex as the ode itself. Instead of being, like a song of Catullus, the impulsive outcry of a sudden pain or joy, an ode is apt to be a nine-years-pondered affair, the product of study and repeated use of the "file"; yet it sings its way into our hearts, and every word, now that it is there, seems to be the inevitable word in the inevitable place. Each ode comes to us trailing memories of

---

[1] *Ibid.*, I, 24, 19–20.
[2] *Ibid.*, IV, 8; IV, 9.
[3] *Ibid.*, I, 1, 29–36; IV, 3; II, 20; III, 30. Cf. Ennius' epitaph; Ovid, *Metamorph.* XV, 871–879; and Shakspere, Sonnets XVIII, LV, LXIII, and LXXXI (I. Gollancz, London, 1906).
[4] Horace, *Odes*, I, 7; I, 12.

the long tradition of Greek poetry, perhaps evoking a definite original of Alcaeus; yet Horace, like Catullus, prefers to call his lyrics not *Odes* (though this name has been given later to the Horatian collection) but *Carmina*, suggesting the simpler, often liturgical or magical chants of the Italian peasantry of an earlier age. Again, though Horace frequently appears in the rôle of hierophant, setting forth religious mysteries or moral maxims, he seeks to create the illusion that it is only Horace, after all, who on some special occasion is moved to address a particular friend in the manner of a familiar letter.

The diction of the *Odes*, moreover, though in general more elevated than that of prose, has little of the splendor and suggestiveness or variety of the Greek lyric; but in the deft arrangement of words in their most effective positions, juxtaposed or interlocked or far separated, Horace achieves surprising effects of contrast and emphasis, of suspense, and climax. "Clever joiner's work" gives a certain novelty even to well-worn words.[1] The effect is one of good luck, but it came by the use of infinite pains, as Petronius suggested by attributing to Horace the quality of *curiosa felicitas*;[2] his phrases have passed through centuries of quotation into the international currency of educated men. Nor should we overlook the skill with which Horace contrives usually to end an ode on a quiet note, frequently with a picture that lingers in the mind.[3]

The same care that Horace spends on word order and the structure of odes enters into the arrangement of the odes within the books; contrasts of metre and of light with serious

---

[1] "Notum si callida verbum | reddiderit iunctura novum." Horace, *Epist.* II, 3, 47 f. Cf. *Odes* I, 9, 21–22, and I, 37, 25–32, for effective interlocked order; III, 11, 35, "splendide mendax," for oxymoron, or violent contrast.

[2] Petronius, *Satyricon* 118.

[3] Horace, *Odes* I, 14; I, 33. Cf. several of Virgil's Bucolics.

subjects explain most of the arrangements. In the first book, the stirring ode on the death of Cleopatra is followed by the slight final ode picturing the poet drinking in a shaded arbor; in the third book the sequence of six odes on the national morals, all in the Alcaic strophe, is deliberately relieved by the graceful poem that follows, to Asterie; and the playful avowals of the introductory poem of the fourth book are placed before the patriotic odes. The editor of the poems of Catullus attempted similar principles of arrangement, but less successfully; the *Bucolics* of Virgil alternate dialogues with monologues, Italian and Theocritean themes; Tibullus and Propertius, too, are skillful in contrasting their elegies.

In many of the odes the thought is simple; the reader has no doubt "what it is about." But in other cases Horace displays a Pindaric complexity of thought. As in dealing with nature and landscape he prefers the telling epithet, the glancing allusion, the vignette, so in setting forth an idea, perhaps a moral maxim or admonition, he prefers to convey it incidentally, or indirectly, or by means of a Parthian dart discharged over his retreating shoulder. This it is that sometimes mystifies his modern readers, who cannot make out what an ode is "about"; it seems to be about two or three things. Unity of some sort, however, an Horatian ode is sure to have, for all its diversity; and the supplying of an English title for an ode is always a game worth playing. The music of the verse, to begin with, is a smooth gliding stream on which the poet sails his ships. Or, to change the figure, the poet amuses himself with a "modulation" from one key to another.[1] The result, for the reader, is a sense of move-

---

[1] "'Modulations' are a very great part of the secret of the *Odes*." A. Y. Campbell, *Horace*, p. 77; see also pp. 4–7, 68–81, and 192–232, an illuminating discussion.

ment from point to point, with something of the exhilaration of a steeplechase. Instead of rotating about a single point and exhausting it, and us, in the manner of many writers of lyrics, Horace develops one theme by contrasting it with another; he is like a painter who specializes in perspectives and reflected lights. A few examples will illustrate some of his methods.

Simplest and most obvious are the poems in which a contrast seems to occur quite naturally.[1] Thus in the spring poems the delight in the beauty of the year's renewal suggests to Horace that the cycle of man's life, once ended, knows no such renewal; best enjoy the present.[2] The attachment of an unworthy lover to a girl suggests by contrast the unbroken happiness of the well-mated.[3] The single dialogue to be found in the *Odes* (III, 9) follows in balanced quatrains the stages of a lover's quarrel, from disdain to reconciliation; the woman scores at each exchange, and has the last word. The close of the "Regulus ode," [4] after dwelling on the heroism of the general in going back to torture and death, ends on a note of absolute and studied simplicity; the struggle of Regulus is over, now that his mind is made up, and he is going, as it were, to his home: "nothing is here for tears," Horace feels of him, as Milton's Manoah of Samson.

Another of Horace's devices is not so much contrast as the artful if apparently discursive association of ideas, perhaps with a myth to lift the horizon. He chides Lydia for ruining young Sybaris by her love; [5] yet it is really the significantly

---

[1] This might be named "psychological transition" (R. K. Hack, "The Doctrine of Literary Forms," *H. S. C. P.*, XXVII [1916], 36); but there are other forms of transition, to be mentioned presently, not so easily to be explained.

[2] Cf. p. 582.

[3] Horace, *Odes* I, 13; cf. p. 486.

[4] *Ibid.*, III, 5; cf. p. 578, and Campbell, *op. cit.*, p. 226.

[5] Horace, *Odes* I, 8.

named lad, of course, who is the butt of the poem; he has given up all manly sports, — like Achilles, concealed in maiden's dress! The seventh ode of the first book shows, on first reading, so slight a connection between its parts that some ancient critics thought they were two separate poems. The reason, it seems, is that Horace is building a deliberate approach to his theme, which is the consolation of Plancus, a native of Tibur, for having to leave this beautiful spot for military service. The thought runs, then, somewhat as follows: There are many famous and beautiful places in Greece, endeared by historic and literary associations; none, in my mind, vies with Tibur, with its grotto, its headlong Anio, its grove and well-watered orchards. Now rains give place to clear skies; have the good sense, Plancus, to put aside your sadness, and cheer yourself with wine, whether you are in camp or in shady Tibur. That is what Teucer did, of old, on the eve of exile, bidding his companions to be of good cheer, to drive care away with wine; on the morrow they would sail anew the mighty sea. Here is movement, a unity in variety, and subtlety in the introduction of an idea.

A deeper, or a more concealed, irony animates other odes. Why does Horace address Asterie, the "star-bright maid"? [1] Primarily, one gathers, to counsel her against forgetting her absent lover and yielding to the serenades and the wooing of her athletic neighbor, Enipeus. How can he tactfully convey the counsel? By dwelling at length on the temptations to which her own true-hearted Gyges may be exposed, across seas, from a scheming, love-lorn hostess, and by dropping in the counsel to Asterie as an after-thought. Why, in another ode, does the poet address Lyde? [2] As a matter of fact he does not address her at all; but he wishes to convey to her

[1] Horace, *Odes* III, 7.
[2] *Ibid.*, III, 11.

the advice that it is high time that she think of matrimony, skittish filly that she is. So he enlists the aid of Mercury, and of his own lyre, asking what theme can reach
obstinate Lyde's ears; for the lyre has the power to charm
beasts and trees and streams, even Cerberus and the
damned, and among them the daughters of Danaüs. Ah!
Yes, that is the famous tale that Lyde should hear, of those
fifty maidens doomed to a fruitless task in the Lower World
for carrying out their father's bidding and slaying their husbands, — all save that one maiden who, "splendidly men-
dacious," spared her spouse and helped him to escape.
Where is Lyde all this while? Not mentioned in the last half
of the poem, but presumably taking to heart the moral: for
Hypermestra was the only one of the sisters to have descendants and to win glory.

Horace is fond of reminding his readers that he is a poet,
one of the guild of inspired singers who guide and humanize
and glorify even a Periclean or an Augustan age; [1] thus he is
under the special protection from childhood's perils, from
battle, from falling tree, of the Muses [2] and of Mercury and
Faunus.[3] That he bears a charmed life he contrives to convey, tongue in cheek, to his waggish friend Aristius Fuscus.[4]
He begins, in the solemn, oracular style, with two quatrains
(which have been sung at funerals) on the safety of the up-
right man whose life is pure; he needs no weapons, though he
travel to the ends of the earth. Horace knows, for while he
was wandering, carefree and unarmed, beyond the bounds
of his farm, singing of his Lalage, a wolf, a portentous beast,
fled from him. Now where'er he go, to the barren, clouded
steppes, or to the scorched desert, ever will he love the

[1] Cf. Horace, *Odes* III, 4.
[2] *Ibid.*, III, 3, 9–36; IV, 3.
[3] *Ibid.*, II, 7, 9–16; II, 17, 27–30.
[4] *Ibid.*, I, 22.

sweetly laughing, sweetly prattling Lalage. Perhaps there are people who think it worth while to discuss whether or not Horace actually met a wolf; such persons will not see in the poem any passing fling at his own pretensions as lover and poet. And they will miss other examples of Horatian irony. They will see in the first ode of the second book only an elaborate compliment to Pollio, not noting that the reference to his projected history of the Civil Wars is only a spring-board for Horace's own rapid but powerful sketch of this tragic period of wicked bloodshed. Horace at last suddenly rebukes his wayward Muse, to be sure, for attempting so lamentable a theme; but the thing has been done, done by Horace, and the poet has not reverted to Pollio. One more example of Horatian art must suffice, the second ode of the fourth book. Horace seems to be responding to the request of Iullus Antonius that he write a Pindaric ode to celebrate the return of Augustus from campaigns in Germany. Rivalry with the swan, Pindar, he responds, is doomed to failure; and he is only a bee. Antonius will better sing of the future triumph of Augustus and his Golden Age, though Horace will gladly add his voice to the chorus of citizens; and when Antonius performs his lordly sacrifice of twenty cattle, Horace will offer a young calf, now feeding beside its mother, with a snowy crescent on its brow like a three-days' moon, elsewhere tawny. Pindar, the swan; Horace, the bee; Antonius, Augustus triumphant, Horace in the throng, the twenty cattle, the calf: all these come into the sweep of sixty verses, — evasive, elusive verses, that rise and just graze the main theme and fall away to a quiet conclusion.

Horace sometimes succeeds precisely because he recognizes his limitations. Within his limitations, however, Horace comes very near perfection, and is unique among Latin lyric poets in having brought to Rome the inspiration of the Greek lyric poetry of the classical rather than of the Alexandrine age. In this sense his claims to originality and his prophecies of immortality [1] may be easily forgiven, because true, even if his boasting offends modern taste. Classical his odes are, organically sound and whole, with a wide outlook on life, and therefore more within the understanding and appreciation of mature readers than of the young. They stand the test of repeated readings. [2]

Other Roman poets we must dismiss more briefly. Catullus is doubtless the greatest, though not the last, of a group of Roman poets who use the elegiac or the lyric form to express the joys and the sorrows of the lover's experience. His was a real experience; it hardly matters for us that most of the others are drawing much on their imagination or on the literary conventions of gallantry. Who really cares, so long as he reads poetry for pleasure, whether the Dark Lady of the Sonnets was a real person? The Delia of Tibullus and the Cynthia of Propertius stand, as a matter of fact, for real people; Ovid's Corinna is probably a fiction. The result, if we are looking not for "human documents" but for poetry, and if we allow for differences of temperament, is not surprisingly different. Differences there are, of course. Tibullus, gentle soul, writes wistfully of his dreams of happiness with Delia, — of "love in a cottage," as it were: a mad dream, as he comes to realize. [3] Lover of peace, he contrasts its blessings with the curses of war. [4] Full of the sentiment of the Italian countryside, he is at his best when he pictures a rustic festival. [5] Propertius, by contrast, lives over intensely the great moments in his love for Cynthia. She was the first

---

[1] Cf. p. 489.

[2] See further J. W. Mackail, "The Odes of Horace," in *Classical Studies* (New York, 1926).

[3] Tibullus I, 5, 19–20.

[4] *Ibid.*, I, 10.   [5] *Ibid.*, II, 1.

to "take" him with her eyes,[1] those great blazing eyes;[2] he
lingers over her birthday,[3] an illness of hers,[4] a dream that
she has drowned,[5] her appearance to him after her death.[6]
Yet he can also air his learning like the Greek Alexandrine
poets (he hopes to be the Roman Callimachus), and deal
with Roman legends; he can even pen the imaginary words
of a noble Roman matron to her family after her death, a
poem that has deservedly been called the "Queen of Elegies." [7]

The facile, brilliant Ovid defies all classification. He begins (in the *Amores*) as a poet of love: not, like Catullus and
Tibullus and Propertius, as the singer of his personal joys
and sorrows, for these poets took life too seriously, but, more
like Horace (yet without the broader outlook of Horace), as
the chronicler of the comedy of love's vicissitudes, sometimes conjuring up Corinna to help him. A soldier he is, but
in Cupid's camp; this is his whole world. He tries his hand at
writing the letters that unhappy ladies of times past, deserted by their lovers, might have sent them, if they had
learned from the rhetoricians how to pen *suasoriae* (the
Heroides). Pathetic, romantic, sometimes tragic they are,
but Ovid's wit is forever breaking in and transforming these
mythical heroines into the sophisticated inhabitants of modern Rome. Yes, modern: to be old-fashioned, to be rustic, is
the unpardonable sin, as Ovid will presently remark.[8] The
Heroides are interpretations, in the light of the newest psy-
chology, of perennial traits in human nature. And now come

---

[1] Propertius, I, 1.   [2] *Ibid.*, II, 3, 14.
[3] *Ibid.*, III, 10.   [4] *Ibid.*, II, 28.
[5] *Ibid.*, II, 26.   [6] *Ibid.*, IV, 7.
[7] *Ibid.*, IV, 11.
[8] Ovid, *Ars Amatoria*, III, 121–122: "Prisca iuvant alios, ego me nunc
denique natum | Gratulor: haec artes moribus apta meis." Cf. *Med. Fac.*
11–30.

the cynical, didactic treatises on the *Art of Love* and the *Remedy for Love*, — scholarly advice to Don Juan on the arts of seduction, with an equivocal palinode as a sequel, — shrewd, witty, and by no means immoral, for the simple reason that in Ovid's world there are no morals to bother about! His world enlarges in the *Metamorphoses*, and exhibits the kaleidescopic changes that have taken place from the Creation to the Augustan age. Protean as had been the earlier poems in their magical handling of old themes and characters, the *Metamorphoses* is the very incarnation of the spirit of change. Perfect master of the hexameter and of narrative style, of transition, of atmospheric effects, Ovid is most himself when deftly producing these transformations of personality and mood. There are gods aplenty, mostly Don Juans at that, and getting as little reverence as they deserve; heroes, treated chiefly in burlesque; mortals, varied as life. Perhaps the mortals come off best; only they afford such pictures of devotion as Cephalus and as Baucis and Philemon. But again we shall miss the charm of Ovid's magic if we raise irrelevant questions of morals; this is a world of bright fancies and images, an irridescent phantasmagoria, all viewed with detached enjoyment, with the intellect rather than with strong emotion. Wit, imagination, genial high spirits, love of the strange, ability to paint good backgrounds of landscape, if not a real love of nature, are in Ovid's quiver: not satire, save rarely. The satirist is apt to write with an ulterior aim; Ovid only to amuse. With Ovid a poem, like a game or a jest, is its own sufficient reason for being. It was no deep religious conviction that moved him to embark next on his didactic poem on the Pagan Year (the *Fasti*), recording month by month the festivals of the Calendar and the myths suggested by them; it was simply his fondness for the beauty of liturgy and his realization that here was another opportunity to exercise his narrative art in a series of dissolving views, scene melting into scene. Not choice but the emperor's will gave him his final themes. The reason for his exile to bleak Tomi, on the Black Sea, we shall never fully know: "a poem and an error" is his twofold explanation.[1] The poem was doubtless the *Art of Love*, published some eight years before, but now regarded by Augustus in his zeal for moral reform as in some measure responsible for the laxness and recent scandals in his own household; even the *Metamorphoses*, moreover, was not altogether calculated to assist the official Puritanism. The error may have involved the witnessing of some indiscretion in the imperial household. Beginning with poems of considerable spirit and interest, often of dignity, the *Tristia* reflects the gradual breaking down of the poet's spirit in his lengthening exile; hope, protestations of innocence and defenses of his "*carmen*," and appeals for clemency give place to complaints about the desolateness of his abode and about his illnesses: elegies, laments, these are in the strict sense. Most of his technical skill remains (though he likes to think not); but the themes are threadbare. In the *Epistles from the Pontus*, darkness has still further closed in on Ovid's bright world; and the longed-for reprieve never comes. Only his devotion to his loyal wife in Rome relieves the gloom.

Wit, *ingenium*, the lambent play of a quick intellect about all things, grave or gay, was Ovid's forte and Ovid's foible. "Ingenio perii Naso poeta meo," he wished to have carved on his gravestone, well knowing that his wit was his undoing.[2] It was also his making: one marvels at his dexterity, as one marvels at a clever figure-skater, not because he travels from one point to another, but because of the grace and

---

[1] "Carmen et error." *Tristia* II, 207; not a *scelus*, he protests, IV, 10, 90.
[2] *Tristia* III, 3, 74.

infinite variety of his evolutions. Ovid's verse is the cul-
mination of a century of Roman experiment in the poetry of
learning and artifice. He knows all the arts of playing with a
theme, varying it by comparison or contrast, by allusion and
oblique glances in other directions. He knows as well as
Horace how to pretend not to deal with a theme, and in the
very act how to say all that he wishes to say about it. *Praeteritio* is indeed the essential Roman device in this period.
And Ovid is the supreme master of transition, — or should
we say, rather, of metamorphosis? Just as he is in danger of
exhausting a theme, presto, and he is off on a new trail,
smiling at our surprise! His versification we almost take for
granted, forgetting how deftly he has mastered all the old
tricks, adding a few of his own and giving the elegiac couplet
its final and standard form. His verse, if it rarely soars to the
heights, never falls below a distinguished level.

Ovid's appeal is far more to the intellect than to the emotions, — a doubtful quality for a poet, and there are those
who would deny him the name of poet. Even if we seek amid
the scintillations of his wit for a positive vein of thought, a
"criticism" of life in the sense in which Chaucer and Shakspere and even Pope give us "criticism," we are for the most
part doomed to disappointment, despite many a shrewd
moral precept. His irony could have existed only in a sophisticated age, when the gods, the myths, the cults, and the
social traditions that he exploited were no longer taken seriously, but were still capable of being used for decorative
purposes, as beautiful survivals of quaint antiquity, or for
the purposes of sheer amusement. Decorative art and
amusement and irony have their place; unfortunately for
Ovid, Augustus was very much in earnest, for political reasons, that the old religion should be taken seriously and that
the old traditions of family life should be revived and puri-

fied. As censor of public morals, imbued with the Roman genius, as statesman in a critical moment in the history of the world, Augustus was undoubtedly correct, if literary censors are ever correct, in sending Ovid to Tomi. There are those whom Ovid could not corrupt; there are those whom strong meat offends or corrupts; statesmen do not like to take chances. It is a pity; for there is only one Ovid. Nor is it clear that Roman society was actually purified by his being exiled.

Nevertheless, Ovid helps us to realize the change that has come over Roman poetry. Even when reading the passionate outpourings of Catullus we feel that we are dealing with a poet who is far from subduing himself to the national *mores* and the expression of social ideals. Virgil, on the other hand, who though apparently himself never scathed by Cupid's arrows was yet able to give the world a Dido, subordinated her, and Aeneas, to the Fatum Romanum. But in the verses of gentle, peace-loving Tibullus and the unabashed love poems of Propertius there is something not Roman, not quite manly. And Ovid gives the impression of one who is without conscience and who glories in his emancipation. With these poets, love, or at least love-affairs imaginary or real, social pleasures, and in general the entertaining surface of life, instead of being subordinated to grave social considerations, are the whole of life; and poetry is no longer the medium of a homogeneous society, but is the pastime of a sophisticated group. No doubt the newly won security of the Pax Augusta enabled men to breathe more freely,[1] to indulge in decorative arts as a luxury, to regard poetry as a world apart, an escape from the humdrum actualities of daily life. But whereas hitherto, during the Civil Wars, a few had indeed toyed with verse as an escape from

---

[1] Horace, *Odes* III, 14.

sterner realities, now the poetry of escape has become the usual thing. Nor is it without significance that whereas Catullus and his contemporaries (the *neoterici* whom Cicero regarded with some contempt) and perhaps even the youthful Virgil found models chiefly in the Greek poets of the Alexandrine age, — clever, labored, learned, eccentric, sentimental, pretty, trivial, in their several ways, — Virgil in his maturity and Horace in the main returned to the Greek poets of the great age, from Homer to Euripides, and were none the less Roman in spirit. But Ovid and the elegiac poets reverted once more to Alexandrianism. Now it cannot be said that their verse lacks charm; some readers may feel that the most appealing portions of Roman poetry are precisely those that are least Roman, — the cry of Italic (or Celtic?) Catullus and Virgil in their more "romantic" or individualistic moods; the precious fragments of the poetess Sulpicia, head over heels in love with her Corinthus, whose poems are preserved with those of Tibullus; and in a later period the richly cadenced music of the *Pervigilium Veneris*, and the pleasantly descriptive *Mosella* of Ausonius. Yet one need not depreciate any of these in order to realize that they are lesser luminaries, inevitably obscured by the greater light of the poets who united the imaginative splendor of Greek poetry with Italic emotional power, under the controlling influence of the Roman will to achieve: Lucretius, Virgil in the *Georgics* and the *Aeneid*, Horace in the *Odes*.

The reason for this difference rests on the fundamental character of classical art. The aim of classical art is to present life as far as possible with an appreciation of the true relations of its parts, in recognition of what is central and normal in human nature and its environment. To this end it tries to profit by previous experience, and curbs and disciplines or satirizes eccentricities however arresting. Standards it regards therefore not as external or arbitrary but as deduced from the constants in human nature. Unlike romantic art, it is unfriendly to the crude, the infantile, the irresponsible, the merely spontaneous, though finding room within its limits for great variety of subject and form and mood. Unlike its pale shadow, neo-classic art, it is not satisfied by mechanical imitations of existing works; rather it encourages a masterful use of such works as preparation for the creation of new and living works, unique yet with a universal quality. Dido is more than the sum-total of her literary ingredients, and she is alive to-day. The Sabine Farm exists wherever we happen to find it, or make it. Classical art, once more, tends to be objective, a little reticent, somewhat chary of exploiting the idiosyncrasies of its practitioners; it eschews posturings and rhetoric and lets the facts speak for themselves. It strives at all costs for organic or architectonic unity in the work of art; surface qualities are not enough. It is aristocratic, not in any snobbish sense, but because it presents, for the enjoyment of all who will make the necessary effort of mind and imagination, the fruits of long ages of creation, — the best. These standards, which are almost as much ethical as aesthetic, may be tested by reference to the really classical works of various literatures, in contrast with others that are less worthy of the name. They suggest, for example, where Catullus succeeds and where he fails; why Ovid is inferior to Chaucer; why sentimental and cynical literature both pall in the end; why Virgil and Horace tower above the poets of the Silver Age.

Poetry continued to be written in the Silver Age; too much, in fact, for social conditions favored the literary ambition of mediocrities. We hear of lyrics; but practically none have survived, unless some of the *Silvae* of Statius may be so described. Satire and epigram flourished, as we have seen:[1] Seneca and others wrote tragedy; Lucan, Statius, and Silius Italicus wrote epic. But their work was vitiated by two fatal defects: they were mechanical imitators of earlier writers, and they lacked the architectonic power. Seneca's plays, intended to be read rather than acted, do not convince one that he has mastered Euripides only in order to produce something independent, that his characters are the result of observation and the creative imagination, that the action is finding words because it must. His plots savor of antiquarianism, his speeches of the library; it is all clever rhetoric distributed among lay figures. Good scenes there are, and powerful speeches of real beauty, and the choral lyrics are sometimes instinct with subdued splendor;[2] but these do not redeem plays that are structurally weak. Even less are the straggling, ill-proportioned epics of the Silver Age redeemed by excellent purple patches. Their authors had the power, perhaps, to negotiate successfully the requirements of the miniature epic, the *epyllion*; but the larger form escaped from their control, and their imitations of previous epics are often barefaced plagiarisms. Lucan may have intended to make Cato Uticensis the real hero of his (unfinished) epic on the Civil Wars; but it is Caesar and Pompey who actually divide the honors. One is tempted to contrast with the *Pharsalia* Shakspere's *Julius Caesar*, which is so deliberately controlled that it is Caesar who dominates the action even to the end, though he has been murdered in the third act. Statius had real talent for the cameo, as he proves in a number of the improvisations in the *Silvae*; but he was so ill-advised as to essay also the monumental, and an epic cannot be built of mosaic.

The result is that though the Silver Age tempts one but

---

[1] Pp. 455–465.
[2] E.g., *Hercules Furens*, 1063 ff.

little to embark upon the reading of its long poems, it invites the maker of anthologies to cull its flowers: scenes, episodes, speeches, and occasional poems. If one enjoys repartee, Seneca provides it;[1] Lucan gives almost satirical character studies,[2] graphic episodes,[3] and bitter political invective.[4] There is pleasant country sentiment even in Petronius, if his are some fragments attributed to him: an autumn picture, in which is fulfilled "all the promise of the year"; delight in a rustic cottage amid orchards and vineyards and well-watered gardens; deep satisfaction in a life by the sea. "I have lived my life to the full; nor can grudging fortune ever rob me of that which her favoring breeze once gave me."[5] Ovid's facility in painting effective landscape backgrounds, with a little of Virgil's pathos, seems now and then to meet us in the *Argonautica* of Valerius Flaccus.[6] Cleverness without sincerity or depth of feeling is all that one can attribute to most of the *Silvae* of Statius; but perfection of a kind he attains in his oft-quoted "Invocation to Sleep."

> "What sin was mine, sweet, silent boy-god, Sleep,
>   Or what, poor sufferer, have I left undone,
>   That I should lack thy guerdon, I alone?
>   Quiet are the brawling streams: the shuddering deep
>   Sinks, and the rounded mountains feign to sleep.
>   The high seas slumber pillowed on Earth's breast;
>   All flocks and birds and beasts are stilled in rest,

---

[1] E.g., *Agamemnon*, 306 ff., with striking verbal give and take; quoted in H. E. Butler, *Post-Augustan Poetry*, p. 56. For the convenience of the reader, most of the following citations have also been made from Butler's work, the best of its scope.

[2] E.g. of Pompey, *Pharsalia* I, 129–143; of Caesar, *ibid.*, I, 143–157; of Cato, *ibid.*, II, 380–391; quoted in Butler, *op. cit.*, pp. 106–110.

[3] E.g. Caesar at the Rubicon, *Pharsalia* I, 185 ff.; Pompey's dream, *ibid.*, VII, 7; Butler, pp. 102–113.

[4] E.g. *Pharsalia* VII, 638 ff.; Butler, p. 119.

[5] Baehrens, *Poetae Latini Minores* IV, 75; 81; 84; Butler, pp. 136–137.

[6] See passages quoted by Butler, pp. 192–200.

But my sad eyes their nightly vigil keep.
O! if beneath the night some happier swain,
Entwined in loving arms, refuse thy boon
In wanton happiness, — come hither soon,
Come hither, Sleep. Let happier mortals gain
The full embrace of thy soft angel wing:
But touch me with thy wand, or hovering
Above mine eyelids sweep me with thy train." [1]

This is the sort of thing that Shakspere might have done in an effortless moment; it is the supreme effort of Statius. There is an almost indefinable difference, after all, between the minor work of a great, or classical, poet, and the best work of a minor poet. Even *juvenilia* sometimes betray inklings of a great poet-to-be, while even a fine poem of a minor poet, like this of Statius, is apt to betray a "literary" surface, rather than to open a window on the poet's world. Yet how fortunate would Statius have been if all the rest of his work had perished, and we had conjectured that the "Invocation to Sleep" was his average level!

The two hundred years that followed the Silver Age produced no poetry of any real importance; triviality and imitativeness mark what remains of the verse of this period. The fourth century witnessed a poetic revival, but still chiefly in minor *genres* and still largely imitative. One notes a curious fondness for the composition of epitaphs and of other epigrammatic pieces, frequently in the vein of the Greek Anthology. The world of these poets is, except in one respect, the library. The exception is a new and highly interesting concern with the description of landscape. Tiberianus describes with tender sentiment a lush spring scene,

---

[1] Statius, *Silvae*, V, 4; Butler, p. 234; *Oxford Book of Latin Verse*, No. 262. The translation is by W. H. Fyfe, printed in *Oxford Book of Latin Verse*, p. 495; it compresses in its eighth line seven lines of the original. It is followed, pp. 496–500, by seven English poems on sleep, all but one being sonnets.

in which stream and flowers, birds and trees and fragrances,
fill the mind, and humanity is all but forgotten.[1] Asmenius
and Claudian and others rehearse the joys of one whose days
are spent in a garden,[2] while the Gaul Ausonius, elsewhere
an elegant eclectic, enumerates in one poem the beauties of
his beloved river, the Mosella.[3] Here humanity and nature
are once more mated. But their most beautiful marriage is
in the poem of an unknown genius, the *Pervigilium Veneris.*
"To-morrow shall the loveless love, and the lover, too, shall
love to-morrow. Spring is new; now spring is singing; in
spring the earth is reborn; in spring do loves find loving
hearts, in spring the birds mate, and the woodland loosens
her tresses under nuptial showers." So the poem begins, and
celebrates the eve of Venus' festival [4] and her universal reign
over all nature and over the hearts of men, till the poet cries
out in his own behalf: "the swallow sings in the poplar's
shade, so that you must needs think it is not her sister's
plight that she sings, but love. . . . She sings, and I am
silent. When shall my spring come? When may I, like the
swallow, no longer be still?" Again and again the first line is
echoed as a refrain, a liturgical refrain perhaps, invoking the
aid of Venus, as in the earliest days of charms, yet surely
giving presage of the secular refrains of mediaeval verse
forms. "Cras amet qui numquam amavit, quique amavit
cras amet!" The very cadence of the trochaic line carries
us forward to the favorite rhythms of Christian hymnody,

---

[1] *Oxford Book of Latin Verse,* No. 315; translation in E. E. Sikes, *Roman Poetry,* p. 133.

[2] *Oxford Book of Latin Verse,* No. 354 and No. 368, the latter with two translations; also translated in Sikes, *op. cit.,* p. 131.

[3] Ed. R. Peiper, 1886, No. X; ed. C. Schenkel, 1883, No. XVIII. On Ausonius, see further E. K. Rand, "Decimus Magnus Ausonius, the First French Poet," in *Proceedings of the (English) Classical Association,* XXIV (1927).

[4] Cf. Ovid, *Fasti,* IV, 1–162.

or indeed both in thought and in cadence to "Locksley Hall": "In the spring a young man's fancy lightly turns to thoughts of love." [1]

Classical Roman poetry, indeed, had run its course. Having grown from the life of the people, and for some centuries keeping step with the national life, it had found its inspiration more and more elsewhere than in Roman life, and had at last become academic. It was in vain that the Egyptian Claudian, a belated Augustan, sought to revive the grand manner; nothing could be more futile than his attempt to confer dignity on contemporary heroes or princelings by reviving the epic machinery and mythology.[2] And if it is interesting to read the tribute of the Gaul Rutilius Namatianus to the greatness of Rome,[3] one realizes none the less that the greatness has departed: Rutilius is living in the afterglow of a sunset. The Roman poetry still to be written is inspired by other motives and ideas: by Christianity, by the new life of the Middle Ages, by the rediscovery of ancient letters in the Renaissance.

[1] The imaginative setting in which Walter Pater placed the *Pervigilium Veneris* is well known (*Marius the Epicurean*, Part I, Chs. VI and VII). He supposes it to have been composed in the time of M. Aurelius by a youthful poet who had caught one April night the refrain of a popular chorus and who feverishly wove it into his song. Even if, as is probable, the poem belongs to a later century, the magic of words is here at its best. See the edition, with verse translation, by C. C. Clementi (Oxford, 1911); and the text, with prose translation by J. W. Mackail, in the Loeb series (together with Catullus and Tibullus).

[2] E.g. *Oxford Book of Latin Verse*, Nos. 366 and 367.
[3] *Ibid.*, No. 373.

CHAPTER VIII

THE MEANING OF CIVILIZATION

Sic rerum summa novatur
semper, et inter se mortales mutua vivunt.
Augescunt aliae gentes, aliae minuantur,
inque brevi spatio mutantur saecla animantum
et quasi cursores vitai lampada tradunt.

Lucretius II, 75–79.

"THE might of the Roman Empire," wrote the elder
Pliny, "has given unity to the world; all must agree
that human life has benefited, both in the general intercourse
made possible and in the common enjoyment of the blessings of peace." We must indeed agree; and we may add that
the Pax Romana permitted, as did no other empire, the development of organized systems of life and thought which
have influenced all later ages. Though we have not found
space in this book, except occasionally, to trace their influence, the book will have failed of part of its purpose if it
has not caused the reader to wish to investigate the consequences of the achievement of Rome in mediaeval and modern times.[1] Regarded simply in itself, however, this achievement constitutes one of the most notable chapters, and in
one respect the most notable chapter, in the history of
civilization. The Romans were not, to be sure, great inven-
tors in things intellectual and artistic; they were not by
nature speculative; and at first they lacked, as individuals,
the more humane qualities; here they yield precedence to

---

[1] Convenient for this purpose are some of the chapters in *The Legacy of
Rome*, and several of the volumes in the series "Our Debt to Greece and
Rome."

the Greeks. Nor had they the spiritual gifts of many oriental peoples. But they had the gifts necessary to mould for
social use their many borrowings, and to devise the framework of a vast and civilized society.

It may be worth our while, therefore, in a brief epilogue
to inquire into the meaning of the word "civilization," which
seems so well to express the specific achievement of Rome.
We shall not discover any complete definition of civilization;
indeed, we may conclude that civilization has never really
existed, and is only a vague ideal, even a will-o'-the-wisp.
Yet even an unembodied spirit may be worth pursuing; and
after all we have practical reasons for wishing to capture it.
Let us range as freely as we please through ancient and modern times. Remembering that the political and military
frameworks of all empires have suffered change and usually
death, we may ask whether civilization is a source of
strength or of weakness, and whether our modern civilization is likely to endure. Observing the ups and downs of
civilization, the golden ages and the dark ages, we may ask
whether there is such a thing as real or continuous progress,
and how progress is to be recognized or measured. What
causes progress? Is it inevitable, or is it the result of deliberate effort? Can civilized individuals exist in uncivilized nations? Or, on the other hand, is it only individuals and
minorities that can be truly civilized, and is it too much to
hope that nations can ever be civilized?

The English word "civilization," to be sure, is not borrowed from any exactly corresponding Latin word, and is a
late introduction from French into English. Dr. Johnson
would not admit it to his dictionary, preferring the older
word "civility." Both of these words, however, emphasize
the thoroughly Roman idea of social relationships and human qualities implied in citizenship, whether in the Roman

state or in the world at large; nor is it perverse to prefer, for our purpose, our English word to such accepted Latin words as in various ways throw light on the idea. *Humanitas* emphasizes the essential qualities of men as men, in distinction both to beasts and to gods. If it is used not so much of the qualities of the primitive, merely "natural," man as of his more developed descendant, this does not imply that any violence has been done to man's essential nature; on the contrary, the real man is the developed man. But *humanitas*, or "humanism," is really more a Greek than a Roman quality. *Urbanitas* calls attention to the fact that man's intellectual and artistic qualities are most rapidly matured in centres of population, where the friction of minds strikes out ideas, and where ideas travel fast; "urbanity," wit and social tact, is largely a matter of environment. "Culture," with its Latin forebears, means a tilling of the soil, not the addition of a veneer. But these words, again, represent ideas of which Rome has no monopoly. What we call "civilization," also, was not invented by the Romans, and it did not die with them; yet they above all other peoples found in the conception of citizenship and institutions the clue to a practical way of dealing with human nature.

Now it is worth while noting that for us "civilization" implies the result of a process. "To civilize" is an active verb; it suggests making a citizen of one who was not a citizen; a "civilized" people, a "civilized" person, would deserve the epithet by having received some sort of treatment, by having been made to conform to some sort of standard. (We are not concerned for the moment with the question whether the treatment or the standard is good.) Something similar is involved when we speak of a person as "cultivated," or "educated"; it is not the same thing as calling him "intelligent," though he may be both. In all these cases we imply the deliberate development of people for definite ends, with all the creation of material aids and means that may be necessary; nor is this distinction invalid if we find that the process (for example of education) seems pleasing and valuable quite apart from ulterior objectives. Certainly the Roman civilization, in its discipline and its subordination of personal vagaries to the social need, was animated by controlling purposes. Even Virgil, conscious as he was of weakness and failure in human life, found in the mission of Rome an ideal worthy of heroic effort and self-denial. Whether the Romans generally were as fully aware of the larger objectives and trends of civilization as of the more immediate, we may doubt; they won battles and wars, and built cities and institutions, but failed to perceive the economic dangers of slavery, of the political trend of senatorial government, and of the weakness of the imperial fabric in its later phases; at least they were helpless to cope with these conditions. The present generation is still witnessing the tragic results of a similar check to our own confident and complex civilization; discipline of character and the will to understand and cooperate with other persons and peoples have not kept pace with the multiplication of scientific discoveries and material contrivances.

Nothing in past history gives us the right to suppose that all phases of civilization must necessarily reach maturity together. If we were to ask in what period of Roman history civilization rose to its zenith, our answer must depend on our special interest. It was in the third century B.C. that the Roman character was strongest, political solidarity greatest, democratic development at its height. Literature reached its greatest perfection in the late Republic and the Augustan Age; sculpture and architecture in the first two centuries of the Empire. If we are in search of the period when military security was greatest, we may choose the century from Augustus to Hadrian; material comfort we shall find especially under Hadrian and the Antonines; law was a continuous growth from the times of the early Republic, but was most successfully interpreted and codified in the last century of the Western Empire, and still later in the East. We may well be cautious in appraising our own age and its tendency by any single criterion; the tide of human affairs ebbs and flows unevenly, growth and decay and new growth appear in unsuspected quarters; to attempt to forecast the future in accordance with a theory of predetermined cycles is a bolder undertaking than history will sanction. The gift of Palestine to Rome was all but wholly unexpected. What we may do is to suggest, in view of past events, the probability that certain circumstances will lead to certain results; we may distinguish between inevitable movements and movements that may be controlled by human activities; and we may attempt to set comparative values on various results in order to guide such activities. So we devise tests for estimating the character of a civilization and for measuring progress.[1]

Any definition of civilization would probably recognize that it brings about the economical satisfaction of a number

[1] Sir W. M. Flinders Petrie attempts in *The Revolutions of Civilisation* (London, 1911) to exhibit the alternations of "summers" and "winters" in history and their successive phases, cautiously suggesting geographical and biological causes, but refraining from making more than general forecasts for the future. His chief test in measuring civilization is sculpture. A more thoroughgoing thesis is put forward in the elaborate work of O. Spengler, *Der Untergang des Abendlandes* (2 vols., 6th ed., [Munich, 1920–22]; English translation entitled *The Decline of the West*, 2 vols., 2nd ed. [New York, 1926–28]), which despite much vigorous argument is vitiated by its deterministic assumptions. Of more than passing interest is an article in the *New York Times*, May 24, 1925, "Will Our Civilization Survive," which incorporates answers to a questionnaire, contributed by G. M. Trevelyan, Ernest Barker, Sir W. M. Flinders Petrie, J. Holland Rose, and A. E. Zimmern.

of human needs. Without attempting to rank these needs in any order of absolute value, we may perhaps set them down in several groups. For life itself man needs food, clothing, and shelter, with at least simple provisions for the maintenance of health. For the perpetuation of life and the enlarging of its boundaries, he needs the gifts of love and the home, the tools of language and other means of communication, the social guarantees of protection and law and order. For the enriching of the quality of life, he needs leisure and recreation, and he needs religion and the arts. These needs and their satisfaction are by no means to be separated into compartments; obviously they interact freely. On the other hand, the fullest development of some of them depends on the previous well-being of others, and suffers in times of stress; a plague, an economic maladjustment, a political tyranny, is reflected in a score of ways. Civilization, then, is the attempt to satisfy all these needs with the greatest economy. It is a social undertaking; this means, or should mean, a saving of waste and friction. As members of social groups, moreover, we do many things which we could not, or at least would not, do alone, things that express our submerged feelings; it usually takes social pressure, for example, to make us give to charitable causes or to observe anniversaries. Civilization builds on the foundations of past achievement, thus saving the loss involved in unnecessary fresh beginnings. Nomad peoples and uncompromising individualists have their rude, pioneer qualities; but a settled, social life and willingness to learn from the past are the conditions of civilization, to which sophisticated recluses form only an apparent exception. Civilization thus appears to be a form of capitalism: the labor of the past and the activities of the present are stored up in institutions as in a reservoir, — political constitutions and law, factories, churches, universities, libraries, museums, hospitals, foundations for research, in a word all the intellectual and artistic traditions and habits of the race that can be transmitted and enjoyed and utilized for fresh creation. In fact the best defense that can be made of the capitalistic system in the limited sense is not merely that it is the most economic form of production but rather that it is the system by which the greatest amount of the world's labor is thus stored up and diffused for the benefit of the future. Governments and their tax-payers and the "man in the street," being hard-pressed with current expenses and the day's affairs, are notoriously reluctant or unable to do much for posterity, especially in matters of intellectual investigation and medical work and artistic creation. It is often the enlightened capitalist who thus endows humanity either by direct gifts or indirectly by spending his surplus on ultimately beneficial work. Of course not all states are blind; nor are all capitalists enlightened. But from whatever source come the material conditions that liberate civilizing energy, the result is the perpetuation and diffusion, through the vicissitudes of fortune, of the means of satisfying human needs.

Let us not be too easily convinced, however, that civilization is a blessing. Granted that it means a concentration and direction of energy, are we prepared to sacrifice to it the independence of individuals? Is not spontaneity a quality too precious to lose? Is the happy child at play less to be envied than his serious, burdened parent? The Indian's eyes are far better than ours. The head-hunter is happy till deprived of his quarry; why civilize him? Chiefly, no doubt, for the benefit of those whose heads are in peril. Yet the sudden "civilizing" of backward peoples, as is well known, often spoils even their good qualities. Some balancing of gains and losses and some compromise is inevitable; it is a pity to lose the Indian's sharpness of vision in our urbanized life, but we cannot eat our cake and have it too. We may be the more easily contented if we remember that even the native of the jungle is no carefree individualist, but a creature hedged about by extraordinary taboos and social restrictions. On the whole we have gained far more than we have lost. Though we can hardly turn back altogether to primitive culture, we can to some extent recapture its advantages during childhood and by our use of vacations; and we do need some moral and physical equivalent for the primitive virtues. The Romans were disciplined in their earlier history by the rigors of war; later their non-militant population found a vicarious thrill, but no discipline, in gladiatorial shows; perhaps we may do better by making the most of out-of-door sports.

The danger of civilization, however, lies deeper. Though it is an economy of effort, its devices may come to be regarded not as means but as ends with an absolute value.[1] And indeed habit and old associations, to say nothing of vested interests, make it hard to abandon social expedients that have outlived their usefulness. A nation is born of the throes of heroic aspiration; it degenerates into a clique of reactionary noblemen. Democracy rescues the world from tyranny, and ties the hands of responsible leadership. An infant industry is given a protective tariff; it never grows up. A benefaction, wrapped in legal shrouds, proves to have no value for a later age; a church becomes the coffin of an outgrown theology; a philosophy becomes a "genteel" survival; the "dead hand" is thus laid on the living. How much easier it is to climb a tree than to get down from it!

---

[1] That many of the failures in civilization are due to our "failure to relate" the "here and now" to the "then and yonder" is a view thoughtfully worked out by Mr. Edmund Noble, in *Our Slumbering World: A Plea for the Awakened Mind* (New York, 1928).

But this is not all. We have just mentioned the sins committed in the name of the sleeping past; the present is not without blame. The tendency of civilization is to emphasize the value of social control, of centralization and standardization, not only as a matter of economy but as conformity with a supposed "best." There is such a thing as a tyranny of "the best." Devoted parents are sometimes too anxious to fashion their offspring in their own image. Even a benevolent government is in danger of riding rough-shod over precious local heritages and aspirations. The Roman Empire wisely did not attempt to force uniformity within its economic and military union; national and regional cultures continued, and under the divine emperor the *municipia* retained a considerable measure of home rule. Under the federal constitution of the United States it is intended that "states' rights" shall be safeguarded in all matters not specifically delegated to the federal government; yet the tendency to-day is to permit encroachments on local and state control. From coast to coast American life is becoming more and more uniform, without necessarily becoming more civilized. The public school system tries nobly to bring a whole people into contact with "the best," and finds that its accomplishment is limited by the capacity of the average. In matters of daily life, we allow ourselves to be standardized by the patterns of advertisers and high-pressure salesmanship: we eat the most advertised foods; we are anxious to wear correct clothes, to see the films that "everybody is talking about." "A million dollars can't be wrong." The regimentation of the reading public by "book clubs" gives a false emphasis to some books and stupefies the public's powers of discrimination. Even universities and intellectual and charitable foundations are a menace if directed in accordance with arbitrary ideas. It is perhaps most of all in the arts that urbanization and standardization may have a deadening influence on all that gives life and variety. The Roman lyric hardly outlived the Republic, though epigram flourished in the Empire, and the provinces sent new blood to Rome. What Josiah Royce called "a wholesome provincialism" [1] is a tonic to the sophistication of the rootless citizen of the world.

For the equivocal nature of civilization, a blessing and a danger, the chief reason lies in the difficulty of distinguishing between ends and means. We have put great faith in the wonderful recent advances in scientific understanding of the physical universe, and in the material devices that it has made possible. Because these gains can be consolidated and transmitted, we have supposed that we were making true progress. Now we are beginning to realize that the machinery of modern life is controlling us. Not science itself, but the false notion that science is enough, without human mastery of ourselves and of science, is our peril. And it is clear that we have not mastered ourselves or learned to apply scientific discovery intelligently. "Evolution" can no longer be supposed to be fighting on our side. Our bodies have not changed for many thousand years; our brains are no better than those of men in Aristotle's day; and whereas past scientific and artistic gains, the accumulated experience of the race, are relatively secure, every individual human being has to begin afresh, for better and for worse, to recapitulate this experience, and if possible to add to it. Nor is it certain that the moral nature of the race has far surpassed that of the cave-man: superstitions, taboos, racial prejudices, cruelty, the survivals of infantile emotions, still crop up, and lead to social and international maladjustments and

[1] Josiah Royce, *Race Questions, Provincialism, and Other American Problems* (New York, 1908).

to wars, with the diversion of scientific discoveries to murderous ends. It is not surprising that civilization suffers retrogression as well as progress.

Even in our more amiable aspects, however, we confuse means and ends. We measure civilization by "prosperity," and "prosperity" in terms of automobiles and plumbing and all manner of "gadgets." A friendly French critic writes of American society:

> Luxury in every-day consumption and the extension to the many of living conditions previously reserved for the few — these are new phenomena in the history of mankind, and are undoubtedly evidence of splendid progress. But what is absolutely new about this society which is accomplishing such marvels is that in all its many aspects — even including idealism and religion — it is working toward the single goal of production. It is a materialistic society, organized to produce things rather than people, with output set up as a god.[1]

Even if materialism does not always involve a preference for quantity over quality, faith in things rather than in human qualities is a sign of degeneration of character. Civilizations, like individuals, are apt in middle life to grow fat and let out their belts; only constant exercise and the active struggle for ends intelligently conceived keeps them healthy; success, complete achievement, is a kind of failure. Imperial Rome, though not industrialized like America, provides the classic instance of the cult of prosperity and of the consequent softening of character which always invites barbarians within and without a country to devour its capital. The Greek tragic poets, and indeed the Roman satirists, recognized in "prosperity" a disease leading to arrogance (*hybris*), and containing the seeds of destruc-

---

[1] André Siegfried, *America Comes of Age*, English translation (New York, 1927), p. 348.

tion. The religious faith of sailors, it has been said, is inversely proportionate to the tonnage of their ship. But they do not think a captain unnecessary because their ship is large. As a matter of fact the intricate economic structure of a modern industrial society is far more frail than that of a self-contained agricultural society; a war is more destructive of its capital, and an economic depression is more widely felt.

More vital than the attempt to control physical forces, then, is the effort to control human nature. Law and government represent one attempt to set up a social control. "Law is the fabric in which the activities of life are carried on; it provides the rules that make social order possible; its perfection is the measure of a civilization." [1] What is true of single states is true also of the society of nations. In Rome we have not only the best example of an ancient society controlled by law but the best example of a single law applied to diverse nations. Here, to be sure, arms stood behind the toga; and there are still those who believe that international arbitration and the offices of the League of Nations can never replace war. [2] What is certainly true both in single states and in international dealings is that mere laws and institutions, however enlightened, will not avail without the force of an enlightened public opinion behind them. "Quid leges sine moribus vanae proficiunt?" [3] Government itself re-

---

[1] A. Lawrence Lowell, in the annual *Report of the President of Harvard College* for 1925–26, p. 21.

[2] The distinguished historian E. Meyer, in a speech before the Harvard Graduate Club on "War and Civilization" (reported in the *Harvard Illustrated Magazine*, April, 1910), defended the naïf view not only of the inevitability and justifiability of war when the vital interests of states are involved but of the moral value of war itself. "The destructive power of war is the creative force of life." One wonders whether such a view could find so distinguished a defender to-day.

[3] Horace, *Odes* III, 24, 36 f.

quires men to work the system, men with a tradition of public service and a code of personal honor. Countries are fortunate that can draw for such purposes on an aristocracy of brains and service, whether hereditary or recruited constantly from their universities and the world of affairs. Rome succeeded moderately well in this respect, and England best among modern nations; America's record is uneven, but gives no ground for despair. Yet leaders, particularly in a democracy, are helpless to lead without a responsible public opinion. What has made doubly tragic the chaotic state of Europe and America in the years following the Great War is the feeling that the leading statesmen of the several countries concerned could have worked out together acceptable and salutary agreements about war debts and reparations and tariffs and armaments had they not feared repudiation by the democracies in their own countries. Yet the alternative to democracy is autocracy, which the world has learned to fear. Rome actually found it the sole means to efficiency; and Italy is to-day prospering under a highly centralized system; countries with northern traditions are likely to revert to autocratic methods only under the greatest stress.

There are large areas of action which we prefer not to give over to the realm of positive law, leaving to the free choice of individuals the control of as much of their lives as possible. We believe in "government by discussion." There are risks in this freedom. It permits organized minorities and business interests to manipulate public opinion; the press, the stage, the moving-pictures are all a prey to such manipulation. Even law is at last affected; lobbying and "invisible government" are often the power behind the throne; special views with regard to history or science or religion dictate the nature of public education; tariff laws are written by interested parties; crime and lawlessness are tolerated. Nevertheless, a long view of things may regard these risks worth taking on the ground that the country that is least governed is best governed, provided that there is, or can be developed, an adequate public opinion and an individual self-control. Old civilizations, though firm and rapid in dealing with actual crime, are apt in other matters to trust a good deal to traditions that cannot be enforced by law, — to a sense of honor and duty, to good taste and manners. No law compels men during a shipwreck to follow the maxim "Women and children first." In most countries it is self-respect, rather than law, that causes moderation in the use of alcoholic beverages. It is chiefly young nations that fill their statute-books with laws for every possible contingency. Yet an enforced morality is of less value than a free and enlightened choice: "mere obedience to law does not measure the greatness of a nation." [1]

Public opinion is seldom intellectual; even intelligent individuals, though they subject their conduct to criticism, seldom act through the promptings of abstract thought. "Civilization develops only where considerable numbers of men work together for common ends. Such unity is brought about not so much by community of bare ideas as by community of the feelings by which ideas are 'emotionalized' and become beliefs and motives." [2] If this is true, the hope of civilization is in a purification and education of the emo-

---

[1] Lord Moulton, "Law and Manners," *Atlantic Monthly* (July, 1924). Cf. Burke, in *Letters on a Regicide Peace*, 1796: "Manners are of more importance than laws. Upon them, in a great measure, the laws depend. The law touches us but here and there, and now and then. Manners are what vex or soothe, corrupt or purify, exalt or debase, barbarize or refine us, by a constant, steady, uniform, insensible operation, like that of the air we breathe in."

[2] G. F. Moore, in Prefatory Note to J. H. Denison's *Emotion as the Basis of Civilization* (New York, 1928).

tions, a heightening of the imagination, a new and applied sense of humor. We should be profoundly distrustful of any schemes for the progress of the world that are founded on improved machinery, whether material or political or even intellectual, without a corresponding advance in the quality of human nature. Money is not enough; technical experts are not enough; the *formulae* of philosophy are not enough. The Augustan Age was created not only by the victor of Actium but by the author of the *Aeneid* and the unknown sculptors of the Ara Pacis. In our own age particularly we need to be on our guard against quack scientists who pretend to reduce to scientific principles the whole of human affairs. In spite of all the similarities of people and events, every human being is unique, and every event in history is unique, as every work of art is unique. History does *not* repeat itself precisely, nor can any one predict what motives will cause any individual, or the race in general, to act under all conceivable circumstances. There is no single type of civilization that is suited to all peoples at all times. Why, then, study history or attempt to deal with human nature and its products, apart from the personal satisfaction that such study brings? Because it is the best, and indeed the only available, means of training one's powers of understanding and sympathy and one's sense of values; and despite the uniqueness of human beings there *are* similarities. Civilization, then, like the rest of life, is an art or a game rather than a science, though it is glad to employ science as a tool; it involves continual adjustments to new situations, and the most experienced artist or player is the most flexible and versatile. The best civilization is that which has developed the most persons with such qualities and makes the greatest use of them.

Just here enters again the ancient quarrel between liberal

and conservative. As soon as we admit that history is not a science but a delicate process of interpretation, that Clio is a Muse,[1] that literature must reckon with the flux of things, so soon do we open the door for a host of honest differences of opinion. Because life is in flux, half of us are the more determined to control it by reference to "the best": standards and conventions, aristocracy and authority, the imitation of masterpieces, the preservation of types, are the means to this control. We feel safe in ruts; we cultivate formality in speech and in dress. Because life is in flux, the rest of us are the more determined to let the flux take its course; traditionalism seems a meaningless subservience to a dead past. We must be tolerant and inclusive, even as Rome assimilated many races and cultures; let us extend the franchise to new ideas, and let us measure civilization by the breadth of its sympathies. Thus we applaud the present because it shows a greater sympathy than the past for the poor and suffering, for women and children, for foreigners (except in times of war), and for animals (at least for domestic, if not for wild, animals). As usual, there is truth in the contentions of both conservatives and liberals. Though they may feel far apart, and dub each other "reactionaries" and "sentimentalists," an enlightened civilization has room for both. Yet history tends on the whole to give the benefit of any doubt to the conservative, because it has seemed logical and economical (and easy) to keep what one has till something else is proved to be better; such a favoritism is not unfair, provided that free opportunity for reasonable experiment is given to the liberal. Choices must be made ultimately by public opinion under trained leadership.

The origination of ideas and the creation of masterpieces of art come almost wholly from individuals and small

[1] Cf. G. M. Trevelyan, *Clio, a Muse, and Other Essays* (London, 1913).

groups; the formation of taste is also the work of minorities, in the past generally of castes. "Civilization has hitherto consisted in diffusion and dilution of habits arising in privileged centres."[1] How far can whole peoples share in these matters? What many believe or hope may emerge in America is a widespread civilization not based on social privileges and inequalities. Certainly wealth is becoming more generally diffused, and is diffusing opportunities for leisure and education. The quantity if not the quality of civilization has advanced; and in many ways taste has improved, in spite of excessive standardization. Though wealth still enjoys privilege, careers are open to talents. But it is not clear that the fundamental differences between men of genius and ordinary men, between leaders and followers, are likely to disappear. Creation must still be the task of the few, and cannot be a matter of mass production. How much the few can accomplish is a problem. They will not constitute a caste, but will constantly be recruited from all available sources. In fact castes have always tended to run out, and societies dependent on them without popular support have degenerated. The Greek successors of Alexander the Great attempted to Hellenize the barbarians of the East, but were too few to leaven the lump, and failed, and the flower of the Greek race died.[2] Marcus Aurelius was helpless to cope with the growing barbarization of his empire; three centuries later the process was fairly complete, and Rome witnessed what has been called by Mr. Rostovtzeff "the

---

[1] G. Santayana, *Reason in Society* (New York, 1905–06), p. 125.

[2] Cf. E. Meyer, *Blüte und Niedergang des Hellenismus in Asia* (Berlin, 1925). Meyer also points out that these Greeks were city-dwellers, and that city-dwellers notoriously fail to reproduce themselves. "Race suicide" seldom threatens whole peoples; but it is well known that the families of men of intelligence are on an average far smaller than those of the ignorant. Human quality is more important than quantity; and we are not likely to have too many sons of those whose heritage is best.

absorption of the higher classes by the lower, accompanied by a gradual levelling down of standards."[1] The same author remarks:[2]

> Our civilization will not last unless it be a civilization not of one class but of the masses. . . . But the ultimate problem remains like a ghost, ever present and unlaid: Is it possible to extend a higher civilization to the lower classes without debasing its standard and diluting its quality to the vanishing point? Is not every civilization bound to decay as soon as it begins to penetrate the masses?

Real progress, real civilization, is not the passive acceptance of external forces, but is an activity and operates from within; people cannot be civilized wholesale any more than they can become good or intelligent *en masse*. They may be exposed together to civilizing influences, such as social institutions and works of art; but it is as individuals that they must grow, mostly by conscious effort, in their powers of understanding and sympathy. Rome became civilized to the extent that she effectively exposed her citizens to these influences; but a large proportion of her citizens remained immune. Nor can a modern society take much pride in a material civilization even if it is widely diffused, unless it is accompanied by a lively and intelligent attitude on the part of its public. A good criterion for this purpose is the character of men's occupations in hours of leisure, especially since the diffusion of leisure is now greater than in any previous age. During their working hours, men are often cogs in the industrial machine, with less personal freedom than their grandfathers had; but in hours of leisure and in holidays they have a chance to cultivate their individual powers

---

[1] M. Rostovtzeff, *Social and Economic History of the Roman Empire*, p. 480; already quoted above, p. 276.

[2] *Ibid*. p. 486.

and tastes not as a means to a living but as ends in themselves: here is their chance for sport and travel and the fuller flowering of personality in conversation and social intercourse and in the cultivation of interests and hobbies remote from their vocations. The pity is that so many do not know how to use their leisure. An appreciable part of the increase of crime in America has been traced to mere idleness. But even of the law-abiding majority too few use their leisure intelligently: while some superficially over-civilized people in sheer boredom revert to a sophisticated primitivism of art and morals (which is the negation of civilization's emphasis on the conscious mind), the unimaginative many surrender to passive and conventional amusements, like the moving-pictures, that demand little of them, and so let themselves be standardized; their intellectual and political and religious attitudes are those of acquiescence. Granted that it is only the few who can originate important ideas and works of art, it is nevertheless obvious that the fortunate people of our day are those who have developed skills, — for example in sports or handicrafts or arts, — or at least have learned to appreciate good work in others. It is more stimulating to play a game than to watch it; it is more fun to play a musical instrument than to listen to (possibly better performed) music that is mechanically rendered; yet one may do both. Only it is clear that we need education for leisure quite as much as for our vocations, if we are to regard the things that we do for their own sakes as having equal importance with the things that we do as means to ulterior ends. And that is in essence the ideal of liberal education, which strives to set men free by making them citizens of the world in the fullest sense.

"Our manners, our civilization, and all the good things which are connected with manners, and with civilization, have in this European world of ours depended for ages upon two principles, . . . the spirit of a gentleman, and the spirit of religion." [1] So Burke wrote in an age when the claims both of religion and of aristocracy were being called in question. From every point of view, and at every level of civilization, the rôle of "the spirit of religion" has been powerful: as a cohesive force in a tribal society, as the sustainer of morale in times of danger and distress, as the creator of ethical standards and the champion of the weak, the poor, and the alien, as the patron and conserver of the arts. It has made men free by making them citizens of a kingdom not of this world. The faults committed in the name of religion have been many, chiefly those of superstition, intolerance, and formalism; they have often been rebuked; and religion, like every human art, must remain forever amenable to criticism.

Hardly less powerful has been "the spirit of the gentleman," the product of ages of ripening. Originating in superior social castes based first on military prestige and later on birth and breeding, the idea of the gentleman came to imply above all the possession of certain moral qualities: courage, courtesy, refinement of manners, with perhaps some artistic or intellectual accomplishments (such as singing). Even when, as among the Greeks and the early Romans, manual labor did not necessarily involve any social stigma, gentlemen held aloof from occupations of a confining or of a mercenary nature, such as would make them narrow specialists or professionals rather than amateurs. But some useful occupations and arts that tended among the Romans to be practised by slaves were on this account avoided by gentlemen; not the least vice in the whole system of slavery was this effect on the masters. With the Greek the *kalos*

---

[1] Burke, *Reflections on the Revolution in France* (1790).

k'agathos tended to be a man of good birth, and must have all-round moral and intellectual qualities. The Roman aristocrat inherited a tradition of patriotic service; the refinements of mind and manners he learned chiefly from the Greeks. Yet Cicero, a "new man," helped enormously to mould the standards of conduct for succeeding centuries; Virgil, a rustic with gifts of heart and mind, gave the world new sympathies; and Horace, the son of a freedman, "gave mankind the type of the man of the world and the gentleman; he showed how it is attainable without birth or wealth, without anxiety or ambition, without either high intellectual gifts or unattainable saintliness." [1] The declining Roman Empire and the Middle Ages, to be sure, attached a new importance to rank and military prowess; feudal lords and their serfs had little in common. Yet chivalry did enhance the ideals of courage, courtesy, and refinement, and especially of respect for womanhood, though within such artificial limitations that it hardly needed a *Don Quixote* to give the *coup de grâce* to the knight-errant. Meanwhile the Church not only mitigated the more cruel aspects of life but sometimes did more than secular society to promote a more democratic conception of the gentleman. Sons of the people might become princes of the Church; and beside the knight stands the monk, who often has the gentleman's qualities of mind and character. A gentleman may, perhaps, be neither a saint nor a scholar, and indeed we use a double expression to characterize "a gentleman *and* a scholar"; but the gentleman has an instinctive understanding of both the scholar and the saint. Dante will serve as an example. Certainly the centuries since the Renaissance have been increasingly reluctant to call the libertine or the ignoramus a gentleman merely because of birth or wealth; and especially in the

[1] J. W. Mackail, in *The Legacy of Rome*, p. 340.

English-speaking world education has regarded intellect and character and manners as inseparable, and has sought to provide the environment in which they may grow harmoniously. If there is any one institution, beyond native endowments, which we should trust in our democratic world to produce "the spirit of a gentleman," it is education. And it is the gentleman, once more, in the true sense of the word, whom we trust to do what no law can compel him to do; to act generously, not sparing himself; to act promptly and resourcefully in an emergency; to be tolerant of others.

Superficially a gentleman is judged by his manners; yet manners are not merely a superficial matter. As the Romans knew, habits become character; *mores* are morals. Manners are the outward indication of the tolerance and consideration which are internal; even when stereotyped, as the social amenities of dress and good form, they serve to minimize the friction of daily life; even when preserved as mere conventions (the traditional Englishman dressing for dinner even when alone in the jungle), they serve to preserve a pattern of life, a morale, which may be precious; they are a protest against carelessness. It is not necessary to be snobbish about these matters; for real courtesy that comes from the heart one can hardly improve on the natural friendliness of many an Italian peasant who is by all academic standards very ignorant. And the hard-working peasant, even to-day, is not in too much of a hurry to enjoy life as it comes, — in the *siesta*, the *festa*, the conversation on the doorstep and from window to window.

The appreciation of leisure, *dolce far niente, genio indulgere*, is one of the earmarks of old civilizations, which realize how many centuries have conspired to produce the present, and how comparatively little one generation can accomplish. Our age of haste and mechanical efficiency may lose something precious if it does not learn how to use leisure, not only for the eager pursuit of hobbies but more casually in the give and take of life. Dining, a characteristic Greek and Roman art, found its finest flowering in the conversation of the guests.[1] How few of us to-day understand the art of conversation, in which social equals, emancipated from mere gossip and anecdote, and too courteous to lecture one another, play with experiences and ideas as with a tennis ball, not necessarily in order to score points, but for the exhilaration of the game! A Socrates or a Dr. Johnson may, at his peril, be allowed to dominate the talk; but the best conversation takes the bit in its teeth, and no man knows when or where it will end. And who knows what new ideas, what discovery of life's ironies, what ripening of personality and friendship may emerge?[2] How few of us find time to indulge in what one of its practitioners has called "the most civilized occupation," the reading aloud of books, followed by the discussion of them by all the hearers! How few of us write letters except to do business or to give news! How niggardly we are of ourselves!

A great weight drops from our shoulders when we come to realize that we are not bound by any moral or logical necessity to change the world overnight by setting up new machinery. Granted that we recognize certain distant goals as desirable, and certain existing types of institution, mostly traditional, as useful in making progress toward them, it is still clear that these institutions, — law and government, economic systems, educational and religious organizations,

---

[1] Cf. pp. 138–140.

[2] Among the not inconsiderable number of books on the art of conversation one of the best is still the little work, almost Aristotelian in its systematic completeness, and abounding in common sense, of J. P. Mahaffy, *Conversation: Practical Suggestions on the Important Subject of What to Say and just how and when to Say It.* (Philadelphia, 1896.)

— are only the framework within which individuals must work and play. These institutions may deserve our support, even our ardent support; certainly there is to-day no more important work to be done than the arousing of the conscience of the world in favor of the means that may best secure international peace and good will. But we may be sceptical of the value of propaganda in favor of mere institutions when we remember that all reform, all education, all civilization, is ultimately of individuals. We can reform ourselves to a certain extent; to a more limited extent we may influence other individuals, if we are convinced that this is worth doing. But it is a matter of common sense to discover what can and what cannot be changed in human nature; this can be learned only by experiment and the opening of the doors of opportunity, and not by undue pressure. There are individuals who cannot be educated beyond a certain point, or who can be educated only in certain directions; there are races and types of people to whom certain forms of culture and of religion are peculiarly suited, and who should not be expected to conform to other patterns. Missionaries have learned to respect native cultures and traditions. We are learning that it may be a mistake to send certain boys to college, though they will do well in some craft or business. It may be no kindness to uproot peasant life. The rights and capacities of personality have a real, if not an unlimited, value.

Even if a people or the whole world shows signs of temporary decadence, civilization is not necessarily doomed. A saving remnant may keep alive the flame for a better day. Though it may seem to be a contradiction in terms to speak of civilized individuals in an uncivilized society, we know that they do exist and that it is they who "like runners hand on the torch of life." [1] At the worst, he who, like Plato's

---

[1] Lucretius II, 79; quoted in its context at the head of this chapter.

philosopher, has beheld the pattern of a city that is laid away in heaven, "may set his own house in order."[1] In an evil society,

he is like one who retires under the shelter of a wall in the storm of dust and sleet which the driving wind hurries along; and when he sees the rest of mankind full of wickedness, he is content if only he can live his own life and be pure from evil or unrighteousness, and depart in peace and good will, with bright hopes.[2]

But the spirit of religion and the spirit of the gentleman have an almost unlimited resilience and power of endurance; if forced for a time to play the part of spectator and kindly critic, they will in the end lead the active forces of regeneration.

In this brief inquiry we have found no simple formula for civilization that recognizes all the conflicting needs of human nature. For civilization is not a state but a constant effort to establish provisionally the conditions under which personality may be set free. Like the craft of the gardener, "it is a warfare upon earth that is never won, for the wilderness always keeps invading the garden and, if the gardener ceases his effort, the wilderness returns."[3] But garden-flowers are no less nature's children than those of the field and woods; they have been chosen to please human tastes and purposes. So, to change the figure, civilization represents a twofold process: the crystallization, by laws and institutions, by customs,[4] arts, and symbols, of those human experiences that have come to seem valuable, for the purposes of economy in use and transmission; and then, as these crystallized forms lose their value in relation to a changed

[1] Plato, *Republic*, 592.   [2] *Ibid.*, 496.
[3] Eoin MacNeill, in *The Irish Statesman* (October 17, 1925), quoted by Padraic Colum, *The Road Round Ireland* (*New York*, 1926), p. 402.
[4] W. Bagehot, in *Physics and Politics*, pp. 27, 53, speaks of "a cake of custom," which is subjected to criticism by discussion.

environment, the throwing of the crystals back into the melting pot, that they may be fused, and that after the dross has settled a new set of crystals may be gained, possibly richer in content, certainly more useful in form. The civilized society is that which has learned, as far as it can in its day and environment, how much it can wisely retrieve from the melting pot, and how much it had better leave in suspense, in reverence to the gods of the flux.

If this seems a mechanical conception, a brutal process, let us remember that it is in part nature's method, and that our wills are not wholly free from hers. She lets the plants die down, to live again. She lets the hills be worn down by secular rains; and from the detritus grow new crops. She lets men die, and their petty idiosyncrasies are swept away; only that part of them is perpetuated in memory and in their works which other men care for. But here, where nature's process ends, man's task begins; we transcend nature by choosing the activities that minister to our needs. In the wisdom and determination of our choice consists civilization.

LIST OF BOOKS

LIST OF BOOKS

THIS list is far from exhaustive. It includes some of the books which have been found useful in the writing of this book, and also provides suggestions to the reader for further reading. Preference is given to works that are easily accessible, and, of these, to books that are readable and intelligible to readers who are not expert classical scholars. The grouping does not quite correspond to the arrangement of the chapters in the text. Within the several lists, the more general and popular works are usually placed first, and more specialized works after them; in some cases parts of the general works are cited again under special subjects. Still other works are cited in footnotes to the text.

I. GENERAL

Bailey, C., editor. *The Legacy of Rome*. Oxford University Press, 1923.

Stobart, J. C. *The Grandeur That Was Rome*. Sidgwick and Jackson, 1912.

Smyth, H. W., editor. *Harvard Essays on Classical Subjects*. Houghton, Mifflin, 1912.

Grenier, A. *Le Génie Romain, dans la Religion, la Pensée, et l'Art*. Paris, 1925 (also in Eng. trans., London, 1926).

Robinson, D. M., and Hadzits, G. D., editors. *Our Debt to Greece and Rome*. A series of about fifty volumes by as many authors (several cited below by title). Longmans, Green (formerly Marshall Jones), 1922–. (In progress.)

Sandys, Sir J. E., editor. *A Companion to Latin Studies*. Cambridge University Press, 1910.

Mommsen, T., and others, editors. *Corpus Inscriptionum Latinarum* (*C. I. L.*). 14 vols. and supplements in progress. Berlin, 1863–.

Dessau, H., editor. *Inscriptiones Latinae Selectae*. 3 vols. Berlin, 1896–1916.

II. ITALY AND ROME

Sandys, Sir J. E., editor. Articles on Geography, Fauna, and Flora, and on Topography of Rome, in *Companion to Latin Studies*.

Baedeker's Northern Italy, Central Italy, and Southern Italy.

The Blue Guides (Northern Italy and Southern Italy), ed. F. Muirhead. Macmillan.

Tozer, H. F. *Classical Geography*. Macmillan, 1891.

Grundy, G. B., editor. Map of Italy and Sicily, with Index. Also of The Roman Empire. Murray's Handy Classical Maps, John Murray, London, n. d.

Showerman, G. *Eternal Rome; The City and Its People from the Earliest Times to the Present Day*. Yale University Press, 1924.

Platner, S. B. *The Topography and Monuments of Ancient Rome*. Allyn and Bacon, rev. ed., 1911.

Platner, S. B., and Ashby, T. *A Topographical Dictionary of Ancient Rome*. Oxford University Press, 1929.

Huelsen, C. *The Roman Forum*. Eng. trans., 2d ed., Rome, Loescher, 1906.

—— *The Forum and the Palatine*. (Eng. trans.) N. Y., Bruderhausen, 1928.

Holme, G., editor. *Rome, Past and Present*, with intro. by W. Gaunt (special number of the *Studio*). London, 1926.

Lanciani, R. *The Ruins and Excavations of Ancient Rome*. Macmillan, 1897.

—— *Wanderings in the Roman Campagna*. Houghton, Mifflin, 1909.

—— Ancient and Modern Rome. Longmans, Green, 1925.

Ashby, T. *The Roman Campagna in Classical Times*. Benn, 1927.

Geikie, Sir A. *The Love of Nature among the Romans*. John Murray, 1912.

Martinengo-Cesaresco, Countess E. *The Outdoor Life in Greek and Roman Poets*. Macmillan, 1911.

Symonds, J. A. *Sketches and Studies in Italy and Greece*. 3 vols. Scribners, 1898.

Gissing, G. *By the Ionian Sea*. Scribners, 1905.

Hewlett, M. *The Road in Tuscany*. 2 vols. Macmillan, 1904.

Trevelyan, G. M. Essays on "Walking" and "The Marches," in *Clio, A Muse, and Other Essays, Literary and Pedestrian*. Longmans, Green, 1913.

Villari, L. *Italian Life in Town and Country*. Putnams, 1902.

Haight, E. H. *Italy, Old and New*. Dutton, 1922.

Sabin, F. *Classical Associations of Places in Italy*. Madison, 1921.

The English Poets, especially Milton, Keats, Shelley, Byron, Browning, Mrs. Browning, and G. Meredith.

Longfellow, H. W., editor. *Poems of Places: Italy.* 3 vols. Houghton, Mifflin, 1882–83.

Charpentier, G. Orchestral Suite, *Impressions of Italy,* 1891. (Explanatory programme by A. Ernst; translation in programme of Boston Symphony Orchestra, Feb. 28, 1924.)

Respighi, O. Orchestral Suites, *The Fountains of Rome* and *The Pines of Rome.*

III. HISTORY

(See also under Politics and Economics)

Jones, H. S. *Companion to Roman History.* Oxford University Press, 1912.

Sandys, Sir J. E., editor. Article on Ethnology, in *Companion to Latin Studies.*

Henderson, B. W. *The Study of Roman History.* Duckworth, 1921.

Ripley, W. Z. *The Races of Europe.* Appleton, 1899.

Peet, T. E. *The Stone and Bronze Ages in Italy.* Oxford University Press, 1909.

Randall-MacIver, D. *Italy before the Romans.* Oxford University Press, 1928.

—— *Villanovans and Early Etruscans.* Oxford University Press, 1924.

—— *The Iron Age in Italy.* Oxford University Press, 1927.

—— *The Etruscans.* Oxford University Press, 1927.

Fell, R. A. L. *Etruria and Rome.* Cambridge University Press, 1924.

Rose, H. J. *Primitive Culture in Italy.* Methuen, 1926.

Bury, J. B., and others, editors. *The Cambridge Ancient History.* (*C. A. H.*) In progress. (Relevant chapters in vols. IV–.) Cambridge University Press, 1924–.

Matheson, P. E. *Outlines of Roman History.* Longmans, Green, 1905.

—— *The Growth of Rome.* Oxford University Press, 1922.

Fowler, W. W. *Rome.* Holt, 1912.

Pelham, H. *Outlines of Roman History.* Percival, 1893; Putnams, 1907.

Rostovtzeff, M. *History of the Ancient World.* Vol. II, *Rome.* Oxford University Press, 1927.

Mommsen, T. *History of Rome.* (Eng. trans., 5 vols.) Scribners, 1898. (Also, in 4 vols., in Everyman's edition, n. d.)

Frank, T. *Roman Imperialism.* Macmillan, 1914.

—— *History of Rome.* Holt, 1924.

Boak, A. E. R. *A History of Rome to 565 A.D.* Macmillan, 1921.

Heitland, W. E. *The Roman Republic.* 3 vols. Cambridge University Press, 1909.

—— *Short History of the Roman Republic.* Cambridge University Press, 1911.

Ferrero, G. *The Greatness and Decline of Rome.* (Eng. trans.) 5 vols. Putnams, 1909–10.

Jones, H. S. *The Roman Empire.* Putnams, 1908.

Bury, J. B. *Student's Roman Empire.* John Murray, 1900.

Mommsen, T. *The Provinces from Caesar to Diocletian.* (Eng. trans.) 2 vols. Scribners, 1909.

Collingwood, R. W. *Roman Britain.* Oxford University Press, 1923.

—— *The Archaeology of Roman Britain.* The Dial Press, 1930.

Haverfield, F. *The Romanization of Roman Britain.* 4th ed., rev. by G. Macdonald. Oxford University Press, 1923.

Gibbon, E. *The History of the Decline and Fall of the Roman Empire.* Ed. by J. B. Bury. 7 vols. Macmillan, 1914.

Hodgkin, T. *Italy and Her Invaders.* 8 vols. Oxford University Press, 1880–99.

Bryce, Viscount. *The Holy Roman Empire.* Macmillan, many editions, the latest in 1930.

IV. SOCIAL LIFE

Last, H. Essay on "Family and Social Life," in *The Legacy of Rome.*

Johnston, H. W. *The Private Life of the Romans.* Scott, Foresman, rev. ed., 1932.

Showerman, G. *Rome and the Romans.* Macmillan, 1931.

McDaniel, W. B. *Roman Private Life and Its Survivals.* Longmans, Green, 1924.

Fowler, W. W. *Social Life at Rome in the Age of Cicero.* Macmillan, 1908.

Tucker, T. G. *Life in the Roman World of Nero and St. Paul.* Macmillan, 1924.

Dill, Sir S. *Roman Society from Nero to Marcus Aurelius.* Macmillan, 1904.

—— *Roman Society in the Last Century of the Western Empire.* 2d ed. Macmillan, 1905.

Friedlander, V. *Roman Life and Manners under the Early Empire.* (Eng. trans. of 7th German ed.) 4 vols. Dutton, 1908–13.

Rogers, H. L., and Harley, T. R., editors. *Roman Home Life and Religion* (in Latin and English). Oxford University Press, 1923. Also new ed., in English, 1927.

Davis, W. S. *A Day in Old Rome.* Allyn and Bacon, 1925.

Morgan, M. H. Essay on "Some Aspects of an Ancient Roman City," in *Harvard Essays on Classical Subjects.*

Mau, A. *Pompeii: Its Life and Art.* Trans. by F. W. Kelsey. Macmillan, 1899.

Wilkins, A. S. *Roman Education.* Cambridge University Press, 1905.

Gwynn, A. *Roman Education from Cicero to Quintilian.* Oxford University Press, 1926.

V. POLITICS AND ECONOMICS

(See also under History)

Abbott, F. F. *Roman Politics.* Longmans, Green, 1923.

—— *A History and Description of Roman Political Institutions.* Ginn, 1901.

—— *Society and Politics.* Scribners, 1910.

—— *The Common People of Ancient Rome.* Scribners, 1911.

Sandys, Sir J. E., editor. Articles on Public Antiquities, in *Companion to Latin Studies.*

Jones, H. S. Essay on "Administration," in *The Legacy of Rome.*

Barker, E. Essay on "The Conception of Empire," in *The Legacy of Rome.*

Fowler, W. W. *The City-State of the Greek and Romans.* Macmillan, 1893.

Greenidge, A. H. *Roman Public Life.* Macmillan, 1901.

Botsford, G. W. *The Roman Assemblies.* Macmillan, 1909

Oman, Sir C. *Seven Roman Statesmen of the Later Republic.* Longmans, Green (1902), 1927.

Ferrero, G. *Characters and Events in Roman History.* Putnams, 1909.

Boissier, G. *Cicero and His Friends.* (Eng. trans.) Putnams, 1897.

Strachan-Davidson, J. L. *Cicero and the Fall of the Roman Republic.* Putnams, 1907.

Froude, J. A. *Caesar, a Sketch.* Scribners, 1879.

Fowler, W. W. *Julius Caesar and the Foundation of the Roman Imperial System.* Putnams, 1900.

Holmes, T. R. *The Roman Republic and the Founder of the Empire.* 3 vols. Oxford University Press, 1923.

Marsh, F. B. *The Founding of the Roman Empire.* 2d ed. Oxford University Press, 1927.

Shuckburgh, E. S. *Augustus: The Life and Times of the Founder of the Roman Empire.* T. F. Unwin, 1903.

Hardy, E. G., editor. *The Monumentum Ancyranum.* Oxford University Press, 1923.

Arnold, W. T., and Shuckburgh, E. S. *Roman Provincial Administration.* Oxford University Press, 1914.

Reid, J. S. *The Municipalities of the Roman Empire.* Cambridge University Press, 1913.

Lewis, Sir G. C. *An Essay on the Government of Dependencies* (originally publ. in 1841). Ed. with an intro. by Sir C. P. Lucas. Oxford University Press, 1891.

Bryce, Viscount. "The Ancient Roman Empire and the British Empire in India," and "The Diffusion of Roman and English Law throughout the World." Both revised and reprinted (from *Studies in History and Jurisprudence*). Oxford University Press, 1914.

Cromer, Earl. *Ancient and Modern Imperialism.* John Murray, 1910.

Lucas, Sir C. P. *The British Empire.* Macmillan, 1915.

Frank, T. *Economic History of Rome.* 2d ed. Johns Hopkins Press, 1927.

Rostovtzeff, M. *The Social and Economic History of the Roman Empire.* Oxford University Press, 1926.

Davis, W. S. *The Influence of Wealth in Imperial Rome.* Macmillan, 1910.

Heitland, W. E. Essay on "Agriculture," in *The Legacy of Rome.*

—— *Agricola.* Cambridge University Press, 1921.

de Zulueta, F. Essay on "The Science of Law," in *The Legacy of Rome.*

Reid, J. S. Article on Roman Law, in *Companion to Latin Studies.*

Morey, W. C. *Outlines of Roman Law.* 2d ed. Putnams, 1885.

Walton, F. P. *Historical Introduction to Roman Law.* 2d ed. Green, Edinburgh and London, 1912.

Mommsen, T., and others, editors. *Corpus Iuris Civilis.* 3 vols. Berlin, 1895.

Robinson, J. J. *Selections from the Public and Private Law of the Romans.* American Book Co., 1905.

Bruns, C. G. (and O. Gradenwitz). *Fontes Iuris Romani Antiqui.* 7th ed. Tubingen, 1909.

VI. THE FINE ARTS

Walters, H. B. *The Art of the Romans.* Methuen, 1911.

Rushforth, G. M. Essay on "Architecture and Art," in *The Legacy of Rome.*

Giovannoni, G. Essay on "Building and Engineering," in *The Legacy of Rome.*

Chase, G. H. Essay on "The New Criticism of Roman Art," in *Harvard Essays on Classical Subjects.* Houghton, Mifflin, 1912.

Strong, Mrs. A. (Eugenie Sellers) *Art in Ancient Rome.* 2 vols. Scribners, 1928.

Robertson, D. S. *A Handbook of Greek and Roman Architecture.* Cambridge University Press, 1929.

Anderson, W. J., and Spiers, R. P. *The Architecture of Greece and Rome.* 2 vols., 3d ed. (rev. by W. B. Dinsmoor and T. Ashby). Scribners, 1927.

Rivoira, G. T. *Roman Architecture and Its Principles of Construction under the Empire.* Oxford University Press, 1925.

Wickhoff, F. *Roman Art.* (Trans. by Mrs. A. Strong.) Macmillan, 1900.

Strong, Mrs. A. *Roman Sculpture from Augustus to Constantine.* Scribners, 1907.

Chase, G. H., and Post, C. R. *A History of Sculpture.* (Chap. VIII on Roman Sculpture.) Harpers, 1924.

Chase, G. H. *Greek and Roman Sculpture in American Collections.* Harvard University Press, 1924.

VII. RELIGION AND PHILOSOPHY

Bailey, C. Essay on "Religion and Philosophy," in *The Legacy of Rome.*

—— *The Religion of Ancient Rome.* Constable, 1911.

Carter, J. B. *The Religious Life of Ancient Rome.* Houghton, Mifflin, 1911.

—— *The Religion of Numa.* Macmillan, 1906.

Halliday, W. R. *Lectures on the History of Roman Religion.* Small, Maynard, 1923.

—— *The Pagan Background of Early Christianity*, 1925.

Wissowa, G. *Religion und Kultus der Römer.* 2d ed. Munich, 1912.

Fowler, W. W. *The Religious Experience of the Roman People.* Macmillan, 1911.

—— *Roman Festivals of the Period of the Republic.* 2d ed. Macmillan, 1908.

—— *Roman Ideas of Deity in the Last Century before the Christian Era.* Macmillan, 1914.

—— *Roman Essays and Interpretations.* Macmillan, 1920.

Boissier, G. *La Religion Romaine, d'Augustus Jusqu'à Justinian.* 2 vols. Paris, 1874.

Dill, Sir S. *Roman Society from Nero to Marcus Aurelius.* Macmillan, 1904.

Moore, C. H. Essay on "Greek and Roman Ascetic Tendencies," in *Harvard Essays on Classical Subjects.*

Cumont, F. *Textes et Monuments Figurés Relatifs aux Mystères de Mithra.* 2 vols. Brussels, 1899, 96.

—— *The Mysteries of Mithra.* Trans. from the 2d rev. French ed. Open Court Publishing Co., 1903.

—— *The Oriental Religions in Roman Paganism.* (Eng. trans.) Open Court Publishing Co., 1911.

—— *After Life in Roman Paganism.* Yale University Press, 1922.

Rostovtzeff, M. *Mystic Italy.* Holt, 1927.

Arnold, E. V. *Roman Stoicism.* Cambridge University Press, 1911.

Bevan, E. *Stoics and Sceptics.* Oxford University Press, 1913.

Santayana, G. *Three Philosophic Poets.* (Essay on Lucretius.) Harvard University Press, 1910.

Masson, J. *Lucretius, Epicurean and Poet.* 2 vols. John Murray, 1907 and 1909.

Munro, H. A. J., editor. *Lucretius.* 3 vols., 4th ed. (Intro. to the 1928 ed. of the 2d vol. by E. N. de C. Andrade.) Bell, 1920.

Pater, W. *Marius the Epicurean.* Macmillan, 1885.

Glover, T. R. *The Conflict of Religions in the Early Roman Empire.* Methuen, 1909.

Rand, E. K. *Founders of the Middle Ages.* Harvard University Press, 1928.

VIII. LITERATURE

See also generally editions and translations of Latin authors; particular mention may be made of the volumes of the Loeb edition, with Latin and English on opposite pages. (Putnams.)

Mackail, J. W. *Latin Literature.* Scribners, 1895.

Duff, J. W. *A Literary History of Rome to the Close of the Golden Age.* Scribners, 1909.

—— *A Literary History of Rome in the Silver Age from Tiberius to Hadrian.* Scribners, 1927.

—— *The Writers of Rome.* Oxford University Press, 1923.

Bailey, C., editor. *The Mind of Rome.* (Selections from Latin literature in English translation, with introductions, by various scholars.) Oxford University Press, 1926.

Garrod, H. W., editor. *The Oxford Book of Latin Verse.* Oxford University Press, 1912.

Sikes, E. E. *Roman Poetry.* Dutton, 1923.

Conway, R. S. *New Studies of a Great Inheritance.* John Murray, 1921.

—— *Harvard Lectures on the Vergilian Age.* Harvard University Press, 1928.

Sellar, W. Y. *The Roman Poets of the Republic.* 3d ed.

—— *The Roman Poets of the Augustan Age: Virgil.* 3d ed.

—— *The Roman Poets of the Augustan Age: Horace and the Elegiac Poets.* All publ. by Oxford University Press, 1905–08.

Rand, E. K. *The Magical Art of Virgil.* Harvard University Press, 1931.

Mackail, J. W. *Virgil and His Meaning to the World of To-day.* Longmans, Green, 1922.

D'Alton, J. F. *Horace and His Age.* Longmans, Green, 1917.

Campbell, A. Y. *Horace, A New Interpretation.* Methuen, 1924.

Fiske, G. C. *Lucilius and Horace.* University of Wisconsin, Madison, 1920.

Showerman, G. *Horace and His Influence.* Longmans, Green, 1922.

Rand, E. K. *Ovid and his Influence.* Longmans, Green, 1925.

Summers, W. C. *The Silver Age of Latin Literature.* Stokes, 1920.

Boissier, G. *Tacitus and other Roman Studies.* (Eng. trans.) Constable, 1906.

Smith, K. F. *Martial the Epigrammatist, and Other Essays.* Johns Hopkins Press, 1920.

Geikie, Sir A. *The Love of Nature among the Romans.* John Murray, 1912.

Everett, C. C. *Poetry, Comedy, and Duty.* Houghton, Mifflin, 1888.

Kroll, W. *Studien zur Verständnis der Römischen Literatur.* Stuttgart, 1924.

IX. THE MEANING OF CIVILIZATION

Santayana, G. *The Life of Reason: or The Phases of Human Progress.* Book II: *Reason in Society.* Scribners, 1905.

Bagehot, W. *Physics and Politics.* Appleton, 1912.

Marvin, F. S., editor. *Progress and History.* Oxford University Press, 1916.

Inge, W. R. *The Idea of Progress.* Oxford University Press, 1920. (Also in *Outspoken Essays,* second series. Longmans, Green, 1926.)

Balfour, A. J. (Lord). *Decadence.* Cambridge University Press, 1908.

Carpenter, E. *Civilization, Its Cause and Cure.* Sonnenschein, 1889.

Bell, C. *Civilization, An Essay.* Harcourt, Brace, 1928.

Ferrero, G. *Ancient Rome and Modern America.* Putnams, 1914.

Babbitt, I. *Democracy and Leadership.* Houghton, Mifflin, 1924.

Siegfried, A. *America Comes of Age.* (Eng. trans.) Harcourt, Brace, 1927.

Nock, A. J. *The Theory of Education in the United States.* Harcourt, Brace, 1932.

GEOGRAPHICAL
EXPANSION
FOREIGN
CONQUEST

PRINCIPAL
PROVINC
APPROXI
DATES
ANNEXA

SOCIAL A
ECONO
HISTOR

POLITI
LEG
LAN

BU

753–500 B.C. Monarchy and (Evolution Etruscan Control)	2000–753 B.C. Invasions of Italy
Alba Longa, Head of Latin League. "Founding of Rome," as Outpost and Market of Latin League (753). Union of Latins and Sabines at Rome. Etruscans in Latium and Rome.	Bronze Age. Pile Dwellings in Po Valley (2000). Italic Tribes Invade Central Italy. Prehistoric Settlement at Rome (1000 ?). Etruscans in N. Italy (circa 900–800). Carthaginians in Africa, W. Sicily, and S. Spain. Greeks in S. Italy and E. Sicily (800–600).
Progressive Decline of Agriculture. Metal Work. Use of Copper Bars in Exchange. Coinage Debased. Oppressive Taxation by Diocletian (305) Crushes Business. Italy, like Provinces, Taxed. Liberty of Occupation Destroyed. Coloni Become Serfs.	Bronze Age. Economic Organizing Considerations. Farming Industry. Iron Imperial (1000 ?). Exchange by Barter. Italian Trading Posts. Recovery of United Italy.
Villages on Palatine and Esquiline. Autocracy. Levelling Process throughout Empire: Romanization and Cosmopolitanism. Citizenship for All Freemen (Edict of Caracalla, 211). Monarchy, Partly under Etruscan Control. The "Tarquins."	Ostrogothic Kingdom of Theodoric (493) Destroyed by Eastern Justinian. Code of Justinian. Lombard Invasion.
The Triumph. Vestal Virgins. Rex (and Pontifex Maximus) (succeeded by Rex Sacrorum and Pontifex Maximus). Divination. Expulsion of Etruscan Monarchy (509). Etruscan Walls, Tombs, Paintings. Metal Work. The Arch. The Calendar. Cloaca Maxima (Begun). Temple of Jupiter Optimus Maximus (Begun).	Religion of the Home. State (political) worship. Public Festivals. Worship of Mandra.
Greek Alphabet Adapted to Latin.	

INDEX

INDEX

Abbott, F. F., 234, 289, 291, 422
Abstractions, 177, 180, 314, 326 f., 346, 387
Accius, 468
Actium, 75, 231, 340, 442, 484
Adam, J., 385
Addison, J., 438
Administration, 241 f., 254 f., 256, 259 f., 282–291, 369
Aediles, 192
Aeneas, 15, 26, 35, 92, 307, 313, 349–354, 388, 396, 414, 417, 501
Africa, 59, 230, 256, 403
Agriculture, 7–9, 117, 118 f., 123, 135, 199, 208 f., 213–216, 219, 242, 253, 258–260, 264–268, 308–311, 465 f., 472 f.
Agrippa, 29, 161, 179, 231, 241, 247
Alaric, 85
Alba Longa, 35–37, 83
Alban Mount, 18 f., 83, 322 f.
Alcaeus, 426
Alexander, 60, 64, 341 f.
Alexandria, 23, 230, 403
Alexandrianism, 497, 502
Alimenta, 252 f., 266
Ambarvalia, 308, 320, 370
Ambrose, St., 366, 371
Amiens, 183
Ammianus Marcellinus, 268
Amphitheatres, 30, 166
Anchises, 172, 349, 351, 388, 414
Ancus Martius, 37, 190
Antiochus III, 61, 63
Antony, Mark, 75, 111, 229–231, 337, 343 f.
Apollo, 29, 172, 244, 245, 323 f., 339 f., 367, 486
Appian, 112
Appius Claudius (Caecus), 153
Appius Clauduis (Crassus), 196
Apuleius, 332, 403 f.

Aqueducts, 24, 28, 153 f., 241
Ara Pacis Augustae, 30, 178–180
Aratus, 385
Arcesilaus, 175
Arches, 30, 159, 169, 180; of Titus, 169, 180; of Trajan, 169; of Septimius Severus, 169; of Constantine, 169, 183
Architecture, 159–172. *See also* Arches, Baths, Building construction, Column, Engineering, House, Temples
Aristocracy, 419 f., 421, 503, 521, 524–526
Aristotle, 371, 386, 417
Arms, 13, 17, 44, 66, 320
Army, 44, 66, 79–82, 84, 108, 195, 204, 216–218, 219 f., 223, 227, 234–236, 244 f., 252, 253, 259, 273–275, 364
Arnold, E. V., 313, 385, 398
Arria, 102, 409, 460
Art, 148–185
Arval Brothers, 320, 339
Ashby, T., 310
Asia (Minor), 214, 235
Astrology, 356, 358, 383, 386
Athens, 62
Atrium, 110, 125 f., 132, 155 f., 173, 312
Attila, 85
Augurs, 188, 319, 321, 336
Augustine, St., 335, 366, 371
Augustus (Octavian), 23, 27, 29, 30, 75–77, 79, 98, 100, 103, 110, 122, 144, 153, 159, 161, 163, 167, 176, 178, 229–247, 320, 337–340 f., 344, 352, 354, 356, 416, 417, 484, 495, 500
Aurelian, 21, 83, 259, 358
Aurelius, M., 82, 170, 177, 182, 255, 274, 355, 390, 396